AMERICA ON FIRE

ALSO BY ELIZABETH HINTON

From the War on Poverty to the War on Crime:
The Making of Mass Incarceration in America

AMERICA ON FIRE

The Untold History of
Police Violence and Black Rebellion
Since the 1960s

ELIZABETH HINTON

WILLIAM
COLLINS

William Collins
An imprint of HarperCollins*Publishers*
1 London Bridge Street
London SE1 9GF

WilliamCollinsBooks.com

HarperCollins*Publishers*
1st Floor, Watermarque Building, Ringsend Road
Dublin 4, Ireland

First published in Great Britain in 2021 by William Collins

First published in the United States by W.W. Norton & Company in 2021

1

Copyright © Elizabeth Hinton 2021

Elizabeth Hinton asserts the moral right to be identified as the author of this work in accordance with the Copyright, Designs and Patents Act 1988

A catalogue record for this book is available from the British Library

ISBN 978-0-00-844383-2 (hardback)
ISBN 978-0-00-844384-9 (trade paperback)

Printed and bound in Great Britain by CPI Group (UK) Ltd, Croydon CR0 4YY

For James Matthews, Leon Mebane,
Willie Grimes, Charles Scott, Arthur McDuffie,
Timothy Thomas, and their families.

CONTENTS

AMERICA
ON FIRE

INTRODUCTION

O N A COLD MONDAY at the start of February, Joseph McNeil, Franklin McCain, Ezell Blair Jr., and David Richmond sat down at a whites-only lunch counter at Woolworth's in Greensboro, North Carolina. A waiter refused to serve the young men and suggested they order take-out instead. The four North Carolina A&T students remained at the counter. The store manager approached and asked them to leave. Still they did not move. A police officer arrived, slapping his nightstick in his hand in an attempt to intimidate. Rather than allow the students' offense against Jim Crow to continue, the manager of the store closed it for the day. Two dozen Black students returned on Tuesday. Over fifty Black students and three white students participated in the sit-in the next day, Wednesday, February 3, 1960.

News of the protest spread, and soon the sit-in movement had expanded to fifty-five cities and thirteen states. By April, over fifty thousand students were involved. Conceived and organized entirely by young people, the sit-in movement ultimately led to the founding of the Student Nonviolent Coordinating Committee (SNCC), which was run by activists such as John Lewis and Stokely Carmichael. As a

Fisk student, Lewis participated in the sit-ins in Nashville, Tennessee, and he would go on to steer the Freedom Rides in the summer of 1961 and speak at the March on Washington in 1963. Carmichael joined the sit-in movement as a high school student and would famously call for "Black Power" at an SNCC rally in Greenwood, Mississippi, in 1966. Together Lewis, Carmichael, and tens of thousands of other young Black Americans signaled that their generation was prepared to risk their lives for freedom and equality. From Greensboro onward, the sit-ins helped build momentum and support for racial justice.[1]

The students in Greensboro engaged in a nonviolent protest to demand full integration, the right to vote, equal educational opportunities, decent jobs, protection against white supremacist terrorism, and an end to police violence. These were the central aims of the civil rights movement more broadly. By the end of the decade, Black students at North Carolina A&T State University were still protesting, but now they were destroying property, assaulting police officers, and shooting in the direction of law enforcement, if not coming close to killing cops in self-defense. In May 1969, after Black students at Greensboro's James B. Dudley High School were arrested, brutalized, and tear-gassed by police during a series of protests against arbitrary disciplinary measures, A&T students came to the teenagers' defense. The confrontations between local police and Black high school and college students led authorities to call the National Guard to A&T's campus, unleashing violence and repression that ended in the killing of sophomore Willie Grimes.

A pivotal stop on the road to the Civil Rights Act of 1964 and the Voting Rights Act of 1965, by the end of the decade Greensboro was a site of sustained violence. It was far from unique in this regard. Between 1964 and 1972, but especially between 1968 and 1972, the United States endured internal violence on a scale not seen since the Civil War. Every major urban center in the country burned during those eight years. Violence flared up not only in archetypal ghettoes including Harlem and Watts, and in majority-Black cities such as Detroit and Washington, DC; it appeared in Greensboro, North Carolina, in Gary, Indiana, in Seattle, Washington, and countless places in between—every city, small or large, where Black residents lived in segregated, unequal conditions. In the north and the south, the east and the west, the rust belt and the Sunbelt, Black people threw rocks and bottles at police, shot at them with rifles, smashed the windows of businesses and institutions, hurled firebombs, and plundered local stores. These events—what we commonly call "riots," or what people who are to the left-of-center sometimes refer to as "civil disturbances"—caused hundreds of millions of dollars of property damage. Most immediately, they shaped the lives of the storeowners whose businesses were destroyed, of the parents who lost their teenage sons to the police, and of the firefighters and cops who were harmed or killed. But ever since, Americans have been living in a nation and a national culture created in part by the extreme violence of the 1960s and early 1970s.

The aftershocks of that era have, at times, taken the form of mass violence to which all Americans have been witness: in Miami in 1980, in Los Angeles in 1992, in Cincinnati in 2001, and in more recent years in Ferguson, Missouri; Baltimore, Maryland; and Minneapolis, Minnesota. The enduring impact of the violence of the 1960s and 1970s has been felt more regularly, and more acutely, by Black people in American cities who faced new policing practices that emerged under the banner of the War on Crime: the routine stop and frisks that attacked people's dignity, the breaking up of community gatherings, the presence of armed, uniformed officers in the hallways of under-resourced public schools, and more. While such strategies helped repress mass violence as a regular phenomenon, they ironically made further "riots" inevitable. These strategies remain in place today.

Mass incarceration is one consequence of the draconian police ethos born in the 1960s and 1970s in response to mass violence.

Another consequence is a semantic habit that hides a deeper reality. A central contention of this book is that the term "riot" is a misnomer. Due to the rhetoric of politicians, media coverage, and much of the academic research on the subject, Americans have become accustomed to think of these moments of mass violence—from Harlem in 1964 to Minneapolis in 2020—as misguided at best, and meaningless or irrational at worst. In either case, these incidents are often seen as being devoid of any political motivation or content. Sympathetic liberals may have believed then, and believe now, that the anger and discontent behind the violence was legitimate. Yet they often concluded that "rioting" was a pathological impulse, rooted in spontaneous, uncontrollable emotion. In this view, the "riots" were ultimately counter-productive: the violence only alienated allies and intensified anti-Black sentiment. Proponents of "law and order" from across the political spectrum, in partial contrast, believe that "riots" should be seen as nothing other than events of mass criminality.

President Lyndon B. Johnson championed the latter view when responding to the first urban "riots" in the 1960s. "The riots—as well as other criminal and juvenile delinquency problems in our cities—are closely connected," Johnson announced following the release of an FBI report on the violence that swept through eight cities in the summer of 1964. "Each riot began with a single incident and was aggravated by hoodlums and habitual lawbreakers," he added. Three years later, Johnson told the nation during a televised address delivered in the middle of the unprecedented violence in Detroit in 1967, which ended in more than forty deaths, a thousand injuries, at least 7,200 arrests, and the destruction of hundreds of buildings: "There is no American right to loot stores, or to burn buildings, or to fire rifles from the rooftops. That is crime."[2]

The 1960s produced an image of "riots" as fundamentally Black. Yet historically, most instances of mass criminality have been perpetrated by white vigilantes hostile to integration and who joined together in roving mobs taking "justice" into their own hands, often with the support of local police. The Jim Crow era was defined by riots. In August 1908, a lynch mob as large as five thousand people, many of them from out of town, descended on the Black community of Springfield, Illinois, wantonly destroying Black businesses, driving Black families from their homes, and executing two Black men. Mobs in East St. Louis, in 1917, forced Black wartime factory workers and their families to choose between being burned alive or shot to death in one of the bloodiest riots of the twentieth century.[3] White supremacist mass violence only escalated as Black migrants fled the terror of the segregationist south in greater numbers during and after the First World War, searching for better opportunities and safety from the white mob—only to meet it again in the North, Midwest, and West. White vigilante violence was a means to police the activities of Black people and to limit their access to jobs, leisure, the franchise, and to the political sphere.

During the Red Summer of 1919, Black Americans—including many veterans of the First World War—exercised their right to defend themselves. White and Black residents fought and killed each other on the streets of Chicago and Washington, DC. Elsewhere, the massacres of Black people continued. In the rural community of Phillips County, Arkansas, where Black sharecroppers were attempting to unionize, white "emergency posses" murdered at least two hundred Black people. Approximately another two hundred would be killed in Tulsa, Oklahoma, two years later, in a massacre carried out by two thousand white men, some of whom were deputized to commit various atrocities against the Black Greenwood community with the full backing of the county government. "Race riots" appeared again in major cities during the Second World War. The worst occurred in Detroit in 1943, when federal troops were deployed to contain the warfare in the streets.[4]

It was only when white people no longer appeared to be the driving force behind rioting in the nation's cities, and when Black collective violence against exploitative and repressive institutions surfaced, that "riots" came to be seen as a purely criminal, and completely senseless, acts. "Law and order" became the main response from the white establishment. As local police began to assume many of the previous functions of the white mob, the terms of urban violence were set.

In the view of President Johnson and others, rioting and crime were two strains of the same disease in Black communities—and could only be cured by more police. "These riots were each a symptom of a sickness in the center of our cities," the McCone Commission determined in its December report on the Watts uprising that took place in Los Angeles in August 1965. Eight days after the violence had subsided, California Governor Edmond G. "Pat" Brown had formed the commission to investigate the "riot" and appointed former CIA director John A. McCone as its chairman. Echoing the famous conclusions of Daniel Patrick Moynihan in *The Negro Family: The Case for National Action*, in March 1965, the commission identified the cause of the "sickness" as "disintegrating" Black families, who set in motion a "spiral of failure" for their children, dooming them to lives of crime and welfare dependency. "At the core of the cities where they [Negroes] cluster, law and order have only tenuous hold; the conditions of life itself are often marginal; idleness leads to despair and finally, mass violence supplies a momentary relief from the malaise."[5] It was the riffraff of the ghetto who fueled the violence, so the theory went: the criminals, the young, the unskilled, and the jobless. They burned and looted, seeking momentary thrills as a break from their tedious lives. Such diagnoses focused on personal and group pathology—a framework government authorities rarely used for understanding white terrorism—and justified lawmakers' decision to enlist the police to manage the disorder.

These views are not artifacts of the past; they are very much still with us. But the diagnosis was wrong then, and it is wrong now. The so-called urban riots from the 1960s to the present can only be properly understood as *rebellions*. These events did not represent a wave of criminality, but a sustained insurgency. The violence was in response to moments of tangible racism—"a single incident," as Johnson said— almost always taking the form of a police encounter. Yet the tens of thousands of Black Americans who participated in this collective violence were rebelling not just against police brutality. They were rebelling against a broader system that had entrenched unequal conditions and anti-Black violence over generations. Convinced that rebellion was an attack on existing American institutions rather than an appeal for inclusion within them, Johnson and many other officials dismissed the possibility that the "hoodlums" who "rioted" shared most if not all of the same grievances as the college students who started the sit-in movement in Greensboro in 1960.

Recently, some scholars who have examined Black communities' responses to the crime control programs of the second half of the twentieth century have argued that Black Americans called for more police on the streets, at schools, and in housing projects. But the history of Black rebellion adds another, dynamic layer and set of actors to the story of the "Black silent majority."[6] Some segments of the Black middle class, political leaders, and clergy did join the clamor for "law and order," yet other Black people—many of whom do not appear in the archives of traditional civil rights organizations, and many of whom were too young to vote—collectively pushed back against the crime wars that targeted their communities. The violent turn in Black protest was often led by Black pastors and sustained through Black churches, which have been vital to the success of the freedom movement historically. In the immediate post–civil rights period, many Black leaders used both the threat and reality of collective violence to make demands for structural change, and to advocate for community control of resources in Black communities.

While the Black Panther Party, the Black Liberation Army, the Weather Underground, and other revolutionary groups aimed to dismantle capitalism and overthrow the government, community-based Black rebellions sought redress from authorities in the form of employment, housing, education, and law enforcement, as well as a reordering of the status quo so that Black people would no longer be treated as second-class citizens in their cities and in their country. Those well-known radical organizations are frequently seen as the sole source of political violence during this period, an assumption that has helped prevent an understanding of the larger, continuous, and community-based rebellions as participants of a related, but different, kind of political violence of their own. Rebellion served as a message to the nation that the civil rights reforms of the mid-1960s, the equal-opportunity and self-help programs of the War on Poverty, and ongoing nonviolent protest were inadequate to solving the problem of racial inequality and its countless manifestations and consequences. Something else was needed.

JOHNSON HIMSELF RECOGNIZED, in the same July 1967 speech about the rebellion in Detroit, that "the only genuine, long-range solution for what has happened lies in an attack—mounted at every level—upon the conditions that breed despair and violence."[7] The president's rhetoric indicated that he favored social programs as the means of attack, but in practice he increasingly looked to law enforcement as a short-term solution to rebellion. Conservatives had favored a tough police response to Black protest through the postwar period, but many liberals started to back Johnson's similar stance in the second half of the 1960s, and as the rebellions only increased in intensity and frequency alongside the rollout of civil rights legislation and new job training, remedial education, and community action programs. Obsessed with "riots," Johnson and other liberals never seriously asked whether the War on Crime, launched one year after the War on Poverty, may have exacerbated the violence. Instead they embraced the expansion of American law enforcement—of surveillance and militarized police in communities of color, as well as the increasing professionalization of officers through training and technology—as the best strategies to handle "race relations." A short-term solution became the long-term reality.

The decision to respond to the rebellions with more police was not a foregone conclusion. As Sargent Shriver, who directed the Office of Economic Opportunity, pointed out to President Johnson in a memo in early 1968: "for all their destructiveness, I can but read the riots as a terrible call. The Negroes want equal access to the fruits of participating citizenship—the opportunity both to earn and to control their destiny." Shriver's observation and the logical remedies were broadcast to a national audience by Johnson's own National Advisory Commission on Civil Disorders, known popularly as the Kerner Commission, which offered an unpursued alternative to the escalation of policing and punitive policies in general. In its final report of February 1968 (which went on to become a national bestseller as a mass-market paperback), the commission warned federal policymakers and the nation that absent a massive investment into poor Black communities, rebellion and "white retaliation" would entrench racial inequality as a permanent feature of American life.[8]

Federal policymakers did not heed the warnings of officials like Shriver and members of the Kerner Commission. Nor did they truly listen to residents of the rebelling communities, who explained to politicians, reporters, and researchers how rebellion could be prevented in the future. The response was not the result of oversight and nor was it a blind spot; the alternatives were clearly presented. But time and time again, the decision was made to pursue a set of policies that were self-defeating at best, and grievously harmful at worst.

THE PEAK OF THE VIOLENCE appeared to last from the summer of 1967 through the 137 separate incidents that followed the assassination of Martin Luther King Jr. in April 1968. Yet public memory of these incidents largely stops in 1968, even though regular rebellions continued for years afterward. Between May 1968 and December 1972, some 960 segregated Black communities across the United States witnessed 1,949 separate uprisings—the vast majority in mid-sized and smaller cities that journalists at the time and scholars since have tended to overlook. Most of the violent encounters involving Black residents during this period began in response to the policing of ordinary, everyday activity. Over these four years, nearly 40,000 people were arrested, more than 10,000 were injured, and at least 220 people were killed. These figures do not take into account the hundreds of prison rebellions in this era, including the protests stemming from the killing of revolutionary icon George Jackson by San Quentin guards in August 1971, and the Attica uprising that garnered national attention just weeks later.[9]

Even less remembered than this second wave of Black rebellion are the Mexican Americans and Puerto Ricans who similarly turned to violence in an effort to secure equal rights, improve unequal conditions, and challenge the emerging crime control apparatus. Although this book focuses primarily on political violence in segregated Black communities, at least two hundred rebellions were carried out by Latinx residents after King's murder, the majority of them in Puerto Rican communities in the Northeast (twenty-one in New Jersey alone) that were often seen and treated as Black in a way Mexican American communities, generally, were not.[10]

The largely forgotten, post-King rock throwing, arson, and window breaking that shook more than a thousand Black, Mexican American, and Puerto Rican communities began after Johnson's Omnibus Crime Control and Safe Streets Act of 1968 went into effect in June.

Johnson had called for a "War on Crime" in March 1965, one week after he sent the Voting Rights Act to Congress. The "war" consisted of an unprecedented investment in local law enforcement. As the United States waged the Vietnam War abroad, federal policymakers built a pipeline to deliver surplus army weapons and technologies to local law enforcement in order to put down domestic political radicalism and Black rebellion.

City officials took full advantage of the newly available federal resources. From the beginning of the War on Crime in 1965 to the signing of the Safe Streets Act in 1968, the federal government allocated a total of $20.6 million to 359 separate programs that modernized police departments. Riot-control training, military-grade weapons such as AR15s and M4 carbines, steel helmets, three-foot batons, masks, armored vehicles, two-way radios, tear gas—these and other techniques, weapons, and tools flowed into cities, even small ones, across the United States. The federal government funded a handful of low-cost, police–community relations initiatives, too, for good measure. The Los Angeles Police Department, still recovering from the Watts rebellion in 1965, received the second-largest grant, as well as a helicopter, in 1967.[11] As Johnson's "first line of defense," police would be prepared to face the domestic enemy within.

Black communities had long been subject to targeted surveillance, frequent encounters with police, mass arrests, illegal searches, and outright brutality, but after the Safe Streets Act, which marked the extreme escalation of the War on Crime, residents in segregated, low-income neighborhoods in big cities such as New York, mid-sized cities such as Phoenix, and smaller cities such as Waterloo, Iowa, would be patrolled by police departments with veritable arsenals at their disposal. The 1968 legislation, with its additional $400 million outlay (or about $3 billion today) for crime control, allowed cities to flood with police those urban areas that seemed prone to rebellion. By 1970, federal policymakers had allocated some $40 million worth (or about $300 million today) of military-grade equipment for local law enforcement.[12]

The images of National Guardsmen on the scene in Los Angeles in 1965, in Detroit and Newark in 1967, and in Washington, DC, in 1968, made those rebellions particularly sensational. Yet the passing of the Safe Streets Act left law enforcement authorities capable of handling unrest on their own. Calling in the National Guard when several hundred teenagers hurled rocks and bottles at police officers and smashed the windows of police cruisers was no longer necessary.

This new self-reliance helps explain why the later moment of rebellion, between 1968 and 1972, has been overlooked: the uprisings often remained local, and of only local interest. Conventional accounts of this period tend to focus on national developments and on major metropolitan centers, particularly on the East Coast. But the lesser-known cities where rebellion frequently occurred, in the plains and in the heartland, declining industrial towns and in the urban south, open up a more comprehensive understanding of American social relations and the contours of racism and inequality.[13]

The crucible period of rebellion in the late 1960s and early 1970s matters not because it has been largely forgotten. It matters because despite being forgotten, it has defined freedom struggles, state repression, and violence in Black urban America down into our own time.

THE REBELLIONS OF the late 1960s and early 1970s were led, by and large, by young people, not just of high school age, but as young as ten and twelve years old. The four North Carolina A&T students who started the sit-ins in Greensboro were their predecessors, in this sense. Yet at the end of the 1960s, the young people rebelling understood their predecessors to have failed. They looked back on the heyday of the civil rights movement, and they looked at the conditions they were currently living in, with police watching them from the other side of the park, and they rebelled.

The persistence of Black rebellion in the late 1960s and early 1970s and into the present forces us to reconsider the accomplishments of the sit-ins and of the civil rights movement overall. The so-called Second Reconstruction, which promised to realize the unfulfilled promises of the Civil War and its aftermath, was supposed to integrate American society and extend full citizenship to those who had long been denied it. The movement secured for Black Americans the rights to an education, to shop at any stores, to eat in any restaurants, and to vote. It made flagrant racism unacceptable in American public discourse and allowed for the emergence of a Black middle class. But the movement's achievements did not fully secure basic needs for most Black people and quickly came up against the War on Crime and its new programs of social control. As the Reverend Charles Koen, a prominent activist who preached the politics of armed self-defense and community control in Cairo, Illinois, pointed out: "voting rights could not be eaten or made into clothing and shelter."[14] The response, by Koen and many other Black people, was not more nonviolence, but violence.

Koen and the rising generation that led the rebellions in segregated urban communities had spent their childhoods witnessing the civil rights movement unfold and were now approaching adulthood in the era of Black Power. The Black Panthers, in particular, provided a new script for resistance.[15] "Pig," the derogatory term the Black Panthers used for police officers, was frequently yelled or muttered during rebellions and in everyday life. Black popular culture had long seen defiance of the police as heroic. Martin Luther King Jr. and other civil rights heroes made defiance of the police legitimate, but the Black Panthers and other militant groups helped validate violent antagonism toward the police, at least among young Black Americans and other young people of color.

It can be difficult to imagine the children and teenagers who threw rocks at police or who looted local businesses as political actors, and this bias has influenced the writing of the history of this era. Even scholars and activists who focus on resistance to systemic racism have been reluctant to take seriously the political nature of Black rebellion. This is, in part, because there were few manifestos or dramatic claims about intentions, from the rebels. But collective action should be understood as political if it is intended to shape the interests of government.[16] As much as nonviolent direct action, with its august lineage going back to Gandhi and others, violent rebellion offered a means for people of color to express collective solidarity in the face of exploitation, political exclusion, and criminalization. Both traditions continue to ground movements for racial justice. Yet the violent conditions that have shaped the Black experience have made violent responses and the politics that fueled them inevitable.

This book centers on the people who participated in violent political rebellions themselves and takes their grievances seriously. Part I focuses on the crucible period of rebellion—from 1968 to 1972—in order to illuminate the mostly forgotten resistance to the escalation of police power during the early years of the War on Crime, and to highlight the evolution of Black protest in the immediate post–civil rights period. Set in secondary cities that are often overlooked in the struggle for racial justice, the chapters in Part I examine dominant patterns of police violence and Black rebellion, the politics of white supremacy and Black self-defense, and the housing projects and public schools where rebellions frequently occurred. This Part draws heavily from the records of the Lemberg Center for the Study of Violence, which was established immediately after President John F. Kennedy's assassination. The Center collected clippings from local news sources, conducted oral interviews with residents in areas that experienced unrest, and analyzed various data sets from 1967 to 1973. These records—previously closed to the public and available now to only a small group of researchers—comprise one of the book's primary source bases. Part I closes with an account of the failed attempts by politicians and officials to explain and address the violence taking place across the nation.

Part II traces the legacies of the crucible period in the nationally televised moments of mass political violence of the past forty years: Miami in 1980, Los Angeles in 1992, and Cincinnati in 2001. Each was set off by an instance of police violence. Each drew calls for more "law and order." Each involved heavily militarized police confronting residents who were fighting against a larger system of oppression. When examined in the context of earlier rebellions, these eruptions can be understood anew, as examples of historical trends that began in the late 1960s. Yet the differences between this later era and the crucible years are instructive. For one, the violence reached a truly unprecedented scale, especially in Miami and Los Angeles. The main difference, though, is that these later rebellions now occurred in reaction to *exceptional* instances of police violence, which is to say, police killings. There are no longer rebellions against everyday policing practices, a sign that the status quo has become accepted, however bitterly. In this sense, at least, national and local authorities won the War on Crime.

The history of Black rebellion across regions and decades demonstrates a fundamental reality: police violence precipitates community violence. This reality escaped policymakers and many of the scholars they consulted then, and it continues to be ignored by them today. Authorities have funneled billions of taxpayer dollars into the War on Crime, the War on Drugs, and the prison system. Rather than contend with underlying causes, this nation's leaders further criminalized entire communities, guaranteeing that rebellions would only continue.

BLACK REBELLION CLEARLY has a future; it also has a long history. That Black people might rise up in violence has been a widespread fear among white Americans for centuries. Slave owners were terrified their human property would defend themselves by running away, or that groups of enslaved Africans would take bloody revenge on their white masters. Slave patrols, America's first system of organized, civilian-based law enforcement, were charged with suppressing potential insurrection by raiding slave dwellings, dispersing gatherings, and patrolling the areas around plantations and towns.[17] Here was the foundational logic of American policing: maintaining the social order though the surveillance and social control of people of color.

Under the terms of the Declaration of Independence, enslaved Africans were justified in rebelling against the forces that kept them in bondage. As its primary author, Thomas Jefferson, understood: "I tremble for my country when I reflect that God is just: that his justice cannot sleep for ever." Jefferson went on to observe in his *Notes on the State of Virginia*, from 1781, that an "exchange of situation" was on the horizon—that slaves were "rising from the dust." He hoped that their "total emancipation" would be realized "with the consent of the masters, rather than by their extirpation."[18]

Black rebellion was a self-fulfilling prophecy, a menace that would persist as long as state violence was used to preserve racial hierarchy. Paraphrasing Jefferson some 180 years later, Lyndon Johnson remarked of the "riots" that followed the assassination of Martin Luther King Jr.: "What did you expect? I don't know why we're so surprised. When you put your foot on a man's neck and hold him down for three hundred years, and then you let him up, what's he going to do? He's going to knock your block off."[19] Racial hierarchy, inequality, and violence are among the oldest American stories. What follows is the most recent act in a saga that goes back to this country's beginnings.

PART I: ORIGINS

1

THE CYCLE

On the afternoon of July 7, 1970, during the third day of rebellion in
Asbury Park, New Jersey, young people throw rocks at police as officers
move in to break up the crowd. (Bettmann Archive / Getty Images)

THE RESIDENTS OF Carver Ranches didn't have sidewalks, fire
hydrants, or a sewer system. They did, however, have police
patrolling their streets. Black Americans from Miami and Black
migrants from the Bahamas first founded the three-hundred-acre
community in Broward County, Florida, in the late 1940s, naming
it after the celebrated scientist George Washington Carver. Teenaged
children of Carver Ranches' first generation were hanging out around
midnight on a Saturday in August 1969, when a Broward County sheriff's deputy drove by. One of the kids threw a rock at the police car. The

small act of defiance provoked an outsized, and violent, reaction. The deputy stopped, stepped out, rushed the rock thrower, grabbed him by the shirt, and threw him in the back seat of his cruiser. The boy's friends were not about to let him get taken away by the county cops for such an arbitrary offense. They opened the back-seat door and pulled him out, and the deputy hauled him back in. After several rounds of this, the children prevailed, and the rock thrower escaped into the growing crowd of people watching the encounter. Outnumbered, the deputy called for help. When reinforcements from three nearby police departments arrived, someone fired five shots at the officers. No one was hit. The sheriff later called the event a "near riot."[1]

In the late 1960s and early 1970s, rebellions usually started when law enforcement meddled, often violently, in ordinary, everyday activity (a group of kids doing what kids do). They happened when police seemed to be there for no reason, or when the police intervened in matters that could be resolved internally (disputes among friends and family). Rebellions began when the police enforced laws that would almost never be applied in white neighborhoods (laws against gathering in groups of a certain size or acting like a "suspicious person"). Likewise, they erupted when police failed to extend to residents the common courtesies afforded to whites (allowing white teenagers to drink in a park but arresting Mexican American teens for the same behavior). "If they would just leave us alone there would be no trouble," said a Black teenage boy who threw rocks in Decatur, Illinois, during an uprising in August 1969. His solution was a straightforward reaction to an obvious issue. Rebellion was always possible when ordinary life was policed, and often the mere sight of the police—who could potentially arrest, beat, or even kill you—was enough to prompt a violent response. Multiple occasions of seemingly arbitrary or unnecessarily aggressive police interventions accumulated into frustration and set off preemptive, violent reactions.

This was "the cycle": the recurring pattern of over-policing and rebellion, of police violence and community violence, that helped define urban life in segregated, low-income, Black, Mexican American, and Puerto Rican communities in the late 1960s and early 1970s. The cycle occurred in cities across the nation, many of them smaller municipalities that are left out of standard accounts of this era. But it was precisely in these secondary cities that the War on Crime unfolded in the most lasting and influential ways, helping entrench racial inequality and put this nation on the path to mass incarceration. While every rebellion had its particular actors and causes, what is remarkable is the broad similarity between them.

THE EXCEPTIONAL MOMENTS of collective violence that occurred between the passage of the Civil Rights Act in 1964 and the assassination of Martin Luther King Jr. in 1968 were similarly ignited by police arresting Black people. The Harlem rebellion of 1964 was the outlier, a six-night revolt that began after a New York police officer killed a Black, fifteen-year-old boy. Coming two weeks after the enactment of the landmark Civil Rights Act, Harlem was the beginning of the "long hot summers" of Lyndon Johnson's presidency. Watts in 1965 and Newark in 1967, though, each began in reaction to the arrest of a Black motorist. A police raid on a speakeasy in Detroit that year culminated in violence that Johnson called "the worst in our history." More than one hundred other cities erupted in the spring of 1968 after the murder of King on April 4. The collective sorrow, anger, and disillusionment that followed King's death was a turning point for the mainstream civil rights movement and its emphasis on nonviolence, a strategy that had failed to protect its most visible proponent from the violent forces of racism, and seemed, to many, incapable of securing true freedom for Black Americans. As Black Panther leader Eldridge Cleaver reflected in his article "Requiem for Nonviolence," shortly after the assassination, King's murder was "a final repudiation by white America of any hope of reconciliation, of any hope of change by peaceful and nonviolent means." For Cleaver the only way for Black Americans "to get the things that they have a right to and deserve—is to meet fire with fire."[2]

The King rebellions were also a turning point for policing. The day after King died, Johnson mobilized federal troops in the nation's capital and in Chicago, Baltimore, and Kansas City, Missouri, soon after. "I don't know how we handle these things," Johnson admitted in a phone conversation with Chicago's Mayor Richard Daley, roughly two weeks after the King-related unrest began. "But I know one thing: we've got to handle them with muscle and with toughness." Johnson believed that the aggressive use of federal troops, more than twenty thousand soldiers in all, was responsible for leaving the country "in reasonably good shape" in the aftermath of the largest wave of domestic violence since the Civil War.[3] Not until the Los Angeles uprising in 1992 would the president summon federal troops to suppress Black rebellions. The lull was not a consequence of concern for the civil rights of American citizens, but a result of the professionalization of the police, a process that began under Johnson, whose administration instituted training programs for riot control and equipped local police forces with military-grade weapons.

The policing of the ordinary had sparked rebellions earlier in the decade: the dispersing of a crowd in Omaha in July 1966; the arrest of a Black bootlegger in a park in Kansas City, Missouri, in 1967; and the breaking up of fights between Black teenagers in Minneapolis and Sacramento that same year. But after King's murder, police became the foot soldiers in a larger mission—the "War on Crime"—and there were more resources and more men than ever to carry it out. The federal allocation for local police forces went from nothing in 1964 to $10 million in 1965, $20.6 million in 1966, $63 million in 1968, $100 million in 1969, and $300 million in 1970—a 2,900 percent increase in five years.[4] As Johnson's Omnibus Crime Control and Safe Streets Act of 1968 fueled the manufacture and national distribution of a riot-control arsenal, the governments and police forces of smaller cities—those outside of the initial beneficiaries, major metropolitan centers with large Black populations including Washington, DC, Detroit, and Los Angeles—were emboldened. The capstone of Johnson's Great Society, the Safe Streets Act broke with the previous two hundred years of American history, establishing a direct role for the federal government in law enforcement and criminal justice at the state and local levels. It was the expansion of policing in response to the violent eruptions of the 1960s that set in motion the cycle that followed in smaller cities like Carver Ranches and Decatur.

President Johnson's new national strategy was premised on preventing rebellion before it occurred and on identifying and arresting potential rioters or criminals. "More police patrols can be an effective, visible deterrent to crime," federal law enforcement officials assumed. "More police patrols also lead to more and speedier arrests, which takes offenders out of action and lessens the chances of escape, thus serving as a deterrent."[5] Increasingly, preventing rebellion "with muscle and with toughness" became the dominant strategy for fighting disorder, although it consistently failed to lead to the desired goal.

The national strategy set the tone, even in places that did not receive federal funds. Policing became more aggressive and intrusive in Black communities everywhere. Police often claimed to be responding to a tip, which the newspapers later reported to justify the officers' actions and their presence in the community in the first place. The rock thrower in Decatur had a different take: "Police, they come out here looking for trouble," he said.[6] What mattered was police were suddenly *there*. They were more likely to cause harm than offer protection, in the judgment of the rock thrower and his friends and counterparts in other American cities. The people being policed frequently refused to follow police orders and fought back, throwing rocks and jumping on officers' backs to prevent arrests from being carried out.

It was a losing battle for a lone policeman or a small unit, and officers were forced to retreat to wait for reinforcements. This came in the form of cops in riot gear, as well as officers from neighboring cities, state troopers, or National Guardsmen who could be called by state governors depending on the size of the home department and the scale of the rebellion. When law enforcement left the area (if only temporarily), some residents did the same, while others turned on local businesses and other buildings, breaking windows and taking food, clothes, tires, and stereos from stores in what some police chiefs described as "hit and runs." The participants in these outbursts outnumbered and often outsmarted the police, and they slipped away frequently, back into their homes or down familiar alleyways, over fences and dumpsters. The police sent in more police. The rebellion expanded. The escalation would often continue for another day or two before the rebellion burned out on its own or enough participants were arrested to have the same effect.

The proximate cause of the unrest did not present itself easily to many officials. "No explanation" could be found for the shooting at cops that began in Carver Ranches weeks after the initial rock-throwing incident in Florida. "We don't know why it started," said the Mayor of Fort Wayne, Indiana, after a rebellion. The Columbus Police Department in Ohio was "unsure" about what had led to the city's revolt. The mayor of Jersey City spoke of "senseless, random acts of violence with no purpose or meaning." Authorities in York, Pennsylvania, gave no reason for a four-night rebellion other than: "they don't have anything else to do."[7] The officials saw the violence as having no cause or meaning. In the rebellions of the immediate post-King era, Black and Brown participants saw themselves as being policed for nothing. They rebelled when the police appeared out of nowhere, and for no apparent reason.

RESIDENTS WHO WERE reportedly fighting one another frequently put aside their differences to battle a common adversary: the police who interrupted them. In Fort Wayne in August 1968, just before the school year began, a dozen Black teenagers started a rebellion at the McCulloch Recreation Center, where kids in the segregated South-east side of the city often gathered. At around eleven o'clock, a Parks Department officer intruded on their evening ("a fight was reported") and asked the group to disperse. The youths ignored him. They bent down and picked up stones and debris from the Center's lawn to throw. In Indianapolis, a two-night rebellion was set off in June 1969 after two police officers tried to break up a fight in the Lockefield Gardens Apartments in one of the city's Black neighborhoods. A group of twenty people attacked the officers, slightly injuring them both. One lost his gun, his nightstick, and his badge. The crowd began to grow steadily from there, throwing stones at passing cars. In Akron, Ohio, in mid-August 1970, police came to the scene of a fight between two teenage girls near a custard stand. People threw rocks for several hours in response; one policeman was struck.[8]

When cops arrived to stop fights, residents did not perceive them as agents of peace and protection. Following the implementation of the national riot prevention strategy via the Safe Streets Act of 1968, which encouraged local police to initiate interactions with residents in targeted areas as a way to find potential criminals or rioters before they engaged in violent acts, cops and Black residents were brought into contact much more frequently. It's possible the officers in Fort Wayne, Indianapolis, and Akron had the best of intentions when they intervened, that they hoped to prevent further injury and act as mediators.

Yet their intentions mattered little to the residents involved. History and hard experience taught them that police were generally antagonistic, less likely to bring peace or protection and more likely to cause harm—either by beating residents (or worse), or by arresting them and carting them off to jail.

In the late 1960s, with the War on Crime in full swing, apprehending criminals or potential criminals, rioters or potential rioters, became the objective—the measure of "success"—of crime control in targeted communities. If police did not receive a tip about a neighborhood fight as in Fort Wayne, parks where young people of color congregated provided a ready-made site to patrol and possibly make arrests. Having no other pretense to stop, interrogate, and arrest Black youth, in mid-April 1968 the police department in York, Pennsylvania, began enforcing curfew at Penn Common after the wave of rebellions in other cities. Black children and teenagers liked to congregate in the park, and the cops wanted them out by ten o'clock or earlier. Police would chase, harass, and beat kids who refused to obey. A Black teenager described sitting with his girlfriend in the park in early July 1968, when all of a sudden, an officer pulled up and shined his flashlight in the young couple's eyes. "Take that light off my face, we're minding our own business," the young man said. The officer got out of his car, billy club in hand, and told the couple to leave the park. He shoved his club in the teenager's back, using it to push the young man as he escorted him and his date off the premises. This violent police encounter itself triggered violence. "Am I supposed to take that forever? What would you do?" the teenager asked a reporter. "Last night I threw a bottle at a cop."[9]

Days after the officer disrupted the teenage date, on July 11, York police began their regular curfew enforcement routine, moving to clear about fifty Black kids and teenagers from Penn Common at 9:15 p.m. This time, the youths refused to leave. "Why do they have to disperse a group of Blacks?" one asked. "What's wrong with congregating in the park?" When the police arrested two people, the rock- and bottle-throwing started. Twelve officers chased after various young people. Another violated proper procedure and fired his pistol in the air to scare them—and this action launched a five-day battle between police and Black residents, most of them in their teens and twenties. A reporter asked a male participant: "Why are young black Yorkers throwing rocks and bottles at policemen?" To which he replied: "Why do police hit people on the heads with their clubs?"[10] The cycle seemed clear enough, at least to this young man.

In Decatur, Illinois, Black teenage boys enjoyed drag racing on a strip that had been used for that purpose since 1964. In the summer, they would gather in nearby Mueller Park when the races were being held. White teens raced freely on a boulevard in the northern part of town, but police would regularly come to the southside park to surveil the city's Black teens. Following a demonstration at the A&P store to demand jobs for Black workers on Thursday, August 7, 1969, the police decided to arrest the Black young people racing that evening. The cops were "mad" about the protest, one of the youths assumed, "so they came in here." The Black teens started throwing rocks when law enforcement arrived. The police used tear gas to disperse them, detaining nine. The teenagers complained that excessive force had been used during the arrests and prepared for another confrontation. They knew what was coming. At about nine thirty the next night, an estimated two hundred people trapped an officer as soon as he pulled up to their block, surrounding his vehicle with four cars. Someone threw a Molotov cocktail at the cornered police cruiser, but it failed to ignite. Police reinforcements arrived and fired tear gas grenades back at the crowd.[11]

At Roosevelt Park in Albuquerque, New Mexico, in June 1971, the arrest of fifteen Mexican American teens for underage drinking touched off thirty hours of violence, a rebellion that was only suppressed in the end by the National Guard. Some five hundred young people had gathered in the park when officers arrived. According to Richard Moore, minister of justice for the Black Berets, a militant Mexican American group, the police "started putting on strong pressure, and some of the guys got fed up." The Black Berets led protesters in a march from Roosevelt Park to the police headquarters to negotiate the release of the fifteen young people, some throwing rocks and breaking windows on the way. The activists won the release of the suspects "on their own recognizance," but by the time they stepped out of the police station the rebellion was well underway. In little more than a day, participants caused between three and five million dollars' worth of property damage and six hundred fifty people were arrested.[12]

In addition to reacting when police appeared for no apparent reason, residents fought back when law enforcement exercised their most basic legal authority: making arrests. Baltimore residents challenged that authority with determination, disrupting officers mid-arrest on three separate occasions in late-June 1968—two months after the week-long rebellion in the city that followed Martin Luther King Jr.'s murder. On June 19, after an officer tried to arrest a young man in the heart of the Black Upton neighborhood in front of a growing crowd, a woman scratched him down his left arm and took his watch. The officer sprayed the woman and others with mace, and the people who gathered at the scene left. Less than a week later, a fifteen-year-old boy grabbed an officer's arm during a disorderly conduct arrest, giving his suspect an opportunity to flee. The officer hit the boy and took him into custody.[13]

The next evening, two dozen teenagers began shouting at officers Paul Karaskavicz and Norman Stamp as they attempted to arrest three people on burglary charges at around eleven thirty in Reservoir Hill. A thirteen-year-old girl jumped on Stamp's back, forcing him to let go of two of the suspects. The men escaped, and Stamp seized the girl, who kicked him, clawed him, and bit him. Eventually he managed to put her in handcuffs for resisting arrest, but suddenly her fourteen-year-old brother attacked the officer from behind. After a struggle the brother was also detained. Another fourteen-year-old boy helped free the third burglary suspect by assaulting Karaskavicz. The suspects, all three of them young men, escaped; the kids who came to their defense went to jail.[14] Viewing the arrests as an injustice, these young people were prepared to take justice into their own hands, and sacrifice their own freedom in the process.

Although the informal arrest prevention campaign in Baltimore did not directly inspire a broad rebellion, in other cities a single arrest could lead to sustained collective violence committed by hundreds of people. In Jersey City in August 1970, about five hundred Black and Puerto Rican residents declared what police called "open warfare on whites" in the downtown area, after two patrolmen stopped a vehicle for a minor traffic violation. Weeks later, a six-hour-long drug raid during which twenty-five people were arrested caused a two-night rebellion in nearby Hoboken, New Jersey. The prominent twenty-one-year-old local activist Luis Lopez came to protest the mass arrest and was subsequently arrested himself for "interfering with police duties" and using "obscene language." Lopez was already known to the Hoboken Police Department for his political activities. In early August, he was arrested in Newark for disrupting a Puerto Rican day parade with the Young Lords Party, an organization founded on the principles of self-determination and community empowerment for Puerto Rican groups and other oppressed peoples, and had been convicted for squatting in (Lopez called it "liberating") two Hoboken tenement buildings that he and his followers occupied. Many people in the community rejected this type of enforcement and wanted to see Lopez freed. By 7:30 p.m. on August 27, three hundred to four hundred "enraged Puerto Ricans," as the Hudson Dispatch described them, surrounded

City Hall demanding Lopez's release. About thirty people sat at the intersection of Washington and First to block traffic. The crowd threw rocks and bottles at police and smashed windows in the area.[15]

Lopez continued to protest the arrest of Puerto Rican residents in Hoboken, leading to another rebellion a year later. It started with an angry confrontation between Luis and Jaime Santana, aged twenty-six and twenty-four, and a store owner whom the brothers claimed repossessed their television set under false pretenses. After the Santana brothers were arrested for assault with a dangerous weapon, Lopez led a small group of activists to police headquarters to demand the release of the prisoners and to request the suspension of the two officers who allegedly used brutal force during the arrest. Soon after Lopez and his group left, police reportedly received calls that people were harassing motorists and passersby outside of City Hall. When local officers arrived, a group of about three hundred began throwing cans, bottles, and bricks at them.[16] The rebellion had begun. Following the enactment of the Safe Streets Act, residents of Jersey City and of many other cities across the nation made clear that if a war was declared on their communities, they were ready for a fight.

FROM CARVER RANCHES to Jersey City, when the rock throwing started, the police called in their fellow officers. As their numbers increased and as they brought more sophisticated weapons to bear on the rebellion, so too did the size of the crowd and the scale of destruction. In Fort Wayne, when a Park officer arrived at the McCulloch Recreation Center to help the first responder clear the area, the kids continued to throw stones. Overwhelmed, the officers retreated and waited for reinforcements. Police Chief Albert Bauermeister dispatched an additional fifteen officers in full riot gear to the scene. By the time they arrived, the crowd had expanded from ten to roughly

two hundred people. No one was seriously injured in the ensuing confrontation, but the "riot prevention equipment" bore the physical scars
of the rebellion: the department's newly acquired mobile crime lab van
suffered dents and smashed windows. "So many rocks were hitting the
van it sounded like bongo drums," the driver said. It took tear gas to
pacify the crowd, at least temporarily.[17]

The lesson the Columbus Police Department took away from
the rebellion of June 1970 was not that their very presence provoked
rebellion, but that the young Black people gained an edge when
police officers retreated to await backup. As officials put it, there was
a "destructive lag between the start of troubles and the deployment
of police." On Thursday, June 4, when Sargent Ed Baker stepped in to
break up a fight between fifty-two-year-old Cecil Butler and another
Black man, Butler drew his gun. Baker took Butler's gun, placed him
under arrest, and walked him across the street toward his cruiser
just as a police van drove by. The van hit Butler, knocking him to the
ground but not causing any serious injuries. Witnesses believed the
van struck Butler intentionally, and a "rock-throwing spree" involving
fifty to seventy-five Black residents began. Baker left the scene of the
nascent rebellion under a rain of rocks and bottles as the department
mustered reinforcements. It took an hour before the "second trick B
Platoon and riot-trained D Platoon personnel" arrived ready to do battle. In the interim, "sixty to seventy-five youths" broke the windows of
several stores and walked away with merchandise from Maury's Drugs
and Wilson-Oak Hardware.[18]

The next night, at about nine thirty, the Columbus vice squad
swooped down Main Street in the Black Wilson-Oak neighborhood,
arresting nineteen people on gambling charges. Whether the goal of
the police was to flex their muscle or to intentionally provoke violence,
the mere sight of them drew the same response they received the previous night, with some twists. When the squad left the area to join

a larger tactical force, a reported seventy-five residents walked down the block and proceeded to throw stones at passing cars and buses, but now they also smashed windows, looted a supermarket run by the Columbus Board of Education, and set fire to Topy's Surplus Store after cleaning out its merchandise. In preparation for another night of violence on Saturday, the police department mobilized the special tactical force early so that it would be "ready to move into the area on a nightly basis immediately."[19] The department was now better prepared to respond to the insurgency with a set of counterinsurgent tactics. But by then the rebellion had already ended.

The Hoboken Police Department would have struggled to suppress the rebellion in August 1970 without the assistance of the Jersey City Tactical Squad, whose fifty-five officers were trained in riot prevention techniques. The force marched down First Street, shoulder to shoulder with off-duty local police, clearing the area and ultimately restoring order. Hoping to prevent future unrest, the police department quickly established a Community Relations Board to handle the community's demands. Staffed by six officers, the board operated out of a storefront office in the Black and Puerto Rican neighborhood.[20] A key development in the new national crime control strategy, neighborhood precincts were created in targeted communities of color. Perhaps the strategy was misguided from the start: neighborhood precincts, often established in storefronts, made patrols and surveillance easier and assigned officers took advantage, even though these precincts were intended to prevent violence that resulted directly from patrols and surveillance in the first place.

Hoboken police "believed that everything was working out well for all concerned," at least until another rebellion struck one year later. On a Friday night in September 1971, three hundred people began throwing cans, bottles, and bricks at police following an arrest. Officers from the Jersey City Police and the Port Authority of New York and New

Jersey Police arrived to help the Hoboken police cope with the situation. On Saturday, seventy-five officers in riot gear—including bulletproof vests, shotguns, and tear gas grenades—were ready when, as the *Hudson Dispatch* reported, "marauding bands of disgruntled Puerto Ricans" resumed the bottle throwing and the window smashing at around ten o'clock. The officers proceeded to arrest as many people as they could (forty-two in all over the two days) and ordered the participants to disperse. "Watch television, there's a good movie on," one policeman suggested to people in the streets.[21]

Law enforcement officials in Akron were outliers in recognizing, during the rebellion in August 1970, that the presence of police in the Black Wooster Avenue district only seemed to provoke violence further. "Black youths reacted angrily to the sight of patrol cars and uniformed officers," in the words of an *Akron Beacon Journal* reporter. On Monday, August 10, Akron police arrived to break up a fight and were met with rock throwing that lasted for several hours. On Tuesday, "gangs of youth" started heaving concrete blocks in addition to the stones and bottles, causing more severe damage to cars and injuring five civilians and one police officer. On Wednesday, the rebellion exploded: one thousand people, mostly of junior high school age, came out throwing rocks and other objects. The police barricaded the area, "read the riot act," and twenty officers fired a total of thirty-two tear gas grenades as they marched through the streets.[22]

After three nights of violence, police turned to a new strategy, one that made officers less visible to the rebels while still allowing them to maintain a strong presence in the area. On Thursday, August 13, police cruisers patrolled the perimeter of the neighborhood to keep the rebellion contained, and a plainclothes force was sent into the blockaded district. Withdrawing uniformed officers from a "riot zone" did not address the root causes of rebellion, of course, but it did appear to curb the violence. Save for a few scattered incidents and reports of civilians roaming the streets with walkie-talkies in hand, the night was tense but calm. Yet on Friday, the police department seemed to abandon the plan as more than one hundred officers confronted a gathering of Black residents after the city's Soap Box Derby parade. According to local papers, "a property destruction spree by black youths" followed; the participants broke windows, stoned cars, looted auto parts stores and supermarkets, and set fire to a butcher shop and a car. Two firebombs were thrown at the Akron public library but did not ignite.[23] Perhaps if the Akron Police Department would have fully committed to de-escalation in the troubled community, this spate of renewed violence would have been prevented.

A COMMON FEATURE of the cycle was the use of non-lethal gas, commonly referred to as tear gas. Officers threw grenades filled with either chloroacetophenone (CN), the tear gas most commonly used to quell rebellion, or o-chlorobenzylidene malononitrile (CS) or "super" tear gas. CS had been initially formulated in the late 1920s, but it became popular among US military and law enforcement officials during the 1960s to fight both the war on Vietnam and the War on Crime. The chemical weapon proved effective in pursuing the Vietcong through underground bunkers and tunnels, and in putting down rebellions in Black American neighborhoods. The use of tear gas in US overseas interventions correlated directly to its use at home: by 1969, the Department of Justice had facilitated the low-cost sale of more than seventy thousand gas masks to local law enforcement, along with other surplus military equipment including body armor, armored vehicles, and rifles.[24]

In a domestic setting, CN or CS gas was seen as a "measured" response to rebellion, a way to prevent violence without resorting to brutality. A combined total of some eighty-five Black residents had been killed by police or National Guardsmen during the rebellions in Watts, Newark, and Detroit alone, and riot-control methods came in for criticism. "Equipping civil police with automatic rifles, machine guns, and other weapons of massive and indiscriminate lethality is not warranted by evidence," the Kerner Commission wrote in its 1968 report. "Weapons which are designed to destroy, not to control, have no place in densely populated urban communities." But as an alternative to brute force, the commission and federal policymakers across the political spectrum agreed: "Chemical agents provide police forces with an effective and appropriate weapon."[25] Now tear gas became a larger part of the police arsenal.

As a nonlethal means of exerting force on a crowd, tear gas offered an ideal technical solution to Black rebellion and the tendency among riot-control police to quickly draw their guns and start shooting. The chemical weapon produced immediate effects, incapacitating people for twenty to sixty seconds and causing, as the Army manual *Military Chemistry and Chemical Agents* described it, "extreme burning of the eyes accompanied by copious flow of tears, coughing, difficulty in breathing, and chest tightness, involuntary closing of the eyes, stinging sensations of moist skin, running nose, and dizziness or swimming of the head." Although tear gas was thought to be harmless beyond the immediate effects, it is now understood that it can cause significant damage to the lungs, liver, and heart, yet it is still used as a crowd control device, and it is still held up as a humane alternative to violently arresting or shooting into crowds of people.[26]

Tear gas was the most frequent police response to rock-throwing protests during the rebellions after 1968 (and remains so today), whether involving a mere dozen or several hundred people, or more. If an angry crowd refused to go home, the chemical was guaranteed to get people moving. But it did not always succeed in quelling a revolt. On the second night of rebellion in Decatur, officers fired their service revolvers and shotguns in the air in an attempt to force a two-hundred-person crowd to retreat. Someone in the crowd responded by throwing a Molotov cocktail at a police cruiser, though it did not explode. Using loudspeakers, law enforcement ordered the crowd to disperse, but to no avail, so officers fogged the area with tear gas and arrested eleven people. With their eyes burning and their throats clogged, the participants still managed to hit several squad cars with rocks and bricks before the night was over.[27]

Throwing gas grenades at people had the tendency to create violence even if the purpose was to end it. When hundreds of teenagers in Albuquerque's Roosevelt Park started throwing rocks at police during the June 1971 rebellion, the police fired their pistols in the air and threw CS gas grenades, but still had no choice but to back away as the crowd grew to more than one thousand strong. With the officers gone, people in the crowd overturned and set fire to their cruisers. They did the same to a van belonging to the New Mexico Rangers, a citizens' patrol group dating back to the nineteenth century. The crowd smashed the doors to the city commission room at City Hall, started a small fire inside it with a Molotov cocktail, and lit firecrackers on nearby streets. Police stationed on top of the nine-story building threw tear gas grenades at the crowd in response, ultimately clearing the area.[28] The tear gas proved to be only a temporary solution, however.

During the second day of the Albuquerque rebellion, as a "roving mob" marched east on the city's main street, breaking windows, flipping cars, and looting stores, more than two hundred National Guardsmen, who had been waiting in the wings since the morning, gathered across the street from Roosevelt Park. People threw rocks and firebombs in their direction. Soon a three-quarter-ton truck with a loudspeaker appeared. A police officer stepped out of it with a microphone, and read aloud from a piece of paper, over and over again: "Leave this area immediately. You are violating the law. If you do not leave, you will be removed forcibly. We do not wish to hurt you, but we will in order to protect lives and property."[29] The crowd in Roosevelt Park shouted back and held their ground, and the Guardsmen lined up down the road: two armies squaring off for combat.

In Indianapolis during the 1969 uprising, rock throwing and fire-bombing on Friday night became looting and sniper fire on Saturday. Law enforcement officials prepared for the second night by sending 295 officers to patrol the Lockefield Gardens area, with another seventy-five sheriff's deputies and one hundred state troopers standing by. After one hundred fifty people gathered in front of the Newbauer clothing store in the heart of the neighborhood—some ripped off the security mesh, smashed its windows, and began to loot it—police and snipers began to shoot at one another. Someone fired from the roof of Lockefield Gardens and hit Detective Al Watkins, grazing his forehead, and twenty-two-year-old Black resident Andrew Martin was shot in the leg during the crossfire. (Martin was later arrested, from his hospital bed, for resisting arrest and disorderly conduct.) The sniping eventually forced the police to withdraw until another technology used in Vietnam appeared: a helicopter illuminated the rooftops of Lockefield Gardens with its landing lights to expose the snipers, who soon withdrew. By the time the rebellion was over, two officers had been injured in addition to Watkins. Beyond Martin, the only non-police officer with a gunshot wound, the local newspapers did not report how many Black residents were hurt by police. Such facts rarely made it into the newspapers, but the names, ages, and addresses of those arrested did.[30]

Sniping was another common feature of the cycle, less familiar and more shocking today than tear gas. If civilians started shooting during a rebellion, they usually did so after the opening rock throwing phase and when officers returned to the "troubled area" with their riot sticks, helmets, shotguns, and an armored vehicle if the department had one on hand. Sniping was overreported and was frequently invoked by those who claimed that America was on the verge of chaos and race war, but in some places, it was, in fact, the main expression of collective violence. Policymakers and law enforcement officials were convinced that snipers intended to kill police indiscriminately, yet, given the relatively low number of police officers who died by sniper fire, it appears to have served as an intimidation tactic more than anything.

Black residents in Carver Ranches, Florida, rebelled primarily with sniper fire in late September 1969, weeks after the "near riot" that resulted when the sheriff's deputy attempted to take the young rock thrower to jail. On Thursday, September 25, a group of Black men were working on a car at the home of Eugene "Dino" Jones and his family. Two white youths approached and looked under the hood, claiming the header pipe belonged to them. The car's owner, Curtis Green, had purchased the header pipe and had a bill of sale to prove it. The white boys left, reported the "crime," and returned with a sheriff's deputy and an officer from the nearby city of Hollywood. "It didn't make any difference that Curtis had proof he bought the parts," said twenty-three-year-old Carol Bohler, one of the young Black men on Jones's lawn. Law enforcement "towed his car away." [31] As Bohler told it, the police were the thieves, having stolen Green's car on the white youths' word and in the face of documentary evidence.

A crowd gathered outside Jones's home, and young people began throwing rocks at the police cars. "Most of us men were trying to stop the kids from throwing stones," Bohler recalled, "but some of them kept on." Beyond a few strikes on the head with police nightsticks, no one was seriously injured. According to Bohler and other witnesses, after most of the police left the scene, a Pembroke Park officer remained stationed on the block. The officer got out of his car, rested his arm on the hood and shot at Jones's house with his pistol multiple times. "At first I thought it was blanks, until I heard a bullet that was parked in the yard," Bohler said. "I was scared for my little kids in that house," who ranged in age from nine months to three years old, "and Dino Jones' old grandmother, who was there baby-sitting."[32]

Two hours later, at around ten o'clock, snipers riddled a number of patrol cars and the Pembroke Park police station with .38- and .22-caliber bullets and shotgun pellets. "You could hear the pellets bouncing off the station," a desk sergeant said. "Then somebody cut down with a rifle or an automatic pistol with hollow points and all hell broke loose." More than one hundred officers came to the scene, some of them riding, along with Florida Governor Claude Kirk, in the Highway Patrol's armored riot prevention vehicle, nicknamed the "Monster Machine." The County had produced a "show of force to let them know we mean business," in Sheriff Ed Stack's words. The gunshots continued into the night, though no one was seriously injured.[33]

In some instances, the army of cops, the warning shots, the tear gas, and the return fire from police succeeded in bringing rebellion to an end. At other times, these escalatory tactics led the crowd to break into smaller groups, making it harder for police to find them even as they continued the violence and property destruction. A line from the Fort Wayne *Journal-Gazette* captures the game of hide-and-seek that frequently resulted: "Police were kept busy chasing down roving gangs of young Negroes, some on foot and some in cars, who threw rocks at windows of cars and stores and quickly disappeared." Participants remained one step ahead of the police, shattering the windows of nearby stores and taking televisions, stereos, whiskey, and clothes. In Columbus, by the time police "platoons" were positioned in the spot where fifty to seventy-five youths had gathered minutes before, the "troublemakers" were gone. The next night, as soon as police stationed marksmen on the roofs in the area and sent their four-man cars out on patrol, the participants—a reported three hundred fifty at that point—had disappeared.[34]

The cycle could be ended through police action, whether overbearing or shrewdly de-escalatory. It could end when the crowd had spent its energy. It could also be brought to an end by ministers, community leaders, and radical activists, who often acted as important intermediaries between participants and the police. In Akron, Willie Clark of the United Services For All organization and local reverend Willie Jackson walked the streets in order to keep young people "in line," while simultaneously asking law enforcement to exercise compassion for the participants, many of whom lived in impoverished households. Meanwhile, the Poor People's Headquarters, which remained open twenty-four hours a day during the rebellion, put out a leaflet titled "Message to a Black Man," which discouraged "members of the black community from engaging in violence for fear of damage and loss of life" and asked the police to "use all human passion possible if young people are found in unlawful situations."[35] These organizations and leaders did not condone the actions of the participants, but they also vociferously critiqued how police responded to community violence with ever-increasing violence on their own part.

In Indianapolis, four Black activists reportedly came to the defense of a white reporter after he was hit in the head by an angry resident. "Hey man, leave this guy alone. He's all right," said one of the peacekeepers. For their efforts, Indianapolis Deputy Police Chief Raymond J. Strattan praised the tenant leaders of Lockefield Gardens as well as the Black Panther Party for "exerting a calming influence on the crowd" after the Lockefield Big 10 Mart was firebombed during the first night of rebellion. Mayor Richard G. Lugar noted that many Black residents "were instrumental in encouraging the crowd that gathered to disperse."[36] Community residents, in Indianapolis and many other cities, were just as if not more successful than police in restoring peace and preventing injury. The police wanted to enforce the law and restore order. The peacekeepers wanted everyone to be safe.

THE AFTERMATHS OF a cycle of police violence and rebellion varied greatly from situation to situation and depended largely on how local authorities responded to Black demands. Even if law enforcement officials tended to pathologize rebellion by labeling participants "hoodlums" and attributing the violence to "a bunch of troublemakers" or "outside influences," many city officials and journalists tried to identify deeper causes. Participants and residents consistently stressed that policing strategies in general, and the way officers treated youth of color in particular, set off the rebellions. "It's those young cops who cause the trouble. They come in with their guns drawn just looking to use them," a young male participant told a *Decatur Review* reporter. "All they're looking for is an excuse to shove you around or to use that gun. When they come in here, it's 'boy' this and 'boy' that."[37]

The "double standard" of law enforcement was clear to this teenage boy, whose views may well have been shaped not only by his own experience but by the civil rights and Black Power movements, which provided him and other young people with language to understand such slights. The Decatur police let the white drag racers get away with the illicit activity. "Like you think, they'll ever arrest those white guys dragging on Eldorado?" a Black racer charged. "You ever see all those white guys sitting in their cars parked in drive-ins or the car washes along there? Just let some black guys do that and the police move right in," he said. "Man, if the police spent as much time on Eldorado as they do here, there'd be no dragging there." And when Black and white drag racers competed against each other, "it's the black that'll get the ticket and arrest. That's the way it always happens for those white guys get off free." The answer to the problem, as the young man saw it, was to "build a drag strip and to leave us alone."[38] The drag racing had never caused an accident, and very few residents complained. Ending the violence would be easy: provide recreational spaces, free from excessive policing, to young people.

In Decatur and other cities, rebellions opened up conversations about the long-standing problem of police brutality. Horace B. Livingston Jr., president of the Decatur Association for Black Action, underscored the drag racers' claims. According to Livingston, police officers beat people "without provocation," they invaded people's homes, and they used mace "indiscriminately and without warning." When residents attempted to file formal complaints against the offending officers, law enforcement officials refused to accept them. In the face of such allegations, local politicians celebrated the police department for its handling of the situation. "Officers should be commended for not overreacting," Councilman Charles W. Gallagher proclaimed. It was a slap in the face. "Now, we know where we stand in Decatur, and it's at the bottom," Livingston told a reporter. "We will act accordingly in the future."[39]

With law enforcement officials dismissing Black residents' grievances, Decatur's local Human Relations Commission took steps to put a response system in place. A week after the rebellion, members voted unanimously to establish a hotline out of the city's Community Relations office that would record complaints and follow up on claims about police violence. Police officials bristled at the idea. Police Chief Harold Lindsten said the hotline was "unnecessary." He suggested the commission members were "acting on rumors" and were "not trained to handle" such matters. Although Lindsten indicated that he had a number of complaints "sitting on my desk" from the two days of disturbances, he refused to comment on them to a reporter.[40]

Officials elsewhere sometimes frankly acknowledged police violence and promised action. "I know we have police brutality in Albuquerque," Lieutenant Governor Robert Mondragon said at a rally attended by four hundred people in Roosevelt Park the day after the Albuquerque rebellion began, and where chants of "Chicano Power" and "People Power" could be heard. "Police brutality is not alleged—it is factual." Mondragon and Attorney General David Norvell pledged to work with city officials to address longstanding grievances. In Hoboken, the mayor, police chief, and other state and city officials sat down with five Puerto Rican community leaders for a five-hour meeting at the Holiday Inn in Jersey City as the rebellion continued into its second night. Hoboken Prosecutor Geoffrey Gaulkin agreed to release thirty-three people who were arrested during the unrest to the custody of an attorney selected by Puerto Rican residents. Gaulkin also assured the community leaders that he would investigate allegations of police brutality in connection with the uprising. In return, the leaders pledged to discuss the agreement with their constituents and take steps to prevent rebellion in the future.[41]

At times, residents brought the root causes to the fore before a rebellion burned out or was put down. In the middle of the violence in Akron, Black residents went to municipal officials and law enforcement to make their case. Akron Mayor John Ballard called a meeting with twenty Black businessmen, government officials, and social service agents to "find out what you people can do to help stop these kids from continuing their rampage." The Black elite offered little advice on how to keep the young people off the streets, and the meeting went nowhere until "four black militants entered the room," as the *Akron Beacon Journal* described them, and the tone of the conversation changed.[42]

The militants had an answer: social services. "The black youth relate to certain cultural projects like bands, speakers, and programs they can understand," they explained, calling for an investment into the young people who were outside throwing rocks. "Mr. Mayor, we can play basketball only for so long." Police Chief Harry Whiddon asked the militants, all of them young Black men, why "innocent citizens were being stoned?" The militants explained that the causes were routine police harassment, the dearth of recreational facilities accessible to Black youth outside of basketball courts, "200 years of repression and frustration from the white man," and a lack of jobs. "Everybody's been turned down this summer for employment."[43]

The question, from the militants, was how Mayor Ballard and other officials would respond "when this rebellion" was over. "Will we just be told to shuffle back to the basketball courts, Mr. Mayor?" Ballard asked for their patience. He couldn't work miracles "for you or for anyone else in the city. There is no one who can wave a magic wand and get rid of the problems," he said, condescending and firm. "It takes planning and hard work with people facing the hard realities of life." The mayor made no promises for change and refused to negotiate, but he seemed open to the idea of cultural programs, which would be less costly and disruptive than the other proposals.[44]

Three days after the sniping in Carver Ranches, Robbie Brayboy, the Secretary of the Carver Ranches Homeowners Association, called a meeting with city officials from the surrounding communities of Hollywood, Miramar, and Pembroke Park, as well as Broward County Sheriff Ed Stack. Residents wanted to give their side of the story, which was that police started everything by shooting "into a house full of children," as resident Ellen Sears charged. The meeting also presented Brayboy and others with an opportunity to ask for better police protection ("without the accompanying harassment"), better recreational facilities, and basic public works. "You are the ones who put a man on the moon in a decade and it's taken 20 years to get one water pipe into this area," twenty-one-year-old Joseph Smith said. "Clean this place up."[45]

THE CYCLE BEGAN WITH the police, who moved through the ghettos of America "like an occupying soldier in a bitterly hostile country," as James Baldwin had observed in 1960, so that their very presence— their perceived callousness to the inequality around them—felt violent in itself.[46] An unnecessary encounter between police and young Black and Brown residents, or an arrest, could tip into community violence. This almost always took the form of rock throwing, initially. In response, police reinforcements dressed in riot gear and carrying high-grade rifles financed by the federal government threw tear gas grenades at the crowds. Often the rebellion would turn more violent from there, with shooting and sniping, firebombing, and arrests. The cycle could play out for multiple nights before the rebellion came to an end in one way or another, followed by some attempts, however meager, to at least look at deeper causes.

As the cycle played out in cities large and small across the United States between 1968 and 1972, it set in motion dynamics between residents in communities of color and police for decades to come, laying the foundation for "zero tolerance" and "broken windows" policing characterized by the aggressive enforcement of misdemeanors in order to prevent future disorder. (Well before the early 1980s, when the "broken windows" theory emerged as the guiding principle of modern American law enforcement, actual broken windows that resulted from political violence could be found in cities across the country). As rebellions persisted after 1972, although not with the frequency of those in the immediate post-King era, the cycle remained unbroken, further demonstrating that aggressive policing tends to incite violence, especially when residents are protesting the very thing they are then subjected to.

Rebellion was a consequence of the all too predictable presence of the police. The late 1960s and early 1970s were the crucible years—the period when the War on Crime pumped resources in police departments and dramatically escalated surveillance, harassment, and violence in American cities. Each element in the cycle had distinctive origins, actors, and strategies on both sides. And without understanding each element in turn, it is impossible to begin to understand this era of rebellion or its persistent legacy.

2

THE PROJECTS

A group of residents in the Pyramid Courts housing project in Cairo, Illinois, gathers for a protest. (From *On the Battlefield: Cairo, Illinois*, ed. Robert Sutherland, 1970)

T HE TOP OF THE Mississippi River levee in Cairo, Illinois, offered a panoramic view of the west side of the Pyramid Courts housing project. On the last day of March 1969, white men stood on the levee, sixty feet in the air, with guns in their hands. The community they surveilled stretched a mere two blocks long and one block wide. The two thousand people living in it, roughly half of the city's Black residents, occupied twenty wood-framed buildings, all in need of a fresh paint job.[1] A rail yard sat between the levee and Pyramid Courts, and a train crew happened to be milling about that evening. When the shooting began at around ten o'clock, residents in Pyramid Courts reached for their guns. Some rushed outside to shoot out the dozen or so streetlights in the project to prevent themselves from being illuminated to their attackers.

The shot-out streetlights went unfixed, and Pyramid Courts remained completely dark at night for years. But this was just as well. Residents would turn off the lamps in their apartments when the sun went down, or they would board up their windows. Children would do homework in the darkness. "It was hard to study without lights," Harry Lee Williams remembered of his childhood in Pyramid Courts, "and it certainly hampered our social lives." When it was deemed safe enough, Williams and his friends would play in the project's basketball court, practicing their jump shots under the glow of the moon and a streetlamp a few blocks away that cast some light toward the hoop. The only way players could tell if they made a basket was if they heard a clinking from the chain basketball net. "Sometimes we'd be arguing about what kind of sound it made. "That went in the hole!" "No, it hit the front of the chain."[2] Williams and his friends learned to improvise, as did everyone else in Pyramid Courts, from that day in March 1969 until the shooting finally stopped three years later.

Located on the fringes of Cairo, Pyramid Courts had been built in an area vulnerable to flooding, on the exact spot where formerly enslaved people were kept in a contraband camp under the Union army's watch. Its construction and that of the other, white housing project in Cairo, Elmwood Place, began in 1939 when the Federal Housing Authority broke ground on new public housing across the country as part of the New Deal. The white elites who controlled the Cairo Housing Authority intended the two projects to be wholly segregated, down to their names: "Pyramid Courts for Africa," "Elmwood Place for the

White American Dream." Authorities selected an uptown location for Elmwood Place, between Thirty-Seventh and Fortieth Streets, around the corner from the grand Victorian mansions that evoked Cairo's glory days in the decades after the Civil War, when steamboats still plied the Mississippi. For appearances' sake, work crews occasionally cleaned up the brick homes in Elmwood, a courtesy the city's Housing Authority did not extend to its Black tenants in Pyramid Courts. By the late 1960s, the apartments in Pyramid Courts were decaying: plumbing failed, ceilings cracked, and roaches and rats proliferated. Tenants had to pay for all repairs with their own money. Families unknowingly drank water contaminated with lead. Conditions in Elmwood Place were only slightly better, but its white residents didn't have to worry about getting shot while they went about their lives. Many Black and white Cairo residents could not even secure an apartment in the subpar public housing. Since 1960, only nine new houses were built and two hundred were torn down in the city, leaving 45.8 percent of all residents in Cairo in deteriorating homes. During the 1960s and 1970s, Cairo consistently ranked first among Illinois cities in the proportion of residents living in poverty, second in the number of people living in sub-standard housing, and third in its levels of unemployment.[3]

Pyramid Courts had been at the center of the rebellion that began on July 17, 1967, just as the flames in Newark had subsided and exactly a week before Detroit exploded. After two days of firebombings and shooting between Black residents on one side and the police and white vigilantes on the other, Mayor Lee P. Stenzel called a three hour meeting with eight young community leaders who lived in the project—during which, as the *New York Times* reported, "City officials and rebellious Negroes exchanged shouts." The night before, one hundred National Guardsmen had patrolled the perimeter of the all-Black community, armed with M1 rifles. Now, in the light of day, the young Black activists sat with city council members, law enforcement authorities, and representatives of the state Migrant Council, the National Association for the Advancement of Colored People (NAACP), and the Illinois Commission on Human Relations in a smoke-filled second-story room in the project's administrative building.[4]

The rebellion was in response to the infrastructure of racial oppression in a town where Black residents, numbering about thirty-eight hundred in total, constituted just under half of the population and yet were locked out of political and economic institutions by design. "We are fighting this discrimination—this economic thing," thirty-year-old Johnny Brantley explained. "This is not Black Power but Negro strategy," twenty-seven-year-old Willie Bingham said. "We need jobs, we got a right to live, same as you people."[5] The eight young men demanded an end to police brutality. They wanted representation in city hall, in the fire department, and in the police department. They wanted jobs in Cairo's industries, its banks, its stores, and its public utilities, all places where Black residents were only hired as janitors, if at all. They asked for an overhaul of Pyramid Courts. "Negroes are living in shacks," they said of the rotting row houses with yards of mud where the city's other half lived, crammed together. "We goin' to keep fighting until we get something around here," Bingham threatened.[6]

Hoping to prevent widespread destruction, Stenzel promised more jobs for Black residents, the hiring of Black police and firemen (there was only one Black officer on Cairo's twenty-person police force, and there were no Black firemen), and to enforce nondiscrimination in hiring (all fifty-five employees of the city-owned public utility companies were white). The mayor pledged to "keep the peace no matter who it hurts," but expressed reservations about meeting the demands the young community leaders had put forth. Stenzel told the press that city hall would "see what in the world we can do and how. But, doggone it, you can't just shove things like this down people's throats."[7] The Black representatives had asked for too much, too soon.

Many of the young men in the room had been involved in civil rights struggles in Cairo since the early 1960s, and they were tired of waiting. Fieldworkers from the SNCC (including John Lewis, who would go on to speak at the March on Washington the following year) had trained activists and advised on an integration campaign in Cairo in the summer of 1962. Working with the local NAACP and the SNCC chapter in nearby Carbondale, sixteen-year-old Charles Koen organized Black high school students and Pyramid Courts residents into the Cairo Nonviolent Freedom Committee. Under the SNCC's guidance, seventy-five Black students held sit-ins at restaurants and formed picket lines. They were assaulted, sprayed with fire hoses, and stabbed by white people, just like their counterparts in the South.[8]

Soon after, the Freedom Committee launched "Operation Open City" to desegregate the city's swimming pool, roller rink, youth center, barbershops, and churches through direct action. The Cairo police threw as many of the young protesters in jail as they could, including Koen and Lewis. The committee shifted strategies, moving from direct action to civil suits against the swimming pool and the roller rink for denying admission to Black patrons; they won both cases. Koen and a group of thirty-eight students went to the rink, which was owned by Cairo police officer Billy Thistlewood, to test whether their victory in court would actually make a difference. The students were attacked by white men with bicycle chains, lead pipes, and baseball bats, and Koen and others ended up in the hospital. Meanwhile, rather than open the pool to Black swimmers following the lawsuit, the owners simply closed the facility, boarding up its doors and windows, and filling the pool with concrete, effectively making it a monument to racism in downtown Cairo.[9]

The 1962 desegregation campaign did at least succeed in integrating Cairo's restaurants and stores, but Black residents remained disproportionately unemployed and underemployed. The fires and the shooting in 1967 presented a new opportunity to draw attention to root causes and force change. Maybe the outcome would be different five years after the initial burst of protests; the city's young Black people could point to new civil rights protections and their own growing militancy as reasons for optimism.

During the 1967 rebellion, with the protests and beatings of his high school days behind him, Koen, then twenty-one years old, boldly asserted to the mayor and other local officials at the meeting in Pyramid Courts: "We have seventy-two hours to meet this emergency." If the city did nothing, Brantley cautioned the city officials, "The next thing you know, Cairo will look like Rome burning down."[10]

Chesley Willis, the sheriff of Alexander County, snorted in response: "You haven't got 10 percent of your own people who will back you." To him, Koen, Brantley, and the other activists were nothing more than extortionists, lacking the power to back up their threats and hiding behind a moralist rhetoric of racism to justify violence.

"If these demands are not met in seventy-two hours, you'll find out how many are backing us," Willie Hollis replied.[11]

"If that happens, you'll find out how many white extremists there are here," the sheriff warned. The demands Koen, Hollis, and the other young leaders made were not met (the Cairo Retail Merchants Association and the Chamber of Commerce did agree to send letters to their members recommending they hire Black workers), and the city's "white extremists" mobilized.[12] The 1967 rebellion came to an end after a total of three days, burning out on its own. Immediately after, white residents founded a vigilante group called the "Committee of Ten Million" to protect their families, homes, and property from the firebombing, and to hold Cairo's rigid color line. The supremacists terrorized Black Cairoites on an everyday basis, driving around Pyramid Courts, pointing their rifles at passersby, and when Black children were on their way to school, they threatened them with German shepherds.

The low-grade terror continued for two years, until March 31, 1969, when the vigilantes fired into Pyramid Courts, Black men fired back, and the railyard crew got caught in the crossfire. Police arrived. More shots were fired, with the exchanges lasting between one and three hours. Cairo Police Chief Carl Clutts insisted that none of his fellow whites were involved, and that Pyramid Courts residents had started the entire affair by firing at the rail crew. A witness corroborated the official story, claiming that he "saw a group of Negroes coming out of a school on Fourteenth Street with a bunch of guns" about fifteen minutes before the shooting began. One Black man was arrested: twenty-five-year-old Jerry Harrod, who reportedly ignored police orders to halt and then was caught with a rifle under his coat.[13] Anyone in Pyramid Courts would have explained that Harrod and others only armed themselves in self-defense.

The shooting in Cairo made the national news. A *Time* magazine headline from September 1969 called these events the "War in Little Egypt." Unlike in many other cities that fell into the cycle of police violence and Black rebellion, the cycle in Cairo did not fizzle out and it was not put down; on the contrary, it would continue on and off again for years, until the spring of 1972. The pocked walls and shattered windows in Pyramid Courts served as a reminder of just how vulnerable residents were to the white marauders and the white cops who often joined together to harass and attack them. "We're going to go out to Pyramid Courts and what we should do is bomb them all out or blow them all up," a former police sergeant recalled his fellow officers saying. When they didn't join them, the police left the white men with guns alone, to do as they pleased.[14]

White vigilantes would shoot into the project from the levee on its west side, and from the increasing number of bombed-out buildings to the north and east. Periodically, the city would institute a curfew at six or seven o'clock for Pyramid Courts residents alone. The state would send National Guardsmen to patrol the perimeter of the project armed with military-grade rifles and a fleet of Jeeps, to "ease Cairo's racial tension." Police would even shoot into the housing project with machine guns from an armored vehicle (dubbed "the Great Intimidator" by Black residents) granted to the Cairo Police Department in 1970 by Illinois Governor Richard Ogilvie; it was intended to help bring the "indiscriminate gunfire and lawlessness to an end." Residents would sometimes sleep in their bathtubs, where they were less likely to be hit by a bullet from the outside forces. And sometimes the residents of Pyramid Courts would fire back. Before long, a firearm could be found in nearly all two hundred fifty households in the project.[15]

Though public housing has acquired negative connotations, Pyramid Courts and other projects built during the New Deal era, or in the early postwar period, offered vast improvements to daily life for their tenants. For many white Americans, public housing was a stepping-stone to homeownership in the suburbs and, by extension, to financial security for generations. For many Black families, public housing was the only decent, affordable shelter available. In Peoria, Illinois, the state transformed temporary barracks for Korean War veterans into desirable public housing for low-income Black families. With their basic modern amenities, Peoria's Taft Homes were a step up from the slums, where residents had to carry wood, coal, and kerosene to the stove in order to eat and to heat water for bathing. "My brother and I envied our friends who lived in the project," Peoria resident John Parker remembered. "As a child I longed to live in the projects so I could take a bath in a real tub." When he was fifteen years old, in 1957, Parker finally had a bathtub at home—along with hot water and gas heating—when his family moved to the Taft Homes near the Illinois River, some three hundred miles north of Pyramid Courts in Cairo.[16]

But by the late 1960s, the initial sheen of modern living had faded
in Black housing projects such as Pyramid Courts and the Taft Homes.
Across the nation, public housing had become the most visible mani-
festation of the consequences of segregation and neglect. Residents sent
their children to sub-par schools in neighborhoods with sub-par recreational facilities. They faced high rates of unemployment and underemployment, as well as over-policing and under-protection.[17] Still, the
ongoing shortage of available housing for low-income Black renters in
Cairo and many other cities made public housing the best of a bad set
of options—if not the only option if they hoped to survive being Black
and poor in America.

The over-policing of Black housing projects, already a fact of
urban life by the mid-1960s, escalated during the early War on Crime.
As "problem areas" with high rates of poverty and reported crime,
housing projects provided law enforcement the opportunity to monitor, patrol, and detain people.[18] These practices were central to the
crime war, which encouraged police to make themselves a continuous presence amid concentrated Black poverty, where criminals and
potential criminals were sure to be discovered. By the late 1960s, residents were growing tired of interacting with officers, of coming into
contact with armed agents of the state on a daily basis. Law enforcement saw everyday contact with Black residents as their duty. The
message was simple: Black people should get used to the police being
part of their pickup basketball games, walks home from work, and
family barbeques.

The conditions within housing projects and their unique designs
led to distinct forms of enforcement and regulation, as well as distinct forms of rebellion. With anywhere between several hundred to
thousands of tenants, housing projects meant large numbers of people
could clearly spot police the instant they arrived on the scene, which
made police even more paranoid when they patrolled these spaces, and

with good reason. High-rise projects such as Cabrini Green and the Robert Taylor Homes in Chicago made shooting down at police from one's own apartment window an option. In one- or two-story projects, including Miami's Liberty Square, the homes were huddled together, yet between them were many alleyways in which to hide. The people in Pyramid Courts had shot out streetlights and boarded up their homes as necessary defensive measures. In Peoria, Illinois, in July 1968, residents of the Taft Homes built barricades in an attempt to block police from entering. That same month in Stockton, a mid-sized city in California's Central Valley, Black residents seized an opportunity to kidnap police officers who were patrolling through the community gymnasium. The kidnapping was the culmination of a two-day rebellion in the segregated Sierra Vista project that began on July 17, 1968, when two police officers came to break up a party just after one o'clock that morning.

This scenario—police arriving to put an end to festivities in public housing—commonly resulted in confrontations with Black tenants. In May 1969, in the northern Los Angeles neighborhood of Pacoima, when police reportedly responded to a call about a party in the San Fernando Gardens housing project, they were met with a "barrage" of rocks and bottles thrown from a crowd of some seventy-five teenagers. One officer was hit on the head with a rock. When twenty-five more officers arrived as reinforcements, the crowd quickly scattered back to their homes.[19]

The Stockton police did not get off as easily as the force in Los Angeles. The partygoers in Sierra Vista started arguing with the officers, waking up their neighbors and drawing more people outside. A crowd quickly formed. The two cops—outnumbered and vulnerable—called for backup. Soon, more than forty white officers, including sheriff's deputies and highway patrolmen, descended on the Black housing project. The escalation of force only fueled the transformation of a party into a protest. Over a loudspeaker, Sergeant Wilson E. Stewart announced that everyone outside of their homes was unlawfully assembled and would be arrested unless they went back inside.[20]

Stewart's threat backfired, as Sierra Vista residents started throwing rocks and bottles, smashing the windshields of police cars, and attacking policemen. Six officers suffered facial cuts or broken teeth. "My face and body feel like I've been run over by a steam roller," officer John Marnoch told a local news reporter after several men knocked him to the ground and began kicking him repeatedly in the head and upper torso. Stockton's *Record* did not report the number of residents who suffered serious injuries, but the paper did mention that police arrested eleven people—all Black boys and men between the ages of thirteen and twenty-three.[21]

White youths had battled with police in the segregated north section of Stockton just three months before the Sierra Vista rebellion, throwing eggs and rocks at officers. Most of these young people taken into custody were immediately released to their parents and did not face charges. Most of their Black counterparts whose actions were indistinguishable (minus the eggs) were unable to make the high three-thousand-dollar bail that had been set for each person charged with resisting arrest and failure to disperse. They sat in jail through the weekend. As local activist Ralph Lee White explained this differential treatment: "If we have a little fun, it's a riot. If they have a little fun, it's a melee."[22]

The next day, July 18, both the police and the project's tenants were on high alert. Police sent additional officers to Sierra Vista, hoping to find more people involved in the previous night's disturbance while heading off another uprising; residents wanted to prevent other young men from being detained. In the late afternoon, twenty-four-year-old officer Richard "Dick" Harmon and twenty-five-year-old officer Charles M. Sargent went to Sierra Vista to arrest twenty-one-year-old James D. Jones for his alleged participation in the previous night's unrest. Residents hurled glass bottles at the officers as they cuffed Jones and put him into the squad car.[23]

Soon after Jones was processed at the jail, Harmon received a call from the dispatcher that someone had attempted to break into the Sierra Vista gym. He drove to the project with twenty-four-year-old officer Doug Wilholt to investigate. As soon as the two policemen arrived and opened the gym's doors, residents locked them inside. News of the kidnapping spread quickly. More people came out of their homes, surrounding the facility, and soon the crowd grew from fifty to two hundred fifty. For more than two hours, the crowd hurled fire-bombs, rocks, and bottles at the building, screaming "Pigs!" and other expletives (the Stockton Police Department at the time said that the anti-police slur stood for "Pride, Integrity, Guts"). "You don't have to do this," was all Wilholt and Harmon could say to the participants through the gym's windows.[24]

Only after the police saturated the area with more than seventy-five local officers supported by twenty sheriff's deputies and twelve highway patrolmen from departments in the nearby towns of Lodi, Manteca, and Tracy, did Harmon and Wilholt go free. Yet after the officers were released, Sierra Vista residents threw twenty-five firebombs, mainly against the roof and walls of the gymnasium, but also into cars and into the nearby elementary school. Stockton Police Chief Jack O'Keefe ordered a number of county and state patrol and probation officers to call parents in the project, in an attempt to get the young people off the streets. The move appeared to work. At two o'clock in the morning the police chief relieved scores of off-duty cops who were standing by in the event the situation escalated even further. The next day, the cover of the *Record* featured a photograph of the parked police car the project's tenants had burned.[25]

Sierra Vista residents had responded to aggressive policing strategies with taunts and firebombs, and by kidnapping cops. Police Chief O'Keefe would assert that the rebellion was completely unexpected, and that "Negroes have never had beef with the police here in Stockton." But the actions of the department had concerned Black residents for some time. The night before the rebellion in Sierra Vista began, on July 16, a local civil rights organization known as the Black Unity Conference, and headed by Black professionals, presented a series of demands to the Stockton city council. Influenced by the Kerner Commission report, which had been released just five months prior in March 1968, the local Stockton group called for a greater voice in public spending, for a community-based public safety mechanism in the form of tenant patrols, and for a grievance board that would hold police accountable for brutality.[26]

In the aftermath of the fiery Sierra Vista rebellion, the Black Unity Conference continued to confront city council on the policing issue. Spokesman Edward Davis pointed out that "if the chief can state there have been no problems in the black community, it is obvious that he is unaware of what is going on in his department." Seeking to end the cycle of violence that led to the fires and the broken windows in Sierra Vista, Davis declared: "We want to make it unmistakably clear that if the police cannot perform their duties without provocation of further violence . . . with the same fervor that [Chief O'Keefe] will strive for law and order, we will strive for justice."[27] Davis hoped his remarks would draw attention to the fact that the violence in Sierra Vista had been sparked by police contact, and was not an inexplicable explosion of Black criminality.

Even if the police department dismissed the relevance of the encounter between the cops and the Sierra Vista residents that triggered the uprising, these events forced law enforcement authorities to listen to the community as never before. On July 19, the night after calm had been restored in Stockton, O'Keefe met with the Black Unity

Conference and other concerned residents in the Sierra Vista project and accepted their proposal to create a role for residents in policing their own community. Now, instead of conducting routine stop and frisks, the police department would enter the fifteen-square block area of Sierra Vista only in response to major crimes, accidents, and fires. Other minor but inflammatory police functions, such as breaking up parties and handling fights, would be assigned to neighborhood patrols of unarmed young men and women between the ages of seventeen and twenty-five.[28]

In what appeared to be a major shift in police-community relations, the city of Stockton had ceded some authority to Sierra Vista residents. But the tenant patrols would prove to be short-lived. Three city council members, including Vice Mayor Mike Evanhoe, who called the strategy a "miscalculation," condemned the police department's approval of the new initiative. Councilmen Emmet E. Ward argued that O'Keefe had "set a very dangerous precedent [by] denying the right of protection through our police department" to Sierra Vista residents.[29] Ward's comment suggested that the only way to maintain public safety in Sierra Vista was to assert police power in the project, and to police ordinary activity (the social gatherings, the familial disputes) in the name of protecting the community (for the residents' "own good")—measures that residents themselves had not requested.

Many Stocktonians recognized the unintended results of police escalation. "This problem is not going to be cured by more guns, more police dogs, more anything," the longtime white resident Ben Parks said at the city council meeting four days after the rebellion. "The only way you're going to solve this is by loving your fellow man. And you'd better start right now. You have no choice." The coordinator of the tenant patrols, John Nisby, suggested a concrete first step toward realizing Parks's ambitious goal. "If the entire City Council were to go out there with the city manager and the chief of police and invite all the residents of Sierra Vista—the old people, the young people, but mainly the young people—and talk about the problems they are having, possibly you can eliminate violence, period."[30] Yet the authorities were unwilling to commit the time or the resources to hear the community's concerns. Ultimately the city council and the police department opted to restore the status quo, leaving the existing power structures and policing strategies intact. Force was the prevailing logic of public safety, and thus policy. Less than a week after the rebellion ended, on July 22, police began to resume their beats in Sierra Vista.

A FEW WEEKS LATER and halfway across the country, on Monday, July 29, 1968, residents in Peoria's Taft Homes rebelled. Law enforcement felt it coming, as young people in the project had been more defiant than ever in the months prior. "Policemen spend most of their shift dealing with teenagers who won't cooperate," Peoria patrolman Jack Beecker explained. Black teens had dared to challenge police impunity and to assert their right to ask why they were being stopped. "You say, 'Come over here,' and they twitch this way and that way and whine something like 'I ain't done nothing. What you want with me?'" The strategy of stopping people for no apparent reason was doomed from the start. As Beecker put it: "Everybody the police comes into contact with is a problem."[31]

To the south, in New Orleans, Louis Sirgo, the superintendent of the city's police, had the same reservations about the task of patrolling housing projects. Sirgo and his force almost always "expected trouble" in the Desire Projects in the city's Ninth Ward, where thirteen thousand residents lived on a one-hundred-acre plot of land. The large courtyards separating one row of homes from another made officers visible, and therefore vulnerable. "Hardly a week goes by," he said, that officers were not pelted with bricks and rocks during a routine arrest. The attacks came "mostly from youngsters" in crowds ranging from twenty-five to fifty people in size that left officers "just powerless." Sirgo believed his cops deserved public commendation "because of the restraint they have shown under these severe situations when you go in to make arrests and bottles and bricks rain on you." As he lamented, "it is a terrible situation."[32] Police repression and Black rebellion—the latter seen as both inevitable and meaningless—became a self-fulfilling prophecy. In Black projects from New Orleans to Peoria, officers expected trouble, and were almost sure to find it for that reason.

As reported in the *New York Times*, the Taft Homes uprising started when "a band of 50 youths began bombarding a neighborhood tavern with bricks, bottles, and firebombs." Police charged at the Black teens. All of them ran, except a pregnant sixteen-year-old named Sirita Hines, who was from Chicago and in town to visit her grandmother, who lived in the Taft Homes. The police informed Hines that she was under arrest for disorderly conduct and creating a disturbance. Hines told the police she hadn't thrown anything. It didn't matter. The police arrested Hines, treating her roughly and thereby putting her baby in danger, all in front of a growing crowd of people. Contrary to testimony from Taft Homes residents, police later claimed Hines violently resisted arrest.[33]

The arrest of Hines and a teenage boy did nothing to curb the violence. On the contrary. The crowd set up barricades on SW Adams Street, the main thoroughfare along the Taft Homes, and continued to throw rocks and bricks at passing cars and nearby buildings. Seven police officers advanced toward the group, wearing their regular, light blue, short-sleeved uniforms along with special riot helmets. When the officers got close to the "band of fifty," someone fired a shotgun at the police from at least sixty yards away. The pellets ripped into all seven cops, as well as a local radio newscaster along for the ride. Al Misener, a twenty-four-year-old rookie who probably wasn't much older than the person who shot him, had the worst of it, suffering wounds to his torso, legs, arms, and face. Misener was in the hospital as the action continued in the Taft Homes. "To me, it was exciting to be involved in that—the adrenaline was flowing," he recalled.[34]

Although the Peoria police force did show a degree of restraint by not returning fire initially, law enforcement quickly went on the offensive. Soon enough, the Taft Homes were completely surrounded by two hundred city, county, and state police. The officers shot out streetlights with service revolvers to conceal their positions, the same strategy Pyramid Courts residents would rely on to protect themselves from the white vigilantes. Sporadic gunfire could be heard for several hours that night.[35]

As in Stockton, authorities and residents had sharply contrasting ideas about the path forward. "We are confident we can work out our differences by cooperation, but not by shooting," Mayor Robert Lenhausen said at a press conference, announcing a dusk-to-dawn curfew for all residents of the project under the age of twenty-one (a curious move if the goal was, in fact, to foster cooperation). "We cannot live in a civil society by taking the law into our own hands," he declared. Like officials elsewhere, Lenhausen apparently failed to consider that Black people might not believe it necessary to take the law into their own hands if the law worked for instead of against them. Acknowledging such an idea would have required a major shift in public priorities and spending, not mere rhetorical appeals to "cooperation" and a few poorly funded social services. As a Black resident told a reporter, "they can spend thousands of dollars to bring in troops, pay policemen overtime, and repair damage, but they can't find the money to prevent these things."[36]

The city and the police department had a plan to prevent future rebellion, even if that plan was insufficient. In the two years that followed the first Taft rebellion, Peoria authorities could boast that they had taken all the right steps to foster "cooperation" as a means of addressing the "problem of racial relations." The local police department had created a two-man police-community relations unit led by a Black officer. An urban renewal program was underway to supplement the shortage of low-income housing and the rapidly decaying conditions in existing public housing. And various private groups had committed to providing job training to Black teenagers as part of a fifteen-thousand-dollar city program.[37]

Yet these measures did not go far enough to prevent another rebellion. Sirita Hines, the pregnant girl whose arrest fueled the first rebellion in the Taft Homes in the summer of 1968, found herself at the center of a second uprising in July 1970. Hines had moved to the Taft Homes shortly after her baby was born. She and another Taft tenant, Dorothy Johnson, had each been late on their rent payments for three months. They also had failed to pay "damage assessments" on their homes (which were already damaged as a result of the city's indifference). The Peoria Housing Authority wanted them out. But rather than handle the matter themselves, officials asked that police remove Hines, Johnson, and their children from the Taft Homes.[38]

Officers showed up to evict the women early in the morning of Thursday, July 23. They knocked on the apartment doors of both women, explaining to each tenant that she was being evicted. Police reported that Hines "gave no trouble." She had already been brutalized by police, and perhaps had been scarred by it. Now caring for a baby, the last place Hines wanted to go was jail. Johnson, however, expressed her understandable displeasure with the situation in a way that offended the police. When her arrest seemed imminent, Johnson pulled a butcher knife on the officers and the manager of the Taft Homes. She was taken to jail (and later, when it appeared Johnson had been injured by police at some point during the interaction, to St. Francis hospital, where doctors did not confirm that she was injured but still gave her an injection of painkilling drugs). The police removed all of the furniture and belongings from Hines's and Johnson's apartments. They walked the sidewalks and alleys of the Taft Homes with their revolvers on their hips, carrying couches, mattresses, nightstands, piles of clothes, and baby cribs. A group of residents watched the eviction unfold from the project's playground, perhaps plotting a response.[39]

When all of the furniture was on the street and the police left, young activists made their move. Horace Jones, the twenty-two-year-old leader of the militant, youth-led United Front organization, and a group of fellow activists broke off the new locks that had been placed on the evicted units. Together the young people picked up the couches, the mattresses, the nightstands, the piles of clothes, and the baby cribs from the street, and moved them right back into Hines's and Johnson's homes. Soon, about two hundred people were gathered outside the apartment duplex, helping the United Front members move the furniture, or simply observing the scene.[40] Before long, the police learned that they would need to return to the Taft Homes to once again remove the furniture from Hines's and Johnson's apartments. They returned and moved the furniture, but this time loaded it into a city garbage truck.[41]

At that point, members of the United Front and other young residents began hurling rocks and bottles in the direction of police officers, launching the rebellion directly in front of Johnson's apartment. Mike Mihm, a police advisor, arrived to inform the "troublemakers" that they were unlawfully assembled. Residents responded by smashing the windows of the Taft Homes management office. Police flooded the area just after six o'clock, and about fifty officers in total arrested as many people as they could on criminal trespassing charges. The officers were especially proud that they captured both the United Front's Jones and twenty-year-old Audobon Walls, the leader of a South Side group called the FBI Rangers, described by the *New York Times* as a "black militant organization" and by local papers as a "gang" of thirteen- to eighteen-year-olds. Longstanding targets of the Peoria Police Department, Jones and Walls now faced numerous charges, including disorderly conduct, criminal trespass, and resisting arrest.[42]

The rebellion raged into the night. Residents and police started knocking each other down with their fists as rocks flew through the air. Every available officer was called to duty as the unrest escalated, bringing the force deployed to the project to two hundred. At 10:10 p.m., Mayor E. Michael O'Brien declared a state of emergency that imposed a curfew for everyone under twenty-one, closed all of the city's bars, and prohibited the sale of gasoline (used in making fire-bombs) until the morning. The police blocked off SW Adams Street in front of the Taft Homes, hoping to keep the rebellion contained. But this did little to curb the violence. The rebels focused on the Taft Homes Offices, breaking its windows and looting it before throwing firebombs at the structure, gutting it within an hour and a half. The firemen who came to save what they could of the building were accompanied by two dozen police officers in riot gear. Non-participating residents who were still awake "peeked from windows or sat on porches watching police and firemen." Police still received reports that people were buying containers of gasoline.[43]

After midnight, the large crowd split into smaller groups and continued the attacks. By that point the rebellion had spread to the Warner Homes and the Harrison Homes on the South Side—the other segregated Black housing projects in Peoria. The participants, while still throwing rocks and bricks and firebombs, now started shooting at the anti-riot police. Snipers fired on a squad car and at two bars near the Warner Homes; two patrons suffered bullet wounds. There were twelve shooting incidents in all, and seventeen arsons reported, mostly against public property such as the Taft Homes offices. Police arrested nearly thirty people, including six juveniles. A series of firebombings the next night, Friday July 24, on the South Side of the city prompted the Mayor to declare another state of emergency. This time, participants in the rebellion mainly targeted dwellings that were already slated for demolition as part of the urban renewal effort. The damage done was thus not considered a serious matter by city authorities.[44]

As the rebellion wore on, residents targeted businesses around the Taft Homes. People broke the windows of Sparky's Cafe, throwing rocks and bricks along with tomatoes and peaches. They smashed the front windows of Couri's Food Town, about a mile down the street from the Taft Homes. And whether or not they knew patrolman Joseph P. Whallen had arrested Johnson during her eviction, snipers targeted Whallen as he drove up MacArthur Street in the direction of the Taft Homes, near Couri's Food Town, firing three shots in his direction. A group of twenty to twenty-five youths reportedly pushed a stolen station wagon down the street and then set fire to the front seat.[45]

By Saturday, the rebellion had largely run its course, save for a few more firebombings, including at the Tri-County Urban League office. Ultimately the police blamed the FBI Rangers for the sniping, the twenty firebombings, and the six injuries the rebellion had caused. In all, more than fifty Black residents were arrested.[46]

The day after the rebellion appeared to be over, finally, the lead editorial in Peoria's *Journal Star* bore a provocative title: "The Black Saboteurs." The newspaper did not touch on the cocktail of socioeconomic exclusion and overbearing policing that made the Taft Homes explode. Instead, the editorial blamed residents for behavior the authors predicted would only deter future investment into the "disadvantaged" communities, such as the modest job training program for Black youth that the businessmen of Peoria had established. "We are certainly in sympathy with those who have called for racial harmony, for understanding, for working together, and for peace in Peoria," the editorial began, assuming that patience and conversation were the primary solutions. However, "permissiveness" for people who "abuse and damage" public housing "pulls the rug out from under both public or private investments" to improve it.[47]

According to this line of argument, the uprisings threatened development initiatives to provide better housing, as taxpayers and private investors would not support "building things that will not be preserved and maintained, but will inevitably be abused and vandalized." Too much attention had been placed on the "over-reactions" of police and politicians to the riot—the hundreds of officers summoned to the Black areas of the city, the declaration of states of emergency and curfews. "Something must be done about the 'over-reaction' of some black revolutionaries and some black gangs," who were making progress "impossible," the editorial argued. "Who is going to step up and oppose the black saboteurs of services, housing, schooling and jobs?"[48] That opposition would not come in the form of better services, better schools, and access to jobs that Black people were fighting for, but in the form of more police and more draconian policing methods, exactly what residents of the projects were fighting against.

WHILE PUBLIC HOUSING WAS and remained a boon for many poor Black Americans into the 1960s, it also came to be seen by many as another source of state oppression, if not the most immediate, alongside the police. When rebellion occurred in housing projects, it often found expression in an attack on the project itself. In the July 1968 rebellion, Taft residents threw firebombs into the project's main office. In late September of that year, something similar happened in the Black East Side of Bridgeport, Connecticut. When police arrived to investigate a group of young people fighting on the grounds of the Father Panik Village project shortly after seven o'clock in the evening, the youths stopped fighting each other and started throwing rocks at the officers. The cycle had begun, but in the setting of the housing project that was home to some fifty-four hundred people, the participants smashed the windows of the housing project's pharmacy, market, and mail center, instead of vandalizing local businesses. They shattered the windows of the project's administrative building, too, before attempting to throw a firebomb on its roof; it landed instead near one of the patrolmen. The rock throwing and the property destruction continued for seven hours.[49]

Both the punitive and social welfare arms of the state weighed on housing project tenants and on other residents who relied on public services. They responded to the forces of state violence in their lives—police patrols and surveillance as well as delinquent housing authorities—by challenging evictions, throwing objects at officers, and destroying the offices and other symbols of authority within the projects themselves. As sites of concentrated poverty, housing projects gave residents good reason to rebel. When new policing strategies starting in the late 1960s specifically targeted these communities, the result was a powder keg.

The rocks and bricks, and the firebombs and bullets that were directed at police officers in most housing projects in the United States in the 1960s eventually stopped flying, even though underlying conditions remained unchanged or worsened. But the rebellion in Pyramid Courts and among the Black residents of Cairo, Illinois, was far from over. The purpose of the shooting that began on March 31, 1969, in Pyramid Courts was to intimidate "militant Negroes" into submission. It had the opposite effect. Charles Koen, local NAACP President Preston Ewing, and other activists who shaped Cairo's freedom struggle in the 1960s came together to establish a new organization—named, like the group in Peoria, the United Front—to continue the struggle against police brutality, systemic racism, and white violence that had inspired the rebellion of 1967. Returning to the tactics used earlier in the decade that succeeded in partially integrating Cairo, activists called for a citywide Black boycott of all stores in the business district, where Black customers were treated with contempt and where storeowners refused to hire Black workers. No longer would Black residents "provide money for the whites to buy bullets to shoot at them," a United Front spokesman later explained. The boycott began on April 7, 1969, with protesters marching through the streets of Cairo. Lasting for almost three years, it became one of the longest protests in American history.[50] The cycle returned, and recurred. In Cairo, from the spring of 1969 into the early 1970s, picketing was a weekly ritual, and gunfire directed at Black residents in Pyramid Courts from the forces of white hate was a nightly routine.

3

THE VIGILANTES

Mayor John L. Snyder walks a police German shepherd through the
streets of York, Pennsylvania, in the late 1960s. The K-9 Corps dogs
were frequently used to intimidate and brutalize Black residents.
(Collection of the York County History Center, York, PA)

THE CYCLE OF police violence and Black rebellion in the late 1960s
and early 1970s often started in, and consumed, public housing
areas. That was the main setting for rebellion within the American city.
But the police and the rebels were not the only people involved in every

case. Nearly two years before the protracted "race war" in Cairo began with shooting from the levee looking over Pyramid Courts, more than four hundred white residents gathered at St. Mary's Park in the city's Northside. It was July, 1967, and they came because their neighbors were attending, or because they saw a flyer calling for a meeting of the "White Citizens' Council" that would discuss how to "protect your life and property," or because they already belonged to such a group (or their ancestors did), or simply because white people usually formed armed groups whenever Black people disrupted the status quo.[1] The scene reminded Mayor Lee Stenzel, who had come to plead with the crowd, of the rampaging violence he witnessed at the age of seventeen during the 1917 riot in East St. Louis, when white people murdered hundreds of Black residents. East St. Louis's labor market had expanded during the First World War, opening up new military production jobs that attracted Black migrants from the South in droves. In cities across the industrial North, white people viewed the newcomers as a threat to their livelihood and turned to violence and intimidation to maintain their political and economic position. In East St. Louis, backed by the state police and local law enforcement, white mobs spent three days pulling Black residents from streetcars and beating them; they looted and burned Black homes. It was a prelude to the anti-Black mob violence in some three dozen cities during the Red Summer of 1919, and in Tulsa in 1921.

"I saw the slaughter and destruction," Stenzel told the white crowd in Cairo, half a century later. White people had killed an estimated two hundred Black residents during the East St. Louis riot, but perhaps even more disturbing to him was that the violence caused millions of dollars in property damage. "East St. Louis hasn't amounted to a damned thing since. If it happens here like it happened there, we won't have industry here for twenty-five years."[2] Stenzel indicated he was sympathetic to his white constituents' concerns, but warned that white supremacist violence had destroyed East St. Louis's future, and that Cairo seemed poised for a similar fate, with its scarcity of jobs for working class Blacks and whites, and with gatherings such as the one he was speaking to in St. Mary's Park.

When Stenzel delivered his warning in July 1967, the city had been engulfed for three days by a Black rebellion that was sparked by the suspicious death of a nineteen-year-old Black soldier, Robert L. Hunt, in the city jail. Police claimed Hunt committed suicide by hanging himself with his T-shirt, but many community members believed the young GI had been murdered by Cairo authorities. That Hunt's bruised body was sent for embalming before dawn only heightened Black skepticism. White homes and shops burned, and Black residents were beaten and arrested. Stenzel explained to the white crowd that he needed time to handle the situation, since "the Negro problem has been building a long time."[3] The transition from segregation to integration involved some growing pains the good people of Cairo would need to accept. Stenzel's emphasis on "communication" sounded weak to his audience, which wanted assurance that the city's Black residents would be put back in their place. They wanted law and order.

For the white people in St. Mary's Park, the solution to Stenzel's "Negro Problem" was straightforward. Ignoring the mayor, they formed the Committee of Ten Million. The job of the vigilante group would be to carry out the heavy-handed response the Mayor seemed unwilling to deliver. Similar groups had been coming together ever since the civil rights movement first gained momentum in the 1950s. Unlike many of the lynch mobs that had terrorized Black communities from Reconstruction to the middle of the next century, these new white supremacist groups attracted a more genteel class. The founders of the Committee of Ten Million included Peyton Berbling, the wealthy, chain-smoking, white-haired lawyer in his early seventies who had served as district attorney and would return to the post in 1968; Larry Potts, the dapper pastor of Cairo Baptist Church; the prominent local businessman Tom Madra, one of the organizers of the rally in St. Mary's Park; and the lumber dealer Bob Cunningham.[4] Like the Citizens' Councils of America that could be found across the South, the Committee of Ten Million used intimidation and violence to counter the freedom movement, relying not only on brute force but also on their political and economic power.

The group took its name from an essay former President Dwight Eisenhower penned for *Reader's Digest* in August 1967, in response to the devastating fires in Detroit and Newark that summer. "These riots are a growing danger to our nation and must be handled without temporizing," Eisenhower wrote. The "savage riots" were due to a "neglect of certain fundamental moral principles," which in turn signaled that the country was "plunging into an era of lawlessness, which in the end can lead only to anarchy." Eisenhower ended his article with a suggestion: "we need a 'Committee of Ten Million' citizens dedicated to law and order in this country." Members would uphold "proper principles" and would participate in community groups "trying to combat the blight of crime and delinquency." Eisenhower did not explicitly call for white mob violence, but it is understandable why Berbling and his cofounders interpreted his words as demanding that very thing.[5]

The Committee of Ten Million quickly organized a force of armed, white residents, who prepared to defend their families and property against Black rebellion. "Its purpose is protective, not punitive," Cairo Chamber of Commerce President Harry Bolen insisted, "nor is it racist, inasmuch as Negroes were invited to join."[6] The white supremacist organization unsurprisingly failed to attract a single Black member, but nearly every white person in Cairo who was anybody enthusiastically joined the cause. Soon the vigilantes became informally known as the "White Hats" for the white helmets they wore. Whether this was an intentional nod to the white hoods worn by members of the Ku Klux Klan was not clear.

The White Hats believed it was their duty to support the local police, and law enforcement officers, many of whom were members, embraced the group. Sheriff Chesley Willis and Alexander County Coroner Donald Turner deputized any white person who wanted to assume police functions, to the point that Cairo businessman Phillip D. Marsden famously bragged that he "could get my dog deputized in this town." Marsden and the White Hats' six hundred members patrolled the streets of Cairo in groups, armed with shotguns, rifles, pistols, two-way radios, and police dogs, conducting paramilitary drills to practice for the impending battles with Black residents. Allowed to openly carry weapons and make arrests, the White Hats, as Berbling boasted to reporters, could "stop everything that moves in Cairo. If they can't move, they can't firebomb." At night, members took part in and amplified ongoing police harassment and intimidation, cruising around Cairo's Black neighborhoods and sticking shotguns and rifles out of the windows of their cars, which were adorned with bumper stickers that read, "Cairo, Love it or Leave it."[7]

Under constant threat from the White Hats, Black Cairoites waited patiently and peacefully for the city council to make good on its promise of police reform and expanded economic opportunities. The city did apply for and received a $75,000 federal grant to improve police-community relations but spent only $6,500 of the funds and was forced to return the rest to the Illinois Law Enforcement Commission. And although several Black patrolmen joined the Cairo Police Department, and a Neighborhood Youth Corps program provided jobs to unemployed Black youth, conditions changed little over the two years after the rebellion of 1967. In fact, the ubiquitous presence of the White Hats on semi-official patrol made the hardship Black residents faced feel even more acute. Because members of the Cairo establishment were either active members, or enthusiastically supported the White Hats' activities, local authorities and white vigilantes together sustained a climate of violence, fear, and resentment. In the build-up to the all-out war that exploded in the spring of 1969, the chant of those protesters boycotting white businesses—and their owners who fired on them with bullets paid for by Black patronage—was clear: "the White Hats must go because the Blacks are keeping the dough."[8]

The grip of the White Hats on Cairo's Black community was finally loosened by a young, white priest named Gerald Montroy who came to the city in August 1968 to address its alarming rate of Black poverty, which was twice the national average and ranked first of any city in Illinois. But even more than the crippling poverty, Montroy was disturbed by the White Hats, and tried to draw attention to their anti-Black violence. Based on an interview with Montroy, the *St. Louis Post-Dispatch* published an article on the organization that appeared on the front page of the March 23, 1969 edition under the headline: "Vigilante Corps in Cairo." The White Hats were using violence to keep Black residents "in line," according to Montroy. "The blacks in Cairo are afraid of the whites and are terribly oppressed by them." Black children required escorts home from school because as they walked by, white people stood on their lawns brandishing shotguns. A White Hats member had recently sicced his German shepherd on an eleven-year-old Black girl just to frighten her. As Montroy described the situation, "Cairo is a keg of racial dynamite."[9]

With the terror of the White Hats newly visible to a wider public, the organization and its local allies went on the offensive. The chamber of commerce dubbed Father Montroy an "irreverent and irresponsible priest" who had viciously slandered Cairo. Montroy was an outsider, a "troublemaker" who "fomented dissension between the races" by riling up Black people and getting involved in matters that should be left to local whites. The White Hats, by contrast, were "good citizens," as Berbling told a *Post-Dispatch* reporter. The white people who stood on their lawns with their shotguns and their dogs to frighten Black children "were protecting their property in an area where Negroes have been throwing stones through windows." Vigilantism was a logical response to Black rebellion, as far as Berbling and others in Cairo were concerned. Indeed, the White Hats were a "good thing," as the conservative pastor of St. Patrick's Church Hugh Kilfoil argued. "We can't have militants throwing bombs."[10]

A different kind of white group emerged to support Montroy and the Black residents living under the White Hats' regime. The day after Montroy's charges made the front page of the *Post-Dispatch*, an organization called the Concerned Clergy was established in East St. Louis. Bishop Albert Zuroweste organized the group because, as he put it, "The situation at Cairo necessarily disturbs every Christian conscience." The clergy wrote to the governor and other state officials about the vigilantes who had put Montroy's life in danger. Within a week, the group sent twenty priests and ministers to Cairo to support Montroy and the Black community. The Reverend Keith Davis, pastor of the Lutheran Inner-City Ministry of East St. Louis, explained that he and other Concerned Clergy members would stay in Cairo "as long as necessary to see to it that black men can live as full citizens and Father Montroy can continue his ministry free of harassment and intimidation."[11] Black residents may have wondered if this outside intervention by white clergy could lead to actual change.

Eight days after Montroy's accusations made headlines, on March 31, 1969, members of the White Hats started firing into Pyramid Courts from the levee to the west. The attack took place during the Concerned Clergy's visit and Black residents risked their own lives that night to guard the rectory of St. Columba, the old Black church in

Cairo that Montroy had assumed, in order to protect the pastors who were sleeping there.[12] The White Hats may have denied they were a vigilante organization, but there was no better term to describe them.

AS THE WHITE HATS TERRORIZED Black Cairo through the summer of 1969, another white vigilante force emerged just over the Mason–Dixon line in York, Pennsylvania. York had thrived as a manufacturing hub in the decades after the Civil War and much of its exemplary Victorian architecture still stands to this day. During the 1920s, York's Black population doubled, as significant numbers of migrants arrived from Aiken, South Carolina—a hotbed of Klan activity—in the mistaken assumption that they could escape white violence. Much like Cairo's United Front, Black residents in York rose up to defend their families and homes against white supremacist groups and law enforcement in 1969. York and Cairo were integrated, in theory, but many stores and restaurants, and white society in general, remained hostile to Black people. Police brutality was common. Black unemployment rates were twice as high as those of whites in both cities. "The black man can't be a technician, even with a college degree," an underemployed Black man from York explained. "He has to be a laborer." In York and Cairo, Black people lived in the areas most susceptible to flooding, and those who didn't make it into public housing lived in deteriorating tenements owned by white slum landlords.[13] The mayors were unresponsive to ongoing demonstrations for jobs and better living conditions, and reluctant to solicit federal War on Poverty funds that might have helped to address these problems.

The conditions in Cairo and York were similar to those in many other cities where Black residents rebelled in the late 1960s and early 1970s. But they were distinguished by the close alliances between law enforcement and white power groups that dominated both cities, and that caused unusually intense and protracted violence. The historian Peter Levy claims that, adjusted for population, the major uprising in York in the late 1960s was perhaps "the most severe of the era," and the Cairo rebellions lasted longer than any others. In Cairo, the sheriff deputized adults who joined the White Hats; in York, police officers provided guns and ammunition to young, white gang members— the Newberry Street Boys, the Swampers, the Yorklyn Boys, and the Girarders—in the name of self-defense and white power. Members would gather to play baseball, drink, fight rival gangs, and attack Black youths. "If there were blacks somewhere, we were fighting them," a white gang member remembered.[14]

From the summer of 1968 through the fall of 1969, Black York was in a state of sporadic war against police forces and white gangs. An encounter between police and Black teenagers on July 11, 1968, led to "five consecutive nights of disturbances by roving teenage bands" in the Black district, as the *Washington Post* reported. On the fourth night of the rebellion, six Black witnesses described two shirtless white men walking down Maple Street in the city's Black neighborhood, firing between four and thirteen shots into a crowd. Police chose not to investigate. The following month, the battle between young Black people and the police resumed, this time after the police demonstrated their allegiance to a white sniper. A group of kids were gathered out on the streets at around eleven thirty on the night of August 3, 1968. Chester Roach, a fifty-eight-year-old white man who lived above a meat market on the block, yelled at them to quiet down. The kids yelled back. Roach retrieved his pellet gun and his shotgun and started firing at them, striking ten and sending one to the hospital. York Public Safety Director Jacob Hose deployed two-thirds of the city's police force to the scene in full riot gear, accompanied by two armored vehicles the department had recently acquired through a federal riot prevention grant.[15]

The officers did not come to arrest the white man who shot the

Black kids. They came instead to confront his victims with a display of force. "Whitey made his statement last night. He said, 'I hate you niggers and I'm going to kill you,'" a male teenager declared. "If whitey is going to start shooting, you better bet I'm firing back." The following night, Black residents ranging in age from their late teens to mid-twenties turned to the tactics they had used two weeks earlier: throwing rocks at cars and, in this case, firebombs at a nearby paper mill and at the meat market below Roach's apartment. The Mayor called it a "planned operation."[16]

York authorities reasserted their power with a symbol of state-sanctioned racist violence from the civil rights era: police canines. Mayor Snyder, who openly referred to Black people as "darkies," was a fan of the dogs and the K-9 Corps. Snyder would walk a German shepherd through the streets of York, intimidating his Black constituents with what was essentially a police weapon on a leash, just as the White Hats did in Cairo. When white gangs and Black students fought after a high school football game in September 1968, the K-9 Corps arrived on the scene and unleashed their animals on the Black teens, sending seven to the hospital. No white gang members suffered injuries. The department's strategy was obvious. "Police dogs are used only against Negroes," the New York Times reported of York.[17]

In the wake of the rebellions in July and August 1968, Black and white residents in York prepared for a larger war. A group of thirty-five Black adults and teens created a new organization called York City Youth to defend the community. Police brutality and white gang activity were increasing, and there appeared to be no other recourse, with city hall taking no action to address the issue. "We are giving this white power structure their last chance," said founder Bobby Simpson. "We don't mind dying." Seeing that Black militancy was on the rise, white people in York went on the offensive, as in Cairo. In the segregated white neighborhood of Salem Square, residents roamed the streets "with weapons, waiting for any Negro to leave his cordoned off ghetto," explained a white man to a reporter. "The police had better get in charge of this situation or we will." The "situation" was the Black struggle for full citizenship and police protection. But as another white man saw it, "They're trying to take over this country." He added, "And we're not going to let them."[18]

The racial strife in York culminated in a period of sustained violence that began on July 17, 1969, after twelve-year-old Clifford Green was hospitalized for burns he claimed resulted from members of the white Girarders gang dousing him with gasoline and setting him on fire. Seeking to avenge the burning of a Black child, members of the York City Youth went searching for Green's assailants. The leader of the Girarders, Gregory Neff, quickly notified the Newberry Street Boys and other white gangs that their Black enemies were "looking for blood."[19]

Soon enough, Black and white teenagers were fighting each other at a swimming pool and on the corner of Newberry and Gay, in the heart of the Newberry Street Boys' neighborhood. The York City Youth won the opening rumble: Arthur Messersmith claimed he was beaten up by seventeen-year-old Taka Nii Sweeney, while other Black teenagers headed to the Newberry Street Boys' clubhouse—a converted old cigar shop with the words "white power" spray painted on the door—and smashed its windows.[20]

When questioned by police, Clifford Green admitted that he had taken a swig of lighter fluid while playing with a friend, in an attempt to spit fire. That the fighting had been set off by a lie mattered little to the participants on either side. Over the next two weeks, the violence escalated from fistfights and rock throwing to armed gang warfare and arson, ending in the deaths of a twenty-two-year-old police officer and a twenty-seven-year-old Black mother. The shooting began at 11:40 p.m. on the seventeenth, when twenty-year-old Robert Messersmith, Arthur's brother, attacked Sweeney and fourteen-year-old John

Washington. As soon as he spotted the Black teen who had presumably beaten his brother the previous night, Messersmith fired his gun, striking Sweeney in the abdomen and Washington in the elbow. John Smith, one of the few Black detectives in the York City Police Department, happened to be talking to Sweeney and Washington at the time of the shooting and escorted them to York hospital. Much like the department's handling of Chester Roach, the other officers who had come to the scene did not question any of the Newberry Street Boys for the shooting and made no arrests. Sweeney remained in the hospital for weeks as he recovered from the gunshot wound.[21]

The following night, as Black people began attacking any white person passing through the West End of the city, more than forty state police joined the York police to suppress the violence. A Black crowd had gathered at the intersection of Penn and College, and at 10:30 p.m. the police department appeared just before a white man was shot in the back while riding his motorcycle. Police promptly dispatched one of the department's armored trucks to the scene. Nicknamed "Big Al," it was manned by three officers. Black witnesses would remember the police yelling from inside the truck, "Niggers, get off the corners, go to your homes," before they fired shots into a group of about twenty-five people. The crowd fired back, and several bullets passed through the one-eighth of an inch steel plating of the vehicle, striking officer Henry Schaad in his torso, legs, and foot. Schaad died from the wounds two weeks later.[22]

In retaliation for the shooting, policemen and white gangs descended on Black neighborhoods together. A Black couple reported that a group of officers stationed on the roof of a factory building "opened fire in the direction of any noise or anything that moved." Siblings Daryl and Jeannette Register, aged three and eight, were hit by stray police gunshots as they reportedly watched an officer beat a Black person. A man named Bennie Carter described an armored truck pulling up on a gathering of Black residents at the corner of Green Street and College Avenue. "All you Black bastards get back in the house!" the officers shouted, before pointing their rifles at them. Shots were fired, hitting Carter's friend Clarence Ausby. Instead of calling in an ambulance for Ausby, the officers brought him into the armored car, drove him to the outskirts of York, and beat him.[23]

Whereas police shot into Black crowds and Black neighborhoods, white gangs appeared to target individuals. Vigilantes fired guns for several minutes into the home of York City Youth leader Bobby Simpson. They firebombed the home of the lone Black couple who lived in the Newberry Street area and shot at two Black women who ventured onto the Newberry Boys' "turf." With a dozen or so white and Black gunshot victims, Mayor Snyder declared a state of emergency in the city and Governor Raymond P. Shafer enforced an evening curfew.[24]

Despite the restrictions, white youth were permitted to congregate freely. On the evening of Sunday, June 20, the Girarders, the Yorklyn Boys, and the Newberry Street Boys converged on Farquhar Park in the name of "protecting their neighborhood." When officer Charlie Robertson and other cops arrived at the park, they did not follow the protocol they would have used to disperse a large gathering of Black youth. No one was chased, no one had the end of a billy club shoved into their back. Instead, the officers chanted "white power" and "we have to stick together" alongside the white gangs. The police passed out bullets to gang members, pledging not to get in the way of the gangs' work. As a member of the Newberry Street Boys put it, the officers made the white teens feel as though they "were on our side," empowering the young men to openly carry their weapons and assault Black people as they wished.[25]

As the forces of white supremacy convened in Farquhar Park, just as they had in Cairo's St. Mary's Park two years before, Lillie Belle Allen and her family were watching Neil Armstrong walk on the moon. Allen had driven with her two children and her parents from Aiken, South Carolina to visit her sister, Hattie Dickson. The family spent the next day fishing in the country, unaware of the ongoing war in the city. That evening Dickson was driving her white Cadillac—with her husband, her parents, and Allen in the car—to the grocery store and decided to take a shortcut on Newberry Street, where armed gang members were patrolling. Dickson tried to turn around, but her car stalled at the worst possible moment, leaving the Black family stranded in the middle of a white mob at the street corner where the warfare had started four days before. Allen got out of the car to help her sister restart the Cadillac. "Don't Shoot! Don't Shoot!" Allen pleaded, her hands in the air. She was shot down. Then dozens of people began firing at the car. "Stay down!" Allen's father cried, as his wife and daughter threw themselves to the car seats and floor.[26]

The shooting continued until Charlie Robertson, who had chanted "white power" with the same mob the night before, appeared with three other cops. Dickson's car had been completely destroyed, its chassis bullet-torn and its windows shattered. It was a miracle that everyone in the car survived with only a few minor injuries and shards of glass in their hair. Allen was taken to the hospital at nine thirty, and she died twenty minutes later from the gunshot wound in the right side of her chest. Robert Messersmith, who shot Sweeney and Washington four days before, and whose father was rumored to be the Grand Giant of the York County Ku Klux Klan, bragged that he tore Allen "in half," the force of his bullet "blowing her out of her shoes." One of Allen's sneakers came off when she hit the ground. Messersmith reportedly took it home as a trophy.[27]

Officer Robertson kept the promise he had made to the white gang members, though his next moves also followed the usual pattern of York's police response to Black victims of white violence. He and the other officers did not confiscate weapons or make arrests. They simply sent the crowd—the witnesses—home after Allen's murder. Instead of an investigation, authorities reacted to Allen's death by deploying six hundred National Guardsmen armed with carbines. They rolled into York in their jeeps and an armored personnel carrier to support the 147 state and city police officers already on duty.[28]

Over the following week, the Guardsmen mainly helped local police raid homes in a search for guns and ammunition. In the Black neighborhood of Penn and College, the police searched eight homes, confiscating ten rifles, shotguns, and revolvers. In the Newberry Street area, the police seized fifteen guns—an assortment of military-grade weapons ranging from rifles with scopes to 12-gauge, pump-action shotguns—and hundreds of rounds of ammunition. This veritable arsenal was found at the Messersmith home. With both sides disarmed, at least partially, the war in York seemed to wind down.[29]

Unlike nearly every other city that experienced rebellion, York eventually achieved a semblance of closure. In 2000, a wave of prominent civil rights-era murders were brought to trial when white people started telling investigators the truth about what had happened in the 1960s, including the killing of civil-rights leader Medgar Evers in Mississippi and the murder of four little girls in the bombing of a Birmingham church, both in 1963. After a series of local news stories in 1999 that commemorated the thirty-year anniversary of the York rebellion and raised new questions about the unsolved murders of Lillie Belle Allen and Henry Schaad, York County District Attorney Stan Rebert launched a grand jury investigation. The process of reopening old case files and reinterviewing witnesses uncovered new evidence that led to the arrest of ten white men for Allen's murder. Most pled guilty and received no jail time in exchange for testimony against gang leaders Gregory Neff and Robert Messersmith, who were given four and a half-to-ten-year and nine-to-nineteen-year sentences, respectively. The two Black men charged with Schaad's killing, Leon Wright and Stephen Freeland, received identical sentences.[30] Both sides of York's war had received justice, it appeared. Yet former officer Charlie Robertson walked free, acquitted of murder charges. At the time of his trial, Robertson was serving his second term as York's Mayor. The white power proponent had risen, over the course of his career, to the very top of the local power structure.

THE PRIMARY STORY officials and the press told about the racial warfare in York, Cairo, and other cities was that groups of Black and white residents alike had descended into "lawlessness." Both sides held extreme views, both sides were racist, and both sides attacked the other. Another view was simply that the problems were overstated, and Black fears were thus not rooted in reality. As Illinois Lieutenant Governor Paul Simon put it: "The White Hats or the Committee of Ten Million have become a source of fear for the black community." But he concluded that "this fear appears to be largely unwarranted."[31]

Simon visited Cairo for two days in mid-April 1969. He spoke with mothers, children, and grandfathers in Pyramid Courts who told him about the White Hats and what happened on March 31, when the vigilantes shot into the housing project for two and a half hours, setting off Cairo's continuing violence. The White Hats, however, made an impressive show of victimhood, ultimately convincing Simon that the group had nothing to do with the attack. Someone called in a threat on Peyton Berbling's life during Simon's first night in Cairo, and the lieutenant governor was summoned to the white supremacist's home at eleven at night. Berbling had resigned from the White Hats in November 1968—when he was elected state's attorney, he said "there might be a conflict"—but he continued to serve the cause from his new perch. Now Brebling was in danger (or so he wanted Simon to believe) and he had the lieutenant governor's ear. Simon left their hour-long conversation persuaded that "law and order must be restored in Pyramid Courts."[32]

As with the white gangs of York, support from authorities and law enforcement only emboldened the White Hats. The Saturday after Simon's visit, April 26, Berbling issued warrants for raids on three Pyramid Courts apartments in search of guns and explosives. This was a calculated move on the state attorney's part: Berbling timed the searches to coincide with the third Saturday protest in support of the Black boycott of white-owned businesses, where hundreds of people carried signs, some of which read: "Don't buy from white merchants downtown. Spend your money where your Soul Brother benefits." The police did not discover any weapons in Pyramid Courts that day. Some protesters returned from the picket line to discover their homes ransacked, forcing them to piece together or simply throw away already meager family possessions, and leaving those who dared to challenge the white power structure, and their families, humiliated.[33]

Then Cairo burned. In the four days following the raids that Berbling orchestrated, the city witnessed an unprecedented total of twenty-eight fires, mostly in the Pyramid Courts area—including in the tavern United Front members frequented near St. Columba Church—and in the vacant building that had served as the Black high school before integration was enforced in 1967. Intermittent firebombing persisted through May, as did gunshots aimed at the police station, the United Front offices, and Pyramid Courts. Neither side claimed responsibility for the violence; both sides believed they were acting in self-defense.[34]

By mid-June, with no end in sight to the sniping and firebombings absent a major intervention, state authorities moved to shut down the White Hats. The Illinois Legislature passed a bill repealing an 1885 state law that permitted the formation of vigilante groups to apprehend "horse thieves, incendiaries, and other felons." Under the threat of injunction, the White Hats officially disbanded. Yet as cofounder Thomas Madra pledged, "we'll continue whether or not the governor signs it."[35] Within a week, Madra and others in Cairo's white establishment organized another rally in St. Mary's Park, where the vigilante group resurfaced in a new guise.

Modeled more directly than the White Hats had been after Citizens' Councils, the United Citizens for Community Action (UCCA) purported to be focused on "community cooperation, not repression." (The group's informal nickname—the "United Coon Control Association"—suggested otherwise.) UCCA leadership was comprised of prominent former White Hats members: Captain Jerry Lebo, the commander of the Illinois National Guard in Cairo; Carl Helt, who owned Cairo News and Music Co. and had just been named the editor of the *Tri-State Informer*, the white supremacist organ of the Citizens' Councils whose slogan was "States' Rights, Racial Integrity"; business-owner Allen Moss; and the Reverend Larry Potts, who in 1968 had killed a seventy-three-year-old disabled Black man he claimed to have caught raping his wife and who had been absolved of all charges by the coroner's jury.[36]

Most of the White Hats became UCCA members, and more than a thousand new people joined, bringing the forces of white vigilantism in Cairo to a reported two thousand people in total. In addition to denouncing "racist blacks"—an oft-used charge against Black people fighting for equal rights that increasingly became part of white rhetoric post–civil rights and that fueled animosity and vigilantism—the UCCA pledged to "find solutions to present problems and set goals for community development by uniting the responsible citizens of Cairo." This was a far more expansive vision than the "protect your homes" organizing principle of the White Hats. The UCCA also soon boasted connections well beyond Cairo. In the fall of 1969, after a meeting with white supremacist leaders in Jackson, Mississippi, the group joined the larger Citizens' Councils of America movement.[37]

Even though most of the violence in Cairo took place in Pyramid Courts and was carried out by whites, many white residents felt as though their lives and livelihoods were in jeopardy. "We will use every force necessary to put an end to the five months of violence the United Front has inflicted on Cairo," Bob Cunningham, the prosperous lumber dealer and a founder of the White Hats, who now led the UCCA, announced. Violence, in this sense, is best understood as any action that challenged white supremacy, including nonviolent demonstrations or armed self-defense. The United Front was nothing but "a half-dozen Negro hoodlums and liars," Cunningham said. A woman who worked at Mark Twain Café, where the UCCA elite frequently gathered to eat catfish and socialize, shared her customers' sentiments. "I'd like to meet 'em with a machine gun. It's going to end up with a civil war," she told a reporter. The small concessions made by the state toward Black residents had given the latter too much power, and the "taxpaying, law-abiding, responsible citizens of Cairo," as the UCCA described its membership, would fight to defend their rule.[38]

THE IDEA THAT "lawlessness" on both sides was responsible for the violence in American cities in this era was based on a more fundamental assumption: that there was no reason to end the domination of political and economic institutions that systematically locked Black people out of jobs, decent housing, and educational opportunities. These beliefs were widely held by whites, and for Black activists already facing a daunting situation, the presence of white vigilante groups made for an even graver challenge. In Cairo, York, and elsewhere, Black activists and militants devised a new set of strategies and responses to protect the community and to fill the void created by the racist establishment by providing clothing, shelter, medical care, and other basic necessities to Black people. The United Front of Cairo, in particular, was successful in both aims. It synthesized the strategies of the civil rights movement—nonviolent, legal, direct-action challenges to discrimination—with the principles of self-determination and Black nationalism that guided the Black Power movement.

The United Front rooted its politics in a radical reading of Christianity. Its symbol—a pistol overlaid on a bible—brought together the spiritual groundings of the civil rights movement with the politics of armed self-defense espoused by the organization's Black Power contemporaries. "The gun was for your protection and the bible was for your direction," as United Front member Clarence Dossier put it.[39] The organization derived its purpose from the parable of the sheep and the goats from the Book of Matthew, in which Jesus calls his followers to "feed the hungry, clothe the naked, house the needy, administer unto the sick, take in strangers, and visit those in captivity." By 1970, the Front had created a food distribution network with the Urban League and other sympathetic supporters in Chicago, who would send tons of canned goods, medical supplies, household items, clothing, and toys down to Cairo on trucks donated by Sears, Roebuck and Company and the Montgomery Ward department store. The United Front offered Cairo residents free legal aid services and (limited) medical care.[40] It established a day care center, a pig farm, a factory that made prefabricated housing, a women's clothing store, and a grocery store, all based on the principles of collective ownership: profits were shared with the community in order to distribute wealth equitably. As longtime local civil rights leader and United Front Founder Charles Koen preached at an organization rally, this work was "larger than Cairo." It was part of a broader movement to "replace the white value system"—capitalism—

with a system based on cooperation and community. It was clear the state would not guarantee Black residents protection or rights, and it would not respond to their basic needs. "It's up to us."[41]

At the center of the United Front's activities during the ongoing conflict in Cairo was its boycott of white merchants. Because they were outnumbered and outgunned by the police and white vigilantes, withdrawing from the city's economy was one of the most potent responses Black Cairoites could mount. In just over a year, eleven white-owned businesses closed as a result of the boycott, sending the town, which was already struggling, into an even deeper depression. The boycott would have been successful without the rallies and the picketing. But the United Front believed direct action fostered solidarity, empowerment, and love in a community under siege. Marching in the streets and seeing downtown stores fold one after another allowed every participant to understand their collective power. Together they were renouncing racism and terrorism, declaring that the old system of oppression was no longer acceptable. White property owners rejected Black freedom just as forcefully, sacrificing themselves in the process. "The white businessmen are willing to put up with the hardships for their own racism," United Front spokesman Manker Harris observed.[42]

Before long, the United Front's Saturday demonstrations were a major weekly event in Cairo and determined the basic functioning of the city. Each demonstration would begin in St. Columba Church, where Koen and other activists would speak to the participants, usually about a hundred or so in total. "We are looking forward to the day we will change society," Koen would say. "We will either change society or die, and it will change anyway." When white people first fired their guns into the Pyramid Courts housing project in March 1969, "something brought us together," Koen would remind the group of that terrifying, clarifying moment. "It was the will to live, the will to walk around in the open." When the community mobilized against the violent conditions, things changed: "Then we really started loving one another. We began to understand that if I got shot, you could get shot. We began to watch out for one another."[43] Protecting Black Cairo meant not only keeping a rifle in the home and meeting people's basic needs for food, clothing, and shelter, but also marshaling collective power to boycott and picket racist businesses.

Energized by the rally, the pickets would march downtown, where groups of white residents awaited, standing on sidewalks and leaning on storefronts. State and local police would array themselves at intersections, blocking traffic to allow the march. A patrol car would follow the marchers, who would be surrounded by hostile white residents and further police. Yet they marched every week. They would march as UCCA leader Carl Helt blasted awful noise at the demonstrators from a loudspeaker he installed at his Cairo News and Music Co. Helt would put on a laugh track, or excerpts from speeches by former Alabama Governor George Wallace. Cunningham, the lumberyard owner, might follow the marches and record anything the participants said. If a white person spoke to any Black person directly, it was almost surely Cunningham. "How you doing, boy?" he would call out. White children would shout at the marchers and Black children among the pickets would shout back. United Front representatives, very often the parents of the children, would scold them. ("'What's the matter with you? Get back in line!' 'She started it. She called us a bunch of—' 'Talk never hurt anybody.'")[44]

The three-mile march would end back at St. Columba Church, where protesters would clap their hands and stomp their feet in the pews. Most of the people at the rallies and in the streets were young, but a few older people could be found, such as the aged Black woman sitting in an aisle seat and supported by her cane, who would tap her blue sneakers on the floor when others clapped and stomped their feet. It was more likely than not that shots would be fired into Pyramid

Courts that night—perhaps from the same white men who sneered when the pickets strode by. Many of the adult activists who marched during the day kept their guns close at night. If the shooting was sustained or became truly dangerous, "we will fire back," Manker Harris warned during an interview. "We are not playing."[45]

The white ruling elite of Cairo weren't playing, either. "If we have to kill them [Blacks] we'll have to kill them," Cairo Mayor Peter Thomas said in an ABC news segment that aired in November 1970, after twenty months of warfare. "It seems to me that this is the only way we're going to solve our problems."[46] Thomas's comment was extreme, even by Cairo's standards. But government authorities and the police had long been complicit in violence against marginalized groups. In both North and South throughout the twentieth century, white vigilantes killed Black Americans and bombed Black homes, businesses, and institutions. They faced little if any consequences for their actions, because this violence was an accepted way of preserving "public safety," meaning reinforcing white dominion when Black people won political and economic gains.

By the era of rebellion in the late 1960s the influence of the Ku Klux Klan had waned, but anti-Black vigilante violence persisted in new forms across the United States. In August 1968, when the police department in Salisbury, Maryland, installed an all-white, 216-member volunteer force to aid the regular 40-man force in the event of a riot, Black residents proceeded to hurl firebombs at buildings and to loot stores in protest. Salisbury's riot-control policy—which gave white civilians the power to police Black people—had essentially caused a riot. In the steel mill town of Aliquippa, Pennsylvania, in May 1970, "open warfare between the races" erupted after a young Black man brushed against a white police officer on the sidewalk in front of a bar. The policeman berated the young man and did nothing as a white crowd began to assault him. Before long, Black and white residents were fighting in the streets with baseball bats, tire chains, and clubs. The next month in Kalamazoo, Michigan, white motorcycle gangs drove through a Black neighborhood, shooting at and injuring several residents. A group of about a dozen people proceeded to smash windows around the city and throw rocks at police and passersby, angered that "police allowed the gang to come into the black area," as the *Ann Arbor News* reported. In the tobacco town of Yanceyville, North Carolina, a fight broke out on Friday, September 18, 1970, between white and Black residents at the Caswell County Fair, ending with the shooting of a Black girl in the hip. According to the *Charlotte Observer*, the next day at around ten o'clock, "bands of blacks, numbering about fifty," ran down the main street of the city, hurling rocks and firebombs and exchanging gunfire with police.[47] The police did not arrest a single white citizen in connection to the violence in any of these cities, even though white citizens had been instigators and perpetrators. White people could attack Black people and face no consequences; Black people were criminalized and punished for defending themselves and their communities.

The forces of anti-Black violence and Black rebellion in Salisbury, Aliquippa, Kalamazoo, and Yanceyville did not reach the scale of that in Cairo or York. Although police in these cities were complicit in white violence and looked the other way when white supremacists spread terror, Cairo's UCCA and York's white gangs were highly organized, heavily armed, and actively collaborated with local law enforcement. As a result, violence in both cities was protracted and particularly deadly: as far as Black residents were concerned, they were fighting for their lives and the safety of their communities. But still, the notion of a general "race war" took hold. In 1970, during the height of the violence in Cairo, the *Atlantic* described the city as split into "two armed camps," white and Black. "With bad faith on both sides."[48]

4

THE SNIPERS

Rice Whitfield, the choir director of Cairo's United Front, surveys
the damage to his car after it was shot up by white vigilantes. (From
On the Battlefield: Cairo, Illinois, ed. Robert Sutherland, 1970)

IN THE SHADOW OF Martin Luther King Jr.'s assassination and the
enactment of the Safe Streets Act, both in 1968, the guiding principle
of Black American protest moved away from nonviolence and toward
self-defense. Although Black people had long armed themselves to protect their families and communities, especially in the 1930s and 1940s,
this shift had been a decade in the making within the mainstream

freedom movement. In Monroe, North Carolina, where Klan rallies attracted fifteen thousand people, the NAACP engaged in armed resistance against white supremacist violence under the leadership of the World War II veteran Robert F. Williams. "There is no law here," Williams declared from the steps of the Monroe courthouse in 1959, after a jury acquitted a white man for the rape of a Black woman. "It is time that Negroes must defend themselves even if it is necessary to resort to violence." Williams founded a rifle club—the Black Guard—to practice what he called "armed self-reliance." As Williams's following grew, and as Monroe became a site of civil rights protests, they were met with violent resistance by local whites. A white mob, some several thousand strong, attacked about thirty demonstrators during a sit-in, inflicting significant injuries on many of the Black protesters.[1] The bleeding people were arrested, the members of the mob walked free, and Williams fled to Cuba, where he began hosting a radio show and publishing a newspaper, the *Crusader*, attracting a wide international following.

Williams's influential 1962 book *Negroes with Guns* made the case for armed resistance as essential to the struggle against white violence and oppression. "When people say that they are opposed to Negroes 'resorting to violence' what they really mean is that they are opposed to Negroes defending themselves," Williams wrote.[2] As he saw it, from Klansmen in Monroe to officials in Washington, white people tended to treat Black people's exercise of their Second Amendment rights as an act of violence.

Black Americans did not "introduce violence into a racist social system," Williams argued. Rather, "the violence is already there, and has always been there." When Williams and his followers challenged "the exclusive monopoly of violence practiced by white racists," they were maintaining their dignity and hoping to promote public safety. "We have shown in Monroe that with violence working *both ways* constituted law will be more inclined to keep the peace."[3] Since law enforcement and the courts had failed to protect Black people from white vigilantes, Williams believed armed self-defense was the best available means to prevent the escalation of violence.

As law enforcement, the press, and much of the white public saw it, Black self-defense was an illegitimate form of protest that was rooted in racism against whites and that undermined public safety. And no form of Black self-defense was more illegitimate or more terrifying than sniping. Black people who shot at police with rifles while hidden from view were imagined to be psychopaths associated with fringe, militant activists who were the true agents of violence in American streets in the 1960s and 1970s.[4] The term "sniping" became shorthand for the shooting—usually targeting precinct stations, firehouses, and other symbols of state power—that very often provided the soundtrack for rebellion. For some Black residents, sniping was a way to intimidate the police into backing down, and to let the officers know that some Black people were prepared to defend their community. For many white Americans, the idea of the "black sniper," hunting police from the rooftops (which did happen on rare occasions) was freighted with political meaning, giving credence to the idea that there was a nation-wide Black conspiracy to kill police.

Any account of the rebellions of the late 1960s and early 1970s requires an understanding of the "Black sniper"—both the reality and the bogeyman stalking the white imagination—not least because this figure seems so foreign in the early twenty-first century. The Black sniper complicates, in important and revealing ways, the cycle of state violence and rebellion that characterized this era. A close look at the sniping phenomenon reveals that the larger system of anti-Black political and economic exclusion was ultimately responsible for violence in this period, and that some police officers themselves became the victims of this system and its consequences.

THE IMAGE OF the Black sniper first took hold during the Newark uprising in July 1967, as calls for self-defense were made with greater frequency and vehemence in the Black community. Before that year's "Long Hot Summer," Black rebellions in Newark and across the country had mainly climaxed in the torching of buildings and police cars with Molotov cocktails. Most of the unrest that summer, though, involved firearms. Law enforcement officials, believing that Black residents were arming themselves and targeting police officers, became obsessed with sniping.

The fear of the Black sniper was prefigured by an older concern, dating back to the Civil War and the First World War, over collective violence perpetrated by Black veterans. And it is not surprising that it grabbed white Americans in the context of the Vietnam War, which many Black soldiers, Black communities, and the Black Power and anti-war movements saw as a failed and racially charged conflict. Authorities viewed Black veterans—who had received the latest training in waging war—as potentially dangerous vectors of resentment, capable of organizing and inflicting violence. Black soldiers had been taught to shoot in order to spread freedom and democracy around the world. What would prevent them from using their skills in the struggle to secure freedom and democracy at home?[5]

Killings of police officers spiked in 1969 and remained high through the mid-1970s, after Black snipers first became a concern. Two fewer police officers were killed in the line of duty in 1967 than in 1962, when seventy-eight were killed, according to FBI Uniform Crime Reports. From seventy-six in 1967, the number rose sharply in 1969 before peaking in 1974, when one hundred thirty-two officers were killed—a number that has not been surpassed since. The claims about Black snipers in the coverage to the rebellions in Detroit and Newark in 1967, and in smaller cities in the years after, added another layer of drama to the unrest and fed into the widespread perception that urban rebellions were part of a larger Black nationalist conspiracy. Network producers at NBC news, planning a TV documentary about the violence in Detroit, allegedly went so far as to interview a group of "Negro rioters" and ask them "which one of you fellows wants to play the part of a sniper?"[6] If sniping was a new problem, its effects were not yet apparent in the numbers of police being killed.

The focus on sniping did distract from escalating police brutality in the summer of 1967. Police, believing their own lives were in greater danger than before, often felt they had license to act without regard to the law or human rights. Between July 12 and July 17 in Newark, police killed twenty-four Black residents. Less than a week later, beginning on July 23 in Detroit—where one National Guardsmen explained, "If we see anyone move, we shoot and ask questions later"—thirty-three Black residents were killed, most if not all at the hands of law enforcement and the National Guard.[7] Police usually claimed they were only returning fire from rooftops or windows, but in many cases they randomly or even wildly fired their weapons, killing Black people who were not involved in the rebellion: individuals who might be sitting at home with their parents, taking the trash out after curfew, or standing in front of a drugstore.[8]

The violent exchanges between police and Black residents during rebellions were subject to the same uncertainties that accompanied any combat situation—the "fog of war." From American soldiers in the rice paddies of Vietnam to police in the courtyards of housing projects, the forces of counterinsurgency did not know where, when, or how their adversary would make their next move. In the late 1960s and early 1970s, when Black rebellion peaked in frequency and scale, long-standing paranoias about Black insurgency created an atmosphere of suspicion and unpredictability; the imagination of white police officers, municipal officials, and federal authorities ran wild.[9]

A *Life* cover story following the Newark rebellion alleged that a fifty-member sniping group affiliated with the SNCC had traveled to Newark, after organizing unemployed sharecroppers in Mississippi, and had ignited the violence. The journalist who wrote the story, Russell Sackett, explained that indiscriminate murder was never the intention of the snipers, who instead tried to distract police in order to provide residents with opportunities to loot. "While the police are busy tearing buildings apart looking to kill snipers, our people are getting color television sets, refrigerators, clothes—what they couldn't afford, they got it," one member of this alleged group reportedly said.[10]

Later, Sackett would admit that the story was partly fabricated: the men he talked to didn't identify themselves as snipers and they didn't even carry guns. Still, his reporting aligned with the story many public figures wanted to tell about the rebellion, and it was picked up by other news outlets and widely discussed. Writing in his nationally syndicated column that appeared in the *Boston Globe*, the conservative public intellectual William F. Buckley cited Sackett's reporting to argue that the riots were "related to civil rights" and were "racist and political in character."[11] The Black snipers, Buckley and other pundits argued, were part of a nefarious social movement that would destroy America if left unchecked.

Bullet-ridden police cars and buildings were the only physical evidence of the existence of Black snipers. There were other possible explanations. One important fact about Newark was that the civilian casualties only started after the National Guard arrived on July 14, when "young and inexperienced Guardsmen began seeing snipers everywhere," as Newark Police Director Dominick Spina put it. Did the snipers truly exist? "I think a lot of the reports of snipers was due to the, I hate to use the word, trigger-happy guardsmen, who were firing at noises and firing indiscriminately at times."[12]

According to Spina, National Guardsmen, not Black residents, were the main perpetrators of the (unintentional) sniping. Officers tended to respond to the sound of a gunshot by haphazardly firing their own guns back. This led to mistaken gun battles between local police and National Guardsmen, and to shooting at civilians. The activist and poet Amiri Baraka would put the question to the Governor's Select Commission on the Newark rebellion: "Where are the snipers? Has anybody caught a sniper? Has anybody brought any snipers to light?" The answer was no. "I think the sniper thing was a ghost created by the white man," Newark activist Willie Wright suggested, a "myth" fabricated by the governor "and his gestapo to commit mass murder in this town." Wright and others in Newark were not faced with white vigilante terrorism like Black people in Cairo, York, and other cities across the country, but police violence during the Newark rebellion led them to take up arms. In anticipation of the National Guard's return to Newark, Wright said, "I want to have every black man in the city with a gun on his side or in his home." As he explained, "It's just a matter of choosing your battleground, to know where you die."[13] Wright represented an emerging generation of activists responding to and elaborating on the calls for Black self-defense that had been raised by Williams from the steps of the courthouse in Monroe, North Carolina, almost a decade earlier, and by Malcolm X before his assassination.

In Cairo, the United Front responded to the conditions of the Black community by helping arm it. As Charles Koen and other United Front members believed, this strategy would serve to correct the "mistakes" made in earlier phases of the mainstream civil rights movement. "People have learned to defend themselves," Koen told a reporter from the *New York Times*. "We have to defend ourselves because no law enforcement body will do it." The United Front established an armed unit called the Black Liberators in the spring of 1969, who were trained by Chicago's Deacons for Defense and Justice leader Fats Crawford, and whose nightly "survival patrols" protected Cairo's Black community from attacks.[14] For Koen, Stokely Carmichael, Huey Newton, and other prominent militants, the philosophy of nonviolence may have had some moral advantages, but it also came with obvious practical failings. As it had for colonized people in Asia, Latin America, and Africa, in the United States, self-defense became a means for Black Americans to contest their second-class citizenship. And as in Vietnam, American authorities launched a counterinsurgency effort against an enemy defined by sniping and "guerrilla warfare."

Though white fears about Black sniping were first voiced during the Newark and Detroit rebellions in 1967, it was only after these bursts of violence, and as the politics of self-defense increasingly defined the Black freedom struggle, that sniping—or, more plainly and accurately, shooting—became a regular feature of rebellion. When police arrived to break up a loud house party in a Black neighborhood in Kankakee, Illinois, in September 1968, residents responded by firing five shots in their direction, wounding one officer in the neck and shoulder. It was a "planned ambush," as Police Chief Thomas Maas put it. An angry crowd surrounded the officers who came to investigate, and four Black residents were arrested. In Roanoke, Virginia, in 1970, two police officers were shot when they arrived to investigate the house where a group of young people regularly hung out after school. After the shots rang out, the injured officers tear-gassed the seventeen youths inside, aged twelve to eighteen, all of whom were arrested on charges of malicious wounding. In Cairo, over three separate attacks in late October 1970, and after nearly twenty months of escalating police and vigilante violence, groups described as "squads of armed black men, some dressed in battle fatigues" riddled the police station with hundreds of rounds of gunfire. Cairo police, sheriff's deputies, and state troopers eventually forced the fifteen to eighteen men back and chased them through the streets of Cairo, with each side firing at the other.[15]

Even if the "snipers" intended to kill or seriously injure police as officials claimed, they rarely achieved those objectives. Like most police who were shot at by civilians, the officers in Kankakee, Roanoke, and Cairo fortunately suffered relatively minor injuries, if they were hurt at all. Yet police officers were getting killed in record numbers by the middle of the decade. The seventy-six police officers killed in the line of duty in 1967 increased to eighty-six the following year. One hundred officers lost their lives in 1970, and the years that followed would prove more dangerous for police than any subsequent decade. Law enforcement pled for assistance to fight the enemy in American cities. "When police are being shot like fish in a barrel, it's time to do something," the president of the Fraternal Order of Police said in July 1968, as he threatened a two-day walkout of the organization's 137,000 members over the "lack of support in dealing with racial violence."[16]

While significantly more officers were being killed, there was also a greater police presence on the streets. According to FBI data, the number of uniformed men and women killed annually more than doubled between 1963 and 1971, a period during which the size of the police force in America also more than doubled. The cycle of rebellion and the escalatory actions promoted by the War on Crime led to a gradual increase in the number of Black men under the age of twenty-five who were killed by police, and members of this demographic group were killed by officers at a rate ten times higher than their white and Latinx counterparts. According to the "Compressed Mortality File" available from the Centers for Disease Control and Prevention (CDC), the late 1960s and early 1970s represented the peak of the killings by law enforcement officers of Black men under the age of twenty-five, with nearly one hundred dying at the hands of police every year. By the 2000s, police shootings of young Black men amounted to about thirty-five annually. Whereas from late 1968 to 1974, Black people were the victims of one in four police killings, between 1975 and 1985 they constituted one in seven, and today the proportion is about one in ten. (The CDC figures may represent underreporting, especially in more recent years. The Mapping Police Violence Consortium and the *Washington Post*'s Fatal Force Database have exposed serious inaccuracies in the federal data, a fact that the Bureau of Justice Statistics has acknowledged. The Mapping Police Violence data indicates that Black people were victims in 1,957 of the 7,627 police killings, or 25.7 percent, between 2013 and 2019 alone.)[17] As in Newark in 1967, many of the Black casualties of police fire throughout the rest of the country were not engaging in violence themselves; they were people who happened to be in the wrong place at the wrong time.

Fatal shootings by police were treated by officials as isolated events, unrelated to the expansion of police force in targeted Black neighborhoods. But the idea of the Black sniper became a national phenomenon. It led to more calls for "law and order" and made it easier to criminalize the post–civil rights Black freedom struggle. Whether real or imagined, policymakers and law enforcement officials responded to the figure of the Black sniper as a terrorist threatening to destroy America or bring the nation to the brink of civil war (if it had not already). As the *Black Liberation News* observed following a series of ambushes on police in New York City in February 1970, "The police who daily patrol the black community as a white occupation army sense that the sniping amounts to a very specific declaration of war."[18] The idea of the Black sniper turned the cycle of police violence and Black rebellion on its head: in this version of racial conflict in the late 1960s and early 1970s, white police were helpless victims of Black aggressors, murdered in cold blood for merely trying to help Black residents in need.

With the Black sniper presumed to be skulking in the American city's urban shadows, virtually all activity by any organizations promoting armed self-defense—from "police the police" programs to community centers to direct-action protest—was deemed, by white officials, to be linked to revolutionary groups that aimed to overthrow the US government. Because Black snipers were viewed as a domestic security issue, the path chosen by policymakers and officials at all levels involved more and better-equipped police. New personal armor; new armored vehicles; new, more fortified police department buildings; new, more advanced weaponry—these were, in part, a consequence of the fears of the Black sniper.[19]

ABOUT THIRTY PERCENT of the uprisings between 1968 and 1972 involved reports of shooting by civilians, a significant figure. Yet at the same time, shooting and sniping fostered a broad atmosphere of lawlessness among police. A grand jury investigation into twenty-five of the deaths in Newark in 1967 concluded that police and National Guardsmen had resorted to "excessive use of firearms." The Governor's Select Commission reported that "the amount of ammunition expended by police forces was out of all proportion to the mission assigned to them." This reality was not unique to Newark or major cities in general. In the downriver Detroit suburb of Inkster, where 40 percent of the thirty-seven thousand residents were Black, the shooting death of a police officer led officials to attempt to undermine the growing influence of local Black radicals, some of whom were active duty soldiers, and set law enforcement down a path of violence that ended in the killing of a fifteen-year-old boy.[20]

Darnell Stephen Summers was one of the Black radicals of particular concern to local authorities in Inkster. On leave from the Army in the summer of 1968, the twenty-one-year-old returned home with specific political objectives in mind. Summers was set to be deployed to Vietnam in the fall, but in the meantime he started an organization called the Black Youth Council and devised a three-point plan, which

the group presented to the Inkster City Council in late July as a program for "averting summer trouble." Before one hundred supporters
and the integrated city council, Summers and his comrades labeled
conditions in Inkster a "state of emergency," and called for the creation of a Black community center, a citywide investigation into police
harassment, and the improvement of parks in Black neighborhoods to
the same level as those in white neighborhoods. During the meeting,
the twenty-six-year-old activist Turhan Lewis took a bullet from his
pocket and placed it in view of the council, as a threat that there would
be bloodshed if the demands were not met. "And they gave up the keys,"
Summers remembered.[21] The city council voted unanimously in favor
of the plan, but only followed through on the cultural center, granting
the Black Youth Council space in a vacant recreation center in the segregated part of the city where Summers and other members lived.

By August, Summers's Youth Council had established the
Malcolm X Cultural Center in the building, intending to strengthen
social bonds and improve the community using the recreation building the city had permitted them. They adorned its walls with images of
Black Power icons including H. Rap Brown, Stokely Carmichael, and
of course the late Malcolm X, the "godfather of Black Power," whose
name appeared on a hand-painted sign in the front of the building. In
life, Malcolm had an important connection to Inkster: after his release
from prison in 1952 he lived in the city with his brother Wilfred Little,
moving up the ranks in the Nation of Islam as he built cars at the Ford
Assembly plant and garbage trucks at Garwood Industries. Within a
year of his arrival, Malcolm became assistant minister at Muhammad's
Temple No. 1 in Detroit and wrote his first sermons from his bedroom
at Wilfred's. In what would be the last public address he delivered, on
February 14, 1965, at Detroit's Ford Auditorium, Malcolm spoke of
"vigorous action for self-defense" as the only means to combat white
supremacist violence from Detroit to Dixie. "I used to live out here in

Inkster," Malcolm said. "And you had to go through Dearborn to get to Inkster. Just like driving through Mississippi when you go to Dearborn."[22] In both places, Black people were vulnerable to the twinned forces of vigilantes and police.

Inkster was surrounded by all-white suburbs with all-white police departments whose job, effectively, was to keep the Black residents out. Inkster had been designed as a segregated city and a company town under the influence of Henry Ford, who developed its sewers, water system, and electrical lines to provide housing for Black employees during the Depression in the 1930s. Although Ford framed Inkster as a humanitarian cause, he deducted the cost of development from the wages of his Black workers. For some families, this "tax" was 80 percent of their earnings. What little was left of Black workers' pay was likely spent at the commissary that Ford built in Inkster, and which posted some of the lowest prices for food and essentials in the area in order to keep everyone buying from him. While Ford established what resembled an urban sharecropping system in Inkster, nearby Dearborn (where he had lived and where he located his company's headquarters) remained a segregationist white enclave. The city's motto—"Keep Dearborn Clean"—could be found on bumper stickers on police cars, a thinly veiled message Malcolm X likely encountered as he drove through the city to work in the plants in Detroit. "Is it still that way?" Malcolm asked his audience in the Ford Auditorium, and they told him that it was. "Well, you should straighten it out."[23]

Beginning on August 2, days after the Malcolm X Cultural Center opened, police reported incidents of rock throwing, firebombing, and sniper fire over several nights. On August 7, city officials sent a police officer to the building to force Summers, who would be sent to Vietnam in September, to change the Center's name and remove its sign, as though the invocation alone of Malcolm X was somehow responsible for the violence. The city council likely faced pressure from Detroit's

Red Squad, a police intelligence unit founded in 1932 to disrupt "subversive" social movements and that, by the late 1960s, was collaborating with the FBI's CounterIntelligence Program (COINTELPRO) to "root out" Black militants. The squad had been investigating Summers and the Black Youth Council for several weeks, and now the center refused to meet the city's demands.[24]

That evening, Inkster Police Officers John Knight and Thomas Freeman patrolled the Black neighborhood in the southwest tip of the city that was home to the Cultural Center. Their shift began with a call to investigate a sniping complaint: someone's car had been shot up. Knight, one of the few Black officers in Inkster, took a statement from a witness and then continued driving through the community with his white partner. As Freeman and Knight approached a Mercury Cougar, they heard a gunshot from the opposite side of the street, presumably aimed at them. The officers passed the Cougar, which had pulled up in front of the Center. Someone in the Mercury fired two shots in Freeman and Knight's direction, sending fragments of flying shell casings into Freeman's face and into Knight's right arm and the right side of his stomach. Freeman returned fire into the Cougar but didn't strike any of its passengers. Instead the officer shot a nearby pedestrian in the shoulder; twenty-one-year-old Gerald Calvin Graham happened to be passing by at an unfortunate moment. On their way to Wayne County General Hospital, Knight and Freeman broadcast a description of the Cougar. Both were shaken, but neither had suffered serious injuries.[25]

The police had a suspect within five minutes of the exchange. Although Knight and Freeman described the Cougar as dark ("maroon, black, or grey"), two Inkster police stopped a light green Cougar on Carlyle Street in front of the Malcolm X Center, where the shooting had taken place. The driver, Black Youth Council member Turhan Lewis—the young man who had threatened the city council with a bullet—had two loaded .30-caliber rifles and a pistol in his possession, and was promptly arrested and charged on two counts: carrying a concealed weapon and assault with intent to murder.[26] Though it appeared the police had found the sniper, the search for Lewis's supposed accomplices continued into the night.

Red Squad detectives assigned to monitor Summers and other Youth Council members joined in the manhunt. As a trained GI, Summers posed a particular threat. Robert Gonser and Frederick Prysby, dressed in plain clothes, drove their unmarked squad car around the area. Gonser had been on the force twelve years but had only been promoted to the Red Squad eight months before. His children—ages three, five, and eight—were old enough for Gonser to assume the demands required of special intelligence officers, which included shifts in the middle of the night.[27]

At around 2:40 a.m. on August 8, as Gonser and Prysby headed south on the Middle Belt service drive, a 1964 Pontiac Bonneville turned directly into their path at an intersection. Gonser swerved to avoid it. "They got a rifle," the trooper announced, speeding up. Three shots came from the car, one of them striking him in the back. "I'm hit! I'm hit!" was the last thing Gonser said. He died almost immediately, one the five police officers across the country whose deaths were attributed to sniper fire in a two-week period. Following Gonser's shooting, Inkster Police Chief James L. Fyke invoked a mutual aid pact to summon officers from the Wayne County Sheriff's Department and from other surrounding white communities including Westland, Dearborn, and Garden City to help with the search for the culprits. The police force in Inkster soon quadrupled to one hundred officers, armed with rifles and shotguns, and was joined by four FBI agents.[28]

Meanwhile, sixteen-year-old Herman Matthews and his cousin, fourteen-year-old James Matthews, were at a friend's house with two other teens about ten blocks away from the Malcolm X Center. Police frequently patrolled their neighborhood, and it was the middle of the night, so the four teenagers didn't think much of the officers' presence. Westland cops approached the group in their squad car at around three o'clock, having just heard over the police radio that one of the snipers suspected of shooting Gonser was wearing a white shirt and dark pants. When the officers saw "four Negro men" standing in front of the house, one of them wearing a white shirt, they assumed they had discovered the shooter and his accomplices. The officers were eager to arrest the person responsible for taking a fellow cop's life. They jumped out of their cruiser, rifles in hand.[29]

The boys' instinct was not to surrender to the white men with guns, but to run. The Matthews cousins sprinted across their friend's backyard toward their own homes, as the other two teens dashed back into the house. The boys ran because they hadn't done anything wrong; the police assumed they ran because they were guilty. Herman Matthews tripped over a garbage can and fell, giving one of the officers an opportunity to catch him. The officer pointed a rifle at the teenager's head, handcuffed him, searched him, and placed him in the squad car as the other officers continued to pursue James Matthews. Herman Matthews recalled hearing gunshots just before he was taken to the police station, where he was held until eleven o'clock without charge and without an opportunity to call his parents.[30]

Alone, James Matthews ran toward home and away from the police, seeking refuge in a field around the corner from where the chase began. One of the officers broadcast over the police radio that "a colored male, wearing a white T-shirt, carrying an unidentified object" was in the field. As the officers closed in on him, Matthews pulled off his white shirt, so as not to be seen as easily, but flashlights still picked his body out of the darkness. According to official reports, the officers commanded Matthews to halt and fired warning shots. According to witnesses, Matthews "looked at the officers, and then commenced running." There were more shots and two of them hit Matthews, causing thirteen separate pellet wounds and killing him instantly. No weapon was found on or near him.[31]

That morning, police wasted no time vandalizing the Malcolm X Center. Beginning at six thirty, a group of state police visited the site to gather evidence that would link its members to the two shootings of police officers. When members of the Cultural Center arrived at the site hours later, they found the glass cover over a bulletin board smashed and photographs of Black Power icons torn from the walls. The police had taken membership lists and other papers, and set up wiretaps in the hopes that they would eventually secure enough evidence to arrest and charge Summers and his associates.[32] In their minds, apparently, the Youth Council's celebration of Malcolm X proved that it was responsible for the violence.

More than one hundred Black residents attended a special city council meeting held less than twenty-four hours after the killings of Gonser and Matthews. The Reverend Aaron Butler, the chairman of the Inkster Ministerial Alliance, made a series of demands, including the immediate suspension of all officers involved in Matthews's shooting. Others objected to the mutual aid pact that brought white officers from other towns into their town. "We don't mind if the State Police and Wayne County Sheriff comes into Inkster," one resident said, "But keep those lily-white police that surround us out!" The "tension charged" meeting lasted for an hour and a half, ending only after the council voted unanimously to reopen the Center and to keep "Malcolm X" in its name.[33]

The police department initially refused to release any details of the Matthews killing, prohibiting officers and administrators from commenting on it. "We can't say whether an officer, many officers or a civilian shot the boy," said Wayne County Prosecutor James Brickley. None of the details law enforcement eventually released about James Matthews' final moments seemed to add up. "I think a frightened child might be captured without the use of firearms," James's twenty-three-year-old brother George Matthews reasoned. "My personal opinion is that the police were looking for a scapegoat." His brother's killing was, as he put it, "an unwarranted assault on teenagers as a means to even the score for an act that was undoubtedly perpetuated by adults." But the police and press *did* treat the Matthews cousins as adults, from the four officers who called in a sighting of "Negro men" to the reporters who frequently referred to them as "men" in their coverage, making the use of deadly force against a child seem less brutal, and more justified. There was only one way that justice for James Matthews could be won, as far as his family was concerned. "I think the person or persons responsible should be charged with murder—cold, premeditated murder. It's as simple as that," George Matthews concluded.[34]

Hosie Matthews, James's father, filed a complaint with the Michigan Civil Rights Commission, and, in response, District Attorney William Callahan called for a special fifteen-person team of prosecutors, police, and sheriff's officers to investigate. Not surprisingly, with no civilian oversight and no stakeholders outside of law enforcement, the team determined that the officer who shot Matthews—the unarmed boy who was running, terrified, home to his parents—had acted lawfully. The killing was a case of "mistaken identity": the police described the sniper as wearing a white shirt, and Matthews, clad in a white shirt, fit the profile.[35]

IN AUGUST 1970, a group of young people living in Chicago's Robert Taylor Homes opened fire on police patrolling the housing project, forcing them into a gun battle. Elsewhere, in the city's Cabrini-Green project—nicknamed "Combat Alley" by the Chicago Police Department—snipers fatally shot two community-relations officers from an apartment on the sixth floor. When police returned to clean up the scene and find the perpetrators, they were met with volleys of gunfire. After the sniping finally subsided, officers searched every apartment in the Cabrini-Green complex, kicking down doors, beating residents, and sending two young people to the hospital with serious injuries. Following these events in Chicago, the *New York Times* boldly declared that "America's cities seem to be on the edge of guerrilla war." National debates ignited about attacks on police in Black communities and about the seeming persistence of sniping, in particular.[36]

In Chicago, the December 1969 murders of Black Panther Party leaders Fred Hampton and Mark Clark during a raid conducted by the Chicago police in conjunction with the FBI and a tactical unit of the Cook County, Illinois, US Attorney's Office had permanently tarnished the reputation of law enforcement authorities for many residents. The police fired at the twenty-one-year-old Hampton, the twenty-two-year-old Clark, and other Panthers between eighty-two and eighty-nine times; the Panthers, who were sleeping when the shooting started, returned one gunshot.[37] Despite the evidence, authorities quickly concluded that the police fired in self-defense and left the crime scene unsecured. Lawyers representing Hampton and Clark's families proceeded to conduct their own investigation in the weeks that followed, and many community members came to see Hampton's bullet-torn apartment for themselves. "Nothin' but a northern lynching," an older Black woman concluded.[38] For this woman and other Black residents in Chicago and elsewhere, the local, state, and federal authorities had conspired to assassinate Hampton and Clark and now faced no consequences for their actions. Law enforcement at every level had demonstrated a pattern of brutal lawlessness in prior incidents, and for some residents, retaliation now seemed to be a reasonable response.

The prospect of retaliatory violence did not escape policymakers. Within the crucible period of Black rebellion in the late 1960s and early 1970s, many federal officials and journalists assumed that, at any moment, Black youth would attempt a large-scale insurrection. Commenting on an FBI report titled "Outlook for Racial Violence in 1970," White House Special Counsel Leonard Garment observed in a memo sent in May that year to President Nixon's Domestic Affairs Advisor John Ehrlichman: "In our urban areas, the ingredients which could precipitate wholesale rioting and violence are present. Tensions in the ghettos remain high." Garment may never have considered the possibility that the increase in aggressive patrolling and the stockpiling of military-grade weapons by urban police forces with the support of the federal government contributed to these tensions. The cause, rather, was the "implacable hostility of black youths to local police." Garment went on to reiterate the FBI's conclusion that "Danger signals pointing to the possibility of racial violence in the United States are as plentiful this year as they have been every year since 1963." The belief that young Black people would only continue to engage in "such acts of violence as snipings, attacks on police, killings, arson, and sabotage" profoundly shaped the strategies Garment and other federal policymakers developed in the years to come.[39]

"This is a war against the police," Mississippi Senator James Eastland declared in October 1970—five months after Garment's memo and in the aftermath of the "guerrilla warfare" in Chicago—as he opened the Internal Security Subcommittee Hearings on "Assaults on Law Enforcement Officers." Eastland, the Chair of the Senate Judiciary Committee and known as the "Voice of the White South" for his staunch opposition to integration, argued that the problem of violence against police was fundamentally a national security issue. There was an "ominous pattern" of deadly violence: "a wave of urban guerrilla warfare which threatens to undermine a pillar of law and order." Because it was a police responsibility to "protect us always from the threat from within," as Eastland put it, paraphrasing former president Dwight Eisenhower, and because sniping was aimed largely at law enforcement, it threatened to undermine "civilized" society. "Every time a police officer dies at the hands of a killer, a part of our legal system goes with him," Senator Edward Gurney said.[40]

Eastland hoped to use the violence in Chicago to build support for a series of legislative proposals he and his Republican colleagues had drafted, including the Urban Terrorism Prevention act sponsored by Subcommittee Vice Chairman Thomas J. Dodd of Connecticut. Together, these bills would empower state and local governments to "stop attacks on police officers, firemen, and judges" by expanding the US criminal code to include a new range of penalties for people who injured or killed an officer "because of his official character." The proposed bills would levy more severe punishments on anyone involved in "urban terrorist acts," broadly defined, including mandatory minimum sentences for suspects in possession of Molotov cocktails or explosives.[41] Eastland and other Senators wanted to bring sniping to an end and offer police on the beat in troubled urban communities a new layer of protection. None of the bills ultimately passed, but the debate in Congress did indicate broad support among legislators for aggressive law enforcement strategies and for the money already flowing from the federal government into urban police forces.

Although the Weathermen, Students for a Democratic Society (SDS), and anti-war activists were mentioned throughout the three days of the hearings, most of the testimony and discussion focused on the Black Panthers, who, as Republican Senator Richard Schweiker (a co-sponsor of one of the bills under consideration) claimed, were behind the "national radical conspiracy to assault and kill law enforcement across the land." Los Angeles Police Chief Ed Davis testified that during the annual summer festival held in Watts beginning in 1966 to commemorate the 1965 rebellion, "there were virtual volley lines of shooting at policemen and policemen returning the fire of people shooting at them," all of it "stimulated by Black Panther activity." A sniping incident during the festival ended in the deaths of two Panthers at the hands of police. The shootout took place far away from the site of the event itself, but in Davis's telling, the festival "turned into a virtual battlefield." Davis went on to share the story of two other Black Panther members, armed with a carbine and a shotgun, who came up behind two Los Angeles police officers and opened fire. One officer was hit and suffered minor injuries. The Panthers did not fare as well, however: one was killed by the return fire and the other was hauled off to jail. By Davis's own account, the Panthers were the ones who were dying disproportionately in the violence. Yet as he saw it, "There is no doubt in my mind that there is a conspiracy to eliminate the police, genocide against the police, to use their own term." He repeated the key claim: "There is organized genocide against the police."[42]

In the Panthers' view, they were the ones under attack, as the slaughter the year prior of Fred Hampton and Mark Clark, asleep in a Chicago apartment, appeared to show. The Panthers organization was founded for the survival of the community, as members saw it. Huey P. Newton and Bobby Seale, both in college at the time, created the Black Panther Party for Self-Defense—as it was originally called—in 1966 to fight back against state-sanctioned violence in Oakland, California. The seventh item in the organization's Ten-Point Program read: "We believe we can end police brutality in our Black community by organizing Black self-defense groups that are dedicated to defending our Black community from racist police oppression and brutality."[43] Deeply influenced by Robert F. Williams and Malcolm X, the Party would emerge before long as the most prominent organization based on the principle of Black self-defense in American history.

One of the first concrete acts the Panthers took was the creation of the "police alert patrol." "If we saw the police brutalizing anyone we would put an end to it," Newton explained in an interview from Alameda County Jail in 1968. Most Oakland police officers did not live in the city, and the force was notoriously violent. "Usually the police wouldn't brutalize anyone if we were on hand because we were armed." If someone was arrested and taken to jail, the Panthers would follow, with money for bail ready. "Policing the police" was an approach to self-defense that intended to keep people safe during police encounters without putting any lives in danger. The presence of Panthers with shot-guns and rifles in their hands was often enough to discourage officers from acting with impunity. As the Panthers gained power and influ-ence in Oakland and other cities, the police alert patrols became one of the cornerstones of Panther organizing across the country, serving as both a means of community defense and a powerful recruitment tool.[44]

In Omaha, Nebraska, Panthers tapped into the police call network, and would show up when the police moved to make an arrest. Waiting for calls to come in, Panther members would sit on the front porch of their homes with rifles on their laps and pistols holstered on their belts. When police drove by, the Panthers would sometimes shoot their guns in the air.[45] As members themselves confronted harassment and vio-lence from law enforcement, the police alert patrols evolved into a self-preservation tactic. According to the Party's own estimates, members were arrested at least 739 times in 1968 and 1969, and paid out a total of nearly five million dollars in bail for party affiliates and community members.[46] In the three years following Hampton and Clark's assassi-nations, ten Panthers and nine police officers were killed during raids and other confrontations across America.[47]

Although activists insisted that they were acting in their own self-defense, policymakers and officials believed that Black Panthers, other "revolutionaries," and Black snipers represented "the greatest adver-sary that has ever challenged the American law enforcement officer," as Illinois State Police Superintendent James T. McGuire testified. He described these groups as consisting of "people more cunning, more evil, more fanatical, more mobile and in many cases better educated

than any other that has ever appeared on the American scene." Even as
McGuire and others remained convinced that the "slaughter of policemen" was part of a larger conspiracy, they contradicted themselves,
dismissing the politics of self-defense as pathological, as mindless terrorism lacking any sound motivation. "To some demented minds a
strike against a public official has become synonymous with a strike
against the problems that exist in our society," said Hugh Scott, the
Republican Senator from Pennsylvania, co-sponsor of the Urban Terrorism Prevention act.[48] This view of sniping and armed self-defense
as a form of mental illness shut down any possibility of understanding
the role of policing strategies or public policies as causes of violence.

The issue was not police pathology, as activists claimed. Policymakers and law enforcement pointed to community pathology. "The
central problem is how the community reacts to the police," James
Frone, the president of the Hamilton County Fraternal Order of Police
lodge in the Cincinnati area, testified. The Cincinnati police had tried
"all types of programs" to improve their standing with Black residents: community relations initiatives, integrated squad cars, a cadet
program for young Black people, and subsidized college tuition for
would-be Black officers. None had worked. And not because individual
police officers held racist views, Frone was quick to add. "Since I first
put on my uniform 18 years ago I have attempted to be fair to everyone
and I believe I am representative of our police force," Frone vowed. "I
assure you, in terms of balance, the problem doesn't lie here with the
policemen, but with the community." If anything, the police had performed admirably during the most difficult moments of "racial strife,"
showing remarkable restraint amid ongoing attacks and harassment
by Black residents—just as the Inkster police force had, in the minds
of law enforcement in that city.[49] The police had acted rationally and
employed violence legitimately, even if sometimes innocent people got
caught in the crossfire or fell victim to cases of "mistaken identity."

At the hearings, law enforcement officials threatened that officers would be forced to use radical discretion in their own self-defense, absent new resources and laws to combat Black snipers and the revolutionary social movements alongside which they appeared to operate. In response to the "guerrilla warfare" in Chicago's Cabrini-Green housing project, the one hundred fifty thousand officers represented by the International Conference of Police Associations pledged to "stand united together in all out retaliation against these senseless killings even if it is in the form of on-the-street justice against those persons organized or otherwise, who injure or kill police officers." Further justifying lawlessness on the part of law enforcement, John Harrington, the President of the Fraternal Order of Police, said he would go so far as to advocate for police to shoot looters "if there is no other way to stop this practice." By this point, police were already shooting and injuring civilians at higher rates than in the mid-1960s.[50]

Charles A. O'Brien, the deputy attorney general of California, spent most of his testimony recounting alarming stories about the widespread distribution of bomb-making instructions, the stockpiling of arsenals by Black revolutionaries and white radicals, and the influence of Gillo Pontecorvo's 1966 movie *The Battle of Algiers*, which depicted insurgent urban guerrillas killing police officers during the Algerian War of Independence and served as "a virtual primer to many of our homegrown terrorists." Yet in O'Brien's concluding statement, he stepped outside the "law and order" echo chamber to offer the senators advice they might not have expected:

A major key to conquering this problem is to stop making the policeman the scapegoat for all of society's ills. We cannot continue to solve all our problems by passing new criminal laws. The policeman today bears the brunt of the failures of government. Poverty, inequality, disease, ignorance, and the alienation of youth were not caused by the policeman, but he is the agent who most often comes face to face with these problems. He is the one who is called in when the system breaks down. He is the one who has to put the lid back on. We must demand that the other segments of government do more—social agencies, educational institutions, college administrators, public law offices. All of these other agencies on which we spend billions must be asked to do more, to bear more of the burden, to act more creatively, to assume more responsibility. I consider this as critical as any portion of our response to the problems of policemen today.[51]

Here was a rare occasion where a white official acknowledged root causes and broad, ambitious solutions. Even if the comment came in amid claims of Black viciousness and conspiracy, it represented a brief, exceptional moment. O'Brien's suggestions went unheeded by the congressional committee and did not appear in any form in the domestic policies of the era.

The irony is that the Malcolm X Community Center in Inkster, Michigan, was doing just what O'Brien hoped new government policies and programs would do: empower and encourage Black Youth. Likewise, the Black Panthers provided a wide range of services in low-income Black communities, including a Breakfast for Children Program, community-based health clinics, and political education classes. Likewise, too, the United Front in Cairo distributed food, clothing, and household goods to impoverished Black families, and organized the community on the principles of love and collective self-determination. All of these measures were meant to ensure the survival of Black people, who understood themselves as vulnerable to violence from police officers and white civilians. None of these activities registered with policymakers and local officials. The belief that sniping, or simply Black self-defense, was part of a larger revolutionary conspiracy or an expression of community pathology prevented those in power from imagining alternatives to further escalation of the crime war. The cycle of violence and rebellion could be broken, but not by the application of more violence.

5

THE POISONED TREE

A New Jersey State Policeman prepares to strike a Black man with his billy club during the July 1970 rebellion in Asbury Park, New Jersey. The man had refused to follow the officer's order to move from the train tracks. (AP / Dave Pickoff)

CLAIBORNE T. CALLAHAN joined the Alexandria Police Department in 1960 at twenty-four years old, after spending his early twenties as a stunt double. Now, at thirty-three, with his Hollywood days long behind him, Callahan taught people how to fly planes in the mornings and patrolled the city's segregated Black community, Arlandria, in the evenings.[1] The husky Callahan saw himself as a fair cop, if aggressive at times. Especially with Black teenagers. "I think I've got a reputation," he admitted, although he believed that his use of force was always justified. If Callahan let certain things go, if he backed off during tense moments, "I would be stealing my money right off the citizens paying me to come out and protect them."[2] For Callahan, getting a little rough sometimes was simply part of good police work.

Officer Callahan had been involved in a number of questionable incidents during his nine years on the force, though no punishments were ever levied. In May 1968, for instance, a seventeen-year-old Black teenager accused Callahan of beating him and calling him "all kinds of names." Callahan denied the charge in court, while the young man was found guilty of resisting arrest and received a thirty-day suspended sentence. A year and a half later, Callahan would commit a similar act, and helped send the city spiraling into rebellion. The officer's superiors would sing his praises. "These people are afraid of him, not because he might hurt them, but because they are afraid he is going to lock them up if they break the law," Sergeant Edgar Cassidy said of Callahan. "We could do our job much better if we had more officers like him."[3] The Alexandria elite would throw a fundraiser in Callahan's honor.

The encounter that foreshadowed a rebellion took place on the first Saturday in October 1969. In the final hours of his routine four-to-midnight shift in Arlandria, Callahan was dispatched to the T-shaped intersection at Edison and Dale Streets, where a group of about thirty young people were playing pickup football. Street football was a popular weekend activity among the teens in the neighborhood, but when Callahan arrived just before ten thirty, he broke up the game and told the players and the spectators to go home. Most followed the officer's orders, but thirteen-year-old Darryl Turner and two of his friends stayed behind to engage with the officer. The young men suggested Callahan refer to them as "Black" or "Negro" instead of as "colored boys." As Turner remembered it, Callahan said that he didn't understand why "colored people got so upset when someone called them colored," and scolded the young men. "We tried to explain to him that it was a matter of respect or something—we didn't know exactly how to say it," Turner said. Callahan once again ordered Turner and his friends to get off the streets, then drove off to a McDonald's parking lot a block away to wait in his car. One job done. On to the next. So far, the night had gone smoothly for Callahan—none of the young people playing football had failed to comply with his orders or to respect his authority.[4]

Segregation was officially over, but Alexandria, Virginia—an important port in the slave trade and the site of at least two lynchings during the late nineteenth century—remained steeped in Southern history and tradition. A statue of a Confederate soldier facing south dominated the city's main downtown intersection. Benjamin James, a Black sixty-five-year-old retired railroad worker, remembered "when a colored man could be arrested for just being in Arlandria after dark. There has been a great change since then. But white people still want to be able to tell us what to do." The end of Jim Crow in the mid-1960s did not bring equality in education, employment, public accommodations, or housing. Alexandria desegregated with reluctance: it was the last city in the Washington, DC, metropolitan area to enact an open housing law, and the desegregation of schools, which began in 1966, sparked massive resistance, as it did elsewhere across the country. More than half of Black Alexandrians—compared to only 4 percent of whites— had an income below $3,200 annually for a family of four and were therefore considered poor based on federal anti-poverty criteria. And of those considered poor, most were at or close to the poverty line, a yet lower threshold. By the late 1960s, some older Black residents still did not know they had won the right to vote, and there were no Black representatives in city government. Locked out of Alexandria's white areas, middle-class Black families lived next door to poor Black families in segregated neighborhoods or public housing. Arlandria, where Callahan patrolled, had been all-white until the early 1960s, when a series of floods in the area depreciated real estate and opened up the modest, brick row houses to Black homebuyers for the first time.[5] White people fled to the suburbs.

Officer Callahan patrolled Arlandria as if it could erupt at any moment. Although Alexandria, a city of 125,000 residents, about 15 percent of whom were Black, did not undergo the kind of large-scale uprising that occurred in nearby Washington, DC, following Martin Luther King Jr.'s murder in April 1968, on the Fourth of July of that year about one hundred Black youths had hurled firecrackers and bottles at police cars and motorists on the main thoroughfare outside of the all-Black Samuel Madden housing project. Police threw tear gas cannisters back, and the battle continued until dawn. As Callahan saw it, the problem was insufficient force. "If we had two-man cars, we wouldn't have incidents like this," Callahan argued.[6]

But the city was "too cheap," in Callahan's words, to effectively double its police force, and that Saturday night in October 1969 he sat alone in his cruiser in the McDonald's parking lot. Waiting for the next call, the next opportunity. Callahan soon heard a Black youth cursing. He called the teenager to his car and asked him why he was using foul language. Someone had hit him on the head during the pickup football game, the teenager explained. Callahan thought he heard the youth call him "motherfucker" under his breath. He treated this as a crime: disrespecting an officer in the performance of his duties. "Well, you're under arrest," Callahan told him. "Catch me," the teen said, and began to run.[7]

POLICE OFFICERS WHO demonstrate a pattern of brutality are frequently referred to by law enforcement officials as "bad apples," as though the problem of police violence is limited to those few particularly egregious offenders within departments. The original twelfth-century proverb from which the term is derived—"A rotten apple quickly infects its neighbor"—warns that bad apples cannot exist in isolation; in fact, the ripening agent apples emit will quickly spoil the entire barrel if they are not removed in time. The term emerged in national debate following the videotaped beating of Rodney King by a group of Los Angeles police officers in 1991, though law enforcement officials turned the original meaning of the term on its head. Rather than treating bad apple cops as an indication that the entire force was compromised, the bad apple argument of the late twentieth and early twenty-first centuries presents police violence as a problem in a select few individuals who happen to be cops, foreclosing any critique of an aggressive policing culture and of systemic racism that devalues Black lives and that is violent to the core.[8]

What often goes overlooked, however, is that though the term appears to have been widely used first by the police themselves, the concept has a longer, more complicated history in the American context. In a sense, the concept originated in Black communities. As Black Americans in the 1960s and 1970—and in every other era—understood, there are police officers (or slave drivers, or overseers) who are particularly cruel and use their protected position to inflict great pain and suffering on Black people. Residents knew these individuals so well that if you mentioned their names or nicknames—"Goldie" in Stockton, "Wee Willie" in Charleston, West Virginia—years or even decades later, everyone remembered them. Even those who weren't around to witness their brutality firsthand had heard the stories, passed down over generations and retold at family barbeques. Bad apples, from the community's perspective, aren't just the officers who shoot indiscriminately, who commit extreme acts of violence and get away with it. Bad apples are the officers who assault residents verbally and physically, in ways big and small, on an everyday basis.

In the cycle of violence that recurred in Alexandria and other American cities in the late 1960s and 1970s, so-called bad apples were frequently involved; more often than not they set off the violence in the first place. But while some police were certainly more vicious than others, the reaction by police departments and city governments to complaints about specific officers revealed that "bad apples" would be defended by authorities, whether or not they agreed that particular officers were problematic, if not lawless. In the present era, many still talk about bad apples in police departments and about the "99 percent who are good cops." But as many Black people understood in earlier periods and understand today, the problem was twofold: the bad apples could only spring from a poisoned tree.

Claiborne T. Callahan was a bad apple. The suspect he chased on Saturday, October 4, 1969, knew that he was, and so did much of the Arlandria community. Darryl Turner and his crew were still standing on the corner of Dale and Edison, fresh off their conversation with Callahan about his use of the term "colored," when the officer raced by in pursuit of the teen he believed had called him "motherfucker." As the young man ran Callahan around a Volkswagen several times, the officer asked Turner and his two friends to help him. Instead they encouraged the boy to jump a nearby fence, which he did. Callahan followed and eventually caught the teen. The officer grabbed the foul-mouthed youth by the collar of his shirt, dragged him back up an alley, and handcuffed him in the McDonald's parking lot. The teen asked, over and over again, why he was being arrested. The officer gave no reason. He didn't have to.[9]

According to the official report, as Callahan walked back to his cruiser with the suspect, "30 subjects started throwing bottles and bricks." As he described it, "anything they could get their hands on." He claimed that a fourteen-year-old struck him with a two-by-four length of wood. Callahan responded by hitting the child in the head with his revolver. "He can't fight us all," Callahan recalled someone in the mob screaming. "Let's get him, let's get him." Then four people jumped him. Callahan fought back. When reinforcements arrived, they pulled his attackers off him and arrested one of them. If the crowd had just "stayed out of it," Callahan could have taken his two suspects—the boy who ran from him and the one who allegedly hit him with the two-by-four—into the squad car and that would have been that.[10]

Though Callahan's own account did not exactly make him look good, his Black victims and Black witnesses offered a far more damning version of the incident. Residents knew Callahan as aggressive and unpredictable, and that a bad apple is more interested in assaulting Black youth than protecting them. As a Black mother described Callahan's disposition to a *Washington Post* reporter: "Callahan will get out here and run and play with the kids and the minute he gets mad with one of them he thinks he can step in and beat the child." Another said of Callahan, "I don't know whether he's playing with the children or not, so I get mine inside as quick as I can." Prior to the incident on October 4, formal complaints had never materialized into charges against Callahan, or even a transfer to a different beat, because the police department did not have procedures for handling citizens' grievances.[11] Collective testimony meant nothing against the word of a single white cop.

The official report leaves out the statements of the young people who lingered after the pickup game, and of the people who lived in the vicinity who saw Callahan pursuing and then aggressively apprehending the young teen who allegedly cursed at him. "The way he was dragging him, we thought he was going to hurt him or something," according to Keith Stickland, the boy Callahan accused of wielding a two-by-four. "When we got close to Callahan, he looked like he was scared." Strickland claimed that Callahan then took out his gun, started waving it around, and told Strickland and several others to get back or he would shoot. All of the youths started to run, except Strickland, who figured if he walked away from Callahan there "would be less of a chance of him shooting." The plan backfired, and Callahan reached Strickland first. "He grabbed me by the collar of my shirt," as he had done to the other boy. "I knew I hadn't done anything wrong, so I pulled away from him. And as I jerked away, he hit me across the head with his gun. I went limp, I was hurting so bad I wanted to fall." Callahan then gripped Strickland by his collar once again and started hauling him to the nearby parking lot. Beaten and terrified, Strickland said that he must have lost consciousness.[12]

News that Strickland had been severely injured by a policeman traveled quickly throughout the neighborhood, and the community came to his defense. Vernell Drummond, who lived across the street from the alley where Callahan grabbed the young men, immediately went to inform Strickland's mother, Sadie Pinn. Drummond and Pinn ran to the McDonald's, "where we found Keith lying with his face on the asphalt," the boy whom Callahan had originally chased lying next to him. Drummond claimed that Callahan put his knees into the backs of the two teens to hold them down on the concrete. Desperate, Pinn yelled at the officer: "You get off my son! Can't you see he's bleeding?" People started throwing bottles, rocks, and bricks. Callahan kept his knees on the teens' backs. Pinn attempted to pull her son out from under the officer. Callahan pushed Pinn with his elbow, knocking her to the ground. He then backed up against a fence and pointed his gun at the growing crowd around him, announcing: "Get out of here or I'll shoot."[13]

As thirty-year-old Arlandria resident Gary Peters approached the McDonald's, he saw Callahan restraining Strickland, the child's head "soaked with blood," and watched the officer shove Pinn. Peters had just left work and had been heading home to his wife and children when he crossed paths with an acquaintance, who mentioned in passing that "it's a shame how that policeman is beating that little boy up there," as though the brutality was merely an unfortunate occurrence, part of normal life in the community. Peters decided to go to the parking lot and was prepared to intervene if necessary. "I don't believe in violence, but I don't think a grown man should be allowed to go around beating up kids," he later explained. When he arrived, Peters asked Callahan to call an ambulance for Strickland and the other young suspect. "What in the hell do you have to do with it?" Callahan reportedly sneered and struck Peters on the head with his revolver. Callahan later admitted that he hurt Peters "worse than anybody, because I could see his skull split open." The two men fought until, alerted by McDonald's employees, three more officers arrived. They pushed Peters off Callahan, handcuffed him, and struck him in the face with a nightstick. As Peters recounted, "after a while, I just gave up." He was placed in a police cruiser and taken to the hospital to get stitches for his head wounds. Peters was eventually convicted of assault and battery—charges he said he planned on appealing—and given a one hundred dollar fine, and a suspended thirty-day jail sentence. There were no repercussions for the police who assaulted him.[14]

Peters's intervention had successfully distracted the officers, providing Strickland and the other youth an opportunity to escape. Once both of the teens were apparently safe, Sadie Pinn called for an ambulance, but none appeared. After twenty minutes, Pinn could no longer wait and took her bleeding son to a hospital. They sat in the emergency room for more than an hour without receiving any treatment, so she took him home and dressed his wound herself. Meanwhile, the crowd went home, and Callahan continued his patrol as if nothing unusual had happened. He returned to the Dale Street intersection, where he arrested a young man for loitering. For his part, Strickland received thirty-one stitches for his head wound.[15]

WHEN CALLAHAN REPORTED for duty the next morning, Sunday, October 5, a number of Keith Strickland's friends were accompanying Sadie Pinn to the police station to help her secure a warrant against the officer. Callahan wasn't surprised; complaints were "normal when something of that nature happens," he said. And nothing ever came of them. Among those with Pinn, Callahan recognized two of the teens from the crowd the previous night whom the officer believed to be "part of the gang coming after me throwing bricks." The teens were arrested on the spot. Both of the youths—one was fifteen years old, the other seventeen—were eventually charged with impeding an officer. Callahan also filed a juvenile complaint for the arrest of the teen who had cursed at him on charges of disorderly conduct and resisting arrest. In all, four Black teens and one adult, Peters, faced charges.[16]

As far as Callahan and the Alexandria Police Department were concerned, the skirmish with Strickland and the other boys was yet another chapter in the force's commitment to upholding the law, equally and fairly. For Callahan the incident in the McDonald's parking lot wasn't a "racial thing," because he treated all suspects the same. "I've had more trouble with white people than black people." Callahan had acted in self-defense. In fact, the officer had shown commendable restraint, given that a mob taunted him and threw rocks and bottles at him during the arrest. "He would have been justified in shooting people under those conditions," said Russell Hawes, who had served as Alexandria police chief for thirty-six years and had enforced segregation for most of that time. Any grievances against the officer were unfounded. "I feel people complain about Callahan and would like to see him fired because he is contentious and does his job," Sergeant Cassidy told a reporter. The officer had fans far beyond the police department: three separate men's organizations in Alexandria quickly adopted pro-Callahan resolutions, prefiguring the celebration in his honor.[17]

For the Alexandria Police Department and its sympathizers, the Black community's reaction, not Callahan's actions, was the problem. Rebellious "hoodlums" shook the "traditional outward placidity of the city's police-community relations," as Hawes put it. Other than a few unruly young Black people, "we don't usually have too much trouble with the colored." There were two Black officers on the force (of 175 in total), and as Hawes described them, they were "well-schooled, intelligent, moderate thinking" individuals. Still, the police chief could not ignore the fact that Callahan was a divisive presence in Arlandria. Black residents had been asking that Callahan be assigned to different duties, and now Hawes finally transferred Callahan from the Arlandria beat to patrol duty in the all-white, western part of city. The move was made not in reaction to Callahan's penchant for violence, but for "his own safety."[18]

Callahan, viewed as a bad apple by Black residents and a hero by many white ones, was the starkest example of the fundamental problems in how the Alexandria Police Department policed segregated neighborhoods. The local Urban League had tried to improve police-community relations by bringing six volunteers from the police department and six Black residents together for a series of discussions that began in January 1969, about nine months before the Callahan-Strickland encounter. After four meetings, the officers refused to participate any further. They were "no longer interested," Chief Hawes presumed. The League had no choice but to cancel the program. That spring, the League's director of community relations, Leo Burroughs, spearheaded an education initiative to inform Black residents, especially older residents, of rights and privileges they might not know they possessed after living under Jim Crow. Burroughs also began organizing residents to protest police brutality. The League had supported a woman named Zelma Carter Kennedy in making a formal complaint against the police officers whom she claimed violently twisted her arm, slammed a car door on her legs, and called her "nigger" repeatedly as they arrested her without informing her of any charge. The officers denied causing the injuries, saying that Kennedy had been "uncoopera-tive." They described her as an angry, "emotionally distressed" woman who had no cause for complaint. "What happened to her probably was her own fault," Police Inspector L. C. Saunders concluded.[19]

The outrage surrounding Keith Strickland's beating by Callahan, though it was just the latest instance in a particular officer's history of violence, presented the Urban League with an opportunity to advance its police reform campaign. Black residents wanted accountability as well as assurances that Strickland would be the last young person Cal-lahan would be able to harm. They would no longer tolerate his pres-ence in their lives. About one hundred Black demonstrators marched to the police station on October 11, demanding the firing of Callahan and Chief Hawes. Burroughs, who organized and spoke at the rally, criticized "the police brutality and injustice that we're all tired of." The Urban League had been pushing for the removal of Hawes for years, and although the latest Callahan incident inspired the protest, resi-dents were demonstrating because, as Burroughs said, "he ain't the only one. I don't say every cop in Alexandria ain't no good, but we got enough. We want to get rid of them."[20]

Local organizers, joined by activists from other parts of the greater DC area, made clear that the lack of official action in response to police violence would itself generate community violence. The issue was big-ger than a "bad apple" on the Alexandria police force. "Our problems do not stop at political or geographical boundaries," the Reverend Douglas Moore, chairman of DC's Black United Front, announced from the podium. He noted that thirty-two Black residents had been killed by DC officers in 1969 so far, and that just two weeks prior, police in Prince George's County, Maryland, shot and killed a man named Rene Richardson as he carried a child in his arms. "The white man only understands one language, the language of violence," Moore concluded, pledging the Black United Front's security force and arsenal of guns to support Black Alexandrians if necessary. Burroughs acknowledged that a shift in tactics was imminent. "They don't want to sit down and talk to black people," he charged, which may have been a reference to the dissolution of the regular conversations between the Urban League and the police department. "When a man is unwilling to talk, you have to fight him."[21]

Chief Hawes was indeed unwilling. He told reporters gathered in his office during the protest that he would be "glad to meet with anyone," but he refused to go outside the police station or to engage any of the demonstrators. As city officials continued to ignore the growing chorus of Black demands for Callahan's ouster, as well as the calls for more Black police officers, compulsory sensitivity training for the police, and weekly meetings between the police and Black residents, Alexandria was rocked by unprecedented disorder.[22]

The sparks of the rebellion were originally lit a year earlier by an encounter between a Black teen and a white policeman near George Washington High School's football field. The site had been the regular location of clashes between students and police, and on Friday, September 6, 1968, "roving gangs of Negro youths," according to the *Washington Post*, fought with white students after a game. A police officer with a canine at his side had arrested Black eighteen-year-old Louis H. Winbush aggressively and, according to seventeen-year-old Washington student Wendell Evans, a group of about seventy-five went to the police station, throwing rocks at police as they marched, leaving only after Winbush had been freed on bond.[23] Evans, a leader of the school's Afro-American Organization, which advocated for a Black Studies curriculum and student-led community patrols as an alternative to police, would later be involved in the events that led to the widespread unrest the following year.

On September 20, 1969, two weeks before Strickland's beating, Evans was among a group of Black teenagers who went to a 7-Eleven near the stadium. The one employee running the store, twenty-one-year-old James Hanshew, refused to let more than five enter at a time, perhaps fearing the youths would attempt to steal merchandise or rob him. The Black teens challenged this seemingly arbitrary rule, and Hanshew called the police. When the officers came, Evans allegedly threw his sunglasses at Sergeant Cassidy—the same officer who would go on to defend Callahan in the press—and elbowed another officer in the nose. One of Evans's friends reportedly jumped in and was hit on the head with a nightstick. A total of twenty officers arrived to restore order. A month later, shortly after the Friday-night football game on October 17 had ended, twenty-four-year-old patrolman Louis Barr was hit by a rock thrown from a group of about one hundred young Black people. Barr, who was there for crowd control, received three stitches, while the windshield of his unmarked police car was smashed.[24]

Sporadic violence against law enforcement authorities quickly evolved into mass violence against businesses, public institutions, and prominent white individuals in the community. From the evening of October 17 to the early morning of October 18, a series of fires were started in Alexandria's fashionable "Old Town" section, many of them by young Black people throwing Molotov cocktails. Police later attributed the damage caused to a total of eight homes and businesses that night to "roving bands of youth traveling on foot or in cars," who were not deterred by local police clad in riot gear nor by a supplemental force of forty-eight Virginia State Troopers. The Urban League's peaceful protests resumed Saturday afternoon as a group of thirty Black residents picketed in front of Chief Hawes's home for ninety minutes, calling again for him and his bad apple, Callahan, to be fired.[25]

When the sun went down on Saturday, October 18, exactly two weeks after Callahan's beating of Keith Strickland, Alexandria continued to burn despite the escalatory moves by the police. Rebels hurled three Molotov cocktails at Vice Mayor Eugene W. Zimmerman's electrical contracting business, in the center of Arlandria, at around nine o'clock that night. Two hours later, a firebomb hit Sloan Furniture Company, scorching the store's carpeting and completely destroying several pieces of furniture. Just before eleven thirty, the Alexandria Redevelopment and Housing Authority's new administration building was struck with a Molotov cocktail, although the bomb failed to ignite. The night of Sunday, October 19, police in riot gear patrolled the area to prevent any "new incidents of terrorism," and Hawes deployed an additional special squad to the scene. The three nights of rebellion ended with a firebomb smashing the front window of a local grocery store without igniting.[26]

The Alexandria City Council had not acted in the face of police violence against Black youth, but the rebellion forced them to reconsider. At the urging of Black community leaders, who continued to demand a public hearing on the Callahan incident and an opportunity to air complaints about police-community relations in general, the council convened a special public session at seven o'clock on the evening of Monday, October 20. Beforehand, council members were divided about how to respond: some felt more force was needed to quell the unrest, while others recognized that fundamental reform of the police department was necessary. "I am confident that the white majority wants to be unequivocally on the side supporting the police," was how an anonymous city councilman described the situation. "The blacks, on the other hand, want absolute condemnation of the police department. If we come down hard on either side, the city winds up in trouble."[27]

About one hundred fifty people came to the meeting, most of them Black youths; some in the overflow crowd stood against the walls of the council chamber or spilled out into the hallway. According to observers, it was the "largest crowd of blacks ever to attend" a city council meeting in Alexandria. Victor Hernandez, the chairman of the Urban League Police–Community Relations task force, presented a petition with nine hundred signatures demanding the firing of Callahan. Hernandez and others complained of the unequal treatment that Black residents received from police in the city, a point that was reinforced by a sympathetic white resident. Noting that a street football game prompted the incident with Callahan that in turn set off the unrest, this person pointed out, "I have kids who play in the street and over six years they have never been warned."[28]

After hearing testimony from numerous residents, the city council agreed to implement a series of police reforms. It committed to establishing an office at the municipal level to handle all citizen complaints against public employees and offices; to supporting the creation of a specially trained, two-person police team that would work to build trust between police and "all elements of the city"; and to requiring officers to participate in regular meetings with community members, in the style of the Urban League's failed conversation program. Ira Robinson, one of the Black residents who addressed the council, pointed out that Black people had asked for these same changes for a year, but the council had remained silent. "A few matches and a little gasoline has gotten implementation . . . it's really shameful," Robinson scolded. Even as it endorsed these reforms, the city council reaffirmed its complete confidence in the "dedication and competence of the Alexandria Police Department."[29]

Many residents were not satisfied by the city council's reforms, believing them too limited to make a difference. At the close of the meeting, about seventy-five young Black people gathered in front of City Hall, breaking a light fixture and overturning trash cans. They listened to speeches by Rufus Mayfield and a handful of other activists from Washington, DC, who, like Reverend Moore, had come to "support our black brothers." Marvin D. Vincent of the Black Revolutionaries Party arrived in Alexandria "in African Dress," as the press described it, and preached Black solidarity from his truck, to which he had attached a loudspeaker. Police apprehended Vincent almost immediately for operating a loudspeaker without a permit, and Mayfield then led about fifty demonstrators from city hall to police headquarters four blocks away to demand that Vincent be freed. Vincent was let go on bond at 11:30 p.m. About twenty of the protesters left city hall and gathered on the streets of Arlandria fifteen minutes later. When police asked the small crowd to disperse, most did. A handful of young men and women remained, all of whom were arrested and charged with disorderly conduct, abusive language, and unlawful assembly violations.[30] Police had arrested them in the belief that this rump group could have restarted the vandalism and firebombing.

Black residents demanded repeatedly in October 1969 that Callahan be arrested on charges of assault, but their concerns were largely ignored. The Alexandria Police Department had never issued a warrant against an officer accusing him of assault and it wasn't going to start now, even facing an uprising. Hawes did order an inquiry into the charges against Callahan, just to "reassure myself," as he put it, that the officer had not resorted to excessive force. Yet the inquiry was run by law enforcement officials, and even though twenty-eight-year-old Albert A. Beverly, the first Black policeman to join the force, in 1965, was among them, they confirmed that Callahan had responded to the situation properly. The FBI launched a brief investigation of its own—the unrest in Alexandria had received extensive coverage in the pages of the *Washington Post*—and the city also brought in a team from Michigan State University to evaluate the "problem of police-community relations." The researchers concluded the violence and animosity was primarily due to the city government's "lack of credibility" among Black residents.[31]

Callahan did not face any repercussions for his actions from authorities in Alexandria. Sadie Pinn did file a three-hundred-thousand-dollar suit in the US District Court against him under a statute forbidding police abuse. On behalf of her son, Pinn sought one hundred thousand dollars from the city for being "negligent" in training Callahan for police work and for failing to "control" him, and two hundred thousand dollars in exemplary and compensatory damages from Callahan. The suit claimed that "without cause, justification or excuse," Callahan used "great force and violence" in his interaction with Strickland, and then subsequently brought false charges against the teen to conceal his "vicious, malicious, and criminal attack." Callahan denied the brutality accusations, and the suit was eventually dismissed.[32]

ON OCTOBER 29, 1969, after the firebombing had ended and the week-long police investigation into the assault on Keith Strickland was complete, the newly formed Alexandria Citizens Committee hosted a three-hundred-person dinner in honor of Callahan and the police department. As attendees saw it, both the officer and his department were the victims of the city's Black community. And as the UCCA had done in Cairo, in Alexandria the white elite mobilized in the wake of Black violence to reinforce law and order. The proceeds from the committee's $5-per-plate dinner (about $35 today) went to the Alexandria Police Boys Club. The well-dressed white diners were mostly local businessmen and their wives, but also present were a handful of police officers and elected officials such as the prominent state representative James M. Thomson, who had consistently lobbied the city council in defense of Callahan and the Alexandria police over previous weeks.[33]

The Citizens Committee circulated a petition at the dinner that was the exact opposite of the demands the Alexandria Urban League presented to the city council in the wake of the rebellion. The all-white Committee called for an end to "considerations leading to establishment of police review boards and the like," the prosecution of "interstate meddlers, exciters and agitators" who encouraged "rioting"—this was clearly aimed at Reverend Moore and Marvin Vincent, above all— and an increase in the size of the police force. The police department strongly supported each of these causes.[34]

Fred Petitt, who served as the Alexandria registrar of voters, opened the dinner by telling the enthusiastic attendees: "We live in a wonderful country, the home of the brave but the gutless," the gutless being those who refused to "get behind the police." Petitt wasn't talking about Black people, explicitly, but about "what I believe is right. I'm not against anybody whether they are black, white, green or pink," as he assured the crowd. "I've got as many friends of the colored race as anybody in Alexandria," and therefore the campaign for law and order was entirely free of prejudice. Petitt's co-host, Glen Faxon, the retired master of the Alexandria-Washington Masonic Lodge, griped about the "decline of the family" and the "American Civil Liberties Union lawyers who are about as American as the hammer and sickle." The anti-Communist remark elicited one of the loudest cheers of the evening.[35]

Callahan was humbled by the tribute, and by the who's who of white Alexandria coming out to celebrate him. The Committee presented Callahan with a plaque commending the officer for upholding "the thin blue line between anarchy and order." Callahan walked to the podium to accept the token of appreciation. "Speaking's not my bag," he said. "I'm more uncomfortable up here than any place I've been in the past month," he added, joking, though his meaning was clear: he was more comfortable policing Black neighborhoods and brutalizing Black teens than he was speaking in public.

The local Juvenile and Domestic Relations District Court further reinforced the white establishment's support of Callahan by condemning his assailants. Judge Irene L. Prescott had presided over the June 1968 case involving the teen who complained that Callahan beat him and called him "all kinds of names." Now, Keith Strickland and a seventeen-year-old who allegedly threw a brick at Callahan during the uprising were sitting in Prescott's courtroom as she heard further testimony on the officer's violent tendencies. When Callahan took the stand, he admitted that he pointed his gun at Strickland and considered pulling the trigger after Strickland allegedly hit him with the two-by-four, but "changed his mind" and instead knocked him to the ground. Once again, Prescott believed Callahan's side of the story over that of the Black teens', finding that Strickland "did commit assault and battery" and resisted arrest, and that the other youth "impeded" Callahan in the performance of his duty. Prescott placed both young men on indefinite probation. Callahan's use of force was fully vindicated.[36]

Glorified by the city elite, Callahan did not face professional consequences for his violent behavior, but municipal authorities did pressure Chief Hawes to step down. In mid-December, Hawes finally announced his retirement at the age of sixty-five, having served in the city's top law enforcement role for close to four decades. As Aaron McKinney, the head of the Black Community Action Council, had explained in October, Hawes oversaw a culture within the police department that effectively gave permission to officers like Callahan to abuse Black residents. "The police force reflects his leadership," McKinney said: "Time has passed him by especially with black people. He still refers to us as 'the coloreds.' He just must be replaced." Municipal authorities agreed that Hawes's approach was behind the times. "I think Major Hawes has been a very good police chief," Alexandria Mayor Charles E. Beatley said, "but he belongs to a generation gone by."[37] It was time for a younger chief, perhaps with slightly less reactionary attitudes, to meet the challenges of crime control in the post–civil rights era.

A middle-aged Black woman "who talked like she has been saving up the words for years," as reporters described her, offered one view of the problem with Hawes. "If you are a racist and your wife is a racist, you can't teach your kids anything else. How can an officer who has never respected a black man teach his policemen to respect them?"[38] As she and many other Black residents understood, the Alexandria Police Department would employ anti-Black policing practices as long as Jim Crow–holdovers like Hawes were at its helm.

But the problem ran deeper than Hawes and the older generation. Roughly eight months after the Callahan incident, and five months after the police chief's resignation, the city experienced another, more destructive rebellion. On Friday, May 29, 1970, a twenty-four-year-old white 7-Eleven clerk named John Hanna shot and killed Arlandria resident Robin Gibson, a nineteen-year-old Black high school junior, after accusing Gibson of stealing razor blades from the store. The ensuing revolt involved an estimated seven hundred people— "irresponsible elements in the Black community," as Mayor Beatley described them—who shouted, threw rocks, and set fires, including at the childhood home of Confederate General Robert E. Lee, which was partially destroyed by several Molotov cocktails. The violence lasted for six consecutive nights, ending in the arrest of fourteen people on charges of disorderly conduct, destroying private property, and using abusive language.[39]

For Black residents, the rebellion was not caused by a trigger-happy 7-Eleven manager, but by city officials who seemed largely unresponsive to their needs—including the need not to get shot. At a city council meeting the week before Gibson's murder, Vice Mayor Zimmerman (whose electrical contracting firm suffered significant fire damage during the rebellion in October 1969) voiced the city's paternalistic stance toward Black Alexandrians. "Look at all we've done for you. Look at all the public housing you have here," Zimmerman argued. "You're a lot better off in Alexandria than Arlington and Fair-fax."[40] In his mind, Black residents should be nothing but grateful to their elected officials. But Black people weren't having it. "They've got to stop saying that because we're black they're doing us a favor to give us a break," as a Black lawyer in Alexandria put it.[41]

Gibson's killing had been "the last straw," Mark Boston of the Alexandria Urban League said, in commenting on the violent protests that had followed. "Now we can hardly control the people because they tried to abide by the system and got nowhere."[42] Despite the range of direct-action tactics that Black residents used to attempt to force change, the Callahan affair confirmed that heavy-handed cops would be exalted and their victims would be punished. Gibson's murder demonstrated just how vulnerable Black people were to violence directed at them from white people in the city—whether uniformed or not.

The double standard in Alexandria was clear: one set of laws and customs applied to white citizens, another to Black citizens. "People don't believe in the credibility of the system of laws," Boston stressed. "I won't call it justice." Even those white people who styled themselves more progressive could not overcome their own blind spots. "There is a feeling that a white man can kill a Negro and not be brought to justice," a city councilman said, "I don't think that is true—not today, not in Alexandria." It was true. Although John Hanna admitted to planting a knife near Gibson's dead body to make it appear as though he killed him in self-defense, an all-white jury of his peers sentenced Hanna to a mere two years in prison for manslaughter. He was released after serving eight months.[43]

The councilman and other white officials may have dismissed or ignored blatant injustices, but Black residents saw them everywhere. They lived in a city where bad-apple police officers with a history of brutality were lauded as heroes, and where white men could murder

Black teenagers without serious repercussion. To the white people of Alexandria, bad cops didn't exist.

The Arlandria community had learned to tolerate the great pain and suffering of everyday life under segregation and poverty—they had little choice in the matter—but after a bad-apple cop seemed to terrorize the community's children, these conditions became intolerable. Yet when their appeals to the city council and nonviolent demonstrations failed to convince officials to implement meaningful reforms, or when a white civilian murdered a Black person and faced almost no consequences, the community rebelled—as they did in hundreds of other cities when authorities demonstrated an unwillingness to provide basic protections. It was clear the bad apple sprung from a poisoned tree, and many concluded that it could only be cut down by violence of their own.

6

THE SCHOOLS

In September 1969, after students at De La Warr High School in New Castle, Delaware, were dismissed early for creating what the supervising principal called "conditions not conducive for learning," the young people threw rocks at police and taunted officers and journalists on the scene. (AP)

WHEN CONSIDERING THE history of racism in the United States, many Americans believe that the North has long been more enlightened than the South, and that the struggle for racial equality is primarily a story of the former Confederate states dragging their feet but eventually accepting Black citizenship. Although explicit laws prohibiting Black people from sharing public facilities with white people did not exist in northern states—where, in theory,

Black people could patronize stores and restaurants or use public transportation as they pleased—there were many commonalities between the two regions, and any kind of moralistic distinctions between them tend to crumble under even modest scrutiny.[1] Segregation defines the nation. Most people across the United States, at midcentury and today, live next door to someone of the same racial or ethnic identity, and this residential segregation both reveals and determines American life, nowhere more immediately than in its public schools. Often seen as a fundamental difference between South and North, school integration played out in similar ways in the southern and northern states, even if segregation was not the law of the land in the latter. On both sides of the Mason–Dixon line, schools were sites of Black insurgency and white counterinsurgency, and of rebellions that began on school grounds before spreading into the streets.

The process of school integration stretched from the *Brown v. Board of Education* decision in 1954, which outlawed racial segregation in American public schools, through the early 1970s and even beyond. Northern and southern schools began to integrate simultaneously following the ruling in *Brown*, and at a similar pace. Segregation of American schools did not begin to decline in a meaningful way until the late 1960s and early 1970s, as federal pressure and incentives established by the Elementary and Secondary Education Act of 1965 compelled school systems across the country to integrate. (After reaching a low point in the 1980s, both residential and school segregation have increased since 1990. The United States is more segregated today than it was before the *Brown* decision, and many areas in the North are more segregated than anywhere in the South.)[2]

As public schools across the United States slowly integrated beginning in the 1960s, cheerleading emerged as a flashpoint. In every region, Black women were regularly excluded from participation in cheerleading squads, and Black students, Black communities, and

Black organizations such as the NAACP consistently challenged these particular discriminatory policies. In September 1967, after a federal court order finally forced the Black and white high schools in Cairo, Illinois, to combine, Black football players refused to play because the student body had not elected a single Black cheerleader. (These sought-after positions were determined by election in many areas of the country, at the time.) A year later, at least two hundred Black students walked out of Argo Community High School in the Chicago metropolitan area to demand a Black homecoming queen and that half the spots on the six-woman cheerleading squad be reserved for Black teens. In Gastonia, North Carolina, in April 1969, two hundred fifty Black students walked out of class at Ashley High School to protest the election of an all-white cheerleading team. The school had started to integrate in 1966, and by 1969 Black students comprised 20 percent of the student body. Nearly half of the young women who participated in cheerleading tryouts at Ashley High were Black (representing twelve of the twenty-six total hopefuls), but the white-student majority easily prevented their inclusion on the team.[3]

Most of the cheerleading-related demonstrations started and ended peacefully. But sometimes the police were called in to contain the Black students, and from there demonstrations could expand into rebellion, or full blown "race war," as the New Pittsburgh Courier described the violence that emerged in Aliquippa, Pennsylvania, in May 1970 after the cheerleading team refused to accept Black girls. Whether efforts to integrate cheerleading squads were based on nonviolent or violent tactics, the protesters usually voiced broad critiques of white supremacy and racial injustice as well as demands aimed at improving public education and the community as a whole.[4] In May 1969, four Black girls tried out for the cheerleading team at the newly integrated Walter M. Williams High School in Burlington, North Carolina, only to be booed by white students during tryouts and denied places on the squad. Soon Black and white students were fighting each other on school grounds, and Black and white parents were complaining to city hall and the police chief. Before long, Burlington was burning, leading to the deployment of the National Guard and the killing of a Black male student by police.

Black students launched protests in this era in response to a range of injustices, pressuring school districts to establish robust Black Studies requirements for all students and to hire more Black teachers. They often rooted their demands in the bedrock principles of pride, equal inclusion, and self-protection that were of the central tenets of Black Power. Black student-activists also frequently demanded the removal of all "prejudiced" white teachers—especially guidance counselors who seemed to intentionally sabotage Black students in their efforts to attend college or vocational schools—and they pressed for Black leadership roles and representation in school organizations. In Harrisburg, the state capitol of Pennsylvania, a student movement that started in February 1969 based its campaign on all of these demands, but included one demand that seemed to go beyond education, at least at first glance: an end to "police brutality," broadly defined to include not only excessive use of force but also routine harassment.[5]

Yet police violence was not unrelated to the experience and prospects of Black students. Like housing projects, urban public schools were sites of new, targeted enforcement during the War on Crime in the late 1960s and early 1970s. Federal law enforcement grants supported the creation of school security forces: groups of police officers who roamed the hallways and classrooms of urban public schools and increasingly replaced school-based disciplinary bodies. Electronic surveillance equipment such as closed-circuit cameras were installed on school buses and on campuses. As schools across the country were slowly becoming more integrated (which, in turn, generated massive white resistance), majority-Black schools became even more isolated; the latter were also more policed and more forti-

fied, long before the "zero tolerance" disciplinary policies of the late
1990s. The origins of the "school-to-prison pipeline" that scholars
and activists have identified in recent years can be found in the era
of Black rebellion.[6]

The tendency on the part of school officials across the nation to
summon law enforcement to respond to disciplinary and administrative matters involving Black students made urban public schools
particularly likely to see rebellions. In September 1970, as Black students pressured school administrators to improve course offerings
in Black culture and history at Asbury Park High School in New Jersey, white and Black students were fighting in the hallways. By the
end of the month, the school closed for two days as rock throwing,
looting, burning, and sniping broke out in the city. When the school
reopened, twenty-five policemen patrolled its hallways. Many Black
students stopped attending. "Why would we show up to a prison? The
police will be patrolling the halls and once we step out of line they'll
throw us in jail," a young woman said. It was a prescient comment;
the police arrested eight students that day. Black and white students
came together to propose a less punitive approach: use student volunteers to patrol the hallways rather than uniformed police officers with
guns. Superintendent Donald E. Smith said the student patrols were an
"excellent idea" but that the police had an important role to play. "At
the moment I believe the situation is too volatile to throw these young
people into it and expect them to cope."[7] Smith and many other school
officials in America could not imagine crossing off the police as an
option to deal with student unrest.

Black rebellion at the turn of the decade frequently began with
young people, in or out of school settings. Yet in many cases rebellions started with young people protesting *as students* and organizing
movements for racial justice within their schools and communities. In
Harrisburg, Pennsylvania, and in Burlington and Greensboro, North

Carolina, among other American cities, student-led rebellions spilled over into the larger community and involved widespread violence. That this violence arose from within the public-school system suggests that these rebellions were not outbursts of criminality, but reactions to unequal educational and socioeconomic conditions. The violence also illuminates, perhaps better than anything else in this period, how the state was increasingly turning to law enforcement to manage the consequences of such conditions. Authorities most often resolved rebellions that originated in schools by arresting and suspending students en masse.

The tens of thousands of Black junior high and high school students who participated in various school-based protest movements had spent their early childhoods watching the boycotts and marches of the civil rights movement, but they were still waiting for change to arrive in their daily lives. Now, approaching adulthood and influenced by the growing militancy of parts of the Black freedom movement, they embraced new strategies and goals to realize the unfilled promises of their predecessors. Public schools, where this rising generation spent most of their days, were in many cases the primary battlegrounds in their struggle.

IN RECOGNITION OF "Negro History Week" in February 1969, the administration of John Harris High in Harrisburg, Pennsylvania, held a school-wide viewing of a film on Black history. Many white students skipped the compulsory event, and many of those who did attend laughed during the movie and walked out before it ended. Black students retaliated by boycotting the next assembly—a presentation to the students of military uniforms by the Women's Army Corps—on Friday, February 14. More than four hundred Black students, representing one third of the student body, went to the cafeteria and the choir room instead of the auditorium. Fights broke out over the remainder of the afternoon. School officials called in the police and dismissed classes forty-five minutes early. That weekend, Black Harris High students met with their peers from Harrisburg's other high school, William Penn. Together they drafted a set of demands for school administrators at both institutions, now that the protest had their attention.[8]

Three hundred Black Harrisburg students came ready to present their vision for a more inclusive system to school officials, teachers, and community members at a sit-in they launched at William Penn first thing Monday morning, February 17, 1969. Principal Paul E. Porter spoke with them. "The school district is trying desperately hard to hire as many black teachers as possible," Porter assured the students, but finding "qualified black teachers" was difficult. "You don't find teachers by just snapping your fingers," he said. The students did not leave the conversation feeling confident that their demands would be taken seriously. John Harris students, who were not afforded a meeting with their principal, adopted more disruptive tactics. They spent the day in the auditorium, hallways, and foyers of the school instead of in class. Students at Camp Curtin Junior High joined the protest by starting fires in a wastebasket, in an air duct, and on an auditorium seat, all of which were quickly extinguished.[9]

The district decided to enlist the police to handle the Black student protesters, a move that pushed the protest out of the classrooms and into the streets. Anticipating "lunch period trouble," Harris High administrators summoned police to the schools, where officers would remain stationed for the rest of the school year. "Our role was to try to keep the crowds under control and disburse them in an orderly fashion," Police Chief Martin Watts explained. When the officers arrived, the students did indeed disperse—hundreds of them spent the remainder of the afternoon throwing snowballs at cars, blocking traffic, and assaulting people. A forty-two-year-old person described as a "suburban Harrisburg man" suffered a fractured nose after allegedly being punched through his open car window near the high school. At 1:30 p.m., about thirty students walked into the Tim Doutrich department store and "helped themselves" to an estimated two-thousand-dollars' worth of merchandise, including a number of eighty-five-dollar suede coats. Five students were arrested on charges of assault and disorderly conduct. That night, City Superintendent David Parker announced that schools would be closed the following day to allow for a "period of cooling off."[10]

As officials saw it, the situation in the schools after they reopened on Wednesday, February 19, "amounted to anarchy." At Camp Curtin, Black students convened "unauthorized assemblies" instead of going to class, while others beat a white student. Four white teachers at the junior high threatened to go home because "they could not control the pupils."[11] William Penn students also held an "unauthorized assembly," where they gave "inflammatory, racist speeches" and burned the school flag. At Harris, two Black students allegedly cut a white student on the arm with a razorblade in the boys' bathroom.[12] Just before noon, three hundred students "swarmed" into the parking lot of a shopping center, "shouting obscenities" at customers and throwing eggs at a hotdog stand. "Roving bands" of students reportedly converged on a lunch counter near William Penn, "shouting and screaming" as they threw rocks. Others defaced their schools with spray paint. Superintendent Parker spoke of "an open rebellion" against white controlled institutions. "What we have here is a group of militant Negroes bent on the destruction of our enterprise." Parker assured residents that the district was "doing all we can to stabilize the situation," but the task was daunting. "The problems we face are the problems of our city plus the country."[13]

With the approval of the school board, the city established a plainclothes police force at Penn, Harris, Camp Curtin, and Edison Junior High School to assuage the fears of white parents, who threatened to pull their children out of school until authorities acted to solve the "breakdown in law enforcement." Most parents still kept their children home despite the arrival of the plainclothes officers the next day, February 20. Less than 50 percent of the students at the city's high schools and junior high schools—and according to some reports, not a single white student at Harris—showed up for school in the morning for several days.[14]

The students who did attend, the majority of whom were Black, found that plainclothes police patrolled inside the now "troubled" schools while uniformed officers cruised the surrounding area, looking for potential rioters. Teachers were expected to use the police as they saw fit. During a vocational workshop at Harris on February 20, an instructor called a plainclothes officer to his class to address an "unruly" student. The officer arrested the student, attracting a crowd of two hundred Black students, who started a "boisterous confrontation." The plainclothes officer used his walkie-talkie to inform headquarters of the situation.[15]

Repressive actions by the authorities fueled student rebellion, and student rebellion fueled repressive actions. In response to the officer's call from Harris, a squad of thirty-five officers in riot gear rushed to the school—this was the moment law enforcement had anticipated. The handcuffed student was taken to jail, and the gathered Black students voiced a "vigorous complaint" about the armored officers in their hallways. They started throwing tables and chairs, using a desk to smash the windows of the assistant principal's office, cleaning out the refrigerators in the home economics department and dumping their contents on the floor, overturning a vending machine, and lighting a fire in the girls' restroom.[16] At Hamilton Elementary School, children reportedly set small fires that day. The rebellion had spread throughout the entire school system.

The city and the police department tried to arrest their way out of the trouble. Harrisburg Mayor Albert Straub called for the detainment of the "known troublemakers" and promised that property destruction at public schools would "not be tolerated." By the end of the night, as stores were burglarized, windows around town were smashed, and white residents continued to report attacks, eight male students from both Harris and Penn were arrested on charges ranging from disorderly conduct to larceny and sent to the Dauphin County Prison, pending action from the probation office. The next morning, February 21, an eighteen-year-old and two younger students were arrested at their homes on charges of "riotous destruction of property" at Harris. A total of twenty-two Black students were arrested for their roles in the rebellion in and around school, and another twenty-seven were indefinitely suspended.[17]

Parents and community leaders on both sides were furious. "We are very displeased and disheartened over the militaristic approach being taken," the Black Coalition of Harrisburg wrote in a statement the evening of the twenty-first. "We feel that both the state and local government have overreacted, turning our communities into armed camps." The Coalition called for the withdrawal of the police from the schools and for the district to meet the Black students' initial demands. While the Black Coalition's meeting was taking place that evening, three hundred white parents gathered at the local Electricians' Union Hall, proposing their own ideas about "how to bring a full return of calm to the schools." Some simply rejected Black residents' claims about police violence. "What kind of brutality exists when police are attacked?" one attendee shouted. Many white parents believed Black students had "terrorized" the hallways and classrooms;

they shared stories of their children being assaulted and made clear that they felt the city had been too lenient. Congressman George W. Gekas offered a well-received solution: a "school police force," which would not be armed with "guns, clubs, and the like," to act as intermediaries between students and their superiors. Mayor Straub assured his constituents that the State Police and the District Attorney's Office had pledged their "full cooperation to whatever degree is required to end this disorder," and that the Pennsylvania National Guard stood "ready" for a confrontation.[18]

Although the violence in Harrisburg's public schools ended before additional police (or even military) force was brought to bear on the Black students involved, the courts and the school system moved forward with punishing the students arrested on charges related to the rebellion. With broad support from their community, Harrisburg's Black students challenged the suspensions and jailing of those who were "sacrificed because they stood up with us," and continued to press their demands with school and city officials. By early March, the school board agreed to create a special committee to investigate alleged acts of discrimination, to convene monthly meetings on the "racist situation," to hire more Black teachers, and to institute a broad educational program in Black history "as soon as possible."[19]

Yet Black students left the final negotiations with the school board believing their efforts had been in vain. To many, the expulsions of six Harris students and five Penn students, and the suspension of twenty-seven others for their involvement in the protest at both schools, were the most tangible outcomes of the entire episode. "The black student morale is low," explained Craig Humes, a Black Student Union representative and chairman of the Youth for the Advancement of Black Studies group. "We feel the situation in the schools has not changed." Harris student Cathy Sims argued that the school board had not communicated effectively with Black students and had "tampered with" and "misinterpreted" the students' demands. "We have no information of what is going on," Sims said of the school board's lack of transparency in implementing the programs it had promised them. Students felt even more isolated, with "nothing concrete for us to hold onto," Emma Givens of Harris High said. "A lot of students have been expelled and teachers have withdrawn from us."[20]

By May 1969, the Harrisburg public school system had hired five Black counselors, and (although the students did not ask for it) had provided new training for teachers, including a course on "the dynamics of urban cultures" and exercises to develop "sensitive concern" around "stereotyping, scapegoating, and racist references."[21] An uneasy calm descended on Harrisburg's public schools for the remainder of the school year after the rebellion. But that summer, Harrisburg would explode. The student protest in February was just the opening act in a larger drama. In late June, an incident of police brutality would set off the cycle of rebellion—police tear-gassed hundreds of Black residents, and residents reciprocated by hurling rocks and bottles, setting fires, and vandalizing property. After two nights, the rebellion came to an end when a Black Harris High student was shot in the back by a white police officer.

HARRISBURG WAS FAR FROM the only city that saw a student rebellion expand into a more general uprising. The violence in Burlington, North Carolina, started out in much the same way as the rebellion in Harrisburg: a very public display of cruelty by white students toward Black students. At Walter Williams High School on Wednesday, May 14, 1969, the day all of the young Black women who tried out for the cheerleading squad were rejected, brawls broke out between Black and white students in the hallways, which prompted authorities to close the school early "because of the tension."²² As in Harrisburg three months before, many white parents kept their children home from school the next day, citing the Black students' behavior.

Furor over the cheerleading team led Black students to call for a new committee at Walter Williams to "relate to the needs of black students": for more Black representation in the school administration, for a Black student newspaper that would "tell it like it is," for an all-Black board of inquiry to investigate violent incidents at the school, and for a Black cultural center on the campus. On Friday, May 16, at around two in the afternoon, the students formed a line and marched across town to the Burlington Public Schools administration building, where they were joined in solidarity by a group of students from the all-Black Jordan Sellars High School. Superintendent Dr. Frank Proffitt spoke with the students briefly as they assembled in front of the building. He refused to negotiate and instead threatened to charge the students with trespassing.²³

Administrators called in Burlington's police, who themselves called in county deputies and the highway patrol for backup. The protesting students stormed the administration building to force a conversation over their demands and were met by uniformed officers. A total of seventeen people were arrested—twelve Black students, five Black men—and charged with disorderly conduct, or damage to a public building, or both. Police drove the remaining protesters from the area. Some allegedly began throwing rocks on Rauhut Street, the commercial hub of the segregated Richmond Hill neighborhood.²⁴

The intervention of law enforcement transformed a student-led protest challenging racism within local schools into a larger conflict between the community and the police. After dark, rock throwing brought officers in riot gear into Richmond Hill. The confrontations with police continued, as did the property damage. One hundred highway patrol officers, fifty Burlington police, agents from the State

Bureau of Investigation, sheriff's deputies, and even prison guards joined forces to attempt to suppress the rebellion. When police in riot gear lined up on Rauhut Street, "a big crowd of black people, must have been three hundred of them, started coming down Rauhut, just raining down bricks, rocks, anything they could throw onto the cops and their patrol cars," as Odell Isley, one of the first Black officers on the Burlington police force, later described the moment.[25]

The first firebomb went off at around ten o'clock on Friday the sixteenth, at the white-owned Fox Fish Market on Rauhut Street. An estimated crowd of two hundred fifty to three hundred Black people threw rocks, bottles, and debris at the firefighters attempting to extinguish the blaze that night. Police brought in a "pepper fog" gas machine, which in seconds could cover a large area with an irritant stronger than tear gas, to disperse the crowd. The chemical weapon cleared the scene, but it did not deter further violence. For nearly two hours, "a crowd of jeering blacks, who cursed and attempted to antagonize the officers, began to gather and grow more and more out of hand," according to Burlington's *Daily Times-News*. Police moved in to "restore order" by firing their shotguns in the air, and they were met in return by sniper fire. With local and state law enforcement struggling to establish order, the National Guard was called in. By midnight, four hundred Guardsmen prowled the streets of Richmond Hill, using floodlights to illuminate the neighborhood and forming small units with police and highway patrolmen to search for suspects. Yet the rebels remained one step ahead of law enforcement. At around one in the morning, another firebomb went off at the white-owned Country Grocery store, also on Rauhut Street.[26] Gunshots could be heard throughout the early morning.

When the rebellion began, Turrentine Junior High School student Leon Mebane and a few of his friends went out into the streets, as did most other residents in Richmond Hill, whether they were participating or not. The fifteen-year-old Mebane, tall and slender, was probably wearing the grey felt coat he "barely took off" and on which he had affixed pieces of cloth spelling out the lyrics to "Mustang Sally"—an homage to James Brown, his favorite singer. At around three thirty, Mebane and other young boys were hanging out in front of the burned-out Country Grocery, perhaps checking out the damage the fire had caused.[27]

Police later claimed that Mebane and about ten other teenagers were looting the store and that Mebane ran into the crossfire during an exchange between police and snipers. "There was a lot of sniper fire coming from inside houses, beneath houses, and the boy was between the sniper fire and police," a National Guardsmen who witnessed the shooting recalled. (He also mentioned that "the boy had been throwing bottles and rocks at police earlier," in an attempt to justify what followed.) Mebane's mother, Zenobia Mebane, didn't buy any of it. Her son never had any disciplinary problems at school and had never been arrested. "A boy who was there told me that they were just looking at the burned-out building. There was nothing left to loot." According to police, the officers ordered Mebane and the other teens to halt, and opened fire when the young men did not listen to them. Mebane was hit a total of seventeen times. He was pronounced dead on arrival at the hospital. He did not have any "loot" on his person.[28]

Assuming the violence would escalate once news spread of Mebane's shooting, city officials decided to round up as many Richmond Hill residents as possible. A strict 8 p.m. curfew was imposed on Saturday, May 17, to be enforced by the four hundred National Guardsmen who remained in the city. The curfew would allow officers and troopers to arrest any person on the streets after the deadline. Hundreds of people were detained for curfew violations.[29]

The seventeen people who had been arrested for storming the

school administration building were each fined one hundred dollars
and slapped with a punishment intended to regulate their behavior.
They were sentenced to three years of probation during which time they
were restricted by a midnight to 7 a.m. curfew. As part of their sentence, they were ordered "not to be involved in any disruptive protests
or demonstrations of any kind at any place," prohibited from using "any
profanity, abusive language or a language calculated to create a disturbance," and instructed to "dress neatly and be clean to the satisfaction
of the probation officers." School officials, hoping to head off further
protests and recognizing the connection between the school uprising
and the general rebellion, obtained a court order prohibiting anyone
from interfering with the operation of city schools. Now only students,
faculty, and staff were allowed on school grounds at any time.[30]

Mebane's family never received a formal apology from the city
or the Burlington police, and there was no investigation into the fatal
shooting. "The mayor was real nasty to me," Zenobia Mebane remembered. "He said Leon was shot down like a dog. He said it was an open-
and-shut case. They never said one word of sympathy. Not one word."
The Mebanes pressed for an investigation, hiring a lawyer and appealing to Governor Bob Scott, Jesse Jackson, and NAACP branches across
North Carolina, but nothing came of their efforts. The police and
autopsy reports are missing now, either destroyed as allowed by law,
or misplaced. In the train depot on Main Street in Burlington, there
is a mural, painted in 1993, depicting scenes from the city's history. It
evokes the rebellion of 1969 with a scene of white policemen handcuff-
ing Black men at the Country Grocery.[31] Even if public memory of the
rebellion lives on, the killing of a Black boy by police has been largely
forgotten. So has the fact that the rebellion began when Black students
fought for full inclusion in a high school cheerleading squad, and simply to be treated with decency by their white peers.

ON MAY 21, 1969, the day after the National Guardsmen deployed
to Burlington were released from duty, six hundred fifty troops were
deployed just twenty-two miles to the west, to the campus of the historically Black North Carolina A&T State University at Greensboro.
"If the blacks shoot we will treat them like an enemy," a Guardsman
said. When the first shots were fired, allegedly by Black students, an
entire infantry company responded with shooting and tear gas.[32] As in
Harrisburg and Burlington, the violence stemmed from the decision
to respond to Black students' grievances with force. And as in Harrisburg and Greensboro, what started as a movement to improve the
educational experience of Black students quickly turned into a more
generalized rebellion against racism and police violence.

    Greensboro had been the birthplace of the sit-in movement in
1960, when four Black A&T students sat down to eat at a whites-only
lunch counter at Woolworth's and ultimately forced the department
store to end its segregationist practices. Nearly a decade later, after the
height of the civil rights movement, the future promised by the victory
in 1960 had not appeared. With a population of one hundred twenty-
five thousand, Greensboro was nearly twice the size of Harrisburg and
four times larger than Burlington. But the three cities were similar in
an important way: in each city, Black residents made up roughly a third
of the population and endured segregated schools (at the primary level,
if not above as well), poor employment prospects, inadequate housing,
and ongoing tensions with the police.[33]

    The violence in Greensboro began in a local secondary school. The
budding activist Claude Barnes, a seventeen-year-old junior at Greensboro's Dudley High School, ran for student council president, aiming
to implement reforms at the almost all-Black school (it had one white
female student) run by all-Black administrators. Barnes was already a
powerful voice in the halls of Dudley, where he led a number of student
groups, and in the larger community as well—he was a member of the

Youth United for Blackness group run by the Greensboro Association of Poor People (GAPP), which organized boycotts, rent strikes, and voter registration drives.[34]

During his campaign, Barnes called out the clear disparities between Dudley and Greensboro's white high schools, which boasted tennis courts, allowed students to leave campus at lunchtime, and didn't require students to follow a strict dress code. (A Dudley student could get sent home for sporting an Afro or wearing a dashiki, among the most popular styles at the time.) Barnes called for a robust African American studies curriculum and student input in the selection of reading materials in English and History.[35] Dudley administrators, most of whom were Black, labeled Barnes a radical who had been corrupted by "outside influences." The school's election committee went so far as to exclude Barnes from the ballot, on the grounds that he "lacked qualifications to be a candidate for student council president." This despite his accomplished record and the fact that he was already serving as junior class president.[36]

The attempt to neutralize Barnes backfired. The morning of the election, May 2, students distributed flyers encouraging a boycott. Barnes and four others walked out in the middle of an assembly as the approved candidates delivered speeches, and the assistant principal ordered the five young men and women to leave campus for the day, to prevent them from voting or interfering with the "democratic" process. Instead the students walked a mile and half north to the campus of A&T State, seeking help from some of Barnes's comrades in GAPP. Meanwhile the election resulted in six hundred write-in votes for Barnes and two hundred total votes for the runner up. Dudley officials refused to accept Barnes's victory, and principal Franklin Brown, a Black man, suspended the five students who walked out of the assembly.[37] Like his white counterparts, Brown would not tolerate "revolutionary" Black students on his campus.

The Dudley students continued to organize with the A&T students, forming the Student Organization for Black Unity (SOBU) at the university five days after the stolen election. In their first action, on May 9, the student activists at Dudley called for a walkout, and one hundred twenty-five students left the school, met up with A&T students, and together returned to Dudley for a demonstration. School authorities had summoned the police, who were now waiting for the students on campus. Students who had not participated in the walkout cheered when the protest returned. As he entered the building with other demonstrators, A&T Student Body Vice President and SOBU founder Nelson Johnson announced: "On the authority of the black community in all its configuration, we install Claude Barnes Jr. as the elected student council president." The police arrested Johnson and two other A&T students on charges of disrupting a public school and disorderly conduct. Seventeen Dudley students were also arrested. Rather than creating calm, as the police and school officials hoped, the arrests only spurred on the protest.[38]

Owen Lewis, the white public relations director of the Greensboro School Board, temporarily removed Principal Brown and put himself in charge of the school. Soon enough, police were patrolling Dudley's campus in full riot gear, and shotguns were prominently displayed by officers circling the campus in their cruisers. Students met with school officials several times over the next week, and although the five suspended students were permitted to return to Dudley, the activists left every meeting even more frustrated. The administration seemed unwilling to respond to the students' demands; the only action it took was to fortify the school with police. On May 16, two hundred Dudley students walked out of class and spent the morning on the corner of streets close to campus, and in nearby Nocho Park, where they reportedly met with SOBU members.[39]

At eight o'clock on the morning of Monday, May 19, Barnes

picketed in front of the school's administration building with eight other students who formed the core group of Dudley activists. Lewis instructed the police to arrest them. The students fought back. "Of course we were resisting," Barnes remembered. "We were getting clubbed. High school students were getting clubbed by the police." The very public display of police aggression only recruited more Dudley students to the cause. "I mean people started joining the protest then," Barnes said. Five hundred students poured out of the school building; some of them broke windows and turned over tables in the cafeteria before leaving, while others threw bricks at police officers once outside. A number of girls tried to beat police with umbrellas, leading to the arrest of more students and several injuries on both sides.[40]

The next day, the entire school shut down as hundreds of students participated in the boycott. The Black students' protests weren't going to simply fizzle out. As the North Carolina Advisory Committee to the United States Commission on Civil Rights concluded after two days of open meetings to investigate the unrest and violence: "the principal and the representative of the central administration misjudged the intensity of the students' feelings and the limits to which the students were prepared to go to make their point."[41]

The confrontation reached its apex on Wednesday. The students started throwing rocks at the officers stationed at the school, and the cops responded by tear-gassing the entire area surrounding Dudley, hitting many students who were not involved. The protesters—"all these little high school kids, bloodied, reeking of tear gas," as Barnes later described it—marched to the A&T campus. "Here we were, high school students, and we were confronted with police in full riot gear, pepper gas," Barnes said. "We were brutalized, basically, we were beaten, locked up." As the protesters walked through A&T and down the street, what started as a group of twenty-five high school and college students quickly attracted several hundred people, angered by the tainted election and the aggressive police response to student activism. A coalition had emerged, organized by young activists in the GAPP, that brought together Dudley students, A&T students, and community members. The mayor requested immediate assistance from the National Guard.[42]

Although initially the only A&T students involved were members of SOBU, police violence had had a galvanizing effect on campus, as it had among the high school student body. A message had been broadcast to A&T students on May 20: "your lives are in mortal danger!" It described police brutality in the language of Black radicalism: "How many of you can stomach the sight of a big, burly, red-neck pig take a little Black child and beat her with a three-foot nightstick, drag her by the hair in the mud and water across the ground, and *throw* her into a pig paddy wagon?" Many Dudley students had been attacked by officers, and it was time for the police department to learn that "they can't beat the black children half to death and expect nothing to be said or *done!*"[43]

The evening of the twenty-first, A&T students threw rocks at cars, injuring several people. By eight o'clock, police had established barricades to keep white residents out of the campus area; tactical units proceeded to tear-gas a group of protesters. The first report of sniper fire came two and a half hours later, at 10:35 p.m., as the National Guard was on its way. It remains unclear who fired the first shot, in this and many other rebellions. As Barnes put it, "People were about not initiating any kind of offensive action, but certainly if someone attacks you, you want to repel that attack." In his view, Black people armed themselves "because we didn't want to be shot down like dogs."[44] Predictably, each side claimed that the other had started the shooting.

At around one thirty the next morning, Willie Grimes, a twenty-year-old sophomore who lived in a dorm at Scott Hall, decided to head out for a snack with some friends, many of whom were fellow members of the Pershing Rifles, a fraternity of Army ROTC members. Grimes hoped to join the Air Force after graduation.[45] As the young Black men walked across campus, they heard gunshots and started running. Grimes was hit in the back of his head and pronounced dead on arrival at the hospital. After Leon Mebane in Burlington, Grimes was the second young man to die in the crossfire of police violence and rebellion in North Carolina's Piedmont Triad in the span of five days. Witnesses to Grimes's death claimed the fatal shots came from an unmarked police car. Law enforcement denied any involvement.

Grimes's killing led to more violence on campus. "It is no more wrong to kill a pig, who is trying to kill you, and he is trying, than it is to eat a meal when you are hungry," proclaimed a letter from SOBU members to Black A&T students that was circulated the day after Grimes's death. The shooting continued that night, with gunfire on both sides resulting in injuries to five police officers and another student, Clarence Count, who was hit in the leg. The next morning, May 23, the National Guard arrived on A&T's campus early, preparing to clear the Cooper and Scott dormitories as though engaged in a military operation. No one from the Guard consulted with university officials before carrying out the raid; they merely informed A&T President Lewis Carnegie Dowdy of their intentions at 5:30 a.m. Their mission began at 7 a.m.[46]

First the troops cleared Scott Hall by kicking in and shooting off doors, then throwing tear gas grenades, some of them from a helicopter. Once the students who lived there were placed in "protective custody" and both dormitories were secured, the Guardsmen swept through rooms, allegedly taking students' personal property with them. The troops did not find the massive weapons arsenal they expected to uncover. They confiscated two guns in total. The assault caused nearly fifty-seven thousand dollars of property damage; in the words of President Dowdy, however, "the damage done to the one

thousand three hundred students who were housed in these two dormitories" was "immeasurable and incalculable." After the raid had concluded, the National Guard and police removed their roadblocks from
the surrounding area and temporarily withdrew, but Guardsmen soon
returned to patrol the A&T campus for an additional two days.[47]

About a year later, on May 4, 1970, the National Guard killed four
white students at Kent State University in Ohio during a protest against
the expansion of the war in Vietnam, a case that drew national attention and intensified the anti-war movement (though the majority of
Americans at the time sided with the Guardsmen). Eleven days later,
at Jackson State, a historically Black college (now university) in Mississippi, state highway patrolmen opened fire on a crowd of one hundred Black students, killing two and injuring twelve others. Authorities
claimed they were being "sniped at," but an FBI investigation did not
find any evidence of sniper fire. Though these events were prefigured
by Willie Grimes's killing and the rampant mistreatment of his fellow students, the earlier case did not attract wide attention or lead to
any changes in how authorities responded to protests and rebellions at
colleges and universities. President Nixon established the President's
Commission on Campus Unrest, known as the Scranton Commission, to investigate the Kent State and Jackson State shootings. In its
final report of September 1970, the Commission determined that the
shootings were not justified in either case. There is no mention of the
Greensboro violence in the five-hundred-page document.[48]

The investigation of violence at Greensboro had been left to a local
Advisory Committee to the United States Commission on Civil Rights.
After the shooting, as one Dudley High School student pointed out to
the North Carolina Advisory Committee in the fall of 1969, the vio-
lence, including the death of Willie Grimes, was entirely avoidable.
The students gave the school administration several opportunities to

come to a compromise on their demands, but none of the authorities rose to advocate for the young activists. (At one point the Greensboro school board believed it could end the rebellion by reassigning to Dudley those Black football players attending predominantly white high schools—a practice intended to improve the white schools' teams.) "The students were left to create situations that would force the officials to take notice," the Committee said in its official report. Principal Brown and other school officials had no interest in discussion, no desire to reach a resolution with the students. The activists at A&T State were the Dudley students' primary defenders.[49]

For their part, city and school officials had dismissed the student movement, arguing that it was led by a group "of not-too-bright black students" who were "being led astray by 'outsiders' and 'radicals.'" This view ignored the underlying problems that motivated the protesters in the first place, the Advisory Committee found. "'Outsiders' cannot create problems although they may exploit them," the Committee observed. It was easier for authorities to scapegoat students for operating in a "Panther-like" fashion than to acknowledge they might have a real point to make.[50]

City and state officials in Harrisburg had likewise clung to the idea that "outside influences" were responsible for the rebellion in their city's schools. Pennsylvania Governor Raymond Shafer had announced at a press conference in the middle of the violence in his state that while there was no evidence that militant groups or federal anti-poverty officials were leading the rebellion, "we are looking into that possibility." The state school superintendent and Mayor Straub also suggested that "outside agitators" were responsible for the unrest. Even if this were true, one Black Coalition of Harrisburg member did not see why it should matter: "Outside agitators are the society." Students were responding to pervasive racial discrimination. "The students have led the way, and we should bury once and for all the 'outside agitators' claim."[51]

In Greensboro, the grievances motivating the uprising were "simple and clear," the Advisory Committee concluded. "The main issue was the unequal treatment of citizens of Greensboro because of their race: discrimination in housing, employment, education, and the delivery of services, coupled with institutional racism and the unresponsiveness of the official system."[52] The schools were but one pillar holding up a larger structure of racial oppression.

THE VIOLENCE IN Greensboro ended when all A&T State University and Dudley High School students were dismissed for the remainder of the school year. That summer the high school and college students as well as the broader community kept protesting, carrying forward Barnes's original campaign platform. In response, Dudley administrators rescinded the strict dress code previously enforced at the school. The school board agreed to invest in new textbooks and improve facilities at Dudley and other underserved campuses in the district. Black history courses were eventually offered as part of Dudley's curriculum.

"That's what we were fighting for," Barnes reflected later. "If that revolt hadn't happened, we wouldn't have had the political progress that was made."[53] It took violent protest—including actions that spilled beyond schools themselves—to force Harrisburg, Burlington, Greensboro, and other school systems in America to respond to the basic needs of Black students. In Harrisburg and Greensboro, though one is a Northern city and the other Southern (and famous as a civil rights battlefield), events played out in a similar fashion and any progress came at a similarly devastating cost: young men had been killed, dozens more students were expelled, and many were left with criminal records. Rather than simply engaging with students putting forward a set of deeply felt and serious-minded demands, administrators often turned to disregard and repression as their chosen tactics. And when this response led to Black political violence, the "solution," even among Black authorities themselves, always involved state-sanctioned counterinsurgency in defense of the existing racial order.

7

THE COMMISSIONS

The city of Columbus, Georgia, witnessed more than 150 fires, sporadic shootings at police and firemen, and frequent incidents of rock and bottle throwing in Black neighborhoods throughout the summer of 1971. Ogletree's Grocery, shown here on June 20, was hit by a Molotov cocktail. (AP)

THE CYCLE OF police violence and Black rebellion appeared in many if not most American cities in the late 1960s and early 1970s, almost regardless of size, region, or the particular history of a given city. And just as the cycle played out in similar ways wherever police violence and desperate conditions prevailed, the aftermaths of these events often followed a template. As in Greensboro, after the unrest and violence in the spring of 1969, a federal civil rights commission or a state or local-level human relations commission would be constituted to investigate, produce a report, and recommend a path forward. Yet even as these commissions succeeded in doing the very thing local officials refused to do—talk about root causes—they can by and large be judged failures. They did not stop the violence themselves, and many of the cities they tried to save went into steep decline despite their efforts. To understand why, the place to start is with the well-meaning attempts to render Black rebellion unnecessary.

The House of Representatives created the first human relations and civil rights commission in 1917, when it sent a special committee to investigate police misconduct during the white riot in East St. Louis that left hundreds of Black people dead. Select committees or commissions were a frequent response to incidents of mass white vigilantism and racial warfare up to and during the Second World War, and to Black rebellions beginning with Watts in 1965. The most prominent and influential "riot commission" was the National Advisory Commission on Civil Disorders established by a Lyndon Johnson executive order in July 1967 during the summer of rebellions in Newark, Cairo, Detroit, and seventy other cities. The Kerner Commission had been named after its chairman, Illinois Governor Otto Kerner, and the task force was given seven months to determine the origins of the violence and to recommend measures to contain future disturbances. When the Kerner Commission released its 426-page report in February 1968, seven hundred forty thousand copies sold within a few weeks—in total, two million Americans would purchase the paperback version of the report.[1] The public wanted to know why "rioting" had occurred and how it could be stopped.

For its time, the Kerner report was a mostly progressive document. Highlighting the role of white racism in perpetuating inequality and segregation, the commission called for the full integration of Black citizens into "the mainstream of American life." Although the report placed the onus on Black Americans themselves to conform to "mainstream" (read, "white") cultural values and practices, the Kerner Commission argued that this goal could only be achieved by directing massive federal investment into "disadvantaged" communities. That effort would need to go well beyond existing War on Poverty programs in order to provide greater access to employment, education, and housing—the same issues that would later be identified by the North Carolina Advisory Committee after Greensboro. But at the time, Johnson viewed these recommendations as unreasonable politically, fearing their radical implications, and refused to publicly comment on the Commission's findings.[2] Still, the Commission had served an important purpose for the president, who had announced its formation in his televised address from the Oval Office four days into the Detroit rebellion. Establishing the task force allowed Johnson to point to a concrete step he had taken to reassure the American people that order would eventually be restored across the nation.

Subsequent state- or local-level investigations into the causes of and solutions to "racial unrest" followed the pattern set by the Kerner Commission: they identified the socioeconomic origins of rebellion and outlined a plan of action by which cities could "improve race relations" and create more equitable conditions, but their recommendations were seldom implemented and ultimately they backed the police. In Minnesota, after St. Paul police tear-gassed some five hundred young Black people in their teens and early twenties at a soul music dance over Labor Day weekend in 1968, a cycle of rebellion began that involved window smashing, arson, and shooting. The local Urban Coalition and Human Rights Department commissioned studies to determine the causes of the uprising, and they interviewed hundreds of witnesses and residents throughout the fall, releasing their reports in February 1969. "The tensions and frustrations of the St. Paul Negro Community have been created by so many factors and been bottled up so long that disorder seemed inevitable," Human Rights Department

Director Louis H. Ervin wrote. "Something had to give." Again, the investigators identified unequal access to decent housing, education, and employment opportunities as the fundamental causes of the violence, while praising the "exemplary conduct" and "discipline" on the part of the police, who injured some thirty residents over the course of the two-day rebellion. The police violence was largely attributed to "some ineptitude, even misconduct" on the part of a few "bad apple" cops, and St. Paul authorities did little to remedy socioeconomic disparities moving forward.[3]

In Harrisburg, Pennsylvania, the state Human Relations Commission held two sets of hearings. Though the city was spared the kind of shattering violence that erupted in nearby Pittsburgh and in Baltimore during the Martin Luther King rebellions in 1968—on April 8, the day before King's burial, "marauding bands of youths" in Harrisburg set fire to a Quaker Oats Company warehouse and the building of a furniture company, but there was not a major outbreak beyond these incidents—many feared it had all the ingredients for large-scale disorder. A week after King's burial services, the Harrisburg Human Relations Council identified the city as a "likely target for riots," due to the inequality and discrimination suffered by its Black residents, who numbered about twenty-three thousand of the city's total population of sixty-eight thousand. The Pennsylvania Human Relations Commission came to investigate and agreed that the city contained "the active potentiality for racial violence."[4]

In their Investigatory Report of May 1968, members of the state commission echoed the Kerner Commission in warning that "interracial tensions cannot be erased without full partnership inclusion in the planning and decision making process of authority." The report encouraged the city to "bring the Negroes of Harrisburg into meaningful inclusion" in the "programs that will affect their families' lives and futures." Specifically, this meant expanding the federal government's

Section 8 vouchers via the US Department of Housing and Development to increase the housing stock accessible to Black residents; stricter
enforcement of the housing code to force slumlords to keep their rent-
als up to basic standards; the expansion of job training programs and
vocational schools to open a pathway for residents into skilled trades;
and the immediate development that summer of swimming pools,
parks, and playgrounds in the "core city" to ensure public services were
"equitably rendered."[5] These measures would not completely overturn
the status quo in favor of Black equality, the report made clear, but
could still help improve conditions in the short-term. About a year
later, the anticipated "racial violence" arrived, in the schools and on
the streets, and the state Human Relations Commission returned, this
time conducting a far more comprehensive investigation and proposing a more ambitious set of reforms.

In Cairo, Illinois, it took two hundred nights of shooting over a
period of three years before a task force arrived and determined the
city was at war with itself. In March 1972, the United States Commission on Civil Rights held a three-day public hearing in Cairo, marking the first time racial oppression and white vigilantism in the city
were recognized by a government authority at any level. Commissioner
Frankie Freeman, the first Black woman to be appointed to the position, understood the stakes. "We have come to Cairo for specific reasons," she explained in her opening remarks. "The Commission has
received allegations . . . that extensive and overt racial discrimination
exists here." Freeman knew the hearings, and the city's problems, were
about more than Cairo. "In turning our attention to the racial situation in Cairo we will also learn a great deal about similar situations in
other communities throughout the country," she said, adding that this
information "will be enlightening and of benefit to Americans everywhere."[6] Black Cairoites were skeptical of the Commission's power to
change their daily lives, but it was the best hope they had had since the

war began on the last day of March in 1969, with local whites shooting into their community from the levee.

EVEN AS liberal-leaning civil rights commissions at the federal level and liberal-leaning human relations commissions at the state and local levels highlighted the socioeconomic roots of rebellion and promoted integration as the primary solution, they tended to pathologize Black residents—and this was central to the ultimate failure of the commissions. A study conducted by the school board in Alexandria, Virginia, in 1970, attributed instances of "black bravado" to the "criminal disruption" of local schools by Black students. The board cast the "discipline problem," much like the Kerner report had, as "ultimately the creature of a negligent white society." While it called for the reformation of existing institutional structures of control and exclusion, the study also pointed to an "unconscious mass paranoia" among Black people that led them to regard all disciplinary actions as "racially motivated."[7] Even as the school board acknowledged the fact of white racism, it concluded that Black Americans' perception of that racism was delusional. The solution lay just as much in changing Black Americans' beliefs in the pervasiveness of discrimination as it did in changing public policy.

The idea that the problem of racism is partially or largely a matter of Black people's mistaken perception appears in the Supreme Court's infamous decision in *Plessy v. Ferguson* in 1896, which established the "separate but equal" clause that enforced Jim Crow segregation. The "badge of inferiority" that resulted from the "enforced separation of the two races" was an "assumption" of Black people's own making, according to the Supreme Court's majority. "If this be so," the Court ruled, "it is not by reason of anything found in the act, but solely because the colored race chooses to put that construction upon it." The problem was not racial exploitation and inequality stemming from slavery, white supremacist violence, and the failures of Reconstruction, but undue sensitivity on the part of the former slaves and their descendants. The *Plessy* decision reduced the "race problem" to mere interpersonal prejudice—to how Black and white people felt about and interacted with one another.[8]

By the 1960s and 1970s, policymakers and social scientists preferred to use the supposedly neutral term "alienation" to describe the psychological impact of racism on Black Americans. As future senator Daniel Patrick Moynihan famously put it in his influential 1965 report, "alienation" was shorthand for "the equally numerous ways in which large numbers of Negro youth appear to be withdrawing from American society."[9] By talking about urban problems, including violence, in terms of "alienation," Moynihan, civil rights commissions, and prominent liberal officials cast racial inequality as a consequence of behavior. This view limited their vision for a more egalitarian America; as many white people did at the time, they had turned to interpersonal and psychological understandings of the causes of Black poverty and violence. The concept of "alienation" united the progressive idea that society treated Black people unfairly with the regressive notion that Black people suffered from a pathology that left them unwilling (as the liberal side of the debate argued) or unfit (as many conservatives suggested) to participate in society. It was a position that undermined the stated goals of the commissions in the first place.

"Alienation" provided a useful framework for the Pennsylvania Human Relations Commission in its attempts to understand the April 1968 rebellion in Harrisburg. "Longstanding patterns of exclusion of the Black resident from participation in the process of local government have resulted in a profound sense of alienation by the Black community," the commission reported. It described alienation as the result of "abrasive contact with agencies or individuals representing governmental authority" that led to the "intensification of real or imagined grievances against the historically insensitive power structure." Trying to make sense of the "riot," the commission elaborated: "Grievances suffered by Negroes take on a deep personal significance far overbalancing the immediate consequences of the grievance." The "alienation" of Black residents led them to view such everyday things as the delay of trash removal in their neighborhood not as an "instance of poor public service but as an example of racial discrimination."[10]

Although the commission clearly understood that the violence was the product of systematic exclusion and discrimination over time, its assertion that at least some Black grievances were "imagined" or that the response to a perceived injustice "far overbalanced the immediate consequence" implied that, to a certain extent, its members believed that racism was a Black problem. Seeing the world as fundamentally racist prompted them to overreact—to rebel—in certain situations.[11]

The commission did address the role of police in provoking the rebellion, but only obliquely. As the "on-the-street representatives of local authority," and therefore the "focal point for overt expressions of disrespect for seemingly insensitive authority by a frustrated minority," the Harrisburg police bore the brunt of the violent manifestations of Black residents' perceived "alienation." The state-level commission borrowed from the recommendations the Kerner Commission had made two months prior to address the "increased misunderstanding and antipathies towards the police." It encouraged the Harrisburg Police Department to establish a complaint review process, to recruit "nonwhite" officers, to offer community-relations and sensitivity training for its rank and file, and to "develop police-citizen rapport and understanding."[12] These recommendations were in line with the prevailing community-oriented reforms police departments across the United States had begun to implement in the late 1960s, especially the turn toward diversifying the ranks.

Following the Pennsylvania Commission's recommendations, in the summer of 1968 the city made good on its earlier promise to expand recreational facilities, building eight new playgrounds and two swimming pools, and the police department opened two new neighborhood police–community relations centers. Staffed by four officers total, two of them Black, the centers were responsible for "establishing rapport with neighborhood citizens," responding to complaints from residents, and developing programming for junior high and high school students. The initiative was good for public relations, but in practice it was treated like the bastard child of the Harrisburg Police Department. The unit was not assigned police cruisers or a clerical staff, leaving the officers to handle all bureaucratic duties themselves. The citizens complaint program was shunned by the rest of the force and given little support from the city.[13]

The Harrisburg Police Department's refusal to commit to improving relations with the community was perhaps best exemplified by the "sensitivity training" it introduced for its officers, which did more to instill a "warrior mentality" than anything else. During the "sensitivity" course, intended to promote understanding of the Black community as a means of reducing instances of police brutality, officers were shown a thirty-five-minute film, "Revolution Underway," produced by the National Education Program, an ultra-right-wing group based in Searcy, Arkansas. Essentially anti-communist propaganda, it warned of a "revolutionary force" that aimed to "destroy" American cities and overthrow the government. It argued that the Kerner Commission, which found that the rebellions were not part of a larger conspiracy, had "suppressed" evidence about the role of "revolutionary Black Power" in stoking unrest. Featuring footage of "traitors" such as Malcolm X, Robert F. Williams, H. Rap Brown, and Stokely Carmichael, the film warned darkly of "outside agitators" who were primarily responsible for the "assault on American institutions from within." The

1968 film was shown to law enforcement officers across the country into the 1970s.[14]

"Revolution Underway" depicted local police as the soldiers of the War on Crime—as the most important line of defense against the violent Black and Brown enemy. Offering few specifics about how to quell rioting beyond the use of paramilitary tactics, "Revolution Underway"—which was also screened at a meeting of the Save Our Schools organization in Harrisburg and at the Market Square Presbyterian Church—heightened the stakes of urban unrest and the role of police in suppressing it. A Black officer called the film "distasteful and destructive" in its "stereotypical" depictions. Harrisburg Mayor Albert Straub, Acting Police Chief Martin Watts, and other city officials endorsed "Revolution Underway" as a necessary element of police "sensitivity" training.[15]

The conflict over "Revolution Underway" illuminated the growing chasm between conservative and liberal officials, and between law enforcement and social services representatives. Both sides understood Black political violence as rooted in pathology and, at best, downplayed underlying socioeconomic causes, but the liberal concept of "alienation" presented a powerful counter to the "outside agitator" thesis, or ideas about innate Black criminality, that police authorities often relied upon to explain the causes of rebellion. Yet by consistently attributing the violence to Black behavior or psychology, or even white racism in the case of the Kerner Commission, officials across the political spectrum ultimately agreed to empower police forces to mitigate the effects of centuries of structural discrimination and exclusion through surveillance, patrol, incarceration, and other forms of social control.

SEVERAL MONTHS AFTER the 1969 rebellion in Harrisburg public schools, on June 23 a crowd of two hundred Black residents gathered in front of the Goodyear Pharmacy at the intersection of Thirteenth and Market Street in the city's Allison Hill neighborhood. By this point, the police already had a plan in place to suppress the "racial disturbance." It had been a year since the visit by the Pennsylvania Human Relations Commission, and housing codes remained largely unenforced, the projects remained segregated (as did, by extension, elementary schools), and no action had been taken to address unemployment issues in a city where the rate of Black unemployment was more than three times that of white unemployment. The people in front of the Goodyear Pharmacy that evening had assembled to watch a peaceful demonstration against police brutality. At the center of the protest was retired schoolteacher Mary Yancey, who carried a sign with a blunt, inflammatory message: "I was brutalized by the pigs." Pamphlets were distributed calling for a boycott of the pharmacy and to "protest the beating of One of Our Black Women!" Two days before, on June 21, the forty-eight-year-old Yancey had gone to the pharmacy to buy a pack of cigarettes and was refused service. Goodyear employees called the police. Six officers arrived, according to witnesses. They grabbed Yancey, one policeman shoving his knee against her back, and threw her into a paddy wagon. The officers did not inform Yancey that she was under arrest, but at the station she was booked on charges of disorderly conduct.[16]

Yancey led the peaceful demonstration on June 23 with a dozen or so others, surrounded by a crowd of mostly younger Black residents who watched the protest unfold. At seven o'clock, when several carloads of officers appeared, along with Mayor Straub and his aides, the spectators joined in the protest. The officials ordered the gathering to disperse. The young Black people responded by throwing bricks and stones at them. The sight of an officer with a shotgun on his hip angered the crowd even more. People marched past the police and started throwing bricks and bottles through the windows of nearby stores. The officer promptly returned his shotgun to his car, but the crowd was already beyond control. The police on the scene responded to the rock throwing by tear-gassing the crowd. About thirty state troopers soon arrived, and the disorder spread from there, through Allison Hill and uptown Harrisburg, down alleys and along main thoroughfares. Windows of stores were shattered and people driving through the area suffered injuries as Black residents threw rocks and bricks at their cars.[17]

The next day, June 24, Officer Raymond Kertulis, an eleven-year veteran of the Harrisburg police force, shot an eighteen-year-old Black youth named Charles Scott three times in the back, killing him. According to Kertulis, he spotted Scott preparing to ignite a Molotov cocktail, and fired after the teenager refused to drop the homemade bomb. A subsequent ACLU investigation did not uncover any evidence that Scott had a weapon in his possession and concluded that Kertulis did not give a warning before he shot him. The rebellion in Harrisburg began with a comparatively minor incident of police brutality—according to Mary Yancey's account, she had been roughhoused by police and arrested for no good reason—and a protest against that brutality. Now police had killed a Black teenager in what the ACLU later termed "a summary execution." Kertulis, charged with criminal negligence, was absolved of any wrongdoing by a coroner's jury six weeks later.[18]

At the urging of Harrisburg's Black Coalition, Governor Raymond Shafer directed the Pennsylvania Human Relations Commission to hold another set of investigatory hearings "into the racial tension situation." As Shafer explained, "the racial tension and the potential of renewed violence in the city of Harrisburg requires that we do everything humanly possible to protect all citizens, and at the same time, seek ways to immediately relieve tension." The idea was that the hearings should be held right away, to "provide a forum" for Harrisburg residents to "air grievances and seek solutions reasonably, away from the inflammatory emotions of the street."[19]

Believing that racism was simply a misunderstanding between Black and white residents and not a systemic matter, Shafer hoped the conversation itself would be enough, that talking things out would lead to a solution. "I appeal to all citizens of the capital city to use the commission hearings as the best way to discuss alleged injustices and find new paths to end the differences that separate the races," the Governor said.[20] But the Human Relations Commission had already visited the city the year before, and Black residents now pointed out that public officials had not abided by or implemented the recommendations made in 1968. People wanted action this time, not more talk. As James Stevens, manager of a market operated by the civil rights organization Ghetto Enterprises in Allison Hill, explained to the commission: "If you had pressed recommendations you made last year this hearing would not be necessary."[21]

THE SECOND ROUND OF Pennsylvania Human Relations Commission hearings began in Harrisburg on Wednesday, July 2, 1969, eleven days after Mary Yancey arrived in front of Goodyear Pharmacy with her sign. Hundreds of residents, most of them Black, gathered in the auditorium at William Penn Memorial Museum to observe the proceedings, which lasted for more than eleven hours, with only two breaks. In Cairo, when the investigation by the United States Commission on Civil Rights began on March 23, 1972, US Marshals searched every person entering the hearing room; the city had the highest per capita gun registration rate in Illinois. Both commissions heard testimony from witnesses and representatives from civil rights, nonprofit, and municipal organizations, and from state agencies. Black witnesses in Harrisburg argued that the "bridges of dialogue" that had been attempted over the prior year—namely, a series of discussion groups sponsored by the local PBS station and the previous Pennsylvania Human Relations Commission hearings—could not address the underlying problems. In Illinois, Cairo's Black witnesses described violent conditions and the terror caused by white vigilantes and police. They voiced the growing refrain: housing, unemployment, the schools, and the unequal delivery of services—these were the pressing issues. But they argued that it was police behavior that needed to be dealt with first.[22]

Black people who appeared before the commissions questioned the purpose of the police, who seemed to introduce violence rather than safety into the community. Activist Richard James charged that the Harrisburg Police Department used "oppressive, repressive, genocidal methods" in its treatment of Black residents. James and other witnesses argued that the police had contributed to the violence in the city's public schools back in February, and more recently had once again "overreacted" to an otherwise peaceful protest. Until the police themselves changed, they would continue to stoke unrest.[23]

Witnesses in Cairo voiced almost identical systemic critiques. "The way we see it from where we stand, is that every time that we strive to do something to help ourselves, that there are more policemen armed with guns, more ammunition is bought to put a stop to the drive to better the condition of the Negro," observed Reverend J. J. Cobb. Recently appointed to the city's three-member Police and Fire Commission, Cobb was the first Black person in Cairo's history to have an official voice in discussions. "This is the way that we see it in this community, and this is the way it is seen across the country."[24] Police tended to respond to any Black protest, regardless of form, with violence. It seemed—to Cobb and to so many other Black people in Cairo, Harrisburg, and across the rest of the country—to be the American way.

Indeed, witnesses at the hearings in both states voiced the belief among some Black Americans that there was a larger coordinated effort on the part of government authorities to keep Black people "in their place." Harold F. Posey, coordinator for the Council of Churches of Greater Harrisburg, went so far as to suggest that there was a "conspiracy at the federal [and] state [levels], and among local officials and authorities to harass black people." Charles Koen, of the United Front in Cairo, was convinced that President Richard Nixon was at the head of a "conspiracy to destroy responsible Black leadership." Illinois Governor Richard Ogilvie and state's attorney and former White Hat leader Peyton Berbling carried out the plan by enabling white supremacists and the police department to terrorize Black Cairoites in general, and United Front activists in particular.[25] While there isn't evidence of a coordinated conspiracy from Nixon down to the White Hats in Cairo, residents could be forgiven for thinking there was. A conspiracy would have had the same results as the widespread violence exacted on America's Black communities. The idea that white authorities were conspiring against Black residents further fueled the notion that Black people were paranoid about the prevalence and scale of racial oppression.

In both Harrisburg and three years later in Cairo, the state proceedings largely focused on accounts of police insensitivity and brutality during the rebellions and in everyday life. Anna Coleman said Harrisburg police beat her son "with a billy club on the head" when they arrested him for "malicious mischief," even though he did not take part in any violence. Several Harrisburg high school students testified about being arrested and held without charges for days even though they had not participated in the school rebellion in February. Witnesses recounted harassment and beatings by police in "normal" times. Their testimony persuaded the Pennsylvania Human Relations Commission that "police officers, in the performance of arrest of Black

youths, have resorted to the use of the club or blackjack with such frequency, that literally all Black citizens are convinced that a primary
police policy and objective is to instill fear of police in Blacks through
the use of club or blackjack on every possible occasion."[26] Even if the
brutality itself was "imagined" or "overbalanced"—the Commission
was shaped by the theory of "alienation"—nearly every Black resident
who testified identified a collective mistrust and fear of the police.
It would be impossible, the Commission concluded, to foster public
safety if policing methods were not drastically revised.

Cairo residents related incidents of police violence in graphic
detail. Former Cairo patrolman Wilbert Beard, one of the three total
Black officers on the police force in the city's history up to that point,
recounted: "In some arrests they [police officers] would have a submachine gun against a black guy's head, begging him to move so they
could kill him." Russell DeBerry, a Black resident of Cairo, revealed
his personal experience with a racist police department. DeBerry was
detained during a mass arrest on September 29, 1971, after a Black
youth allegedly struck a white woman—the relative of a police officer—
and stole her purse. According to DeBerry, when he arrived at the station house, Police Chief Bowers announced: "I want every nigger in
Cairo rounded up, and if that means busting heads to bring them to
jail, I want them brought in." As DeBerry and a group of young Black
people stood with their arms raised overhead, Bowers continued his
rant. "I'm not going to take anything from any nigger," he said. "None
of my police officers' wives, mothers, or grandmothers get knocked in
the face or their pocketbook snatched. If they do, some nigger is going
to die for it, you know."[27]

DeBerry also talked about white vigilantes and how they partnered with police. In one instance, he watched an officer initiate a traffic stop of a Black man for a defective taillight, when a group of white
men—"local whites, some merchants from some of the boycotted areas

downtown"—appeared, surrounded the car, and drew their guns. The White Hats had been disbanded three years earlier, but vigilantes continued to listen to the police radio, operating as a shadow force and often with the tacit consent of law enforcement.[28]

Local officials in both cities refused to credit criticism of police departments or Black residents' grievances. Harrisburg's Mayor Straub and Police Chief Watts were present during the testimonies of abuse, and on the third day of the hearings, July 9, they came prepared to defend the department and its officers. Watts was "amazed by the amount of criticism my department took from witnesses appearing here," because he could not "have enough praise" for his officers "in the past trouble." As Watts explained, cops tended to utilize force when they felt they were under attack—when young Black people cursed at them, called them names, and threw objects at them in the course of their duty. "For some reason or other, policemen are supposed to go at it twenty-four hours a day, take all sorts of verbal abuse and turn a deaf ear," Watts said, and admitted that "we all make mistakes, believe me . . . We're human beings like everyone else." Straub echoed the chief of police. The city had a "great police force," and "everybody makes mistakes because we're all human," he said. Straub chided the witnesses for their "demeaning and derogatory remarks against our police, who are a last line of defense facing civil chaos."[29] Police work in a "racially troubled" community was always difficult, and the police department wasn't perfect, but the mayor and the chief were proud of the way police comported themselves during the rebellion. They did not address the fact that an officer had killed a Black teenager under questionable circumstances. They implied that "derogatory remarks" directed at police justified violent retaliation even as they deemed Black violence in response to abusive policing entirely illegitimate.

Members of the Cairo establishment likewise denied charges of discrimination and defended the actions of the police department.

Former White Hat Jimmy Dale, now Cairo's police commissioner, insisted that "the racial aspect of this has been far overblown" and that "antagonism between the black and white races" was far less prevalent than "in many other towns who haven't had the notoriety and the publicity we have in Cairo." The cause of the "racial difficulties in Cairo," he argued, was Black protest, led by the United Front, which involved relentless shooting at police and caused a great deal of property damage—actions he described as "in the nature of civil rights." A movement for civil rights could be nothing *but* violent, in Dale's view. Police Chief Bowers maintained that his officers "bent over backwards" to work against the public image of racist Cairo police, "for the simple reason as many of us know the pendulum has swung terrifically to the left and it's impossible for an officer to do the things that have been said has been done without losing his position."[30] The civil rights insurgency was the cause of the city's problems, and movements for social justice and anti-racist policies made it impossible for police to perform basic duties. "Mass paranoia" about racism had effectively paralyzed the police, as they saw it.

Harrisburg officials could dismiss the testimony of Black witnesses during the Pennsylvania Commission hearings, but they could not ignore the critiques of the police department that came from within its own ranks. On the fifth day of the hearings, July 15, 1969, two Black officers from the police–community relations team, Sergeant William H. Dickey and patrolman James R. Pitts, testified to the ineffectiveness of the initiative. The team was tasked with developing relationships with community members, investigating allegations of police misconduct, and handling the threat of mass disorder—its two officers were expected to quell any incipient rebellion by themselves. When the crowd formed at Goodyear Pharmacy, the community relations officers should have been immediately deployed. Yet no officials called them. Dickey and Pitts would have known that it was a bad idea for police to brandish shotguns if they hoped to disperse the protesters. Not only did the violent police response provoke community violence, but as Dickey reminded the commission, "Shotguns certainly can do more harm than bricks." The community relations officers were brought in only after the tear gas had been used, when the situation was already "out of hand," according to Dickey.[31]

Although Straub and Watts frequently cited the community relations unit as an example of the department's earnest effort to foster better relations with Black Harrisburg residents, Dickey and Pitts contradicted them. The community relations officers lamented their lack of influence within the department, where fellow cops often referred to them as "drones" and "do nothing fellows." The police evaluation board, which had been established to handle citizens' complaints, was rendered entirely ineffective. Dickey explained that it was "just about impossible to get a police officer to come in" for questioning, and therefore "impossible to navigate a complaint against a police officer." Both Dickey and Pitts made clear that the problem was not in the community, but in the police. "We have found that we can relate to the community," Dickey said. "If we are going to work effectively, the police department has got to clean up its own backyard."[32] Community relations meant little if the police department did not fully invest in the initiative and commit to changing the department's culture from the administration down to the rank and file.

While the city of Harrisburg made (largely empty) gestures toward improving police-community relations, the white ruling elite of Cairo vehemently resisted the very concept. Less than 10 percent of the seventy-five-thousand-dollar federal block grant awarded to the Cairo Police Department for such purposes in late 1969 had been spent by 1972. The Illinois Law Enforcement Commission rescinded the remaining money when it learned that the police department had apparently used the funds it did spend to purchase submachine guns.

Commissioner Dale and other law enforcement administrators dismissed police-community relations as a "total failure." An editorial in the white supremacist *Tri-State Informer* revealed the general attitude among cops and other authorities. "Community and police relations boards are nothing more than police control which in the end only handcuffs police and increases the strength of criminals." The editorial called for more support for elected officials and local police "who stand firm on law and order."[33]

In Harrisburg, after six days of hearings the Pennsylvania Commission concluded that the police department practiced "two standards of treatment of people and two standards of law enforcement: one standard for the white and another standard for the Black." It determined that police "resorted to illegal force in specific circumstances." It demonstrated that the department was "insensitive to civil rights and the individual and collective feelings of Black Citizens," and in this way was no different from "nearly every city police department in America"—a claim that "review of the Kerner Report substantiates." The Harrisburg police and their conduct were the product of entrenched hierarchies, "the reflection of the insensitivity and racial bias of the white society that employs, trains, controls, and directs them from which the majority of police are recruited," as the Commission wrote.[34] Individual officers behaved as they did because they had been trained and conditioned by a racist system.

Yet even as it admonished the police department, the state's Human Relations Commission was just as if not more critical of "alienated," "irresponsible youths" who "added to chaos, fear and racial hatreds in this tense situation." The commission recognized that police brutality plus desperate socioeconomic conditions equaled rebellion, but it also depicted the rebels as emotional and senseless, incapable of fostering "effective and rational communication" between the community and city authorities. The commission theorized that a "small militant core of Black youths" were seeking "an outlet for pent-up hostilities" that police were unable to contain or control. Soon after this hard core group tipped into violence, a "carnival atmosphere induced normally quiescent youths to join in the vandalism; assaults upon and harassment of police and firemen."[35]

The Pennsylvania Commission did not suggest that outside agitators were involved, but it came close in attributing the violence to a "militant core" who recruited other, more impressionable kids. This assumption had become a lodestar of liberal social policy: officials highlighted underlying conditions, and, in the case of the Kerner Commission, concluded that white racism was the source of Black Americans' suffering. But the commissions contradicted themselves, in that theories of "alienation" and a "militant core" of Black radicals in reality precluded an understanding of the conditions that precipitated violent collective action. The liberal commissions wanted to have it both ways. Members cast the forces of anti-Black racism and Black pathology as the twinned sources of the violence. In reviewing the aftermath of Charles Scott's fatal shooting, the Pennsylvania Human Relations Commission concluded that "the venting of hostilities and uncontrolled emotion overruled common sense and decency."[36] Although the Commission disapproved of the heavy-handed response—officers walking the streets with "riot control weapons, helmets, gas masks, and other such paraphernalia"—ultimately it was Black people's reaction to such things that made "police the focal point for group hatred."[37]

In the view of the state-level commission, the violence in the city was the product of "a radically different conception of the police role and function" on the part of Black and white residents, the policed and the protected. "When resistance is encountered and the officer then must use force," the Commission wrote in its report, "any degree of force is applauded by the majority white community as 'law enforcement' and condemned in the Black community as 'police brutality.'"

The violence could "be contained or set aside in only two ways; either by the application of overwhelming raw force or, by positive meaningful action to remove the inequities that have created it. Harrisburg has a choice."[38] The city could either prevent violence by improving conditions for Black people or continue to rely on the police to crack down when rebellions occurred in the future.

To a certain extent, Harrisburg and other cities that confronted rebellion were constrained by declining tax bases, state legislatures that were often hostile to urban areas, a national politics of law and order, and deregulatory economic policies from the federal level down to the local level. But as the commission itself pointed out, the cost of rigorously enforcing housing codes, creating incentives for the private sector to hire Black people, and providing quality low and middle-income housing—not to mention founding a local human relations commission to quickly respond to charges of discrimination and promote equal opportunity for all residents—"will be much less than continuing loss of tax dollars and direct costs to the City that will result from continuance of racial tension." As the commission understood, white flight and the failure to attract industry were themselves the product of "the human relations atmosphere in the city," or the reality of racial inequality that could only be solved by meaningful social welfare intervention.[39]

Yet in Harrisburg, Cairo, and across the country, officials at all levels ultimately pursued the punitive path. After the violence of the late 1960s and early 1970s, policymakers attempted to relieve police-community tensions by pacifying the over-policed and unruly community. The strategy of managing the problems caused by systemic racism with crime control measures left Harrisburg economically stagnant, segregated, and with a failing school system. Throughout the 1970s, Harrisburg lost 21.7 percent of its residents, as middle-class and white people accelerated their exodus to the suburbs. By the early

1980s, high rates of reported crime and unemployment made it one of the most distressed cities in the country. It was not until 1983 that local authorities established a separate Human Relations Commission in Harrisburg—over a decade after the state-level Commission argued that such a body would be the most "meaningful or effective" action the city could take to "reduce racial tensions."[40]

Echoing the Kerner report's famous warning that the United States was swiftly moving toward two societies, Black and white, "separate and unequal," the Pennsylvania Human Relations Commission had spoken of the "wide gap in understanding and inter-group communication that has created and will unless changed perpetuate two distinct and disparate racially circumscribed communities." The commission had hoped the proceedings had served a "useful purpose," as it had provided, if nothing else, "the means by which persons who ordinarily do not engage in person-to-person communication were able to exchange ideas and suggest or commit means to overcome the cause of grievances." Members followed the Kerner Commission in arguing that the full and equal partnership of Black Americans in all facets of society "cannot reach fruition with the present racist attitudes of the white majority." There existed an "increasing need for the development of understanding among peoples" in order to attain "racial harmony."[41] In short: separate and unequal conditions had produced two different worldviews, two different realities that somehow, despite rampant inequalities that bred violence, could be stitched back together through "inter-group communication."

Although airing grievances may have given Black communities a modicum of solace, the talk and discussion offered by post-rebellion commissions was only that. Venting did not change conditions; it created more unkept promises. Harrisburg and other cities could not talk their way out of inequality. Officials could have used their influence to remedy prevailing conditions while simultaneously acknowledging the power of racism historically and in the present. Yet the actual outcome was ambivalent—not intentionally malicious, but mealymouthed and noncommittal. In a sense, the responsibility lies with liberalism itself— in the premise that goodwill, educational opportunities, markets, and limited anti-discrimination laws will solve inequality "in due time." The consequences are still with us today.

"THE IMPACT OF civil rights legislation has still not reached Cairo nearly a decade later," the Illinois State Advisory Committee to the United States Commission on Civil Rights wrote in its 1975 follow-up report on the 1972 hearings, referring to the laws passed in the middle of the previous decade. If anything, the situation in Cairo had gotten worse. The state's Advisory Committee had come to Cairo for the first time in 1966, holding the first set of hearings to focus on racial inequality in the city and producing a study entitled, "I Reckon It's On Its Way But It Ain't Got Here Yet: A Report on Federal Civil Rights Programs in Southern Illinois." In both 1966 and in 1975, public housing was segregated, city and county employees were uniformly white, and the public-school system was on the verge of running out of funds. The economically stagnated county descended even further as young people in search of jobs, and older people with the means, left Cairo; between 1950 and 1970 the city's population dropped by 50 percent.[42]

As the Advisory Committee observed in 1966, the burden of decline fell disproportionately on Black residents: three-quarters of Black families and one-quarter of white families in Cairo lived in deep poverty, defined as an income below 50 percent of the federal poverty level. Racist practices were so entrenched in the Cairo Police Department that officers beat a Black sheriff's deputy for arresting a white man. Local, state, and federal agencies had "joined a vicious circle of racial discrimination and economic depression," the committee concluded.[43] Amid a complete breakdown of law and justice, Black Cairoites rebelled a year after the 1966 commission finished its work, the National Guard was called in, and white vigilantes mobilized.

Later authorities failed to act on the warnings from the earlier commission, pursuing instead a set of responses centered on draconian policing. As a result, the "vicious circle" identified by the committee in 1966 had persisted for a decade, as had the violence. State and federal authorities were aware of the rampant civil rights violations in Cairo but did not intervene with the force necessary to stop them. The primary "aid" officials provided had come from the federal level in the form of the United States Commission on Civil Rights. Authorities had arrived in March 1972 and held a public conversation about violence and racism. In the end, the commission made recommendations to improve conditions and help the city meet civil rights standards. By 1975, barely any of the 1972 commission's recommendations had been implemented. The Cairo city council refused to even pass a resolution stating, as the federal commission had urged, "its intention to ensure the independence of the Cairo Police Department," to at least formally distance itself from the white vigilantes. It would be a step toward making the department appear "responsive to the law enforcement needs of the entire community."[44] And yet there was no progress. Nonviolent protest hadn't worked. Neither had violence.

Although Cairo was no longer in a state of active war by the mid-1970s, residents weren't counting on public officials to improve their lives. Even before the federal Commission on Civil Rights hearings, Cairo's United Front increasingly focused its energies on economic development. Beginning in 1971, and operating through the Egyptian Housing Corporation, the United Front provided homes and jobs for low-income families—Black and white—as the city clearly would not. Even though the corporation tried to help all Cairoites, the white ruling elite resisted its efforts. The city council denied the corporation's bids on vacant land owned by the city in 1971 and 1972, essentially trapping Black residents in shacks or under the gunfire in the otherwise more desirable Pyramid Courts.[45]

Any changes in Cairo after its war would have to be made by Black residents and their allies. The Egyptian Corporation went around city authorities, acquiring land on which it built homes with seed money from the Illinois Housing Development Authority. Soon enough, Cairo residents could own homes for sixty-five to eighty-five dollars a month with no down payment. By 1980, the corporation had constructed about two hundred houses and created hundreds of jobs in the process. United Front members also secured jobs for Black residents through the Pyramid Courts Tenants Council, which received subcontracts from both the Department of Housing and Urban Development and Alexander County to build new roofs and make other improvements to the existing housing project.[46]

The Tenants Council worked with the Lawyers' Committee for Civil Rights Under Law, filing a class action lawsuit that finally led to the desegregation of public housing in Cairo. The Lawyers' Committee, a team of white liberal attorneys who arrived in Cairo in September 1969, proved to be a critical line of defense against racial oppression in the city. Over the following decade, the Lawyers' Committee successfully challenged unconstitutional ordinances—including one that prohibited "gatherings" of two or more people—in Federal District Court, contested disciplinary decisions handed down by Cairo school administrators, and provided assistance to residents who had been arrested or abused. By 1974, thirty Black families lived in the previously all-white Elmwood Place, and five white families had moved into Pyramid Courts.[47] The shootings from the nearby levee, the junkyard, and the police department's armored "Great Intimidator" vehicle had ended.

The Lawyers' Committee's final case in 1980 effectively secured Black representation on the city council for the first time in Cairo's history, offering a new degree of political power to Black people even as the city fell deeper into economic depression. The Committee's suit challenged the at-large city council elections that prevented Black residents, who at that point made up just under half the city's population, from electing their preferred candidates. Charles Koen was elected to the council in 1983, which with his arrival had three Black and four white representatives. Although they were no longer fighting with their fists in the streets, or exchanging gunfire, Koen consistently sparred in the council chambers with Mayor Allen Moss—a former White Hat and prominent member of the UCCA. Moss won the mayoralty in 1976 and held it for fifteen years. "It seems crazy to think that just because the mayor hates me he's going to let his whole town dry up," Koen told a reporter in 1985 of Moss's strategy. As Koen saw it, Moss "perceives his role as trying to keep what they have, and the way to do that is to do nothing."[48]

Koen understood perhaps better than anyone else that the sustained violence against Black people in Cairo in the past decade led to the slow death of the city consumed by its own racism. Everyone lost. Unemployment consistently topped 20 percent through the end of the 1980s, with Black residents still unemployed at a rate three times that of their white counterparts. One third of Cairo residents lived below the poverty line. An adult vocational school was still open and training welfare recipients for nonexistent jobs as oil-rig operators and furniture upholsters. The roller rink Koen and others had fought to desegregate with John Lewis and other SNCC activists in the early 1960s closed, as did the disco and the movie theater.[49]

The history of Cairo across this era is both exceptional in its violence while at the same time broadly representative of the violence of American racism, and the lengths white Americans would go to retain their power. The United Front's three-year boycott had led by the early 1970s to the closure of seventeen discriminatory, white-owned businesses downtown—about one third of the city's stores—and nothing replaced them. The city bid for one of two new state prisons in the late 1970s—a twenty-five-million-dollar prison construction project that would have created four hundred jobs—but Cairo was passed over due to its economic instability and declining population. By the mid-1980s, its hospital closed due to lack of funds. Cairo began to gain the reputation of a ghost town. "I don't think Cairo's ever coming back," said Gerri Gibson, the white owner of a business that was one of the few left standing in the downtown district. "There's so much hate here. There's always so much hate in Cairo."[50]

In 1968 the Kerner Commission had clearly described the racial dynamics in Cairo and other cities in post–civil rights America. Yet with little incentive from government authorities to follow the recommendations of its report, state-level human relations commissions, the United States Commission on Civil Rights, lawmakers, and other officials had since then avoided taking steps that might have led to meaningful change. Even with an entire city's health on the line, officials did not act. As the Kerner Commission had predicted, absent a massive redistribution of resources carried out at the national level, rebellion would remain a fact of American life, as would "white retaliation." The commission suggested that continued inaction by the federal government "could quite conceivably lead to a kind of urban *apartheid* with semi-martial law in many major cities, enforced residence of Negroes in segregated areas, and a drastic reduction in personal freedom for all Americans, particularly Negroes."[51] This exact scenario played out in Cairo, Harrisburg, and many other communities of color across the United States in the years after the civil rights movement.

"We started with some very great hopes," longtime Black activist Preston Ewing reflected in 1985 on the movement in Cairo. "Now there are a lot of awful ironies in this town." The decision by local authorities to respond to egalitarian demands by shoring up white supremacy—

decisions exacerbated by state and federal inaction—killed the city, in the end. "It is no longer blacks against whites in Cairo," said Mayor Moss, the former active white supremacist, in 1987. "It is Cairo against the world." Today Cairo has just over two thousand remaining residents, and two-thirds of them are Black.[52] Whites escaped in the decades after the war in the city, while Black residents on the whole still live with the violent legacies of American racism, and of the paths not chosen.

PART II: LEGACIES

8

THE SYSTEM

A group of young people walk away with a piece of furniture on Northwest 56th Street in Miami during the 1980 rebellion. (From *The Miami Herald* © 2021 McClatchy)

EIGHTEEN-YEAR-OLD Michael Kulp spent Saturday, May 17, 1980, at the beach with his older brother, twenty-two-year-old Jeffrey Kulp, and his brother's girlfriend, twenty-three-year-old Debra Gettman. The Kulp brothers had recently moved to Miami from Spring City, Pennsylvania, finding work in the shipping center at the department store Burdine's, while Gettman worked as a waitress at a fast-food restaurant. After leaving the beach, and with their lives before them, they drove through the heart of Liberty City, Miami's largest Black neighborhood. As the white trio approached Sixty-Second Street and Thirteenth Avenue near the Liberty Square Housing Project at around seven o'clock, people started pelting Kulp's Dodge Dart with rocks and bottles. Then a concrete block crashed through the windshield, and the car careened across the median, hitting seventy-five-year-old Albert Nelson and slamming eleven-year-old Shanreka Perry against an apartment unit in Liberty Square. Perry had been playing softball with friends. The car crushed the girl's pelvis, sending her to the hospital for six months; she would lose her left hip and leg.[1] Bystanders didn't know the extent of Perry's injuries at the time, but the sight of her blood on the wall and her crumpled body was enough. Some immediately began attacking the Kulp brothers.

Over a period of about fifteen minutes and with hundreds watching, Black residents punched and kicked the young white men. The assailants, ranging in age from twelve to forty, hit the Kulp brothers with bricks and a twenty-three-pound concrete slab, and dropped a newspaper dispenser on Jeffrey Kulp's head. Someone cut off his ear and part of his tongue. One man drove over their bodies with a green Cadillac, then proceeded to stab them with a screwdriver to the cheers of the crowd. The violence finally came to an end when a homeless man known in the community as "Ernest" placed a red rose in Jeffrey Kulp's blood-covered mouth. The elder Kulp brother died nearly a month later. Michael Kulp survived, as did Gettman, who had taken off running through the housing project as soon as the car had come to its abrupt stop. On the other side of Liberty Square, a Black taxi driver took the young woman out of the area.[2]

In the crucible years of the late 1960s and early 1970s, rebellions usually began after an encounter with a police officer or in direct response to police brutality or other violent acts committed by whites against Black people. Rebellions could take numerous courses. Some fizzled out after the rock- and bottle-throwing phase. Others expanded to looting, throwing firebombs, and sniping. Miami's 1980 rebellion, by contrast, started with random assaults by Black civilians on white civilians. An hour after the attack on the Kulps, and in the very same intersection, a group of Black people fatally beat a white man in his early twenties as well as two white high school freshmen.[3] Four other people, all of them white except for a light-skinned Guyanese immigrant mistaken as white, were murdered by bricks, cars, and fire in Liberty City that evening.

Black people attacked white civilians during the rebellions in the late 1960s and early 1970s, and in later rebellions, including Los Angeles in 1992 and Cincinnati in 2001. But none of this violence approached the level seen in Miami in 1980, when harming white people was a primary objective from the start of the uprising. After the rebellion, the Ford Foundation produced a report titled "Miami, 1980: A Different Kind of Riot," which called the indiscriminate attacks "unprecedented in this century." The nation had not witnessed this kind of anti-white violence since Nat Turner's rebellion in 1831; as the historian Manning Marable wrote shortly after the uprising, Miami's violence was a "twentieth century slave revolt."[4] In all, two hundred fifty white people across Dade County sought medical attention due to the attacks, suffering injuries ranging from cuts and bruises to severe head trauma. All told, eight white civilians were killed.[5]

To officials in Washington, DC, and the statehouse in Tallahassee, and to much of the American public, the violence in Miami appeared out of nowhere. The post–civil rights rebellions had largely dissipated by the time Richard Nixon resigned from the presidency in 1974. In those eruptions, Black residents collectively responded to the escalation of police patrols and surveillance in their communities with political violence. Yet by the mid-1970s, amid deindustrialization, disinvestment, and the increasing police presence in low-income urban communities, rebellions were far less frequent.

The beginning of mass incarceration helped bring the uprisings to an end. The systematic imprisonment of young Black men that started in this era effectively removed from cities a significant portion of the young people who had committed and sustained the violence. By the mid-1970s, 75 percent of Black people in American prisons were under the age of thirty.[6] Although Black Americans have been disproportionately incarcerated since the Civil War, until the 1970s they amounted to about a third of the nation's prison population. This changed in the mid-1970s, when Black and Latinx groups began to approach majorities in state and federal prisons. As people of color were getting systematically locked up, the total number of Americans incarcerated in state and federal prisons ballooned from just under two hundred thousand in 1970 to just over three hundred thousand by 1980—a 50 percent increase in a decade.[7]

The mass incarceration of Black Americans that started in the 1970s can be partly attributed to the socioeconomic conditions that lay at the root of the rebellions, and that became even worse as the decade wore on with the end of the War on Poverty and the simultaneous escalation of the War on Crime. In 1972, when Black Americans represented 12 percent of the nation's population, 42 percent of all Americans behind bars were Black, while 34 percent of Black Americans lived below the poverty line, compared to 10 percent of white Americans. Access to educational and employment opportunities declined further still, as the federal government, and then state and local authorities, withdrew from social welfare programs. More than any other factor, including even race, the absence of employment and educational opportunities—resulting from the new politics of austerity that hit Black communities particularly hard—determined the likelihood of future incarceration. By the mid-1970s, 64 percent of Black prisoners in state prisons did not possess a high school diploma.[8]

Even as Black Americans were sent to prison in greater numbers and for longer sentences, another, in some ways opposing, trend became evident: they were making significant gains in political representation. During the era of rebellion, there were few Black faces on city councils, in state legislatures, and in the federal government. But as the number of Black Americans of voting age increased from 10.3 million in 1964 to 13.5 million in 1972—and with the Voting Rights Act of 1965 and voter registration drives creating many more Black voters—the number of Black politicians soared.[9]

Whereas at the height of rebellion, Black Americans appeared to be locked out of political power and to have no advocates in government positions, by the mid-1970s this had changed, with levels of Black political leadership resembling those of the Reconstruction era a century prior. The formation of the Congressional Black Caucus in 1971 represented the shift. An emerging cohort of thousands of new Black politicians serving at all levels of government promised to reform the system, which many had critiqued as racist, from the inside. Some of them would attempt to bring about the changes that both nonviolent and violent protesters demanded through official channels. Black elected officials began campaigns to bring job training programs, welfare provisions, health care, and social services to their constituents. It seemed the Black freedom struggle had shifted from direct action to formal politics.[10]

Yet even as Black Americans were sent in greater numbers to cell blocks in prisons, to the halls of Congress, and to state capitol buildings, violent political rebellion did not stop entirely. Nor did state-sanctioned violence. The overbearing presence of police could still lead to rupture, and some residents continued the practice of throwing rocks and bricks at officers when they arrived to monitor and detain people. But Black Americans had more or less resigned themselves to the policing of everyday life. In the last decades of the twentieth century and into the twenty-first, major rebellions tended to break out only after exceptional incidents of police brutality or miscarried justice.

The precipitating incident in Miami was an example of the latter, although police violence played a decisive role in the buildup to rebellion. The Black residents of Liberty City, as well as Overtown, Coconut Grove, Brownsville, and other enclaves in Dade County, were reacting against an entire system—policing, the courts, the prisons—that offered them little hope of justice. In Miami that year, in Los Angeles in 1992, Cincinnati in 2001, Ferguson, Missouri, in 2014, and Minneapolis and other cities in 2020, rebellions started in response to extraordinary moments of official violence or disregard, not to everyday encounters with law enforcement. And in part for the same reason, all of these latter-day rebellions received widespread national coverage in the news media. While Cairo, Harrisburg, and other cities attracted the attention of the national press, the reporting tended to be surface level and, in sites of ongoing rebellions, sporadic. Of course, the advent of cable news and, later, of social media, allowed for the dissemination of information, and of imagery in particular, to a degree that was impossible decades earlier.

With sustained national attention came federal action. The government in DC did not directly participate in putting down rebellions after the spring of 1968, but beginning with Miami in 1980, the scale and the stakes of the events required commitment above the state level. Whether through federal "riot relief" grants (Miami), the deployment of federal troops (Los Angeles), or Justice Department investigations into police violence (Cincinnati), rebellions since 1980 have not been mere matters of local pacification and administration. The differences in these later rebellions were not limited to origins and responses. The results, too, suggested that a new era had arrived. By the 1980s, law enforcement authorities and police unions enjoyed even greater power and influence, further constraining reform efforts of the kind that had been proposed by the liberal-leaning commissions from Kerner on down. Where once transformational change had seemed merely unlikely, now it appeared to be impossible.

THE CUMULATIVE ORIGINS of the Miami rebellion simmered through the fifteen months prior to the attacks on the Kulp brothers and the others that followed. In that period, a number of high-profile cases of police violence managed to shock a Black community that had otherwise become inured to such acts. In early January 1979, a white Florida Highway Patrol officer named Willie T. Jones stopped an eleven-year-old Black girl, informed her that she "fit the description" of a candy thief, ordered her to get into the back seat of his car, and molested her. Jones failed a lie detector test but was released on his own recognizance and was not sentenced to prison. A month later, Dade County Metropolitan officers (Metro Police) terrorized, pistol-whipped, and punched a Black junior high school teacher and his son during a raid on the wrong house. The father and son were charged with resisting arrest, obstructing a police officer in the performance of his duties, and with battery on a police officer. While these charges were eventually dropped, no action was taken against the uniformed men involved. In November 1979, twenty-two-year-old Randy Heath was shot and killed by a white off-duty police officer as he urinated next to a warehouse. The officer who killed Heath, Larry Shockley, did not face serious repercussions even after a judge found probable cause that Shockley had committed manslaughter; he was briefly suspended for mishandling his weapon. Soon after the incident, Shockley received

a merit pay increase based on the "high degree of initiative" he exhibited.[11] Black Miamians believed their neighborhoods were under siege
by police, and they had no one to appeal to for help.

State's Attorney Janet Reno declined to prosecute the child-abusing
state trooper or the police officers who violently attacked or killed
Black residents. Reno did, however, vigorously pursue a criminal case
against Johnny L. Jones, the superintendent of Miami's public schools
and the highest-ranking Black official in the city. Jones, charged by
Reno's office in February 1980 with second-degree grand theft for
planning to steal nine thousand dollars' worth of luxury plumbing
fixtures from Bond Plumbing Company for his vacation home, was
immediately suspended from the school board. Many Black residents
believed Jones had been framed, that the case was part of a larger plot
to remove him from office. The trial aired in its entirety on Miami
public television; the scandal was consumed by thousands of people in
Miami of all races. On April 30, just over three weeks before the rebellion broke out, Jones was convicted by an all-white jury and sentenced
to three years in prison.[12]

Yet the most egregious development—the one that directly precipitated the rebellion—was the acquittal of four Metro police officers by
an all-white, all-male jury on charges stemming from the fatal beating of Black Liberty City resident Arthur McDuffie on December 17,
1979. McDuffie, a thirty-three-year-old divorced insurance executive,
father of two young daughters, and a former Marine, had borrowed his
cousin's black and orange 1973 Kawasaki 900 motorcycle and, after an
evening spent visiting friends, was heading home. According to the
police, at one fifteen in the morning McDuffie failed to stop at a red
light and allegedly waved his middle finger at an officer in a nearby,
parked cruiser. An eight-minute chase ensued, with twelve officers
pursuing McDuffie through the streets of Northwestern Miami before
he finally came to a halt. McDuffie allegedly fought back as a group of

officers swarmed him. For at least three minutes some of the officers viciously assaulted him with heavy eighteen-inch flashlights. McDuffie died several days afterward. As the coroner would later testify, they had shattered his skull, inflicting injuries equivalent to "falling from a four-story building and landing headfirst . . . on concrete."[13]

The officers had immediately tried to cover up their crime by staging the incident as though the victim, still alive at the time and lying on the street in a coma and with his head split open, had been injured in a motorcycle accident. They ran over McDuffie's borrowed Kawasaki with their cruisers, then used their blood-stained flashlights to bang up the bike some more. When other officers arrived to investigate the "accident" around five o'clock, they quickly realized that evidence had been tampered with or destroyed. As news reports drew attention to the inconsistences surrounding McDuffie's death, and as Black Miamians grew suspicious, for one of the officers involved, Charles Veverka, the pressure was too much. He turned himself in at police headquarters on December 26, nine days after the killing, and claimed to be overcome with guilt that McDuffie's children were without their father on Christmas.[14]

Believing that the officers could not receive a fair trial in Miami, defense attorneys had the proceedings moved to Tampa, where, in a case that strongly resembled the killing of McDuffie, a white police officer had been recently acquitted by an all-white jury for beating a young Black motorcyclist to death following a routine traffic stop. Local Miami news stations did not air the trial in its entirety, as they had for Johnny Jones's trial, but they did broadcast clips, including Veverka's graphic account of the beating. After four weeks of testimony that exposed the viciousness of the officers involved, as well as their obvious attempt to cover up a brutal killing, the all-white jury in Tampa delivered a verdict of not guilty after less than three hours of deliberation. Black Miamians held Janet Reno largely responsible for the outcome. "We were all waiting for the verdict in the McDuffie case," an older Black man explained, "because down here Janet Reno is a cold Hitler to the Black people."[15] During the Clinton administration, thirteen years later, Reno would become the first woman to serve as Attorney General of the United States.

Black people in Miami had protested peacefully in January 1980, after it became clear that police had killed McDuffie. Then they watched as the criminal case against the officers involved worked its way through the justice system. Black Miamians hoped that the preponderance of evidence would lead to convictions. They were more than outraged by the results. The verdict seemed to confirm that Reno, and the legal system she represented, were incapable of protecting Black people against police violence. Compared to the vigorous prosecution of Jones for mere theft, the double standard was glaring. "I watched the McDuffie case and the Jones case on the TV. You could see that Jones didn't get no justice," said nineteen-year-old Aaron Mack. "But they did let those polices [sic] go and they killed somebody. All Jones was accused of was trying to steal something. You know that ain't right." The apparent impunity of the police reinforced the sense among Black Miamians that they were all, each and every one of them, vulnerable if not in danger. "All the McDuffie thing did was to make it crystal clear to them that even a middle-class nigger who supposedly has made it can be jumped on, stomped on and done in by the white power structure," said longtime Miami activist Wellington Rolle.[16]

The verdict was announced in Tampa just before noon on Saturday, May 17—five months to the day after McDuffie's killing. When the news reached Miami in the mid-afternoon, people began to gather together for support and solidarity. At the James E. Scott homes, the massive housing project in Liberty City that had one of the highest crime rates in the state of Florida, a nineteen-year-old man in the crowd could be heard saying: "We watched the trial every night. All those pictures and descriptions explaining how they beat the man

Two residents walk hand in hand as Miami's Liberty City burns during
the 1980 rebellion. (From *The Miami Herald*, © 2021 McClatchy)

to death, and they found those guys guilty of nothing? Not nothing?
That's like saying the man didn't die." The McDuffie rebellion was
sparked not by police violence itself, but by the courts' authorization
of that violence. "Let it be an eye for an eye and a tooth for a tooth,"
another young Black man said. "When we try it their way, look what
they do to us."[17] The justice system had proven, time and time again, to
function primarily as a means to lock Black people away for increasingly long prison terms, and to sanction relentless police brutality. The
young people protesting at the James E. Scott homes were now prepared to take the law into their own hands.

"THE DECADE OF the 1970s," wrote Senator Daniel Patrick Moynihan,
who had become one of the nation's leading experts on Black poverty,

"was the first in which, as a group, black Americans with respect to white Americans were better off at the beginning than at the end." By 1980, fifteen years after the formal end of Jim Crow and the extension of citizenship rights to Black Americans, record numbers of Black college graduates flowed into elected office, and people like Arthur McDuffie entered the white-collar industries newly opened to them. Yet as a formidable Black middle-class emerged during the 1970s, Black unemployment and infant mortality rates remained twice as high as those of white Americans. Whereas Asian, Cuban, and Latin American groups had begun to successfully integrate into white communities, for Black residents in major US cities including Miami, segregation remained as much a fact of life in 1980 as it had been in the 1940s. Living conditions had improved somewhat—by 1980, only 6 percent of Black households lacked an indoor flushing toilet, whereas the figure was about half in the 1950s—but overall the housing available to low-income Black families was of poor quality. And although Black poverty rates had fallen in the 1960s, reaching a low of 30 percent by the early 1970s, the recession in the middle of the latter decade saw many Black Americans descend back into poverty. Even as a fortunate few Black families enjoyed upward mobility and political representation, the 1970s was a time of regression and decline for low-income Black communities across the United States.[18]

Miami illustrated these downward trends perhaps more starkly than any other city, in part because of the rapid demographic transformation it went through during those ten years. As migrants fleeing Communist Cuba found refuge in Miami—about twenty-three thousand arrived in the month preceding the 1980 rebellion alone—many got jobs Black Americans had historically filled in the city's tourism and service industry, as well as in clerical and factory work, and in household service. Unemployment among Black Miamians nearly tripled between 1968 and 1978, exceeding the national average for Black

Americans by 1980. In some Black neighborhoods, 85 percent of young people were believed to be out of work. Tracking with national trends, the number of semiskilled and white-collar Black workers in Miami doubled during the 1970s. But Black-owned businesses spiraled into a sharp decline. According to Ford Foundation researchers, Black residents owned 25 percent of all gas stations in Dade County in 1960. By 1979 that figure had dwindled to 9 percent, while Cuban and South and Central American-owned stations quadrupled from 12 to 48 percent.[19]

The federal government was partially responsible for these developments, in that it favored Cuban and Latin American entrepreneurs for contracts and Small Business Association (SBA) grants. Between 1968 and 1979, Latinx applicants received $47.3 million, or about 47 percent of the total SBA grants in Miami, while Black applicants were awarded a paltry $6.5 million. As Cuban and other Latin Americans built a flourishing economy in Little Havana, and opened up meat markets, laundromats, dry cleaners, and grocery store franchises in Liberty City and other segregated Black areas, the average annual gross of these businesses was $83,890—twice that of Black-owned businesses in the city.[20]

US immigration measures reinforced the new and rigid racial hierarchies in Miami. In contrast to the "open-arms, open-heart" stance the federal government and local authorities took toward Cubans fleeing Fidel Castro's regime, Black Haitian refugees were met with hostility and exclusionary policies. Between 1978 and 1980, about thirty thousand political refugees from Haiti arrived in the Miami area, fleeing the US-backed dictatorship of Jean Claude Duvalier. They were denied due process upon entry, systematically refused asylum, and many were deported. Black Miamians linked their own second-class status to the nation's policy toward Haitians. "It is unconscionable," Florida NAACP President Charles W. Cherry said of Jimmy Carter, "that a President who admits the black vote was a decisive factor in his electoral victory would choose to ignore the pleas of the black community who look

upon the [Haitians'] treatment in direct correlation with [his] insensitivity to the needs of black Americans." When violence broke out after
the McDuffie verdict, demonstrators folded critiques of immigration
policies into their rebellion against the criminal justice system.[21]

Even as Black Miami grew more isolated during the 1970s, law
enforcement authorities believed they had created a "good working
relationship with the black community," in the words of Miami Chief
of Police Kenneth Harms. In the 1960s and early 1970s, Black Miamians had lived under the regime of Walter Headley, who famously
declared at a press conference in 1967, "when the looting starts, the
shooting starts," and bragged about police violence: "We don't mind
being accused of police brutality, they haven't seen anything yet.
They'll learn they can't get bailed out of the morgue." Chief Headley's
"get tough" style led to an uprising in August 1968 during the Republican National Convention—nine hundred fifty National Guardsmen
were deployed, and the rebellion ended with the wounding of a Black
child and the deaths of two Black men at the hands of police officers.[22]

After 1968, the Miami Police implemented new community-
relations initiatives, as did many departments across the country. The Miami Police Department started discussion groups
with community members, sensitivity training sessions for officers, and crime watch programs whereby community volunteers
patrolled neighborhoods in an effort to discourage criminal activity. The department also created a new role for police in public
schools (its primary effect was to criminalize Black students) and, following a federal order, actively recruited Black officers to the force. Yet
regardless of how committed the police were to these programs, the
impact was limited. "What the riot showed was that, when it all hit the
fan, the openness of the department and all the effort at good police-
community relations made no difference," said Captain Larry Boemler
of the 1980 rebellion.[23] The challenges in Miami and other cities did

not begin and end with the police, and the measures to relieve tensions between the community and law enforcement were insufficient considering the broader challenges Black residents faced.

In any case, and despite the ostensibly friendlier approach taken by the Miami Police Department under Chief Harms, police violence was still a regular occurrence, as the McDuffie killing demonstrated. In 1979, the primary new measure taken by the Miami police was to withdraw. The officers, most of whom lived in the new suburbs in the south and southwestern part of Dade County, usually did not come into contact with Black people outside of police work and, even while on the job, now avoided contact whenever possible. As a result of the new "hands off" approach, arrests for traffic violations had declined by more than 50 percent in the year prior to the rebellion, and interrogations in the field decreased by 80 percent in the Liberty Square housing project between 1979 and 1980.[24]

When police did assert themselves in segregated Black communities, groups of residents—mainly young people who were occasionally joined by adults—would frequently taunt officers and hurl various objects their way. "It was not unusual for cars to be rocked-and-bottled on Friday and Saturday nights," Chief Harms said. "What usually happens," Metro Police Captain Douglas Hughes explained, is that people would start yelling "Get Whitey" or "Get the mother" and then a bottle would crash near the cops. "And no matter what you're doing—usually just trying to arrest someone and get him out of there—they start yelling, 'He's beating the man! He's beating the man!'" The community's reaction to the mere presence of police put officers in a difficult situation. "If you stand there and make a confrontation, you'll escalate it; it can easily get out of control," Harms concluded. "Time and time again when making arrests within a black area, the possibility of conflict is escalated."[25] So the police retreated.

In the James E. Scott homes, police stopped responding to all but the most serious incidents. The maze-like design of the housing project—made up of one- or two-story apartment homes separated by small alleys—frustrated attempts to patrol the area effectively. Residents would try to throw up barricades against police by pushing dumpsters into the alleys to trap officers or block them from entering. A single 911 call was suspect and often ignored, as it could be a ruse to attack an officer. During daylight hours, if several emergency calls came in, police would show up in teams of two to investigate. If the calls came at night, three separate cars would arrive at the Scott homes: one to look for traps, one to respond to the situation, and one to provide a quick escape if a crowd gathered and violence appeared likely. "God forbid, they should have a conflict with a Black citizen," Hughes said, his sarcasm perhaps indicating the common belief that Black residents were paranoid about racism and overly sensitive to policing. The decision to withdraw, to create further distance between officers on the beat and the citizens they were charged with keeping safe, only contributed to fear of the police among residents and made state-sanctioned violence more likely. As Hughes admitted to researchers: "It's always easier to shoot people you don't know."[26]

THE PRINCIPLE OF self-defense had guided earlier rebellions, and Black Miamians saw their own violence as a declaration of dignity in the face of unequal conditions and a deeply unjust legal system. "The riot was when we got back our self-respect," Miami Urban League President Willard Fair said, after the fact. "What do you think would happen in this community if black folk just sat back?" asked Clyde Pettaway, the assistant director of the James E. Scott Community Association, a federally funded anti-poverty agency. "We would have been living in human bondage again."[27] Fair's and Pettaway's views were shared by most Black residents.

The participants in the rebellion represented a surprisingly class- and age-diverse group, particularly in comparison to the large-scale uprisings of the mid to late 1960s and early 1970s. The *Miami Herald* partnered with the Behavioral Science Research Institute at Coral Gables to conduct a survey of 450 randomly selected people in Miami after the unrest, a sample size similar to the 437 Detroit residents the Kerner Commission interviewed after that rebellion in 1967. In Miami, more than twice the number of people aged sixteen and over claimed to have participated in the revolt when compared with Detroit, where the uprising was considered one of the most age-diverse of its era. Some of the middle-class Black professionals who had condemned the violence in Miami in 1968 joined the rebellion twelve years later. Defying the public stereotype of the "rioter" as a poor and unemployed member of the "criminal class," only 32 percent of people arrested in Miami during the rebellion had prior arrest records, compared to 74 percent in Watts in 1965 and 74.2 percent in Newark in 1967. Older Miamians may not have actively participated, but many reported setting up lawn chairs in front of the stucco buildings of the Scott homes in Liberty Square to watch the roiling violence unfold.[28]

Among the seemingly unexpected participants was a thirty-two-year-old Black lawyer employed by the state of Florida, who attended an evening rally that had been hastily organized for eight o'clock by Black leaders and the NAACP, shortly after the McDuffie verdict was announced. Three thousand residents gathered for the protest at the County's Criminal Justice Complex bearing placards that read, "America is a Damn Lie," and chanting, "Reno Must Go!" "We Shall Overcome," they sang. The lawyer became "consumed with rage," according to his own account, like many others at the protest. When reports hit the airwaves about the attacks on the Kulp brothers and other white residents in Liberty City and Coconut Grove, which had occurred about an hour before, several young men began taunting police inside

the Justice Complex, and soon shattered a portion of the glass entry-
way before leading a crowd to occupy the first floor of the building. The
Black lawyer, clad in a three-piece suit, felt compelled to join in and "do
something. I didn't want to let the moment pass." As he recalled, "All I
could think about was how the criminal justice system I respected put
its foot on my neck and face." Although the lawyer did not help overturn police cruisers and set them on fire, he did tear antennas from
their hoods.[29]

The destruction at and near the Justice Complex lasted until
around ten o'clock, when Miami police mustered a force of seventy officers who marched in, ten-across, equipped with helmets, face shields,
and three-foot riot sticks. As soon as they saw the officers in formation,
the rebels dispersed, moving north to Overtown and Liberty City.[30]
Across Dade County, residents in the working-class communities of
Perrine and Homestead, and in the middle-class enclaves of Opa-locka
and Carol City, joined the rebellion. Once the uprising spread outside of Miami proper, the violence changed. Businesses replaced white
civilians as the primary targets.

As the rebellion continued through Sunday, May 18, residents
looted stores for basic necessities including food and clothing, as well
as Harley Davidson motorcycles and television sets. That afternoon,
a forty-seven-year-old unemployed laundress and mother of seven
whom interviewers called "Willa J." was arrested with her husband,
"Henry," a construction worker. Henry had ventured outside and said
to Willa when he returned: "My God, it looks like the world is on fire."
Willa wanted to see the action for herself, so she convinced Henry to
drive through the flames in Liberty City. "Old people was just carrying
chairs, lamps, you name it. Everybody was just really helping themselves," as Willa described the scene.[31]

At a seafood market, people grabbed as many boxes of frozen
shrimp as they could possibly carry, but Willa's eyes were drawn to

a stove and a freezer sitting outside the store. "Henry, let me get this freezer," she pleaded. He hesitated at first, but eventually gave in to his wide-eyed wife. As he prepared to load the freezer in their truck, a policeman told them to "halt." The officer had instructed others with stolen goods to do the same, but according to Willa, "they just looked back and laughed at him and kept on going." Willa and Henry were arrested, as they put it, "with our mouths wide open. We hadn't even put the freezer on the truck." The officer took them to Dade County jail at four o'clock, where they remained until six the next morning before being released on their own recognizance.[32]

Although Willa herself had never had a bad encounter with the police, an officer had shot and killed her twenty-year-old son during a drug deal in 1971, while another son was beaten by police in her own backyard in a separate incident. "Black people have a *right* to hate," Willa concluded. "They really have a right. It's so many things these people do and get by with it. So many years they beat up poor people you'd think it would get better, but it's no better." Many other Black residents seemed to share Willa's position, "helping themselves" to goods that were systematically inaccessible to them—the act of looting their "right" in a racist society.[33]

Roughly twenty-four hours after the rebellion began, the commercial district of Liberty City had been decimated, with nearly every business on a three-mile stretch of Seventh Avenue cleaned out and torched (most would be bulldozed, not rebuilt). Some Black-owned businesses were hit, but for the most part the rebels left them alone. Only one of the 102 stores burned to the ground during the rebellion was owned by a Black person, and it happened to share the same building as Tony's Trading Post, a white-owned business that was targeted. Several warehouses that employed large numbers of Black workers were also spared. This had been the practice from the Watts uprising onward, when Black owners placed "Soul Brother" or "Black Owned" signs on their establishments. The appeal to solidarity did not always succeed. Samuel Watts's clothing store in Liberty City, which had operated for twelve years, was left barren. Rather than focus on the people who took underwear, shirts, and shoes from his shelves, however, Watts expressed outrage at the Miami police, who watched the whole thing happen. "They were just standing there," Watts said, "as if they were telling the people, 'Take your best shot. We're not going to do anything.'"[34]

This was not an isolated incident. At times during the rebellion the cops retreated and left residents to their own devices, a continuation of their general approach to policing Liberty City. The rebellions of the late 1960s and early 1970s had taught police officials that a heavy-handed response tended to exacerbate the violence, but in Miami, the scale of the uprising—18 deaths, 370 injuries, 787 arrests, and $100 million in property damage—meant that local law enforcement would not have been able to extinguish the rebellion even if they had wanted to. City and county police lacked the manpower and there weren't enough shotguns, face masks, riot sticks, and walkie-talkies for the hundreds of officers on duty. The arrival of one thousand National Guardsmen just after midnight on Sunday, May 18, helped keep residents in their homes, but law enforcement still struggled to maintain control. Officers did not understand their own weapons, for one. They hurled incendiary grenades—which release heat on discharge and can start fires—into stores in an effort to disperse looters, only to destroy the stores in the process. "Triple Chaser" tear bombs discharged their chemical load in three directions, and the Miami police often gassed themselves. Miami Assistant Chief of Police Michael Cosgrove and other law enforcement administrators would conclude that police training had been deficient: officers needed to be taught how to properly apply "nondeadly" force.[35]

Complaints about widespread police brutality quickly emerged. "One cop would hold your hand down on the ground, and another one would smash it with the butt of his gun," a young man said of his arrest. Other residents reported a festive aspect to policing during the rebellion (at least when the cops weren't gassing themselves). "We saw the National Guard lob grenades into stores just for kicks," a Black witness claimed. After police arrested a group of suspects who took food and other essentials at Zayre's Department Store, National Guardsmen and Miami police officers smashed the windows, wrecked the engines, and slashed the tires of a dozen cars they assumed belonged to the suspects. Every car was spray-painted: "Looter," "I am a Cheap No Good Looter," "Thief," and so on. A Black witness observed: "They were getting a kick out of it." Miami Mayor Maurice Ferré suspended four of the officers involved, calling them "bums," but after police protested the decision—their own signs read "I'm a bum too"—Ferré overturned his own decision.[36]

Very few police officers were attacked or suffered serious injuries. "The violence was not directed at us," said Lieutenant Billy Riggs, head of the Special Threat and Response Unit, the Miami Police Department's SWAT team. "They didn't really want to get us. If they did, and at one point we had fifty or sixty police officers against five thousand or six thousand rioters, why was no one hurt?" Even the sergeant who ran through sniper fire with a small team to retrieve the Kulp brothers, and other dead or injured white victims on Sixty-Second Street, made it out without a scratch. A man pointed a shotgun at him from close range, but intentionally shot the dome light of his police cruiser instead. "They harassed the hell out of us," Major Clarence Dickson, a Black officer who headed the Miami Police Department's community relations program, concluded, "but I don't think the main object of this riot was to retaliate against the police. If it was, they could have picked us off at random anytime they wanted to."[37]

The participants in the rebellion, as always, did not fare as well. Within a few hours of the Kulp brothers' assault on the seventeenth, police had shot and killed four Black men, including a forty-three-year-old father of five, two young men in their early twenties, and a seventeen-year-old high school student. The second day of the rebellion, Miami police shot and killed thirty-nine-year-old Haitian minister LaFontant Bien-Aimé as he was driving with his thirteen-year-old son.[38]

At the same time, white civilians decided to take the law into their own hands. White Miamians erected a burning cross in a Black neighborhood. Others torched a Black-owned grocery store in an integrated area. Still others simply wanted to kill Black people. On Sunday afternoon, as fourteen-year-old Andre Dawson went to find his sister, who had disobeyed their mother's warning to stay inside, a blue pickup truck raced down Eighty-Third Street in the Larchmont Gardens housing project. Three shots rang out, two of them hitting Dawson in the

Three white men stand guard at a trailer park on Northwest Twenty-Seventh Avenue in the middle of the Miami Rebellion. The night before, May 17, this self-appointed security force turned a suspected looter over to police. (From *The Miami Herald*, © 2021 McClatchy)

head and killing him instantly. The white vigilantes in the truck also murdered forty-four-year-old Eugene Brown as he waited for his wife and two children to purchase groceries at the U-To-Te'm Store. A thirty-five-year-old man was shot in the back when white men started firing at a Black crowd on 103rd Street and Thirteenth Avenue.[39] By Monday, May 19, with more than three thousand National Guardsmen and police from all twenty-seven incorporated towns and cities in Dade county stationed throughout the zone of violence, the rebellion came to an end. Ten Black people had been killed, in addition to the eight whites who had been murdered.

WITH THE CRISIS IN Miami making the headlines of major media outlets and on the nightly news, Jimmy Carter responded hesitantly. His campaign for a second presidential term against challenger Ronald Reagan was tightening, and Carter needed Black voters if he was to win the election in November. He wanted his administration to appear as though it was acting decisively in reaction to Black Miamians' grievances without alienating conservative white voters whom Carter was courting with pledges to cut domestic spending and by generally laying low on civil rights issues. The president dispatched Attorney General Benjamin Civiletti to Miami before the rebellion ended. To great fanfare, Civiletti announced on Monday, May 19, that the Department of Justice would launch a sweeping investigation into thirteen allegations of police brutality in Dade County, from the McDuffie killing to the four Black men who had been shot by police during the rebellion. "There is a great perception of injustice which has brought a sense of frustration and rage," Civiletti said at his press conference, presenting racism as a belief held by Black people rather than a practice and a structural fact—much like the commissions that investigated the rebellions of the late 1960s and early 1970s. "We hope no one feels so outraged and revengeful that they will not give the United States Government a chance to investigate the death of Arthur McDuffie." Of course, the Justice Department had not investigated the McDuffie case back in December 1979, when it first became clear that a cabal of at least five police officers had covered up the fact that they beat a Black man to death with their fists, their feet, and with heavy flashlights following a traffic violation. But to Black residents, it was better that federal oversight come late than never. The gesture gave hope to many that the federal government would secure a just outcome.[40]

In the first act of its crusade against police brutality in Miami, the Department of Justice punished the policeman who bravely exposed the cover-up. When the federal grand jury reviewed the McDuffie case, it indicted only one officer: Charles Veverka, who had admitted his role in the killing and testified against the defendants at trial. "I can't see any cop going forth and telling the truth after this," Veverka said regarding the federal charges against him. If the goal was to end police violence and encourage transparency and accountability, as Civiletti and the Carter administration claimed, the decision to prosecute the whistleblower was perhaps not the most effective strategy. After Veverka was acquitted, he offered to work with federal prosecutors if they chose to bring charges against the other officers involved. The Justice Department ultimately declined to pursue the case any further.[41]

Carter did not visit Miami until three weeks after the fires had been put out. The president arrived on June 9—the day of a previously scheduled speech at a conference in Miami Beach. During Carter's brief stay, which he believed would "show leadership and concern" for the people of the city, he met with a small group of prominent businessmen, with Mayor Ferré and other local authorities, as well as with a handful of carefully selected Black leaders at the James E. Scott Community Center in Liberty City. Black Miamians looked forward to the president's arrival, hoping he would announce a major relief package. Carter brought no such news. Instead, he scolded the city officials and Black leaders for not presenting a comprehensive recovery plan (although none of the local representatives were informed the president anticipated one) and told them they could not expect the federal government to bail the city out. After a ninety-minute discussion, Carter stepped back into his limousine. People threw rocks and bottles at the motorcade as it pulled away. Some mocked the president, who had grown up on and owned a peanut farm, by stomping on peanuts.[42]

The federal government did eventually send some relief. It offered small business loans, including a total of forty million dollars for the rebellion-torn area. But in the year after the uprising, just over half of that money had been distributed, 90 percent of which went to white, Cuban, and Latin American business owners, most of whom reopened their businesses outside Black neighborhoods. In addition to the small business loans, the Carter administration increased support for the Comprehensive Employment and Training Act in Miami, a program that trained unemployed, low-income young people. The federal government allocated $6 million dollars to this remnant of the War on Poverty, but the youths who participated never found work. When Ronald Reagan took office, his administration moved to terminate the training program and slashed the funding allocation for Miami's post-rebellion relief.[43]

Without a robust federal intervention in the service of justice or reconstruction, Black residents in Liberty City and Overtown grew ever more isolated. After the rebellion, with three thousand fewer jobs in the area and most stores burnt out, and with weeds sprouting up amid the rubble, residents were often forced to venture some thirty blocks to buy a pound of hamburger meat, pay bills, or cash welfare checks. Employers were even more hesitant to hire Black workers; overall, the city had difficulty attracting new businesses. Two years after the unrest, 70 percent of young Liberty City residents were reportedly out of work.[44]

In these austere conditions, further rebellions in Miami were inevitable, as was the continued killing of Black men by police. In December 1982, Officer Luis Alvarez took a trainee into a video arcade in Overtown, one of the few supposedly safe places for young people in the community to go in the evenings. Alvarez, who joined the force the summer of the previous year, had, among other complaints, already been the subject of five internal investigations for excessive use of force. The aggressive officer and the rookie approached eighteen-year-old Nevell Johnson Jr. as he was playing an arcade game, and Alvarez shot the young man in the head at point blank range. Having initially said the shooting was an accident, Alvarez later claimed Johnson was reaching for a weapon (Johnson was later discovered with a pistol in his pocket). As news of the killing traveled through Overtown, residents took to the streets, firing guns, smashing windows, and plundering stores. Although the rebellion was far less extensive than the eruption in 1980, several hundred people participated over two nights, during which a seventeen-year-old Black high school student, Alonso Singleton, was fatally shot eight times by police for allegedly looting.[45]

Johnson and Singleton were killed amid a period of intense police violence in Miami that was directed at Black men. In October 1982, fifty-eight-year-old Ernest Kirkland and thirty-year-old Anthony Nelson were killed in two separate incidents. The two officers who shot them were eventually acquitted by all-white juries. In March 1983, Metro officer Robert Koenig fatally shot twenty-one-year-old Donald Harp while the latter was sitting in the passenger seat of a car that had just been involved in a hit-and-run accident. When officers tried to remove Harp from the vehicle, Koenig claimed Harp made a sudden movement with his left hand. "I thought he was going to kill me," Koenig testified at his trial. But the autopsy proved otherwise: Harp was highly intoxicated at the time of his death, and the young man did not pose a threat to Koenig when he fired at close range. The evidence was strong enough to secure a rare outcome: an all-white jury found Koenig guilty of manslaughter. Less surprising was that an all-white jury found Alvarez not guilty in March 1984, sparking sporadic rock and bottle throwing, looting, and firebombing in Liberty City, Overtown, and Coconut Grove.[46]

As Ronald Reagan settled into office in 1981, public service announcements began to air on Miami radio stations that served large Black audiences. The messages encouraged listeners to refrain from making "sudden moves" (of the kind that cost Donald Harp his life) and to "please avoid arguments" during interactions with police officers. "When you see a flashing light, pull over to the side of the road the first chance you get and do nothing," the broadcast instructed. "Answer precisely and only what you are asked."[47] To some the announcements seemed to hold the fallen responsible for their own deaths, when the real problems were policing practices and systemic racism. The message was clear enough, at least to those for whom it was intended—the police wouldn't change, and the legal system would continue to sanction their lethal behavior. It was up to Black residents themselves to ensure their safety and livelihood through compliance. To do otherwise was to vastly increase the chances of becoming the latest police victim.

And yet compliance did not always offer an effective shield against law enforcement officers with a license to kill. On Martin Luther King Jr. Day in 1989, a Columbian-born officer, thirty-year-old William Lozano, fatally shot twenty-three-year-old Black motorcyclist Clement Lloyd with a 9-millimeter semiautomatic Glock while Lloyd was driving. Lloyd's passenger, twenty-four-year-old Allen Blanchard, died of head injuries from the resulting crash. Once again, hundreds of Overtown residents took to the streets, throwing rocks and burning build-ings as heavily armed police attempted to quell the unrest with tear gas and shotguns. The rebellion lasted for four days.[48]

Lozano's trial in the fall of 1989 generated substantial press cover-age, and local authorities anticipated a repeat of the McDuffie rebellion. Miami Chief of Police Perry Anderson lobbied to delay the announce-ment of the verdict in order to allow the department time to mobilize off-duty officers and armored vehicles. In "preparedness for the pos-sibility of a civil disturbance," the police department had purchased seven hundred gas masks and other riot essentials with seventy-two thousand dollars in emergency funds from the city.[49] Lozano was con-victed of manslaughter in 1990 and given the minimum sentence of seven years. An appeals court overturned the decision in 1991 on the grounds that the Miami jury found Lozano guilty because they feared an acquittal would ignite a riot. There was no major reaction to the decision made by the appeals court, and there has not been a rebel-lion in Miami on the scale of the 1989 uprising since. Nor has there been anything quite like the murder of Jeffrey Kulp and the brutal kill-ings of other white civilians during a moment of Black collective vio-lence. Similar to Arthur McDuffie, Jeffrey Kulp had been the target of lethal violence due to his skin color. One killing was sanctioned by the state, the other was committed by an oppressed community; both were products, in different ways, of a criminal justice system fundamentally opposed to fairness and justice for Black Americans.

9

THE PROPOSAL

Former rivals Spud the Blood (*left*) and Center Park Crips member
Gangster Todd embrace during a unity rally on May 5, 1992, the day
after the Los Angeles rebellion had ended. (AP / Bob Galbraith)

A PEACE MOVEMENT took hold in Los Angeles during the most
deadly and destructive rebellion in American history. As in
Miami over a decade earlier, the uprising was a reaction to systematic
injustice rather than a direct response to police violence. The acquittal
of four police officers for the March 1991 beating of twenty-five-year-

old Black motorcyclist Rodney King—a two-minute assault captured
on video and watched by millions of Americans on the nightly news—
set off a rebellion that lasted for five days, involved the deployment
of 10,072 National Guardsmen and 2,000 federal troops, and caused
an unprecedented $1 billion (just under $2 billion today) in property
damage. Over fifty people died, surpassing Detroit's grim record of
forty-three.[1] Yet in the Watts section of the city, where in 1965 stores
had burned, helicopters had hovered, and police and National Guardsmen had killed dozens of Black residents, in 1992 warring Crip and
Blood gangs understood the rebellion not as a moment of wanton
destruction, but as an opportunity to transform themselves and their
community. By moving to end the violence, the gangs hoped to win
political influence and to control scarce resources on their own terms.

The Bounty Hunter Bloods, Grape Street Crips, Hacienda Village
Pirus Bloods, and the PJ Watts Crips had intermittently discussed a
ceasefire in the years leading up to the rebellion. But it took a series of
discreet meetings supported by the Amer-I-Can program before any
of the Crips and Bloods involved were prepared to make meaningful
steps toward peace. Run by the former NFL star Jim Brown, Amer-I-
Can offered "urban life management skills" classes based on the principles of responsibility and self-determination. Most of the young men in
their twenties who would organize the truce in 1992 had participated
in the program and had often met in Brown's living room.[2]

The Crips and Bloods in Watts had been at war with each other and
with police in Southern California for three decades. In Los Angeles and
other major cities, collective violence in the 1960s and early 1970s was
directed against external state forces—most often the police, who represented the frontline of government authority in segregated urban communities. After the rebellions of that era were repressed by an increase
in uniformed presence on the streets and by mass incarceration, an
internal form of collective violence surfaced. With few opportunities for

formal employment, even within the lowest levels of the service sector, young Black men began to form groups commonly referred to as gangs to claim and guard territory, protect themselves, and keep neighborhoods safe from outsiders. Gang members defaced businesses, schools, parks, churches, and public walls with graffiti. By force or theft, they acquired sneakers, leather jackets, and cash, establishing protection rackets to extort money from local businesses. And they clashed with one another, throwing Molotov Cocktails, attacking rivals with fists and switchblades, and firing cheap, "Saturday Night Special" handguns.[3]

In the early 1970s, the Black Panthers and other radical organizations were no longer seen to pose a major threat, and law enforcement agencies at all levels started to concentrate on gangs, the new "public enemy number one." Beginning in 1972, the County Sheriff's Departments received federal funding to create a special "Street Gang Detail" squad to combat the groups. In 1973, the Los Angeles Police Department formed the "Total Resources Against Street Hoodlums" unit, otherwise known by its acronym, TRASH.[4]

As fears of "black youth gangs" grew, so did gang enforcement. And as gang enforcement expanded, so too did the gangs themselves, which needed increasing numbers of recruits in their push for self-protection amid the crackdowns, and in order to sustain their flourishing informal economy. Whereas in 1972, only eighteen known and active gangs existed in South Central, Compton, and Inglewood, by 1978 that number had more than doubled. And with the expansion of gangs has come the expansion of violence and killing. From 1980 to the present, Black men have constituted half of all America's homicide victims, the vast majority of whom were killed by other Black men. By the time Ronald Reagan officially launched the War on Drugs in 1984, gang members carried Uzis, MAC-10 submachine guns, and semiautomatic rifles to enforce contracts in the underground economy. The most tragic consequence of this arsenal was the prevalence of drive-by shootings, which frequently resulted in the deaths of innocent bystanders and hastened an increasingly aggressive police response. In 1992, the reported number of gang-related homicides in LA County peaked at 803, representing a 77 percent increase over the 1988 figure. Between 1987 and 1992, the state of California expanded its spending on policing and incarceration by 70 percent. By conservative estimates, a quarter of Black youth in South Central had been arrested at some point in the years leading up to the rebellion.[5]

By the spring of 1992, it seemed that nearly two decades of gang control measures had failed under the leadership of Mayor Tom Bradley, who had been elected in 1973 as one of the first Black mayors of a major US city, and who served in that position until 1993. As with the rebellions of the late 1960s and early 1970s, more enforcement seemed to only precipitate more violence in response. But the consequences for low-income Black communities were now more dire. These communities, in LA and other cities, were under attack, caught in a war among rival gangs and between gangs and the police.

Rising crime and mistrust within communities themselves—exacerbated by federal policies—are factors that generally made rebellion less frequent in the last decades of the twentieth century and into the 2010s. As President Ronald Reagan oversaw the "War on Drugs" in the 1980s, he simultaneously supported the removal of half a million families from welfare rolls, one million Americans from food stamps, and 2.6 million previously eligible children from school lunch programs. At the same time, violent crime increased alongside the zero-tolerance policing of the drug war and mandatory minimum sentencing provisions; together, these factors rendered mass incarceration a foregone conclusion. The higher probability of getting harmed or shot led parents in vulnerable areas to call their children home after school. The higher likelihood of getting robbed led grandparents to install additional dead bolts and chains on their doors. The prospect of retaliation led people to be careful about the clothing they wore and kept victims from talking openly with police (whom they probably didn't trust anyway).[6] People learned to comply with officers during routine encounters—to keep both hands on the steering wheel, to answer questions politely—in order to stay alive. They armed themselves in case they had to shoot their neighbor. Yet as the 1992 rebellion raged and the city burned, members of the Crips and the Bloods in Watts set out to bring the internal warfare to an end, and to face a common external enemy—systemic racism, embodied most immediately by the police—as a united front.

FORMAL TRUCE TALKS started three days before the rebellion broke out. On April 26, 1992, a dozen Grape Street Crips, led by two Amer-I-Can participants, twenty-five-year-old Daude Sherrills and his twenty-three-year-old brother Aqeela, drove the two miles south from the Jordan Downs housing project to Imperial Courts, where their PJ Crips rivals lived. The two groups made a peace pact and partied together afterward, marking the end of two decades of violence and fear. On April 28, the two Crip groups approached the Bounty Hunter Bloods of Nickerson Gardens and struck another truce, shaking hands with former enemies, restoring friendships torn apart by the gang wars, forgiving one another. "We started celebrating, 'The peace treaty is on! The peace treaty is on!'" remembered Aqeela Sherrills. "It was an unbelievable release."[7]

Los Angeles blew up the next day, Wednesday April 29, 1992. Roughly ten minutes after it was announced that the four officers who brutalized Rodney King had walked free, crowds gathered at the Pay-Less Liquor and Deli on Florence Avenue in South Central. The police started making arrests, prompting more people to join in to protest the police. Some went to LAPD Headquarters, smashing windows and

chanting "No Justice, No Peace." Others looted stores at the intersection of Florence and Normandie or attacked motorists. Most of the
victims of the random attacks were Latin American or Korean, but a
news helicopter captured the beating of white truck driver Reginald
Denny by a group of Black men, and this incident—presented as the
counterpart to the Rodney King video—became the iconic image of
the rebellion.[8]

When the sun went down, the mass looting and arson began.
Across Los Angeles County, from the San Fernando Valley to Long
Beach, stores were ransacked and burned, ultimately causing damage to more than one thousand buildings and leaving more than two
thousand people injured—both participants and bystanders. Although
non-Black-owned businesses were hit in South Los Angeles, much
of the violence targeted the immigrant communities of Koreatown
and Pico-Union. Tensions between Black and Korean residents had
increased since mid-March the year before, when, two weeks after Rodney King's assault, Black ninth-grader Latasha Harlins was fatally shot
by a Korean storeowner over a $1.79 bottle of orange juice. Harlins's
killer, Soon Ja Du, received probation, community service, and a five
hundred dollar fine after facing charges of voluntary manslaughter. In
April 1992, the Rodney King verdict was the national story, but Harlins
was on the participants' minds. "Rodney King? Shit, my homies be beat
like dogs by the police every day," a member of the Bloods explained.
"This riot is about all the homeboys murdered by the police, about the
little sister killed by the Koreans, about twenty-seven years of oppression," he said, invoking the 1965 Watts rebellion as an origin point.
Rodney King was "just the trigger."[9]

In stark contrast to most prior rebellions, the collective violence
in Los Angeles was multiracial and multiethnic. Just over half of those
arrested were of Central and South American descent; overall, this
demographic made up roughly 40 percent of the city's total popula-

tion, and many within it linked the Rodney King case to the police brutality they faced, too. In August 1991, five months after the King video circulated around the world, LAPD officers and sheriff's deputies gunned down two young Latino teenagers in separate incidents, sparking a wave of protests in East LA. "Fuck the police! They diss us just as much as the blacks," a Salvadoran teenager announced to reporters outside two looted stores in Koreatown during the 1992 rebellion. While many Latin American participants spoke of a shared struggle when they took to the streets, the media mostly depicted them as "illegal aliens" who exploited Black protest for their own personal gain, conjuring a racist stereotype that obscured the scale of police violence in Black and Brown communities and, by extension, their legitimate political grievances.[10]

On Friday, May 1, the third night of unrest, President George H. W. Bush addressed the nation, just as Lyndon Johnson had during the Detroit rebellion in 1967. Bush referred to the King beating as "revolting" and said that he and Barbara Bush were "stunned" by the verdict. Many white Americans shared the first couple's reaction to the sight of officers pummeling King some fifty times with weighted batons and shooting him with their Tasers. This was the first viral video of police brutality, exposing white Americans to state violence in Black Los Angeles and Black America. Bush was not prepared to offer a critique of police brutality or the justice system, but he admitted "it was hard to understand how the verdict could possibly square with the video."[11]

Professing to be disturbed by the King verdict, Bush also assured the American people he would use "whatever force is necessary to restore order." His administration sent two thousand riot-trained federal officers to Los Angeles and placed the three thousand National Guard troops already stationed there under federal command. Attorney General William Barr invoked the Insurrection Act to quickly organize the federal force, which consisted of FBI and Border Patrol agents, special SWAT teams, US Marshals, and prison riot squads, in addition to thousands of Marines and Army soldiers, all of whom were stationed in the city for ten days. In total, more than twenty thousand law enforcement officers and soldiers cooperated to arrest an incredible 16,291 people and put down the rebellion.[12]

The possibility that the "riot" in Los Angeles was a political act did not factor into Bush's analysis. "What we saw last night and the night before in Los Angeles, is not about civil rights," the president told the nation. "It's not about the great cause of equality that all Americans must uphold. It's not a message of protest. It's been the brutality of a mob, pure and simple." The Bush administration explicitly linked the "mob" to gang violence. "The President wanted to know what the violence was about," Barr later remembered. "I told him that there were a lot of street gangs involved and this was primarily centered on street gang activity . . . Crips-type gangs."[13] In the 1960s and 1970s, authorities had blamed communists, "outside agitators," and militants for the destruction. Now Barr and other authorities held gangs and undocumented immigrants responsible, viewing the violence as a problem endemic to those groups.

Federal, state, and local officials also saw the chaos as an opportunity to advance repressive campaigns against the "gangs" and "illegal aliens." "A number of aliens have come into this area and are involved in crime," Chief of Police Daryl Gates claimed in an interview. "They were participating in this riot in a very, very significant way." During the rebellion, police officers would stop possible gang members or undocumented migrants without cause other than to assess their status. Those found to be gang members were added to police and FBI databases, while those determined to be "illegal" were prosecuted by Immigration and Naturalization Services (INS) and the Border Patrol, which had dispatched four hundred agents to Los Angeles. Some INS

A man walks past a building engulfed by flames during the 1992 Los Angeles rebellion. (David Butow / Corbis via Getty Images)

officers went to the county jail to identify undocumented people and haul them away. The INS's campaign continued through June and led to the deportation of more than one thousand Mexican, Guatemalan, and Honduran migrants.[14] Arrest and deportation became yet another tactic government authorities used to manage the violence resulting from unequal socioeconomic conditions and racial oppression. And as in every prior rebellion, a harsh response led more people to rebel. It was, in a sense, the antithesis of the plan the Crips and the Bloods in Watts proposed for South Central.

WHEN THE REBELLION STARTED AT Florence and Normandie, graffiti in Watts already announced the truce agreed to the day before. The uprising had the effect of cementing it. Unity parties in Imperial Courts and Nickerson Gardens went on as the surrounding areas burned. On May 3, the day before the rebellion ended, the Pirus Bloods in the Hacienda Village housing project entered the accord, meaning that there would be peace throughout Watts going forward. Even during the rebellion, the truce made a difference. Compared to South and East LA, property damage in the area was light. Shootings continued among gangs in other neighborhoods, but police alone were responsible for the three deaths in Watts.[15]

There had been prior attempts to negotiate a cease-fire, but the 1992 truce succeeded because it was the first initiated by Crips and Bloods themselves. In 1972, the year "black youth gangs" started making headlines in the Los Angeles Times, the city's Commission on Human Relations sponsored a day-long seminar at the LA Convention Center for gang members from South Central and the segregated Black city of Compton. The boys and young men believed that "black people should have more control over their own community," and agreed to "come together in unity" to organize a broader truce if they were provided with jobs, better schools, and better recreational facilities.[16] These investments never materialized, and so the young people did not hold up their end of the bargain, either.

The official response to the "gang problem" was draconian. New anti-gang policing measures revolved around surveillance, violence, and incarceration. In 1973, the Los Angeles Police Department had established its TRASH unit to combat gang violence in Black and Brown neighborhoods. After complaints about the acronym, it was changed to "CRASH," for "Community Resources Against Street Hoodlums." More moderate in name only, CRASH adopted a strategy of "total suppression," which in practice meant the monitoring and arrest of residents who "fit the profile" of a gang member, and often the violation of their civil rights in the process. CRASH officers were known for picking up gang suspects and dropping them off in enemy territory in order to provoke violence and eliminate the people they were otherwise supposed to serve and protect.[17]

Under the leadership of Darryl Gates, who served as the LAPD chief of police from 1978 until he was forced out after the 1992 rebellion, the department prosecuted a vigorous war on drugs and gangs that was deeply racist in its premise and methods. In a May 1982 interview with the *Los Angeles Times*, Gates famously remarked on the use of choke holds by police: "We may be finding that in some blacks when it is applied, the veins or arteries do not open up as fast as they do in normal people." This and other racist beliefs were widely held throughout the LAPD; some officers informally referred to "Black on Black" homicide cases as "NHI," for "no human involved." Amid the police war on "abnormal" and "inhuman" people of color, between 1980 and 1990 the number of misconduct charges nearly doubled, as did the number of reported gang killings.[18]

Beginning in the spring of 1987, more than a thousand LAPD officers would sporadically swoop into South Central to carry out mass arrests as part of a recurring campaign called "Operation Hammer." The purpose of the program, as Gates explained, was to "make life miserable for gang members." Over the decade's remaining years, more than fifty thousand people, most of them Black, were interrogated and detained for parking fines, traffic citations, curfew violations, outstanding warrants, and "gang-related behaviors." Officers exhibited "gang-related behaviors" themselves. In one particularly violent raid on two apartment buildings—during which police ransacked homes, tore up family photos, smashed toilets, and poured bleach on residents' clothes—officers tagged the community with their own graffiti. "LAPD Rules," they wrote, threatening: "Rollin' 30s Die."[19]

Operation Hammer created or extended criminal records for significant numbers of Los Angeles residents. Only ten percent of the people arrested during the sweeps ended up facing criminal charges, but police classified the majority of those they arrested as gang members and entered them into the computerized database which eventually had over one hundred thousand names. At the time of the 1992 rebellion, 47 percent of Black men and teenagers in Los Angeles were classified by law enforcement authorities as gang members. Names appeared in the database multiple times, leading to a distortion of the gang problem.[20]

During the summer of 1988, in one of the largest sweeps conducted under the banner of Operation Hammer, fifteen different Blood and Crip sets from the Watts, Compton, Crenshaw, and South Los Angeles neighborhoods came together for a series of "peace summits." The gatherings had been organized by Reverend Charles Mims Jr., the fifty-year-old pastor of the Tabernacle of Faith Baptist Church in Watts. Initially, Mims brought rival factions to hotels in the neutral areas of Carson and Long Beach for several days of discussion. The participants would hash out past incidents of violence, each side viewing the other with suspicion and expressing ambivalence about whether a cease-fire could be effectively enforced. Yet by late October, fifty Bloods and Crips members appeared on the steps of Los Angeles City Hall, pledging to the gathered press that they would put down their weapons and act as "silent warriors" to prevent gang killings. Moving forward, they intended to serve as "positive role models for our younger brothers and sisters." The "silent warriors" linked disarmament to community development. "We plan to put our words into action by working in our neighborhoods and removing graffiti, cutting lawns and protecting senior citizens to put pride back into the areas where we live," explained truce activist Twilight Bey.[21] The "silent warriors" were too few in number to maintain a broader armistice, but the summit laid a foundation for the 1992 agreement.

Another foundation, this one unexpected and unplanned, came in the form of the Los Angeles rebellion itself. As residents and gang members understood, the mass violence and arson had the effect of fostering a sense of solidarity and unity among previously warring neighborhoods. "We are coming together because we are Black," said a twenty-three-year-old who identified himself simply as "Anthony." "We are tired of being divided." The truce meant members would no longer have to live under the constant fear of getting shot, or with the belief that it was necessary to shoot someone themselves. They would not have to face the prospect of being sent to a faraway prison for decades, if not forever.[22] The rebellion was a moment when internal violence was set aside in favor of fighting an external threat. Even when the violence stopped, the focus on the police and the larger system remained.

As the truce came into effect, organizers planned programs in the Watts community to promote it. Over the weekend of May 16 and 17, as Governor Pete Wilson withdrew the remaining three thousand National Guardsmen from Los Angeles, the Crips and Bloods sponsored a Saturday "unity picnic" and a Sunday family event, inviting the entire community "to come out for a peaceful day of food and recreation." More than five thousand people showed up, men and women from both sides of the war as well as people who were not involved in it except as bystanders. People played football and danced together. Congresswoman Maxine Waters made an appearance, applauding the peace agreement and vowing to create more jobs in South LA and Watts.[23]

Organizers went beyond parties, picnics, and speeches, in the knowledge that the problems went deeper than violence. The larger goal was to restore Watts, with the support of local organizations including the Coalition Against Police Abuse (CAPA) and Community Youth Gang Services. "We will clean up our community from graffiti and trash and prove to media, police and everyone else that we are not outcast just out to do wrong," a flyer promoting one of the new initiatives

proclaimed. Community Youth Gang Services helped launch training programs that were intended to equip gang members to compete
for jobs. CAPA established an "Off the Roaches" program—a riff on
the Black Panthers' "Off the Pigs" slogan—to train and employ young
people at up to two hundred dollars a day to kill cockroaches in the
community with nontoxic, environmentally safe chemicals, as well as
a speakers' bureau to connect the Crips and Bloods with organizations
across the country, so that the gang members could share their expe-
riences and drum up wider support for the truce. The gang-involved
young people who worked with CAPA increasingly recognized the
need to "come together rather than fight each other," in the words of
former Black Panther and CAPA Chairperson Michael Zinzun, and to
instead "fight police abuse."[24] Within two weeks of the rebellion, walls

Shortly after the acquittal of the four officers who beat Rodney King was
announced on April 29, 1992, residents in South Los Angeles took to the
streets in protest. (Kirk McCoy / *Los Angeles Times* via Getty Images)

that were once covered with gang tags were painted over and discussions about how to build political and economic power were underway.

THOSE WHO STRUCK the truce understood that its success depended on whether the drug and black-market opportunities that lured people into gangs could be replaced with jobs in the formal economy. "The gangbangers that are in the community, that are slinging drugs—put an economic plan together and then they'll quit selling drugs," said PJ Crip Tony Bogard, a key figure in the peace negotiations. "You have to substitute something."[25] Reconstruction would have been necessary, in the minds of those pushing for it, even if the city was not undergoing the largest rebellion in American history. Bogard and other organizers took the rebellion as an opportunity to push the city for a massive investment in health care, education, and employment, and they called for residents themselves to have a say in how it was apportioned.

Local authorities had other ideas in mind. On May 2, the day President Bush declared Los Angeles a disaster area, Mayor Bradley announced the formation of Rebuild LA, entrusting the fifty-four-year-old businessman Peter Ueberroth, a resident of Orange County, with directing the program. Ueberroth had chaired the 1984 Olympic Committee and was named *Time*'s Man of the Year for overseeing the first privately funded Olympics, which had taken place that year in LA. For many Black and Brown residents, the Olympic Games had not been a cause for celebration. On the contrary, they marked the beginning of a new level of police surveillance and violence. In a precursor to Operation Hammer, Ueberroth, Bradley, and other officials supported Chief Gates in expanding gang sweeps and patrolling targeted communities, a strategy that resembled a military occupation. Many of the military-grade weapons the city purchased (from the federal government and with federal funds) to control crime during the Olympics—

machine guns, infrared surveillance equipment, and a V-100 armored vehicle that had been used in Vietnam—became permanent features of policing in Los Angeles.[26]

In mid-May 1992, as Ueberroth vetted candidates for the Rebuild LA board, members of the Crips and the Bloods drafted a comprehensive proposal for a $3.728 billion investment into the community that would accompany the end of the internal warfare. The ten-page document became known for its memorable closing line, "Give us the hammer and the nails, we will rebuild the city." The majority of the funds, or about two billion dollars, would be spent on "LA's Face Lift": building new community centers and recreation facilities to replace burned and abandoned structures, erecting more street lights ("we want a well-lit neighborhood"), properly maintaining the landscape ("new trees will be planted to increase the beauty of our neighborhoods"), and improving trash removal and pest control. The proposal also called for universal health care and the construction of new hospitals, health care centers, and dental clinics; for an end to welfare through new jobs for able-bodied workers; and for free daycare for single parents.[27]

There was another request, too: $700 million for the complete transformation of the Los Angeles Unified School District. The funds would be used for the renovation of derelict public schools, including remodeling and repainting deteriorating buildings and upgrading bathrooms to make them "more modern." Students would have access to computers, supplies, and up-to-date textbooks—and enough copies so the books would no longer need to be shared. Some of the money earmarked for schools would go toward college preparatory courses for teens from South Central (who would now experience "a curriculum similar to non–economically deprived areas"), and mandatory after-school tutoring for students with poor grades. Another portion of the money would take the form of federally funded bonds for high-performing students to help them attend college. The gang members also asked for an end to the well-intentioned liberal practice of forced busing. People no longer wanted their kids to be shipped off to schools outside of their communities; they instead wanted significant investments in their own schools.[28]

The Crips and Bloods also no longer wished to be policed by a gang of outsiders. "The Los Angeles Communities are demanding that they are policed and patrolled by individuals who live in the community and the commanding officers be ten-year residents of the community in which they serve," their proposal explained, putting forward residency requirements as a straightforward step to improve police-community relations. To promote community oversight of policing, former gang members would have a role in "assisting the protection of the neighborhoods" through what the drafters conceived as a "buddy system": former gang members would accompany officers during every encounter, in what would have essentially represented the institutionalization of the Black Panthers' Community Alert Patrol from the 1960s and 1970s. The community members involved in the program would undergo police training and "comply with all of the laws instituted by our established authorities"; they would be issued uniforms but not guns. Instead, "[e]ach buddy patrol will be supplied with a video camera and will tape each event and the officers handling the police matter."[29] The idea was that if an officer was knowingly filmed, he or she would be less likely to engage in brutality or lawlessness—the premise behind the police body cameras that would become relatively common across the country in the twenty-first century.

The drafters of the proposal recognized that change needed to come from both the community and the authorities. In order to build a vibrant formal economy in place of the existing, underground economy in communities with high rates of unemployment and underemployment, the proposal urged federal and state authorities to make loans available to "minority entrepreneurs interested in doing business in these deprived areas"—in other words, to give illicit organizations an opportunity to establish legitimate businesses. Entrepreneurs who received these loans would be required to hire 90 percent of their workforces from within the community. "In return for these demands," the proposal promised, "the Blood/Crips Organization will request the drug lords of Los Angeles . . . to stop drug traffic and get them to use the money constructively." The drafters of the proposal gave authorities seventy-two hours to commit their support in writing, thirty days to begin implementation, and four years to construct three new hospitals and forty health care clinics, as well as to renovate the schools.[30]

Over the summer of 1992, the organizers of the truce also worked to formalize the verbal peace agreements in an official document. Anthony Perry, a thirty-year-old organizer and Amer-I-Can member, went to the Von KleinSmid Center for International and Public Affairs at the University of Southern California (after being turned away from the UCLA Library) to look through old United Nations treaties for inspiration. The document he found most useful was the 1949 armistice agreement between Egypt and Israel, which had been mediated by civil rights leader and South-Central native Ralph Bunche. Perry later explained that he "knew from the Bible and Koran that the Jews and Arabs were Semitic, they were related, both children of Abraham, it was tribal bloodletting." He translated the document into street terms on his yellow legal pad. "The establishment of a cease-fire between the armed gangs of all parties is accepted as a necessary step toward the renewal of peace in Watts, California," his draft treaty stated. It modified a crucial line in the Egypt-Israel treaty—"No element of land, sea or air military or paramilitary forces of either parties . . . shall commit any warlike or hostile act against the military or paramilitary forces of the other party"—as follows: "No element of the land drive-by shootings and random slayings of any organization shall commit any warlike or hostile act against the other parties, or against civilians under the influences of that gang." [31]

The final, complete treaty included a code of ethics authored by Daude Sherrills, one of the leaders who forged the truce. "I accept the duty to honor, uphold and defend the spirit of the red, blue and purple," Sherrills's preamble read, referring to the colors of the Watts gangs, "to teach the black family its legacy and protracted struggle for freedom and justice." Aligning the truce with the civil rights and Black Power movements, the code encouraged gang members to register to vote and to pool their investments to sponsor cultural events, establish a food bank, and provide hardship funds to families in need. It prohibited the use of the "N-word and B-word" as well as "hoo-riding," or throwing up gang signs. [32]

Well before it was formalized, the truce had a measurable impact in reducing violence that went beyond the five days of rebellion, when onetime rivals had had more reason to unite. For years, Black male gunshot victims had filled the emergency room at Martin Luther King Jr. Community Hospital near Nickerson Gardens and Imperial Courts on weekends—the US military trained surgeons at the site in order to prepare them for combat duty—but in the first weekend after the rebellion and the truce, doctors did not operate on a single Black male with gunshot wounds. "Usually there's an onslaught" of Black victims, said Kelvin Spears, an emergency room physician at the hospital. In May and June, only four people were killed, down from twenty-two during the same period in 1991. Drive-by shootings fell by nearly 50 percent from 1991 to 1992, and gang-related homicides by 62 percent. [33]

Almost overnight, Watts enjoyed a new kind of simple, straightforward freedom, with residents now trusting each other more. Children could play in their front yards without their parents worrying that they would be caught in the crossfire. "Now it's quiet, peaceful," said Watts resident Kecia Simmons. "You can take a walk, water your grass. You don't have to worry about anything." People no longer felt constrained in choosing which colors to wear or which neighborhoods to visit. As one resident put it, the truce gave those in Watts "a better chance to live like people." In August, the Ashley-Grigsby Mortuary, the only funeral home in Watts, had not buried any gang members—previously a staple of the business's revenue—since early May.[34]

Most in the community saw law enforcement as the biggest challenge to the endurance of the truce. "I don't have to worry about the gangs," said a former gang member named Duke at a press conference. "I have to worry about the police." The LAPD had maintained their existing tactics, despite the drop-off in violence. The police had even seen the parties celebrating the truce as an opportunity to arrest large groups of people, in some cases in the hopes of causing a violent reaction. In Nickerson Gardens, Monster, a twenty-seven-year-old member of the Bounty Hunters, claimed that police "come in here wearing blue rags on their heads like they're Crips. They know we're Bloods, man. Half this . . . is provoked by the cops." Helicopters continued to hover over Nickerson Gardens, Imperial Courts, and other areas of concentrated poverty, shining search lights at all hours to uncover potential criminals or anyone who "fit the description."[35]

Yet the Crips and Bloods who had signed on to the peace agreement remained committed to unity. "More police are patrolling because they cannot believe that Bloods and Crips are hangin' together," a twenty-six-year-old named Kenneth, who had been a gang member since his teenage years, assumed. "They say things to try to push us, but we know that they are trying to divide us and make us do something that will cause bloodshed. We ain't even sweatin' them though. Our whole thing is to get organized and to love one another."[36]

The truce movement—with young people working together to clean up the community and increase public safety while demanding jobs and justice from the authorities—was puzzling to law enforcement, who viewed the decline in violence in Watts and South LA with cynicism. "Time will tell whether or not we are dealing with a real situation where they definitely want to return to society," said Detective Bob Jackson, one of the LAPD's "gang experts." Sergeant Wes McBride admitted to a reporter that, "To be quite honest with you, we just don't know why black gangs are not killing each other." McBride and others concluded that the sole purpose of the truce was to unify against the police. "I'm concerned as to the true motives of the gang members as to why they would make peace," McBride said in a separate interview. "Is it so they can better fight with us, so they can better deal dope or so they can better be constructive in their neighborhoods? That would be the last item I would choose because gang members have a thug mentality. I'm very suspicious of any peace pact . . . I suspect it won't last long because of this intense hatred they have for each other."[37] McBride viewed the gang members as inherently violent, governed by a criminal mentality, and therefore irredeemable. From this position—one shared by officials from McBride and other officers to the US Attorney General—policing, surveillance, and incarceration represented the only acceptable strategy toward poor Black communities.

The LAPD claimed to have intelligence from informants that the truce movement promoted violence against the police. Even though officers allowed that just as many informants told them otherwise, they embraced the "war on police" narrative. Officials cited a gang-produced flyer as evidence. It allegedly read: "Open Season on LAPD. To All Crips and Bloods. Lets unite . . . and let it be a black thing for the little black girl and the homey Rodney King. An eye for an eye, a tooth for a tooth. If LAPD hurt a black we'll kill two. Pow. Pow. Pow." Crips and Bloods members said the flyer was fabricated by authorities, in the style of COINTELPRO practices during the 1960s and 1970s, when FBI agents spread fake propaganda to undercut popular support for the

Panthers and other Black Power organizations, and to justify the raids, surveillance, shootings, and other repressive measures unleashed on the movement. In LA in 1992, the police needed to keep the gang war alive. If there was peace in the community, and no need for the war on gangs that had shaped policing strategies in Los Angeles for nearly a decade, what would police do?[38]

In the face of testimony from residents about how the truce had improved their lives, LAPD officials insisted that Black people in South Central and Watts still lived in fear and they moved to increase police patrols. "It's not as if the truce means that the gang members have found God or suddenly seen the light," South Bureau Homicide Detective Jerry Johnson argued. "They are just as violent, but they have shifted their activities away from each other and toward the community," Johnson asserted, pointing out that drug deals, robberies, and other street crimes had not entirely vanished. The LAPD deployed a large "crime suppression task force" to aggressively patrol gang neighborhoods. Citing a party at Jordan Downs where residents started throwing rocks and bottles when police showed up, reportedly causing injuries to thirty officers, a police memo called for the transfer of forty officers from the Westside and the San Fernando Valley to maintain a "highly visible police presence in the area" in an effort to "stem this violence." As LAPD spokesman Bob Gill explained of the latest crime suppression strategy: "It's an attempt to properly police the city."[39]

Community members and police officials themselves questioned the utility of heavy-handed tactics amid the historic decline in violence. "Now is the time to start communicating and building a better relationship," said VG Guinses, director of the gang outreach program Save Every Youngster Youth Enterprise Society. "If you come in waving sticks saying, 'If you get out of hand, we gonna go upside your head,' all you're doing is creating a problem. Nobody's gonna win." A high-ranking police official who spoke to reporters off the record expressed similar reservations. "We're almost issuing a challenge to the gangs by trying to show them how tough the police are," the official said, recognizing that the officers would "go in there and want to knock heads together. I'm generally in favor of the cops. But . . . this is not the way to go."[40] Though presented with promising alternatives, including the programs the Crips and Bloods had proposed, authorities could not see a solution outside of more police. If crime was down, they would have to look harder to find it—or create it.

ALTHOUGH THE "Bloods/Crips Proposal" did not make an impression on the authorities, its drafters established business ventures of their own in the months after the rebellion. As the LAPD was reinforcing its crime suppression task force, leading organizers partnered with the sneaker company Eurostar, headquartered in South Los Angeles, to develop a line of shoes promoting the truce. The shoes, to be manufactured in Korea, would feature either the red, black, and green colors of the Black Liberation Flag or the red and blue of the Bloods and the Crips, respectively, with a label reading "TRUCE" on the heels. The various sneaker designs were given names such as "The Motivator," "The Educator," and "The Facilitator." The sneaker enterprise offered Crip and Blood factions hope that the truce would translate to real economic gains, and was initially heralded by city officials as a model job program for former gang members. Rebuild LA Director Peter Ueberroth praised the shoe line as an example of "doing it right"; President Bush even sent a letter to the founders applauding their efforts.[41]

Eurostar, which reported $57.4 million in sales in 1991, invested $600,000 in the sneaker line. The money was supposed to go toward paying rent and training employees, with the idea that the former gang members would eventually assume control themselves. The company hired Ray-Ray, a twenty-four-year-old ex-Crip from Watts, and his best friend, twenty-eight-year-old Gregory "High-T" Hightower, to oversee the venture. Within two weeks of starting operations, the two men were selling an average of sixty pairs of shoes per day at twenty-five dollars a pair from a tent on Figueroa and Eighty-Eighth Place in South Central. "We're not saying that these shoes are gonna make you feel like Michael Jordan or Magic Johnson," High-T said. "But you will feel good knowing that the funds are putting food on somebody's table from your own community." The number of jobs created would depend on how well the sneakers sold; and the goal was to bring in enough revenue to pay employees $15 an hour. With Eurostar's backing, as well as support from Maxine Waters and local businessmen, Ray-Ray and High-T opened a space on Florence Avenue they called the Playground, where, in addition to selling shoes, they offered after-school tutoring and organized basketball tournaments.[42]

Daude Sherrills and other key figures in the truce tried to create other opportunities for young men who had demonstrated their business acumen in the drug trade. Two months after the rebellion, Sherrills founded a nonprofit corporation called Hands Across Watts, one of the slogans he and other organizers had used in forging the truce. The organization sold T-Shirts and set up car washes to provide jobs for former gang members. "This is our first step," Sherrills explained. "We are going to get into the mainstream. This here is to open the door." The hope was that corporate donations would support job training programs, childcare services, and recreational activities in South Central. "We're going to use them like they use us," said Hands Across Watts Vice President and truce organizer Tony Bogard, of the efforts to court private funding. "The difference is we're going to put the money back into our community." The program seemed to be the next logical step, after the truce and the decline in violence. "We are empowering people who have never been empowered before," Sherrills said.[43]

Empowerment, at least in the commercial sphere, would have to wait. The market-based approach to recovery that won the praise of the president and the local business community came to little, in the end. Eurostar never delivered on its promise to put the sneaker line into mass production, and the business faltered by the summer of 1993. "It was in vogue to get involved," Alan Issacs, a Eurostar employee, explained of the company's fleeting support for the former gang members. But with "the cameras gone" and the free advertising gone with them, Eurostar's enthusiasm faded.[44] The company was representative in this respect; Hands Across Watts never received the substantial corporate backing it sought, though it did help maintain the peace before dissolving in 1995.

Rebuild LA met with a similar fate. Ueberroth and other officials showed little interest in partnering with Crips, Bloods, and other community representatives, despite making rhetorical gestures to grassroots empowerment. So, it was little surprise that Rebuild LA failed to deliver on the promise of jobs and relief for businesses damaged during the rebellion. It invested less than $400 million in the revitalization effort, falling far short of its lofty goals and the sums—in the $4–$6 billion range—that would have been required to set South Los Angeles on a meaningful road not just to recovery, but to transformation. Ueberroth resigned from Rebuild LA after only one year, following an internal evaluation that found the organization was little more than "a convenient excuse for inaction."[45] By 1997, it had disbanded.

Despite the broken promises of the business community and politicians, the truce between the Crips and Bloods in Watts not only held but spread. Violence continued to decline in the communities that embraced the new politics of unity. In the year after the rebellion, homicides throughout Los Angeles County dropped by 10 percent, the first decrease since 1984.[46] In Jordan Downs, Nickerson Gardens, and

Imperial Courts, gang-related deaths declined from twenty-five in 1987 to four in 1997, with the treaty still in effect by the latter date.

It would not last much longer. That year, one of the original organizers of the armistice said, "I think this community is more hopeless now that it was before," even if violence never returned to the disastrous earlier levels. "They have no hope that anything is gonna change. They see nothing has been done within that five years." A veteran gang probation officer named Jim Galipeau offered a similar assessment: "The only tragedy of the truce was that society needed to reward" the gang members who created it, yet "didn't do a damn thing."[47]

Given the continued lack of jobs, substandard housing, limited educational opportunities, and police harassment—all of the conditions that precipitated the rebellion in the first place—the old status quo seemed destined to reemerge. Crime, collective mistrust, and exhaustive policing ultimately prevailed. "We are seeing people going back to what they used to be doing, the familiar ways of surviving— selling drugs, robbing, gambling, stealing, hustling," truce organizer Dewayne Holmes said. "People do all sorts of things to live, to survive, to pay their rent and their bills." Geri Silva, a leader of Mothers Reclaiming Our Children, which was established in 1992 to protect young Black and Latino men against police abuse and discrimination in the criminal justice system, drew a conclusion that could have been made about the government response to the 1965 Watts rebellion, at the height of the War on Poverty. "It is this illusion of change where government or business or Rebuild LA come in and say, 'Look what we've done,'" Silva said. "And down the line, when things don't work, they will blame the people who live in the community."[48]

That the armistice in Watts held for a decade was remarkable. Its legacy can be most clearly seen today, however, in the gang intervention programs that became a permanent part of the LAPD. "I feel like law enforcement has successfully co-opted the movement because now gang intervention has to be validated in a sense by law enforcement," Daude Sherrills observed in May 1997. Sherrills was referring to the former gang members who were employed by the city starting in the late 1990s. These men would defuse violence by discouraging victims from seeking revenge, and by brokering peace agreements between rivals. The embrace of gang intervention programs and similar strategies in Los Angeles and other cities marked a step toward empowering residents to solve crime control problems themselves. Yet even this promising approach offered little tangible change in Sherills's Jordan Downs. "We want to tear all of this down and build it back up. But we want to do it ourselves," Sherrills said, continuing to voice the goals of the truce. "You see any improvements around here?" asked Nickerson Gardens resident Greg Brown. "Now the future in Watts and South Central is jail. You see that new Seventy-Seventh Street station?" Brown asked, referring to the thirty-million-dollar LAPD station that opened in 1997. "It's beautiful. You see anything else in the community that looks better than that jail?" The Bloods and Crips had asked for a mere six million dollars to transform policing in South Central. "Give us the hammer and the nails, and we will rebuild the city" their 1992 proposal had begged.[49]

Like the 1960s and 1970s rebellions, the massive, nationally televised rebellions from 1980 onward were carried out by people who wanted not only an end to police violence, but a chance to rebuild their communities and live their lives on their own terms. Yet policymakers consistently resisted socioeconomic solutions, focusing instead on increasing the scale of crime control resources and ultimately supporting the expansion of the prison system to contain troublesome groups. While many Americans understand the period from the 1960s to the 1990s and into the present as one of transformation and even of progress on many fronts—including the diversification of numerous workplaces, increased political representation for people of color, and general prosperity—the rebellions across these decades indicate that for many low-income communities of color, there was more continuity than anything else.

10

THE REFORMS

A young man turns away from a protesting crowd to voice his
anger at police during the 2001 Cincinnati rebellion. (Jimmy
Heath for the Greater Cincinnati Homeless Coalition)

THE VIEWING AT Timothy Thomas's funeral lasted for nearly two
hours. An uninterrupted stream of people flowed through New
Prospect Baptist Church in the heart of Cincinnati's Over-the-Rhine
neighborhood, walking past the open coffin to pay their respects. The
mourners prayed over Thomas's body; they reached out and softly

stroked his face; they embraced one another and sobbed together. Some young men wore white T-shirts bearing an image of Thomas and the letters "RIP," or shirts with slogans cursing the police. Thomas had been killed by a cop one week before. Now the nineteen-year-old was being laid to rest on a white satin pillow before nearly one thousand family, friends, and community members, as well as national civil rights activists who had flown to Cincinnati for the service.[1]

At around two o'clock in the morning of April 7, 2001, two off-duty officers moonlighting as security guards at a bar in Over-the-Rhine had spotted Thomas on his way to buy cigarettes and attempted to stop him. Thomas bolted, the off-duty officers couldn't keep up, and they called ten officers for backup. The young man led the dozen policemen on a seven-minute chase over fences and between abandoned buildings, through empty lots and back alleys. Officer Steven Roach, twenty-seven years old and a four-year veteran of the force, was the one who caught him; he found Thomas hiding behind a building. Thomas made a "sudden movement," Roach later claimed, and the officer assumed he was reaching for a gun in his waistband. Roach fired his own weapon. Thomas was unarmed.[2]

"They keep asking me, why did my son run?" Thomas's mother, Angela Leisure, told a reporter. For Leisure the answer was simple: "If you are an African [American] male, you will run."[3] Thomas's police record showed that he had run from officers on two other occasions in the months before his killing. He ran to avoid being captured and detained, to protect himself from possible violence. He ran because it seemed his best option to stay free and alive. To Roach and the eleven other officers who pursued Thomas, the young man ran because he was guilty of something, and therefore dangerous.

Leisure had moved with her family to Cincinnati from the South Side of Chicago four years earlier to prevent Thomas and her other children from getting involved in that city's gang warfare. "In Chicago, I never worried about police killing my children," as she put it. Cincinnati was supposed to offer Thomas a long, full life and better opportunities. "This was worse than my worst nightmare," Leisure said, after the killing. At the time of the shooting, Thomas split his time between his mother's home in Golf Manor and the home of Monique Wilcox, his fiancée. Wilcox lived with Tywon, the three-month-old son she shared with Thomas, in Over-the-Rhine, where 89 percent of residents lived at or below the poverty line. Jobs were difficult to come by, but things were beginning to turn around for Thomas, who had recently earned a high school general equivalency diploma. He hoped to become an electrician, though had so far only found work as a temporary laborer—work he was scheduled to start the Monday after he was killed.[4]

Like many other Black men in Over-the-Rhine, Thomas not only struggled to secure a decent job, but was the victim of constant police surveillance and harassment. The cops would spot Thomas driving his green 1978 Chevy and pull him over for no reason, issuing him citations for violations that could only be detected after the officer had initiated contact, such as driving without a license or failing to secure Tywon in his car seat properly. Thomas received twenty traffic citations during the spring of 2000 alone; different officers even pulled Thomas over twice in one day. Thomas ignored most of the tickets, and by the time of his killing had accumulated fourteen misdemeanor arrest warrants for failure to appear in court or pay fines. Thomas's record—which consisted of a conviction as a juvenile for receiving stolen property—would convince Judge Ralph Winkler to clear Officer Roach of all charges five months later. "Timothy Thomas was not unknown to the Cincinnati police," Winkler explained in his decision. "Police Officer Roach's history was unblemished prior to this incident. Timothy Thomas's history was not unblemished."[5] Thomas had no real history of criminal, let alone violent, behavior.

The "blemishes" on Thomas's record were the product of an aggressive, "zero tolerance" policing strategy that, in practice, created police records for Thomas and other Black residents and strengthened the case for their incarceration (or killing) down the line, while simultaneously imposing exorbitant fines and court costs that filled municipal coffers. Between March 1999 and December 2000, Black people in Cincinnati—who made up about 43 percent of the city's 331,000 residents—were issued 81 percent of all citations for driving without proof of insurance, 72 percent of citations for driving without a license, and 70 percent of tickets for driving without a seat belt. Seventy-nine percent of people accused of jaywalking in Cincinnati in that period were Black. Anti-Black practices extended into the city's public schools, where suspension and expulsion rates of Black students consistently ranked among the highest in the United States.[6]

As in so many other cities and municipalities across the country, from the 1960s to the present day, in Cincinnati the aggressive policing of low-income men of color was widely regarded as the most effective means of controlling crime. With little or no concern about the civil rights violations or the collateral damage of these practices, the police were free to treat Black men as both guilty and dangerous, an assumption that led directly to police violence, as it had with Thomas. Thomas was the fifteenth Black man to die at the hands of Cincinnati police since 1995. The majority of the killings were of suspects who posed an active threat: bank robbers, kidnappers, and people who started firing at the police. Five of the deaths, including Thomas's, involved unarmed suspects as young as twelve who did not appear to pose an immediate threat to the officers who killed them. For the loved ones of the dead and for increasing numbers of concerned Black residents, the overall death toll demonstrated that, at minimum, police had a fundamental disregard for the lives of Black men. No other Cincinnati residents were killed by police during this period.[7]

Beatings and killings of unarmed suspects all led to protests.

Demonstrations began after police punched and kicked Pharon Crosby, an eighteen-year-old high school honors student, when he refused to disperse as part of an "unruly" crowd of teenagers gathered at a downtown bus stop in April 1995. The incident was captured, like Rodney King's beating, in a two-minute video. In February 1997, Cincinnati police shot Lorenzo Collins, a twenty-five-year-old with a history of mental illness, multiple times. Anti-police brutality protests resumed in November 2000, after police attempted to arrest twenty-nine-year-old Roger Owensby Jr. on an outstanding warrant and suffocated him to death in the process. Timothy Thomas's killing the following spring seemed to underscore that the existing options (peacefully demonstrating and seeking justice through conventional legal channels) were completely inadequate against entrenched police violence and a system that was racist to the core. Three other Black men had been killed by police over the five months prior to Thomas.[8] When he was killed, the community erupted into the largest rebellion the country had seen since Los Angeles nearly a decade prior.

As the uprising drew national attention, the federal government would get involved, as it had in Miami in 1980 and in Los Angeles in 1992. Yet Cincinnati received a starkly different federal response. The rebellion came in the early years of a new era of civil rights enforcement that had begun in the mid-1990s and lasted through the presidency of Barack Obama, ending in January 2017. An increasingly diverse Department of Justice (including the first Black Attorney General, Eric Holder, from 2009 to 2015, and his successor, Loretta Lynch, the first Black woman to assume this role) started focusing on reforming violent police practices. Tracking cities where Black residents rebelled—including Ferguson in 2014 and Baltimore in 2015—or that suffered from alarming levels of brutality and were therefore likely on the brink of rebellion, as was the case in Cleveland in 2015, the Justice Department during the George W. Bush and Obama administrations sent attorneys and investigators to attempt to fix policing and improve police-community relations. The federal intervention in Cincinnati lasted for eight years. By 2015, the community's trust in police had increased and the kind of routine stops that ended in the death of Timothy Thomas had declined; misdemeanor arrests in Cincinnati decreased 57 percent between 2000 and 2014.[9] The Kerner Commission and other post-rebellion task forces in the late 1960s and early 1970s had merely offered recommendations, most of which were simply ignored by policymakers. Now, in Cincinnati, the federal government itself oversaw the implementation of new policing reforms. Yet like the earlier efforts, police killings of Black men persisted, nonetheless. In 2015, a Black man in Cincinnati could still get pulled over for a missing front license plate and end up dead, and the officer who pulled the trigger could walk free.

A police officer on horseback patrols rows of boarded-up buildings in Cincinnati's Over-the-Rhine neighborhood during the 2001 rebellion.
(Jimmy Heath for the Greater Cincinnati Homeless Coalition)

THE 2001 REBELLION in Cincinnati and its aftermath represented the last iteration of the twentieth century uprisings and at the same time anticipated a shift in Black protest that would emerge fully in Ferguson and other cities later in the new century. For residents who were old enough to remember, the violence in 2001 recalled the rebellions of the late 1960s. Cincinnati's rebellion in June 1967 began as a protest against an anti-loitering ordinance that the police selectively used to arrest Black residents: 70 percent of the 240 people arrested under the law between January 1966 and June 1967 were Black. As the crowd threw rocks and bottles, looted stores, and set fires, activists demanded an end to the ordinance, the release of all those arrested in connection to the uprising, full employment, and equal justice. Authorities responded by bringing in seven hundred National Guardsmen, who rolled through the city in armored vehicles, machine guns in hand. The next year, fifteen hundred National Guardsmen were called in to suppress violence following a memorial service in honor of Martin Luther King Jr. on April 8, 1968, when much of the country was on fire. The King rebellion in Cincinnati caused nearly three million dollars' worth of property damage and ended in the death of a thirty-year-old white civilian, who was dragged from his car and stabbed to death by a group of Black residents.[10]

The uprising in Cincinnati thirty-three years later shared many features with these earlier events. A protest against racial injustice spiraled into confrontation with a militarized police force, followed by a turn to window-breaking, looting, fire setting, and general property destruction. On Monday, April 9, two days after Thomas was killed, and with no answers from authorities, Angela Leisure led several hundred angry people to city hall, where a meeting of the city council's Law and Public Safety Committee was taking place. A group of protesters stormed the building and occupied the meeting, demanding an explanation for Thomas's death and keeping the council members inside the room for three hours. "I remember asking myself," Leisure recalled of the disruption, "how many times have people come down to these meetings and asked peacefully for changes to be made in the police department?" The city and police officials at the meeting refused to say anything to Thomas's family or the community about the circumstances of her son's killing, claiming the incident was "still under investigation." Withholding critical information only raised suspicions about a cover-up. Leisure later asked, "How many people will die before these changes will actually have to be made?"[11]

Stymied by the Public Safety Committee, the crowd, now eight-hundred strong and made up of Over-the-Rhine residents as well as Black Cincinnatians from elsewhere in the city, proceeded to march on police headquarters. When they arrived, someone threw a brick through the glass entrance to the building, while another person took down the American flag from the flagpole in front and rehung it upside down. The crowd, which had grown to one thousand people, hurled rocks and bottles at police, and the police fired tear gas bombs and bean bag rounds in response. As the violence on both sides escalated, chants of "Stop the Killing!" and "No justice, no peace!" filled the downtown streets of Cincinnati until midnight.[12]

The rebellion gained momentum the next day, Tuesday, April 10, when dozens of young Black men marched together through Over-the-Rhine, trailed by police. As the protest grew to several hundred participants, marchers threw rocks, bottles, and trash at the officers patrolling them. In the afternoon, some residents continued the march downtown, overturning newspaper racks and garbage cans along the way. The police—on horseback or in riot gear—continued to fire tear gas, bean bags, and rubber bullets into the crowd. By dusk, rebels were smashing the windows of businesses, taking merchandise, and setting fires, the most devastating of which burned the city-owned, open-air market in the heart of Over-the-Rhine called Findlay's.[13] The violence spread to other Black neighborhoods on Wednesday, expanding into random attacks on white residents, including a woman who was dragged from her car and beaten and a male truck driver who was severely assaulted. Someone also reportedly shot a police officer in Over-the-Rhine, but his bulletproof vest saved him from serious harm.

Mayor Charlie Luken declared a state of emergency and a citywide curfew on Thursday, April 12, the first time such measures had been imposed since 1968. "The violence on our streets is uncontrolled and it runs rampant. The time has come to deal with this seriously," Luken said at a news conference held on the fourth afternoon of the rebellion. "There's gunfire here like you might hear in Beirut. It's dangerous and it's getting more dangerous." Treating a Black neighborhood like a warzone, officers on horseback patrolled the streets leading out of the Over-the-Rhine community, while riot gear–clad police fired rubber bullets and bean bags at the assembled crowds. That evening, local police in helmets and bulletproof vests, state troopers and sheriff's deputies with shotguns, and a helicopter flying above showed that law enforcement was prepared for a major confrontation. But it never came. Outside of sporadic bottle and rock throwing, the occasional gunshot, and a fire at a deli, the violence had subsided significantly, as most people stayed home when the curfew went into effect.[14]

The residents in Over-the-Rhine and other Black neighborhoods who didn't stay home that Easter weekend ended up in jail. Police arrested eight hundred people for curfew violations during the rebellion, as well as sixty-three more who faced yearlong prison sentences on charges of aggravated rioting, breaking and entering, or weapons possession. (Officer Roach would receive a lesser punishment than all 863 of them. In March 2002, an internal probe determined that Roach "mishandled his revolver and gave conflicting statements to investigators." He could have been fired for these infractions, but Roach had already quit the Cincinnati police to work for a suburban police

department. By that point, the killing of Timothy Thomas had been
erased from his record.) Although the rebellion had almost completely
died out by the time Thomas was buried on Saturday, April 14, and
although Chief of Police Thomas Streicher Jr. withdrew officers from
the immediate vicinity of the funeral to allow mourners "room to
grieve," police in full riot gear could still be found protecting stores in
downtown Cincinnati from potential vandalism.[15]

Thomas's service, which was attended by NAACP President Kweisi
Mfume and Martin Luther King III, among other national civil rights
leaders, was necessarily political. The New Prospect Baptist Church
was led by the Reverend Damon Lynch III, who was also president of
the Cincinnati Black United Front and the city's most powerful voice
for racial and economic justice. Serving as Thomas's pallbearers were
members of the New Black Panther Party, a Black nationalist organization more similar to the Nation of Islam than the Panthers of the 1960s
and 1970s. Other New Panthers stood shoulder to shoulder in the pews
during the service, letting out intermittent cries of "Black Power!"
Although some speakers urged those in attendance not to "get angry
and trash your neighborhood" but instead to "get angry and register to
vote," the largest applause of the afternoon was for New Black Panther
Party Chairman Malik Zulu Shabazz. The events over the previous five
days were "not a riot," Shabazz suggested, but a "righteous, divinely
ordained rebellion." Shabazz received a standing ovation when he
invoked popular slogans of the civil rights and Black Power eras. "We
must continue to resist by any divine means necessary. We ain't going
to let nobody turn us around."[16]

During the funeral, hundreds of people outside the church prayed,
chanted, and hoisted placards demanding justice. "Let my people go,"
read the sandwich board Peter Frakes, a thirty-nine-year-old carpen-
ter, wore during the protest. "People have taken as much as they can
take," Frakes explained to a reporter. "We've had protests before. Noth-

Members of the New Black Panther Party carry Timothy Thomas's coffin out
of New Prospect Baptist Church in Over-the-Rhine, after his funeral on April
14, 2001. (Jimmy Heath for the Greater Cincinnati Homeless Coalition)

ing ever happens. As soon as everything quiets down, there will be
another dead body."[17] Still, Frakes kept protesting. He felt he had no
other choice.

A BOOMING STOCK MARKET, large tax cuts for the wealthy, and
record corporate profits made the 1990s a highly lucrative decade for
Cincinnati's almost entirely white upper-middle class. The Fortune
500 companies headquartered in the downtown business district—
Procter & Gamble, Chiquita Brands International, and Kroger, among
others—prospered, as did the city's rising technology companies.
Alongside growing affluence came cutbacks and repression, as Bill
Clinton's administration continued Ronald Reagan's attacks on welfare and social services, and supported the dramatic expansion of the
nation's prison system. Many lower income people of all races were

working longer hours, often in multiple jobs, and falling into increasing debt. Local boosters claimed that Cincinnati had rebounded from the devastating loss of automobile production jobs in the 1970s and 1980s to become a shining example of post-industrial growth. The city's own public relations campaign did not mention the fact that despite the all-white golf clubs in the northeastern suburbs of Cincinnati and the Saks Fifth Avenue near the riverfront downtown, two-thirds of the city's Black residents lived in poverty. According to the 2000 Census, Cincinnati was the sixth most segregated city in the country in terms of income.[18]

Class divisions deepened across the United States during the Clinton years, but in Cincinnati inequality was particularly dramatic: the economic chasm between the wealthiest 5 percent and the poorest 5 percent was exceeded only by Tampa Bay, Florida. In contrast to the $26,774 median income in Cincinnati and the $54,800 median income in the Greater Cincinnati Metropolitan Area, the median income among Over-the-Rhine residents in 2001 was a meager $8,600—at a time when the national poverty line was $17,029. The rows of abandoned buildings and groups of unemployed young men who gathered on street corners in Over-the-Rhine were less than a half mile from Saks.[19]

Municipal authorities may have been reluctant to invest in improving living conditions in Over-the-Rhine, but they did enthusiastically support the transformation of the downtown riverfront area along the Ohio River that the neighborhood bordered. The city allocated about one billion dollars for the construction of new football and baseball stadiums, a basketball arena, upscale establishments, and affordable, middle-class housing downtown.[20] The city's solution to Black poverty and abandonment in nearby Over-the-Rhine was to "revitalize" the area—to gentrify it—by offering tax incentives to tech start-ups, real estate developers, and corporations to set up shop in the neighborhood.

The city paired the push to redevelop the downtown area and "revitalize" Over-the-Rhine with more persistent crackdowns on homeless people and Black youth. The enforcement of misdemeanors such as loitering and breaking curfew, together with frequent drug sweeps that led to hundreds of arrests, helped remove "undesirables" from the streets. The private sector hired officers as security guards or even paid police overtime costs directly—the latter being the approach of Hart Realty, landlord to hundreds of residents in Over-the-Rhine.[21] These practices were not unique to Cincinnati then, or today. But given the rising toll of Black men killed by law enforcement and with no apparent consequences for police transgression, many Black residents saw violence as the only thing that would compel authorities to scale back the "zero tolerance" strategies and redirect resources to actually help the city's poor.

"The priorities in this city is all wrong," said Steven Wheeler, the father of Adam Wheeler, one of the fifteen boys and men killed by the Cincinnati Police Department in the six years leading up to Timothy Thomas's killing. "We can take millions of dollars and pour it into a new stadium to support a bunch of losers," Wheeler said, referring to the Bengals, Cincinnati's NFL team and a perennial laughingstock, "but we can't take some of that money and put it into schools where we can build some potential winners." The underfunded schools, the displacement of poor Black families from Over-the-Rhine to make way for "Silicon Alley," the extractive practices of the police department—these were manifestations of the "system of economic apartheid at work in Cincinnati," as the Reverend Lynch often said.[22]

Even before the 2001 rebellion, Mayor Luken acknowledged that the city was a tinderbox, and pledged to make "improving race relations" his "number one priority." It was an area where, Luken admitted, "we have a long way to go." In July 2000, during the annual Cincinnati Jazz Festival, an event known for attracting young Black concertgoers from across the Midwest, some restaurants and stores closed their

doors to attendees. Hotels increased their rates, demanded cash payment at check-in, and reportedly removed more expensive towels and
linens from rooms. Perhaps the most obvious expression of the racism that shaped social relations in the city was the Ku Klux Klan rally,
which started to be held annually as recently as 1996. In their white
robes and hoods, Klansmen would erect and burn a cross in Fountain
Square at the heart of downtown Cincinnati. Year after year, the police
stood guard near the flames in order to prevent anyone from trying to
douse or take down perhaps the starkest symbol of white supremacy
in America.[23]

Although the Reverend Lynch and many other social justice activists in Cincinnati did not actively participate in the 2001 rebellion,
they viewed it as an understandable response to decades of injustice.
Even the Black residents who threw rocks at police and randomly beat
white people seemed to be making a point, in the view of some. As the
Thomas family Attorney Ken Lawson bluntly said, the assaults "gave
whites a better understanding of what it feels like to be a random target
of violence just because of the color of your skin." "You don't condone
violence," Lawson emphasized. "But it took violence to get the attention
of the city. I hope they hear the cry."[24]

MAYOR LUKEN APPEARED as one of the speakers at Timothy Thomas's funeral, using the moment to advocate for reconciliation and
change. "I ask that today be a catalyst for a new Cincinnati," Luken said
to the packed church, which applauded that line, at least. But they had
heard similar promises before. "Don't just say something, do something!" some mourners shouted at the Mayor from the pews. The violence in the streets had already pushed Luken to take unprecedented
steps to address police brutality. It seemed the city's best option was
to call in the Justice Department, headed by Attorney General John

Ashcroft, a staunch religious conservative whose dubious views on race had been raised during his confirmation hearings in January that year. As Governor and Senator of Missouri, Ashcroft had opposed school desegregation, blocked the appointment of Black officials to public office, and praised Confederate heroes like Robert E. Lee and Jefferson Davis, calling them "Southern patriots."[25]

On the fourth day of the rebellion, April 12, Luken wrote a letter to Ashcroft asking for help. "The state of police-community relations in Cincinnati is not healthy," Luken explained. "We could use an independent review of practices, procedures and training as one tool to improve the situation." Ashcroft assured Luken that the matter was "a high priority" and pledged to send a team of lawyers from the Civil Rights Division to Cincinnati.[26]

A few weeks later, the Department of Justice opened a "pattern or practice" inquiry, a new power granted to the Attorney General by Congress under the terms of the Violent Crime Control and Law Enforcement Act of 1994. The largest and most draconian crime bill in American history, the Act's most notable features included a $10.8 billion program to support the hiring of one hundred thousand new police officers in cities nationwide and another $10 billion for prison construction. Prison populations kept skyrocketing as a result of the legislation: in 1970, fewer than two hundred thousand people were incarcerated in the United States; by 1990, this number had increased more than fivefold to reach 1.1 million; and by 2000, the figure had doubled to a record 2.3 million people.[27] The Clinton White House and Congress cemented the status of the United States as home to the most expansive prison regime in the world—as a country defined, in part, by mass incarceration. Yet at the same time, after Los Angeles in 1992, the federal government could not completely ignore the conversation about police violence.

The Act created a mechanism by which the Justice Department

could investigate "a pattern or practice of conduct by law enforcement officers" that appeared to violate Constitutional protections against discrimination, excessive force, unreasonable stops and searches, and arrests without warrants or sufficient cause. Within a decade, the Justice Department had opened twenty-five civil "pattern or practice" cases, and had forced police departments from Pittsburgh to Puerto Rico to address systemic misconduct for the first time.[28] In Cincinnati, Justice Department investigators spent the summer and fall of 2001 reviewing police records and conducting interviews with officials and community members. Finding that the Cincinnati Police Department practiced unconstitutional methods of enforcement, the investigators recommended better training, better oversight, and improved "use of force" policies.

These were among the reforms proposed by the Kerner Commission in 1968, which had looked at the 1967 uprising in Cincinnati, among others. Over the following decades, seventeen other commissions, task forces, and blue-ribbon panels had examined Cincinnati and arrived at similar if not identical conclusions. In a 1979 report on an eighteen-month period that saw four Black residents killed by police and four police officers killed by Black civilians, the Mayor's Community Relations Panel asked "whether or not the Police Division can police itself, and, more seriously, whether elected officials and appointed officials are willing to control police." It appeared that municipal and law enforcement authorities "neither really care nor are willing to do anything about reported incidents of misconduct." Proving the panel's observation correct, when law enforcement and its powerful allies mobilized to protest the spate of police killings, the city responded by purchasing .357 Magnum revolvers, a further stockpile of lethal ammunition, and bulletproof vests for the department.[29]

Two years later, with the warnings still unheeded and with police enjoying their new arsenal, the United States Commission on Civil

Rights concluded after an investigation that excessive force and harassment were pervasive within the Cincinnati Police Department, and it imposed a consent decree to address the systematic abuse.[30] The Cincinnati Police Department, like many other urban police forces across the country, would undergo sensitivity training, create "community-oriented" policing programs, revise its rules around the use of deadly force, and take strides to increase diversity within its ranks.

Yet the city did not institutionalize most of these reforms, and the various new programs eventually withered. After a 1987 federal consent decree, the police department did manage to double the number of Black officers on the force by 2001. On paper, Cincinnati's effort looked impressive: Black officers constituted 28 percent of the police force in that year, making it one of the most diverse departments in the United States. Yet the city's Black residents, who made up close to half of the overall population, remained underrepresented. Not only that, but Black officers were forced to establish their own union and were often overlooked for promotion. Black officers also found themselves the targets of racial profiling while driving off duty. Whatever challenges they faced, however, the community was not sympathetic. "The black police are just as bad as the white police officers," Black resident Henry James said. Black officers had been involved in some of the fifteen fatal shootings of Black men between 1995 and 2001. The issue was the police, no matter the race of individual officers, and the policing culture the department sustained—which Scott Johnson, a Black Cincinnati cop, characterized as an "us against them mentality."[31]

Even as police departments diversified in the late twentieth century in reaction to pressure to enforce Affirmative Action policies and improve police-community relations, the fundamental tensions between police and low-income residents of color remained. Although open racism by officers was less accepted than it once had been, ordinary citizens were still largely excluded from making decisions about their own public safety, and officers and departments were seldom held accountable for their discriminatory actions. Crime control efforts remained fixated on repressive strategies that led to excessive force, if not extreme violence. Law enforcement continued to treat low-income communities of color with suspicion. Absent a more open, transparent, community-based approach, most police officers—even those working for departments that subscribed to what passed for a "community policing" ethos—continued to view their primary job as "getting the bad guys," instead of thinking of themselves as public servants whose mission was to help people and keep vulnerable communities safe. In Cincinnati, this policing culture would face an unprecedented challenge after Timothy Thomas's killing.

Civil rights groups had called into question local policing strategies in the city through lawsuits and protests since the Kerner Commission visited in 1967, and their efforts had taken a promising new turn just before Thomas's death and the rebellion that followed. In March 2001, the Cincinnati Black United Front filed a joint, federal, class-action lawsuit with the ACLU charging that the police department had systematically targeted and illegally harassed Black residents for more than thirty years. The suit, brought on behalf of a Black businessman who alleged that two police officers violated his civil rights by pointing a gun at his head during a traffic stop in 1999, accused police of "stopping African American citizens without reasonable suspicion of criminal activity," and of frequently resorting to violence. The plaintiffs presented as evidence the seventeen previous investigations in Cincinnati and the 214 total recommendations those task forces and panels had produced, in order to demonstrate the "pattern and practice" of discriminatory enforcement on the basis of race by Cincinnati police. Echoing the conclusions of the Mayor's Community Relations Panel in 1979, the plaintiffs argued that officials had "tolerated, acquiesced in, ratified and been deliberately indifferent to practices by members of the CPD" by failing to supervise or discipline officers who violated residents' civil rights.[32]

In an attempt to prevent the lawsuit from exacerbating the conflict between the police and the Black community, Federal District Judge Susan J. Dlott moved to settle the case through an "alternative dispute resolution." Dlott brought together representatives from the city's Black United Front, the ACLU, the police department, and the local chapter of the Fraternal Order of Police to negotiate a solution to police violence against Black residents. The parties named in the lawsuit, known as the "Collaborative," met with Dlott and mediator Jay Rothman, the president of the ARIA Group, a conflict resolution, training, and consulting firm.

The law enforcement representatives and city attorneys in the Collaborative immediately shut down any discussion of confronting racism in policing. As far as the defendants were concerned, racial profiling did not exist and therefore did not need to be fixed. If racial discrimination was put front and center in negotiations, the police leadership threatened to withdraw from the process and take the case to court, where the department would simply deny all the accusations. In order to keep law enforcement at the table, Dlott and Rothman backed off from an explicit focus on systemic racism. The Collaborative would instead set out to improve "police-community relations." It was the only framework that would allow the parties to work together.

While the Collaborative's early discussions were adversarial, after the rebellion, and with the Justice Department in town, police leadership began to take the charges of police misconduct and abuse more seriously. The Black United Front and other civil rights leaders were cautiously optimistic. If the federal court enforced the reforms reached by the Collaborative, so that they would not become yet another dead letter, it had the potential to transform the police department. Even

in late March, weeks before Thomas's killing and the resulting explosion, an advisory group within the Collaborative had been established,
bringing together such potential enemies as Reverend Lynch and Keith
Fangman, the president of the Fraternal Order of Police.[33]

The Collaborative marked an important new beginning for police
reform in the United States. The proposals it made were based on community input rather than solely on crime statistics and policing theory.
The opposed interests within the Collaborative invited their respec-
tive constituencies to join the effort to reshape police-community relations. Roughly thirty-five hundred residents completed surveys online
and participated in interviews conducted by local organizations and
churches, allowing the people of Cincinnati a stake in the resulting
policies and their outcomes.[34]

Even with officials taking these steps, many residents kept protesting, in the belief that racist policing was a symptom of racist institutions and unequal conditions, and that the Collaborative could not
bring about the necessary transformation of the *city*. As the Collaborative began its work in April and May, residents and activists representing the Black United Front, the white-led Coalition for a Humane
Economy, and Stonewall and other LGBTQ groups developed a strategy to fight for social and economic change. On June 2, thousands
of mostly white protesters marched through downtown Cincinnati
shouting "No justice, no peace, no racist police" and calling for Chief
Streicher to resign.[35] It was one of the first interracial protests directly
linked to a Black rebellion.

After the March for Justice, as it was called, a number of religious
and political groups came together to form the Coalition for a Just Cincinnati and to promote an international boycott of the city, focusing on
a tourism industry that discriminated against Black people. On Saturday, July 14, the Coalition called for an immediate and total end of
travel and tourism in Cincinnati and demanded funding for neigh-

borhood development, amnesty for all people jailed for riot-related charges, and the end of racial profiling by city police. Organizers reached out to tourism and business groups, and to Black celebrities in a massive letter-writing campaign, critiquing the "level of racism, discrimination, tyranny, and general oppression in every area of life here," and charging that "police are killing, raping, planting false evidence." In just two years, the boycott cost the city more than an estimated ten million dollars, and led to the cancellation of conferences and conventions sponsored by Black organizations and of performances by Bill Cosby, Whoopi Goldberg, and Wynton Marsalis.[36] The boycott was intended to force authorities to invest in the people. Instead the city decided to invest in the police.

IN EARLY 2002, as the anniversary of the Timothy Thomas rebellion approached, the city and the Fraternal Order of Police found themselves under intense pressure to settle the case brought by the ACLU and the Cincinnati Black United Front. After the Collaborative's community outreach work had been completed by the end of 2001, both sides then threatened to withdraw from negotiations at various points during the winter of the new year. To prevent the effort from unraveling, Judge Dlott held sessions that went as late as three in the morning, ordering food to prevent anyone from using hunger as an excuse to leave. The attorneys representing both parties signed the Collaborative Agreement at 2:04 a.m. on April 3, and the city signed it about a week later, one year to the day after the rebellion started. Separately, the Department of Justice entered into a Memorandum of Agreement (MOA) with the city and the Cincinnati Police Department on April 12, 2002. The two contracts complemented one another, as intended: the Collaborative Agreement required law enforcement to remake police culture and strategies—to change the "us vs. them mentality"—

while the MOA required new standards and training modules to meet constitutional safeguards on the use of choke holds, chemical weapons, and canines.[37]

At the time, the Collaborative Agreement looked as though it established the most comprehensive and ambitious police–community relations initiative in the nation. It called for the entire city to "work together to address such problems as crime, disorder, and quality of life issues in Cincinnati" through a "Community Problem-Oriented Policing" approach. Instead of relying on arrests, the goal was to encourage officers to seek other options during encounters with residents. This required a shift in the worldview of the police, in that they would need to get to know residents and listen to their concerns. The Collaborative Agreement, in short, reimagined police as social service providers. A federal monitor, Saul Green, and a small team of Justice Department investigators would remain in Cincinnati for five years to try to make sure the Agreement was implemented and maintained.[38]

Yet even as the Cincinnati Police Department entered into both the Collaborative Agreement and the MOA, publicly deeming them "fair and progressive," Chief Streicher and other officials remained skeptical. Officers, on the whole, had always followed proper procedures, so the agreements would "not fundamentally change what our officers are already doing," as Assistant Police Chief Richard Janke asserted.[39] All of the recent incidents that ended in the deaths of Black men were determined by internal review boards or the courts to be justified, absolving the police department of wrongdoing. As officers continued to see it, they were simply doing their jobs, and sometimes that meant getting rough.

Fangman offered a list of reasons why the Justice Department's proposed reforms were not only ill-advised, but futile. Regarding controls on the use of guns during citizen interactions, Fangman indicated he would continue to unholster his weapon in "high crime" areas. "If people are offended at that, tough. This is the real world. My safety is more important than their feelings." On the use of mace, Fangman said the public "ought to consider themselves lucky that we have chemical irritant, because if we didn't, a lot more people would be going to the hospital before they go to jail." And as for the police dogs, which were known to attack Black residents, Fangman insisted: "This isn't Birmingham, Alabama, 1963. We don't unleash our dogs and say: 'Go get 'em.' But if a suspect refuses to follow verbal commands, of course the dog may be deployed." The dogs, the mace, and the unholstered guns were necessary for the officers' own self-defense when patrolling a dangerous community. "If anyone has a problem with that, they need to have their head examined."[40]

Given these attitudes, implementation of the stipulated reforms— reforms the police themselves had agreed to, however reluctantly—was a slow and challenging process. The police department treated the federal monitors with outright hostility. In December 2004, about halfway through the contract's term, Saul Green wrote in a progress report that "a CPD Deputy Chief spent much of the meeting with Monitor Team members deriding the competence of the Monitor Team, criticizing the Monitor Reports, and complaining about the [Collaborative Agreement's] reporting requirements." During Green's visit, Chief Streicher also blocked the federal officials from attending training sessions and scheduled ride-alongs, banishing one monitor from police department headquarters. At the end of 2004, the Monitor Team determined that the city had failed to comply with the Collaborative Agreement and the Memorandum, and extended oversight by two years.[41]

In part because the Justice Department was more interested in asserting its investigative power than in actually forcing the implementation of the required solutions, the new, "problem-solving" approach to policing did not take hold right away. For their part, rank-and-file officers basically rejected it. A 2005 evaluation conducted by the conservative-leaning RAND Corporation revealed that Cincinnati police were still aggressively stopping and searching residents in Over-the-Rhine and other Black neighborhoods. But perhaps even more importantly, an independent civilian review board—a necessary check on law enforcement that Black activists had demanded for years and that both agreements had pledged to create—did not materialize in any form that police would have had to reckon with, making it difficult to identify and punish officers with violent records.[42]

In summer 2006, the police department appeared to throw the Collaborative Agreement's problem-oriented approach out the window with "Operation Vortex," an intensive crime control program targeting drug dealers and criminals in Over-the-Rhine. The mission was linked to the city's ongoing drive to gentrify and attract private investment to the neighborhood. The elite cadre of "Vortex" officers flooded the community and used many of the same practices that helped push Black residents to rebel in 2001: frequent pedestrian pat-downs and vehicle stops, misdemeanor arrests for infractions such as loitering, and generally operating under the old "zero tolerance" mantra. By the fall, the department had made more than twenty-two hundred arrests, nearly half of which occurred in a single, twenty-five-day period. Arguing that Vortex officers were "improperly employing arbitrary arrest sweeps in the City" and violating the terms of the Collaborative Agreement, the ACLU filed another lawsuit.[43]

While it took several more years, the Cincinnati Police Department did adopt many of the programs required by the Collaborative Agreement and the MOA, in the end. (The department should not have had any choice in the matter.) By December 2008, at the close of the seven-year oversight period, Green issued his final report on the police department's progress, concluding that the city had made "significant changes in the way it polices Cincinnati" and was "now in a very different situation than in 2002." A 2009 RAND follow-up study further supported Green's claims, pointing out that although residents of color still came into contact with police at disproportionate rates, racial profiling was less common and Black residents expressed more trust in the local police force than before. Remarkably, after decades of little change, police violence declined, too. By 2014, twelve years after the MOA and the Collaborative Agreement were finalized, police use-of-force incidents had dropped by more than half since 2000. In the same period, the number of annual misdemeanor arrests fell from 41,708 in 2000 to 17,913 in 2014.[44]

The Cincinnati Police Department was reformed, but it had not reformed itself; the process had required constant support and oversight from the federal government and had almost collapsed at various points due to resistance from within. "This does not occur without federal intervention," the now-former Police Chief Streicher admitted in 2015. "You can very easily slide back into the same problems and issues you had in the past, unless your feet are held to the fire and the person you're answering to is a federal judge." Compared to cities such as New York and Chicago, where zero tolerance policing continued through the 2010s, Cincinnati emerged as one of the nation's most notable "progressive" alternatives as a result of the sustained and relatively vigorous federal intervention. Policymakers and law enforcement authorities across the country heralded the Collaborative Agreement in Cincinnati as a model of effective policing reform and of community-based policing measures. Especially in the wake of the killings, in 2014 and 2015, of Michael Brown in Ferguson and Freddie Gray in Baltimore, Cincinnati was held up as the poster child of police reform. President Barack Obama's "Task Force on Twenty-First Century Policing," as well as a separate task force convened by Ohio Governor John Kasich, reportedly incorporated some of Cincinnati's community-based strategies into their recommendations for reform.[45]

But for many Black people in Cincinnati, the reforms had brought welcome yet still limited change. Activist groups had envisioned a structural transformation. "People need help in the streets—they don't need help from the police," a man called Big Quartar told an *Atlantic* reporter in 2014. "They can't give you a job."[46] Police harassment and violence were only one aspect of political, economic, and spatial exclusion in Cincinnati and other cities. Even improved policing could not resolve decades, if not centuries, of inequality and racial oppression.

Instead of responding to the demands the Coalition for a Just Cincinnati put forward in its boycott of the downtown area, or the perspectives of residents such as Big Quartar, the city and its corporate elite memorialized the Black freedom movement and the long struggle against racial injustice by spending $110 million to build the National Underground Railroad Freedom Center. The museum, which opened in August 2004, celebrated Cincinnati as a haven for escaped slaves; it was a transparent attempt to address the city's poor reputation on matters of race. Shaped by corporate interests, the Center curiously presented figures including Carl Lindner—at one time the wealthiest man in Cincinnati, who had headed Chiquita Brands International when it was accused of mistreating workers and contaminating the environment—as a civil rights hero.[47]

For many residents, it was obvious the museum was a public relations effort. A cartoon ran in the *Cincinnati Enquirer* depicting a white man shouting, "Free at last!" in response to the Center's opening. Reverend Lynch and the Black United Front protested on the Center's opening day by organizing a "People's Underground Railroad Freedom Center" that brought historical documents and photos from anti-racist movements to Fountain Square in downtown Cincinnati. Reverend Lynch and other activists had been organizing for years to bring better jobs and housing to Black residents, not for a museum on the riverfront funded by corporations.[48] Many Black residents boycotted the Center for years.

IN THE LATE 1960s and early 1970s, the federal government responded to Black rebellions by providing urban police departments with military-grade weapons and patrol techniques so that they could more efficiently wage the War on Crime. In the early twenty-first century, the federal government responded to the rebellion in Cincinnati by attempting to counteract the anti-Black violence it had nurtured in the earlier era. Instead of preventing crime and rebellion with armored cars and bulletproof vests, now these problems would be prevented with "community-oriented" and trust-building strategies, as well as non-lethal technologies such as Tasers and bodycams.

Although such "soft" measures may have improved everyday interactions between officers and residents, they did not stop police violence, in Cincinnati or elsewhere. The August 2014 rebellion in Ferguson, Missouri, following the killing of eighteen-year-old Michael Brown by a police officer, had been a bitter rebuke to the argument that the nation was making progress under its first Black president. The people of Ferguson drew attention to the fact that poverty, unemployment, and police brutality had not gone anywhere. What started as a peaceful protest the day after Brown's death escalated when one hundred fifty police showed up in riot gear. Some residents, in turn, burned down businesses and looted stores. Over the next eight days, the nation was witness to the militarization of local police. Assisted by the National Guard, heavily armored police used tear gas, smoke bombs, and rubber bullets against the protesters.

Representing Cincinnati's Black United Front, activists Iris Roley and Reverend Lynch went to Ferguson three days into the rebellion there. "We're here to share Cincinnati's story of struggle and success," Lynch explained. "I'd hate to see Ferguson lose this opportunity for change." When Lynch and the other Black United Front members arrived in Missouri, they went to an Office Depot to print one hundred copies of the Collaborative Agreement, stuffing each copy of the historic document into a white envelope with the words "A Way For-ward" and their contact information scrawled on the outside. Lynch and Roley stayed for four days, as the violence persisted, handing the packets to activists, officials, civil rights advocates, and academ-ics while protesting in the streets at night and getting tear-gassed for the first time since the Cincinnati rebellion in 2001. Ultimately the Black United Front's efforts inspired the formation of the Ferguson Collaborative in the aftermath of the protests. The Ferguson Collab-orative went on to work with the Justice Department during the con-sent decree negotiations that followed the uprising, and it organized to empower the community and defend residents who were arrested or fined for arbitrary reasons.[49]

LESS THAN ONE YEAR after Ferguson erupted, on Tuesday, July 28, 2015, more than five hundred people attended the memorial service for Samuel DuBose at the Church of the Living God in Cincinnati's Avon-dale neighborhood. They walked by DuBose's open casket, decorated with red mums, his head resting on a white satin pillow. DuBose, aged forty-three, had been stopped nine days earlier by a University of Cin-cinnati police officer—off campus—for driving without a front license plate. The officer, twenty-five-year-old Ray Tensing, asked DuBose for his driver's license. Tensing's body camera footage shows DuBose disobeying the officer, putting his car in drive instead of unbuckling his seatbelt as requested. Tensing, who was wearing a T-shirt depict-ing the Confederate flag under his uniform at the time, shot DuBose in the head at close range. The details of the killing were for another day, however. The funeral service was an opportunity to celebrate DuBose's life. "Today is about solidarity," preached the Reverend Ennis Tait during the service, echoing the words of Reverend Lynch some fourteen years before him. "Fill this house with love."[50] Justice, it was hoped, would follow.

Because DuBose's final moments were captured on video and widely distributed across social media, his killing—like that of forty-three-year-old Eric Garner in July 2014 in New York City, of twelve-year-old Tamir Rice in Cleveland in November the same year, and of fifty-year-old Walter Scott in North Charleston, South Carolina, April the next—stoked debate about policing and the emerging national protest movement, Black Lives Matter. Demonstrations were held across the country in response to DuBose's death, with participants chanting "I am Sam DuBose." During the funeral, and as they had done for Timothy Thomas, a group of protesters gathered outside of the church. "This is democracy. This is what democracy looks like," said December Lamb, a member of the Black Lives Matter movement. "I ain't anti-cops at all. We need good cops. We don't need bad cops." In contrast to the response to Timothy Thomas's killing, the protest in 2015 Cincinnati did not turn violent—in part, officials claimed, because the Collaborative Agreement helped to hold the peace.[51]

Like Angela Leisure and the Thomas family, DuBose's mother, Audrey DuBose, wanted more than anything to see police violence punished. "There is no justice if someone can get away with murder and walk away," she said. Although Tensing was eventually charged with murder and voluntary manslaughter, after two mistrials due to deadlocked juries, County Prosecutor Joe Deters—who called the incident "the most asinine act I've ever seen a police officer make"— dropped the case.[52] Tensing, like Steven Roach, walked free.

Between Michael Brown's shooting in 2014 and Tensing's second mistrial, only six of nineteen cases charging police officers with murder or manslaughter led to convictions nationally. Tensing actually received a $350,000 settlement from the University of Cincinnati for wrongful termination. DuBose's family, who reached their own $4.85 million civil settlement with the University of Cincinnati, saw Tensing's "reward" as the ultimate injustice. "I'm very upset with UC paying that murderer Tensing," DuBose's fiancée, DaShonda Reid, texted to a *Cincinnati Enquirer* reporter. "He's officially a paid assassin who has not shown one ounce of remorse for killing an innocent man."[53] As Reid recognized, and as the thousands of Black people knew when they took to the streets in Cairo, Illinois, in 1969 or Kenosha, Wisconsin, in 2020, justice is not often forthcoming for Black Americans—and reforming the police, though a rare and difficult accomplishment, is never enough. Until this nation imagines a different approach to public safety, beyond police reforms, it is not a question of if another person of color will die at the hands of sworn, even well-trained officers, or if another city will catch fire, but when.

CONCLUSION

A protest for racial justice in Cairo, Illinois, during the summer
of 2020. (Byron Hetzler / © 2020 *The Southern Illinoisian*)

L IKE THEIR FOREBEARERS in the late 1960s and early 1970s,
Black residents in Cairo, Illinois, marched through the streets
calling for an end to racism and discrimination in the summer of
2020. Charles Koen, a significant figure in the earlier movement, died
in 2018. Now, standing "on the shoulders of one who fought the good
fight here in Cairo," his daughter, Robbie Koen, delivered the event's
main address in her father's honor at the Heartland Unity March and

Juneteenth Celebration that took place in the streets of downtown Cairo on June 19, 2020. "The question I ask you today is, 'What are you going to do?' And the question I ask myself is, 'What am I going to do?'" she said. "We have a responsibility as Black people to stand up for what is true."[1]

Between fifteen and twenty-six million people participated in that summer's nationwide demonstrations for racial justice, the largest social movement in American history. Every city discussed in this book and at least twenty-four hundred others across all fifty states and Washington, DC, witnessed protests. Although the vast majority were peaceful—only about 5 percent involved violent forms of protest, according to one study—all were in response to state-sanctioned violence, like Black rebellions that came before. People took to the streets in the days after a group of Minneapolis police officers suffocated a forty-six-year-old Black man named George Floyd to death. The killing of Floyd in late May, caught by a number of bystanders holding phone cameras, was the immediate cause for the rebellions. Yet his death also helped bring awareness to two other horrific incidents of anti-Black violence that local authorities had brushed aside in the months before: the fatal shooting of twenty-five-year-old Ahmaud Arbery by a white father and son who spotted the young Black man jogging through their southern Georgia neighborhood in February 2020; and the shooting by six plainclothes Louisville police officers, of twenty-six-year-old Breonna Taylor in a botched raid the following month, killing her after rousing her from the bed where she was sleeping. Protests demanding justice for all three victims peaked in the first week of June, and eighty-seven hundred demonstrations across seventy-four countries around the world marched in solidarity.[2] These protests marked the arrival of a global movement for racial and economic equality.

The demonstrations lasted for several weeks in Fort Wayne, Indiana, where police had used tear gas during the rebellion in 1968.

Hundreds of protesters paired their outrage over the deaths of Floyd, Arbery, and Taylor with a set of policing and sentencing reforms that Black Americans have long demanded in the city, including banning the use of choke holds and establishing a citizens' review board to be elected by Fort Wayne residents themselves. In Peoria, Illinois, where rebellion was a regular occurrence in the last years of the 1960s, protesters chanted a new slogan: "Defund the police." A call for government authorities to invest directly in low-income communities, the idea of defunding the police put front and center the education, employment, and housing measures that Peoria residents had fought for a half century prior, through both nonviolent and violent means.[3]

The protests in Cairo, Fort Wayne, and Peoria, and in thousands of other cities in the summer of 2020 have, at the time of this writing, marked the latest chapter in the Black freedom struggle. During the key years prior to and after King's assassination, and into the early 1970s, rebellions were rooted in political and economic grievances, but were usually triggered by the policing of ordinary, everyday activity. Beginning with Miami in 1980, Black Americans rebelled in response to moments of exceptional violence and challenged the justice system in its entirety. Along the way, the militarization of American police and the criminalization of Black and Brown communities only continued. While mandatory minimums for drug crimes and "three strikes and you're out" sentencing practices systematically targeted low-income people of color, police officers still rarely faced consequences for their violent actions. The contemporary movement for racial justice has built upon earlier traditions, creating a type of militant, nonviolent protest that blends the direct-action tactics of the civil rights movement with the critiques of systemic racism that are often identified with Black Power.[4]

While many Americans celebrated the massive protest movement ignited by Floyd's killing, that direct action was even seen as necessary—and that so many people were moved to participate— points to dispiriting linkages to the immediate post–civil rights era. For many years it appeared that "riots" were a thing of the past. The violence in Cincinnati in 2001 was treated by the national press as an anomaly, a footnote or coda to the era of mass Black protest. At the time, it appeared that the nation had not confronted a major rebellion in almost a decade, since Los Angeles in 1992.

But by 2020, the nation had already tipped into a new era of protest. The fires returned in Ferguson, Missouri, in 2014, after the killing of Michael Brown by a police officer. Between then and 2020, numerous police killings drew national attention. Among the dead were Laquan McDonald, a seventeen-year-old Chicagoan who was shot as he walked away from a police officer in October 2014, and whose murder was covered up by the city's liberal political establishment; Tamir Rice, the twelve-year-old boy who had been playing in a park with a toy gun and was shot and killed by Cleveland police in November 2014; and Sandra Bland, a twenty-eight-year-old woman who died mysteriously in the Waller County, Texas, jail in July 2015. Eric Garner was killed in New York City only weeks before Brown. There were many others including Freddie Gray, Natasha McKenna, and Philando Castille. And beyond.[5]

One reason for the return of rebellion is technology. Many, if not most of us, have cameras in our phones. Surveillance cameras have become a ubiquitous part of modern life. Outrage over police violence has long existed in Black communities, but the videos—the proof— supported claims that had been disregarded or simply denied for many years. With the fundamental neglect for Black lives now undeniable, countless white Americans were driven to outrage, too. The Rodney King beating in 1991 was the first to broadcast what the police do to Black people when they think no one is looking; two decades later numerous videos of police officers brutalizing and killing civilians could be widely shared across social media platforms. The nine-minute video of George Floyd's murder has been viewed an estimated 1.4 billion times as of this writing.[6] Although the flood of videos has fueled calls for justice among white Americans, increased awareness of widespread anti-Black violence has not resulted in swift systemic change. And so, the struggle continues.

At the forefront of the new generation of activists and organizations is the Black Lives Matter movement, which formed in July 2013 after George Zimmerman was acquitted for the senseless killing of seventeen-year-old Black high school student Trayvon Martin. As an organizing principle, social media hashtag, and idea, Black Lives Matter received national recognition during the uprising in Ferguson and has since inspired worldwide demonstrations. Founded on the argument that the wars on crime and drugs in low-income communities of color constitute a "war on Black and Brown people," Black Lives Matter, the Black Youth Project 100, We Charge Genocide, the Dream Defenders, and similar groups have called into question the decision to invest in policing, surveillance, and incarceration over schools, jobs, and decent shelter for poor people. Two generations removed from the era of rebellion in the 1960s and early 1970s, the young activists at the center of the contemporary freedom movement have forced us to reckon with anti-Black racism and how policing and incarceration in America anchor totalizing systems of political and economic oppression.[7]

That the movement for Black lives began during the second term of Barack Obama, the first Black American president, shattered the illusion that the United States had become a fully inclusive society and had perhaps shed its racist past. Obama's victory was a legacy of the civil rights movement—of the growth of the Black middle class and the rise of Black professionals and elected officials. Yet despite the displays of Black wealth in popular culture, the seats Black executives enjoy in corporate boardrooms, and the fact that, overall,

Black families started to do better, economically, after 1965, in 2020 the typical Black household still earned a fraction of the income of white households—59 cents for every dollar, or about $29,000 less a year. In 1965 and in 2020, unemployment and poverty rates among Black Americans were roughly twice that of their white counterparts. Today, three-quarters of white families own their own homes, while less than half of Black families do. Disinvestment over the last fifty years has left urban public schools in shambles and, as a result, a disparate proportion of low-income Black and Latinx children remain undereducated. Although the incarceration rate for Black Americans has dropped in recent years, it is still six times that of white Americans.[8] These grim figures underscore the ongoing fact of racism and its consequences, a reality that sits uncomfortably alongside the progress made by some Black people in the half century since the legislative victories of the mid-1960s.

During Obama's presidency, in addition to Ferguson, other cities—including Oakland, Baltimore, and Milwaukee—witnessed peaceful protests and vigils as well as violent encounters with police, property destruction, and looting, highlighting the structural shortcomings of 1960s civil rights legislation and the liberal reforms that followed in subsequent decades. The videos and the fires made clear that injustice and inequality had not vanished. People of color were still being killed by the police, and the legal system still demonstrated complacency if not hostility when faced with this fact. Even if most of the new protests were peaceful, collective political violence returned on a scale not seen since the 1960s and 1970s.

Both strains of Black protest have served important purposes historically. Any successes of the nonviolent, direct political action of the civil rights movement depended on the threat of violent, direct political action. As Martin Luther King Jr. himself recognized, the power of

On August 13, 2014, after police fired tear gas canisters at a group of protesters
in Ferguson, Missouri, Edward Crawford Jr. hurled a canister back at the officers.
An unarmed, Black teenager, Michael Brown, had been shot to death by a local
policeman four days before. (Robert Cohen / © *St. Louis Post-Dispatch*)

mass nonviolence arose in part from its capacity to suggest the coercive
power of violent resistance should demands not be met. The violent
and nonviolent expressions of Black protest are entwined forces, and
rebellion must be understood on its own terms, as a type of political
action that has been integral to the history of the freedom movement
in America.

THE WAVE OF PROTESTS in the summer of 2020 diverged in critical
ways from the rebellions of the late 1960s and early 1970s, and from
the massive conflagrations that came after, from Miami to Los Angeles. Unlike earlier rebellions, which typically began with demonstrators throwing rocks, bottles, and other objects when the police arrived
to patrol their communities, the protests started as peaceful marches
and vigils in response to flagrant acts of police violence. When police

responded aggressively to those nonviolent protesters, some of the demonstrations quickly turned violent.

Three days after George Floyd's killing, protesters in Minneapolis seized the city's third police precinct building and set fire to it. Protestors in many cities set police vehicles ablaze. Yet most of the violence—or more specifically, vandalism—in the summer of 2020 was not directed at police officers or businesses, but at the nation's most obvious symbols of oppression: monuments across the country celebrating individuals who promoted conquest and genocide, who held generations of people of African descent in bondage, or who fought to defend the institution of slavery, were defaced or destroyed. At least thirty-eight demonstrations resulted in significant damage to or the complete destruction of memorials around the United States, most of them tributes of some kind to Confederate military leaders. Where the demonstrators did not pull statues down or tarnish memorials with spray paint, the protests pressured authorities to remove symbols that seemed to celebrate injustice, and to rename schools, libraries, and other public facilities that, through their names, were monuments themselves to darker episodes in this country's past.[9]

Rebellions throughout America, from those in the 1960s to Cincinnati in 2001, mainly involved Black protesters, yet the most sustained collective violence in 2020 did not emanate from Black ghettos. In a reversal that would have been unthinkable not so long ago, it came from majority-white cities and suburban communities. Most of the looting in 2020 took place in upscale neighborhoods, and it targeted high-end retailers like Gucci and Tiffany & Co. on Rodeo Drive in Beverly Hills, not the white-owned mom-and-pop stores along Central Avenue in South Los Angeles, as it had in 1965. Confrontations between protesters and police were most intense and protracted in cities like Portland and Seattle, among the whitest cities in America. This matched, broadly, the demographic profile of protesters across the nation—in recent years increasing numbers of white Americans have taken to the streets to fight racial injustice, and very often in places where few (if any) Black people live. An estimated 95 percent of counties where protests took place were majority white, and three-quarters of these counties were 75 percent white. In some cases, white participants protected Black protesters from the police, using their bodies to shield them from potential brutality, and chanting "Black Power!"[10] These developments suggest that, as the country becomes more diverse and as the history and fact of systemic racism is further brought to light, rebellions led and comprised almost solely by Black people and taking place in segregated Black communities may be a thing of the past.

The 2020 demonstrations revealed that racial justice champions, environmental activists, LGBTQ-rights advocates, and labor unions appear to be stitching together a new coalition. In Cincinnati, almost two decades after the March for Justice organized by social justice organizations following the rebellion there, left-wing activist groups now called for a redistribution and redirection of resources away from police departments and prison systems and toward programs that would improve mental health services, address climate change, and provide better housing, education, and job opportunities for all Americans. By emboldening white extremism, the hostile rhetoric and policies of President Donald Trump's administration only emboldened progressive white Americans to forge new alliances and take action.

Another, even more recent shift is that, unlike the heavy-handed riot-control strategies from Harlem in 1964 and on, in 2020 some public officials and police officers participated in the demonstrations to express support for the anti-racist cause. In a number of cities, including Stockton, California, where residents trapped two police officers in the gymnasium of an all-Black housing project in 1968, a few police officers joined Black Lives Matter demonstrations and took a knee to memorialize George Floyd and recognize police brutality.[11] In some cities, these actions reduced tensions and prevented the escalation of violence on both sides; in others they were taken as "PR stunts" that papered over the structural forces that lead to police brutality. Even within the same departments, extremes exist—some officers have expressed solidarity with anti-police brutality protests while others have supported brutalizing peaceful protesters. In Buffalo, New York, one group of officers kneeled alongside demonstrators, while another was captured on video pushing an elderly white man to the ground and fracturing his skull.[12]

Corporate and political leaders offered a notable set of responses to the protests, taking steps "toward progress on racial equality," as a Quaker Oats spokesperson explained the company approach on June 17, 2020, when it decided to change the name and imagery of the Aunt Jemima brand of syrup and pancake mix. Major financial institutions pledged their support; Bank of America alone said it would donate one billion dollars to "strengthen economic opportunities" in communities of color. Walmart, "the world's largest retailer," and pharmacies such as CVS, ended the practice of placing Black beauty products behind anti-theft cases. Former president George W. Bush—who was criticized for his insensitivity to the plight of Black New Orleans residents killed or displaced by Hurricane Katrina in 2005—recognized the protesters as marching "for a better future," and posed the question: "How do we end systemic racism in our society?"[13] An emerging national dialogue moved discussions of racial justice away from individual prejudice and action, and toward the political and economic institutions that perpetuate inequality. The new, multiracial, broadly popular protest movement appeared to signal a break from the past, when Black rebellion—"riots"—were widely feared by white America and seen as a pathology distinct to Black America.

Yet the country had been here before, perhaps not in every respect, but almost surely in the most important respects. From the Kerner

Protestors attempt to take down the statue of Andrew Jackson in Washington, DC's Lafayette Square on June 22, 2020, during the wave of protests for racial justice in the spring and summer. (Drew Angerer / Getty Images)

Commission onward, task forces and commissions frequently identified the structural causes of collective political violence and highlighted the dangers of entrenched racism. Corporations are not new to social justice rhetoric; the Eurostar sneaker brand promised to turn former Crips and Bloods into entrepreneurs after the 1992 rebellion in Los Angeles, but when the news cycle moved on, the company lost interest. Acknowledging the reality of systemic racism, renaming a Robert E. Lee High School to a John Lewis High School (as happened in Fairfax County, Virginia), making donations to social justice and anti-poverty organizations, and using the #BlackLivesMatter hashtag on social media—these are insufficient substitutes for the structural transformation that Black Americans have long been calling for.

ALTHOUGH THE HISTORIC DEMONSTRATIONS in 2020 resembled the civil rights marches of the first half of the 1960s more than the violent protests later in that decade, authorities frequently responded as they had in those later years. As they had then and in Miami in the 1980s, in Los Angeles in the 1990s, and in Cincinnati in the 2000s, they fired rubber bullets, used pepper spray, beat protesters with riot sticks, imposed curfews, made arrests, and in some places called in the National Guard. In Harrisburg, Pennsylvania, protestors surrounded police cars and began shouting obscenities at the officers inside until reinforcements arrived in full riot gear and tear-gassed the men, women, and children at the scene—just as the chemical weapon had been liberally used by the Harrisburg police back in 1969.[14]

In a moment of national eruption over racial inequality, when tens of millions of people were on the streets calling for the country to envision a different kind of society, the Trump administration eagerly championed the escalation of police force as the only viable response to the protests. "These THUGS are dishonoring the memory of George Floyd," President Trump declared on Twitter on May 29, four days after the killing, as mostly peaceful protesters were in the streets across the country. "When the looting starts, the shooting starts," the president wrote in a Tweet, quoting word for word (knowingly or not) Miami Chief of Police Walter Headley's response to the city's rebellion in 1967. Trump called governors "weak" for permitting people to exercise their first amendment right to protest, instructing state officials to summon the National Guard to "dominate" the demonstrations. In Minneapolis, in the president's words, the troops "cut through [protesters] like butter."[15]

Other prominent conservatives joined Trump in advocating for a militarized response to the protests. In a *New York Times* op-ed published June 3, Arkansas Senator Tom Cotton drew comparisons between 2020 demonstrations and the "rioters" of the 1960s who "plunged many American cities into anarchy," in an "orgy of violence." Echoing the distinctions Lyndon Johnson drew between peaceful civil rights protests and violent "hoodlums," Cotton claimed that "the rioting has nothing to do with George Floyd." The only way to "subdue" the "rioters," Cotton concluded, was "an overwhelming show of force to disperse, detain, and ultimately deter lawbreakers."[16]

As in the late 1960s and early 1970s, when blame was laid on "outside agitators" and "Black revolutionaries," Cotton, Trump, and other officials attributed the violence to Black Lives Matter and to the loosely affiliated groups of anti-fascist activists collectively known as "Antifa." In the words of Senator Cotton: "nihilist criminals are simply out for loot and the thrill of destruction, with cadres of left-wing radicals like Antifa infiltrating protest marches to exploit Floyd's death for their own anarchic purposes." In the style of the anti-communist film "Revolution Underway" that had been shown to local police across the United States to discredit the Black Power movement, officials and conservative-leaning media outlets launched disinformation campaigns that classified Black Lives Matter activists as violent extremists and Antifa as a terrorist organization. These labels helped cut into public support for the protests, which peaked the week after Floyd's killing and sharply declined thereafter. Even as the majority of Americans expressed a degree of support for the Black Lives Matter movement, one poll found that 42 percent of respondents believed that most of the protesters against racial injustice "are trying to incite violence or destroy property."[17]

The Trump administration and its allies branded the protests anti-American, criminal, and violent. They backed their rhetoric with action, and attempted action. Federal troops had been deployed to a number of cities during the rebellions that followed Martin Luther King Jr.'s murder in 1968 and to Los Angeles after the acquittal of the police officers who brutalized Rodney King in 1992; now the Trump administration revived the idea that the federal government should intervene directly. On June 1, US Park Police and Secret Service agents used tear gas, riot batons, and other weapons against nonviolent protesters in Lafayette Square near the White House to make way for a photo opportunity for President Trump in front of St. John's Church nearby. By the end of June, as books about anti-Black racism surged to the top of bestseller lists and protestors toppled monuments to Christopher Columbus and Jefferson Davis, President Trump issued an executive order that authorized federal agents to pursue people who damaged statues or federal property. The order led to the establishment of the Protecting American Communities Task Force (PACT) and the deployment of Department of Homeland Security agents to protests in Portland, Oregon, Washington, DC, and other cities. In July, the Trump administration folded these efforts into "Operation Diligent Valor," which, to the great ambivalence of many local officials, sent federal agents into the streets to aggressively police demonstrations.[18]

Unsurprisingly, this strategy only inflamed the protesters even more (that may have been Trump's goal, in the belief that further unrest would increase public support for his reelection campaign). Prior to Operation Diligent Valor, police intervened in about 24 percent of the protests in Portland, and rarely used violent force. But with the arrival of federal agents, reported incidents of official violence nearly doubled to 40 percent. Before the deployment of the federal force, only 17 percent of demonstrations in Portland involved violence. For the remainder of the summer, just under half, or 42 percent, of the protests turned violent. The cycle of police violence causing community violence was in motion. By fall 2020, the federal government had deputized Oregon State Police to help suppress the demonstrations as part of a coordinated response with US Marshals, indicating that the highest levels of the federal government were involved in the effort.[19]

The Trump administration targeted Albuquerque, New Mexico—where Mexican American youth had engaged in violent political protest to challenge policing measures in 1970—with "Operation Legend," a counterpart to Operation Diligent Valor whose mission was to reassert "law and order." In mid-June, after a crowd attempted to tear down a monument celebrating Spanish conquistador Juan de Oñate, an extremist member of a local militia group shot and wounded a demonstrator. Attorney General William Barr oversaw the deployment of thirty-five federal troops to Albuquerque and dozens of agents to New York, Chicago, Baltimore, Detroit, Oakland, and Kansas City, MO. The goal was not to protect residents against white supremacist violence, but to suppress the protesters. In hindsight, Barr's 1992 invocation of the Insurrection Act and rapid deployment of federal forces in Los Angeles while Attorney General under George H. W. Bush was a rehearsal for the larger response in 2020. In addition to dispatching agents from the FBI, DEA, and Bureau of Alcohol, Tobacco, Firearms and Explosives to the city, Barr's Justice Department granted Albuquerque $9.7 million to hire forty new police officers, even as local activists and politicians called for a divestment from law enforcement and investment in educational programs for young people.[20]

Historically, protests against racial injustice have not only come in response to the forces of white supremacy, but have helped mobilize those forces, and 2020 proved to be no different. Acting individually or in connection with organized white power hate groups, white extremists drove their cars into groups of protesters. In Austin, Texas, and Kokomo, Indiana, among other cities, these "car rammings" were perpetrated by military and law enforcement officials themselves. The tactic first appeared at the Unite the Right rally held in Charlottesville, Virginia, during the first summer of Trump's presidency. Militia groups and neo-Nazis marched through the streets of Charlottesville in August 2017, chanting racist slogans, brandishing assault rifles, wearing swastikas, and waving Confederate flags. One white supremacist at the rally rammed his car into a group of counter-protesters, injuring nineteen people and killing a thirty-two-year-old white woman named Heather Heyer.[21]

The rise of Donald Trump and of his divisive and authoritarian politics empowered white supremacists. His campaign slogan in 2016 ("Make America Great Again") and explicit encouragement (telling members of one white hate group to "stand back and stand by" during a presidential debate in 2020) made Lyndon Johnson look tame by comparison. At a press conference held in the aftermath of Heyer's killing, President Trump said that "there were very fine people, on both sides" of the Charlottesville protests—much like the violent White Hats in Cairo had been deemed "good citizens" by officials in the 1970s.[22] Back then, white people stood on their lawns with their shotguns and German shepherds to intimidate and harass Black residents for fighting to be treated as full citizens, or simply for existing in their vicinity. In late June of 2020, a white couple in St. Louis was photographed on their lawn pointing a pistol and an assault rifle at Black Lives Matter protesters, only to be celebrated two months later at the Republican National Convention.

The Trump administration did not hand out bullets to white supremacists like police officers in York, Pennsylvania, had in 1969, but it did give the children and grandchildren of those same extremists other forms of support for their anti-Black campaigns. Although incidents of violence during the protests in the summer of 2020 were minimal, much of the violence that did occur resulted from clashes between white supremacist groups, egged on by Trump, and demonstrators associated with the Black Lives Matter or anti-fascism movements. In Minneapolis, a member of the white supremacist prison and street gang known as the Aryan Cowboys smashed store windows in one of the earliest reports of property destruction in the city. According to police investigators, this man, who many assumed was a protester against police killings, "wanted to sow discord and racial unrest." In Portland, members of Patriot Prayer, the Three Percenters, and the Proud Boys all demonstrated in support of President Trump. They drove trucks around and through demonstrations, using pepper spray and shooting paintball guns at the protesters. During one such protest, Patriot Prayer member Aaron Danielson was shot and killed by white Antifa supporter Michael Reinoehl. Members of a US Marshals task force later apparently executed Reinoehl in front of his car, an action Barr called a "significant accomplishment." In Oakland, an Air Force Sergeant named Steven Carrillo, who belonged to the anti-government Boogaloo Boys militia, allegedly shot and killed a security officer and wounded another in front of a federal courthouse; he apparently saw the city's May protest as an opportunity to spread his extremist views and foment a race war.[23]

Following a historical pattern, local law enforcement welcomed the presence of white supremacist forces in various cities, even actively encouraging them to take the law into their own hands. On September 29, 2020, the House Committee on Oversight and Reform's Subcommittee on Civil Rights and Civil Liberties acknowledged the extent of this problem by convening a hearing on white supremacists infiltrating police departments. Roughly one month before, during protests against police brutality in Wisconsin that followed the shooting of twenty-nine-year-old Jacob Blake—a Black resident who was shot seven times in the back at point blank range by police while in front of three of his young sons—a newly organized civilian group calling itself the Kenosha Guard had taken to social media to encourage armed citizens to help its members to "protect lives and property." This was the same slogan Citizens' Councils had rallied behind in the late 1960s and early 1970s. Many people traveled to Kenosha to support the cause, among them a seventeen-year-old high school student named Kyle Rittenhouse. He shot three people with an AR-15 rifle in what he later claimed to be self-defense. Two of his victims died. After his firing spree, video captured Rittenhouse walking past several armored police vehicles with his hands in the air and his weapon hanging from his neck. Rittenhouse was not arrested until after he returned to his home in Antioch, Illinois, some twenty-one miles away.[24] From Cairo and York in the late 1960s to Kenosha in 2020, individual police officers and sometimes entire departments have proved, time and again, to support the forces of white hate, whether implicitly or explicitly, while abusing protesters who seek racial justice.

IF NOTHING ELSE, this book has striven to show that what were long assumed to be urban, Black "riots" were, in fact, rebellions—political acts carried out in response to an unjust and repressive society. This redefinition leads, necessarily, to an examination of the failures of the civil rights era, whose unfulfilled promises resulted in continued poverty and skyrocketing imprisonment. "Defund the police," the slogan that came to the forefront of the Black Lives Matter movement following the killing of George Floyd, raised urgent questions about government spending priorities. If the goal is to realize the incomplete legacies of the struggle for racial justice, the first step is to move beyond reform.

From the police–community relations programs championed by liberal commissions in the late 1960s and early 1970s, to the federal interventions that introduced sensitivity training and accountability for officers in more recent decades, to the use of body cameras that are meant to keep misconduct in check today, reforms have not stopped the killing in the past, and they won't stop more killings from happening in the future. "When you see a police officer pressing his knee into a black man's neck until he dies, that's the logical result of policing in America" wrote the abolitionist organizer Mariame Kaba. "When a police officer brutalizes a black person, he is doing what he sees as his job."[25] The logic of American policing—searching for potential criminals in low-income communities of color, protecting property in the middle-class and wealthy white areas—increases the likelihood of police contact with Black and Brown people and, with it, police violence.

To end policing in its current form and create a more humane approach to public safety will require convincing many millions of Americans of the righteousness and practicality of the cause, especially since law enforcement officials have generally been resistant to any policies that might alter the balance of power. When residents demand to patrol their own neighborhoods ("community policing" in its truest form) and call for citizen review boards to hold violent cops accountable, police administrators and unions argue that such measures would prevent officers from maintaining safety and securing order.[26]

Yet the history of police violence and Black rebellion in postwar America demonstrates that patrolling low-income neighborhoods with outside forces does not promote public safety. On the contrary, it establishes a dynamic where residents and officers view each other as the enemy, rendering both sides *less* safe.[27] If anything, embracing policing and incarceration as a policy response to racial and economic inequality appears to function as a crime *promotion* program. The approach has not prevented the gun violence and crime that pervades the very same neighborhoods that are energetically policed. Young Black people continue to live at greater risk of harm or death with police lingering in their community—either from each other or from an officer whose job is ostensibly to protect them. Breonna Taylor's killing is a legacy of this policy path, sustained over five decades. So too is the death of nine-year-old Janari Ricks, who was killed in late July 2020 when a person began firing gunshots in a parking lot in Chicago's Cabrini-Green neighborhood, where policymakers feared "urban guerrilla warfare" would explode in 1970. Instead of building policies around the needs of the community, this nation has built them around controlling communities and, at the same time, has erected the largest prison system in the world to warehouse Americans who exist at the margins. Public safety mechanisms are essential to promote community vitality, but these mechanisms cannot and should not take the form of a uniformed officer, an outsider to the community armed with a gun.

Given the resistance to the idea of defunding the police by many Americans across the political spectrum, the struggle to disinvest from law enforcement will be a difficult and protracted one. Yet there are other paths that can be pursued to change how the nation addresses poverty and inequality. For one, the unfair American system of taxation undergirds glaring economic and racial disparities and is a possible source of investments that are urgently needed. The tax revenue pie in the United States is simply too small. Over the past fifty years, as the nation witnessed sporadic rebellion, the rise of mass incarceration, and the growing power and influence of the police, tax rates have fallen sharply for the richest Americans, while tax rates increased for the middle and working classes as wages stagnated and debts mounted. The Americans in the bottom 50 percent of the income bracket pay higher taxes than billionaires. This nation gives hundreds of billions of dollars in welfare to corporations in the form of grants, tax breaks, and bailouts—a sum that far exceeds the amount put into public assistance programs and food stamps. The United States offers tax abatements to the ultra-rich and settles for collecting only small portions of the money held in offshore bank accounts.[28]

Defenders of the regressive tax system argue that if wealthy people are taxed too highly, they will identify loopholes to avoid paying what they owe. It is certainly true, at least, that authorities tend to defer to white collar crime while arresting people like Eric Garner for allegedly selling loose cigarettes, and George Floyd for using counterfeit currency. As with the decision in a number of states to allocate greater portions of taxpayer dollars to facilitate the incarceration of young people rather than provide an education for them, the tax schemes and lax enforcement of white collar crime seem to contradict the nation's stated values and its commitment to the rule of law.

In the face of the best available research, and at a greater cost to taxpayers, policymakers at all levels continue to resist investing in alternative measures that would strengthen communities and improve safety overall. For instance, data indicates that children who participate in early childhood education programs are less likely to be arrested as teenagers. Yet funding for Head Start, the most visible remnant of the War on Poverty and a program that helps the nation's poorest children prepare for school between ages three and five, continues to shrink. Similarly, research has consistently shown that expanding job opportunities for young people living in vulnerable communities can reduce arrest rates and violence. The federal government spent about $2.7 billion on employment programs for low-income youth in 2020, while investing more than double that number, or $6.1 billion, on grants and assistance to law enforcement, on top of the $115 billion state and local governments already spent on police that year.[29]

The most effective approaches to crime prevention involve programs that respond to community needs and grant control of public safety to residents, especially in the areas where the state has failed. In addition to new investments into preschool programs and job-creation measures, mental health treatment and college scholarships would make for a safer society and a stronger democracy. As would establishing a justice system based on the principle of repair instead of retribution. Police are the default response to violence and other crises in low-income neighborhoods of color, but community needs can and should be met by the people.[30] The paths not chosen previously—from the structural blueprint the Kerner Commission developed in 1968 to the proposal made by Crips and Bloods in South Central Los Angeles in 1992—are well worth returning to, for inspiration and for the discrete policy proposals themselves.

"There's a recurring trend in this country," observed protester Jordan Michael at the Peace Monument near the US Capitol Building in early June 2020. "It's uprising, the demanding of rights, it's peaceful protests, it turns to violence, and then we get a response." Looting and arson push authorities to act, "and then to appease us, we get handed something. But it's a crumb. We're asking for a loaf of bread and we get a crumb, and they're like 'Look, we fed you,' but no, this is not sustenance." Michael went on to say that sustained political action and sustained visibility—as in the civil rights era and the crucible years of rebellion that immediately followed—forced lawmakers "to actually listen."[31] Some lawmakers are listening again, and the challenge of the twenty-first century is to actually bring about change. As Michael's comments imply, America will continue to see the fires of rebellion—perhaps by a new, more diverse generation of protesters—until the forces of inequality are finally abolished and the nation no longer empowers police officers to manage the material consequences of conditions that are beyond their control.

ACKNOWLEDGMENTS

THIS BOOK WOULD NOT have been possible without the research and generosity of Professor Christian Davenport. In the summer of 2016, I attended a barbeque at the home of Heather Ann Thompson and Jon Wells, in Detroit, where I met Christian, who had recently joined the Department of Political Science at the University of Michigan. We started talking about the many rebellions that took place into the 1970s—rebellions that kept popping up as I researched my first book. Christian happened to be working on a quantitative study of these later uprisings and had the archives from the Lemberg Center for the Study of Violence in his possession. I had previously encountered various Lemberg Center reports in the Nixon White House Files and jumped at Christian's invitation to come take a look. Before long, I was standing in Christian's office at the Center for Political Studies at Michigan, scouring through a treasure trove of tens of thousands of clippings. For the remainder of the summer and well beyond, Christian became more than a colleague and collaborator. I consider him part of my extended family; even our mothers are close friends. I must also thank Christian for helping to formulate the list of Black rebellions included in the timeline.

The research and writing of this book was a collective labor of love, involving a group of dedicated people starting with Christian, who lent me their minds and their time. No single person deserves more credit than my superb editor at Liveright, Dan Gerstle. Dan planted the seeds of this book by encouraging me to pursue the topic, after years of sitting on the archives and wondering what to do with the stories they contained. His dedication and wisdom from the very beginning helped me figure it out. Deepest thanks also to Steve Forman and Justin Cahill for championing my work for nearly a decade, to Haley Bracken for keeping everything on track, and to Cordelia Calvert for helping to bring this book to the world. I was also extremely fortunate to have the gifted Rebecca Strong serve as copyeditor. My agent, Adam Eaglin, helped me see what this book could be and offered consistent encouragement and advice. The entire team at Elyse Cheney Literary Associates and Emma Patterson helped make it all happen. Thanks also to my editor at William Collins, Shoaib Rokadiya, who consistently provided invaluable feedback through multiple drafts and tight deadlines.

I am eternally indebted to Robin D. G. Kelley and Brandon Terry for sharpening my framework and analysis. I share all of the best ideas with them, any shortcomings are entirely my own. In the spring of 2017 and the fall of 2018, I also received crucial suggestions on early chapter drafts at Princeton University's American Political History Seminar, the Legal Theory Workshop at Yale Law School, and the US History Workshop at the University of Chicago. Boundless thanks go to my colleagues at YLS, who engaged my arguments with rigor and care, and to Keeanga-Yamahtta Taylor and Destin Jenkins, who served as lead commentators during discussions at Princeton and Chicago. I am also grateful to the scholars whose books provided me with an important foundation. In particular, the work of Bruce Porter and

Marvin Dunn on Miami, Kerry Pimblott on Cairo, Peter Levy on York, Max Felker-Kantor on Los Angeles, and Stuart Schrader's examination of tear gas and police militarization proved indispensable.

Funding for the research and writing of this book came from the Ford Foundation, the Carnegie Corporation of New York, and the Oscar M. Ruebhausen General Fund at Yale Law School. Joe McClure, a reporter in the Harrisburg area, provided another important source of support. In addition to sharing his vast knowledge of the city's history, Joe helped me secure articles from the *Harrisburg Patriot-News* archives that would have been impossible for me to obtain otherwise. Robert Sutherland gave me new insights on Cairo and trusted me with personal archival documents, and Tim Kornegay shared key perspective on Los Angeles. My ingenious research assistant, Benjamin Schafer, helped me pull together necessary loose strings as I completed the manuscript. I cannot thank Benjamin enough.

One of the highlights of writing this book has been getting to know Darnell Stephen Summers, who exposed me to new realms of the freedom struggle and deepened my commitment to the fight for justice. Darnell was incredibly considerate with his time over the summer and fall of 2020, even as he faced continued persecution. Although I did not discuss the specifics of his case in the book, authorities unsuccessfully attempted to convict Darnell for the August 1968 shooting of Michigan State Police Detective, Robert Gonser, during the rebellion in Inkster, Michigan. Darnell faced murder charges in 1969 that carried a maximum penalty of life imprisonment and that were dropped "without prejudice"—meaning he could be re-charged. He was retried in 1983. Law enforcement officials decided to reinvestigate his case in late summer 2020. Michigan State Police obtained a search warrant in October, which allowed them to swab Darnell's mouth for DNA and confiscate his cell phone. Darnell says officers have harassed and intimidated him, members of his family, and his close comrades. The continued attempt to oppress Darnell is a reminder that the aftershocks of rebellion, and anti-Black state repression, are still very much with us.

Through the last push in writing the manuscript, during various lockdowns and through a move to a new city and the start of a new job, my amazing colleagues and friends in New Haven helped to lift me up. Jason Stanley and Njeri Thande deserve special mention in this respect. I could not have survived the transition and the completion of the manuscript without their kindness, as well as (socially distant) gatherings with Leah Mirakhor and Navid Hafez, Tracey Meares and Ben Justice, and Monica Bell and Yaseen Eldik. Thanks also to Emily Bazelon and Paul Sabin, Crystal Feimster, Beverly Gage, Doug NeJaime, Marci Shore and Timothy Snyder, and to Titus and Julianne Kaphar. Dixa Ramírez D'Oleo and Ren Ellis Neyra have become staple sources of love and support in recent years. Along with Sarah Robbins, they fed me and made me laugh when I needed it most. And my dear friend and advocate Vanessa Díaz kept my head above water through it all. Thanks to all my other close mentors, colleagues, friends, and family members. I love you and I've acknowledged you before. My mom deserves special mention again, though—I couldn't have done any of this without you.

Odessa Pearl, you are my biggest inspiration and source of pride. Brandon, you pushed me to achieve what I didn't think I could, and you helped make me a better historian, mother, and human along the way. You encouraged me to keep perspective through the most chaotic and discomforting year of our lives and brought warmth and joy into our home on a daily basis. Everything I do is for you, our family, and our people.

TIMELINE OF BLACK REBELLIONS

The rebellions included in this timeline from 1964 to 1967 were compiled by the Senate Committee on Government Operations in *Riots, Criminal, and Civil Disorders Part I: Hearings before the Subcommittee on Investigations*, 90th Cong., 1st sess. (November 1, 2, 3, 6, 1967). Professor Christian Davenport's Radical Information Project at the University of Michigan's Center for Political Studies collected the list of cities from 1968 to 1972, based on data from the Lemberg Center for the Study of Violence. Lemberg researchers stopped tracking the rebellions after 1972, and no other comprehensive study exists to account for incidents between 1973 and 1979. It is clear, however, that by 1972 rebellions had already begun to wane, occurring at a frequency slightly above the 1967 levels.

1964: 4 REBELLIONS
HARLEM, NEW YORK, NY, *July 16–July 22*
ROCHESTER, NY, *July 24–July 26*
DIXMOOR, IL, *August 15–August 17*
PHILADELPHIA, PA, *August 28–August 30*

1965: 4 REBELLIONS
SELMA, AL, *March 5–July 5*
BOGALUSA, LA, *May 20–July 17*
WATTS, LOS ANGELES, CA, *August 11–August 18*
CHICAGO, IL, *August 12–August 15*

1966: 17 REBELLIONS
LOS ANGELES, CA, *March 15–March 17*
BAKERSFIELD, CA, *May 22*
POMPANO BEACH, FL, *June 25–June 26*
OMAHA, NE, *July 3–July 5*
GRENADA, MS, *July 10–July 30*
CLEVELAND, OH, *July 18–July 24*
PERTH AMBOY, NJ, *August 2–August 5*
LANSING, MI, *August 8–August 11*
DETROIT, MI, *August 9–August 11*
MUSKEGON, MI, *August 13*
BENTON HARBOR, MI, *August 26–August 28*
DAYTON, OH, *September 1*
CICERO, IL, *September 4*
ATLANTA, GA, *September 6–September 7*
ATLANTA, GA, *September 10–September 14*
SAN FRANCISCO, CA, *September 28–October 2*
OAKLAND, CA, *October 19–October 21*

1967: 75 REBELLIONS
OMAHA, NE, *April 1*
NASHVILLE, TN, *April 8–April 10*
LOUISVILLE, KY, *April 11–April 24*
MASSILLON, OH, *April 15–April 21*
JACKSON, MS, *May 12–May 14*
SAN FRANCISCO, CA, *May 14–May 15*
HOUSTON, TX, *May 16–May 17*
BOSTON, MA, *June 2–June 4*
TAMPA, FL, *June 11–June 13*
CINCINNATI, OH, *June 12–June 18*
MONTGOMERY, AL, *June 12–June 26*
DAYTON, OH, *June 14–June 15*
BUFFALO, NY, *June 27–July 1*

CINCINNATI, OH, *July 3–July 4*

WATERLOO, IA, *July 8–July 9*

KANSAS CITY, MO, *July 9*

NEWARK, NJ, *July 12–July 16*

NEW YORK, NY, *July 14–July 20*

FRESNO, CA, *July 15–July 17*

PLAINFIELD, NJ, *July 16–July 20*

CAIRO, IL, *July 17–July 21*

GREENSBORO, NC, *July 17–July 20*

ERIE, PA, *July 18–July 20*

MINNEAPOLIS, MN, *July 19–July 20*

ENGLEWOOD, NJ, *July 21–July 25*

HATTIESBURG, MS, *July 22*

BIRMINGHAM, AL, *July 23*

NEW BRITAIN, CT, *July 23–July 24*

PHOENIX, AZ, *July 23–July 24*

ROCHESTER, NY, *July 23–July 24*

TUCSON, AZ, *July 23–July 24*

KALAMAZOO, MI, *July 23–July 26*

LIMA, OH, *July 23–July 26*

TOLEDO, OH, *July 23–July 28*

DETROIT, MI, *July 23–July 31*

NEW YORK, NY, *July 23–August 3*

PONTIAC, MI, *July 24–July 25*

CAMBRIDGE, MD, *July 24–July 26*

MOUNT CLEMENS, MI, *July 25*

MOUNT VERNON, NY, *July 25*

SAGINAW, MI, *July 25–July 26*

SOUTH BEND, IN, *July 25–July 27*

FLINT, MI, *July 25–July 30*

SACRAMENTO, CA, *July 25–August 1*

LONG BEACH, CA, *July 26–July 27*

CHICAGO, IL, *July 26–July 28*

GRAND RAPIDS, MI, *July 26–July 28*

SAN FRANCISCO, CA, *July 26–July 31*

PEEKSKILL, NY, *July 27*

ALBANY, NY, *July 27–July 28*

CINCINNATI, OH, *July 27–July 28*

PASSAIC, NJ, *July 27–July 29*

WATERBURY, CT, *July 27–July 29*

WICHITA, KS, *July 27–August 7*

POUGHKEEPSIE, NY, *July 28–July 29*

ROCKFORD, IL, *July 28–July 30*

WILMINGTON, DE, *July 28–July 30*

ELGIN, IL, *July 29*

HAMILTON, OH, *July 29*

NEW YORK, NY, *July 29–July 31*

RIVIERA BEACH, FL, *July 30*

PORTLAND, OR, *July 30–July 31*

MILWAUKEE, WI, *July 30–August 8*

WEST PALM BEACH, FL, *July 31–August 2*

ERIE, PA, *July 31–August 3*

SAN BERNARDINO, CA, *July 31–August 4*

WASHINGTON, DC, *August 1*

PROVIDENCE, RI, *August 1–August 2*

PEORIA, IL, *August 2–August 3*

ELGIN, IL, *August 4*

HOUSTON, TX, *August 15–August 17*

SYRACUSE, NY, *August 16–August 20*

NEW HAVEN, CT, *August 19–August 23*

HATTIESBURG, MS, *August 25*

NEW YORK, NY, *September 4–September 8*

1968: 504 REBELLIONS

RICHMOND, VA, *January 13*

WILLINGBORO, NJ, *January 13*

NEW YORK, NY, *January 16*

EAST ST. LOUIS, IL, *January 19*

NEW YORK, NY, *February 1*

WILMINGTON, DE, *February 3–February 4*

CHICAGO, IL, *February 5*

NEW HAVEN, CT, *February 5–February 6*

ORANGEBURG, SC, *February 5–February 8*

MILWAUKEE, WI, *February 6*

WASHINGTON, DC, *February 8*

SOCIAL CIRCLE, GA, *February 14–February 16*

MILWAUKEE, WI, *February 15*

MOUNT VERNON, NY, *February 16*

NEWARK, NJ, *February 19*

CHATTANOOGA, TN, *February 20*

WASHINGTON, DC, *February 20*

LORMAN, MS, *February 20–February 21*

CHICAGO, IL, *February 21*

MEMPHIS, TN, *February 23*

MILWAUKEE, WI, *February 26*

CHICAGO, IL, *February 26–February 27*

TRENTON, NJ, *February 28*

SAN FRANCISCO, CA, *March 1–March 2*

CARTERET, NJ, *March 2*

OMAHA, NE, *March 4–March 7*

SAN FRANCISCO, CA, *March 6*

EL DORADO, AR, *March 6–March 7*

MAYWOOD, IL, *March 7*

NORRISTOWN, PA, *March 9*

LOS ANGELES, CA, *March 12*

MAYWOOD, IL, *March 12*

TAMPA, FL, *March 18–March 19*

WASHINGTON, DC, *March 21*

CHICAGO, IL, *March 22*

HARTSDALE ,NY, *March 25*

LINDEN, NJ, *March 26*

DOVER, DE, *March 27*

MEMPHIS, TN, *March 28–March 29*

FRANKFORT, KY, *April 3–April 8*

*MARTIN LUTHER KING ASSASSINATED,
April 4

DENVER, CO, *April 4*

ITHACA, NY, *April 4*

ITTA BENA, MS, *April 4*

JACKSON, MS, *April 4*

LITTLE ROCK, AR, *April 4*

MONTICELLO, NY, *April 4*

NEWARK, NJ, *April 4*

RALEIGH, NC, *April 4*

ST. LOUIS, MO, *April 4*

TAMPA, FL, *April 4*

TYLER, TX, *April 4*

WILMINGTON, DE, *April 4*

CHARLESTON, SC, *April 4–April 5*

PINE BLUFF, AR, *April 4–April 5*

SAN FRANCISCO, CA, *April 4–April 5*

TALLAHASSEE, FL, *April 4–April 5*

WINTER HAVEN, FL, *April 4–April 5*

NEW BEDFORD, MA, *April 4–April 6*

HARTFORD, CT, *April 4–April 7*

NASHVILLE, TN, *April 4–April 8*

GREENBURGH, NY, *April 4–April 9*

NEW YORK, NY, *April 4–April 10*

WASHINGTON, DC, *April 4–April 10*

BERKELEY, CA, *April 5*

BOSTON, MA, *April 5*

BUFFALO, NY, *April 5*

DENVER, CO, *April 5*

GAINESVILLE, FL, *April 5*

GREENVILLE, MS, *April 5*

HELENA-WEST HELENA, AR, *April 5*

HOUSTON, TX, *April 5*

JEFFERSON CITY, MO, *April 5*

MISSOULA, MT, *April 5*

NEW HAVEN, CT, *April 5*

PALO ALTO, CA, *April 5*

PITTSBURGH, PA, *April 5*

SAVANNAH, GA, *April 5*

SOUTH BEND, IN, *April 5*

SPOKANE, WA, *April 5*

ST. LOUIS, MO, *April 5*

TUCSON, AZ, *April 5*

TUSCALOOSA, AL, *April 5*

WICHITA, KS, *April 5*

WILMINGTON, DE, *April 5*

DETROIT, MI, *April 5–April 6*

FLINT, MI, *April 5–April 6*

OAKLAND, CA, *April 5–April 6*

ST. LOUIS, MO, *April 5–April 6*

CHICAGO, IL, *April 5–April 7*

JOLIET, IL, *April 5–April 9*

PITTSBURGH, PA, *April 5–April 9*

LEXINGTON, KY, *April 5–April 10*

ATLANTA, GA, *April 6*

CLINTON, MD, *April 6*

DUNBAR, WV, *April 6*

FREDERICK, MD, *April 6*

FORT VALLEY, GA, *April 6*

PEORIA, IL, *April 6*

CHICAGO HEIGHTS, IL, *April 6–April 7*

GUM SPRING, VA, *April 6–April 7*

ROCKVILLE, MD, *April 6–April 7*

TAKOMA PARK, MD, *April 6–April 7*

BALTIMORE, MD, *April 6–April 9*

POMONA, CA, *April 6–April 10*

RICHMOND, VA, *April 6–April 11*

BATTLE CREEK, MI, *April 7*

CAMBRIDGE, MD, *April 7*

DES MOINES, IA, *April 7*

HOT SPRINGS, AR, *April 7*

MALVERN, AR, *April 7*

ROCKFORD, IN, *April 7*

TUSKEGEE, AL, *April 7*

WHEELING, WV, *April 7*

ALBION, MI, *April 7–April 8*

COLUMBIA, SC, *April 7–April 8*

FORT PIERCE, FL, *April 7–April 8*

POMPANO BEACH, FL, *April 7–April 8*

NEW ORLEANS, LA, *April 7–April 10*

CINCINNATI, OH, *April 8*

DUNBAR, WV, *April 8*

GARY, IN, *April 8*

GENEVA, IL, *April 8*

GIFFORD, FL, *April 8*

HAMILTON, NY, *April 8*

PENSACOLA, FL, *April 8*

PORTSMOUTH, VA, *April 8*

RAHWAY, NJ, *April 8*

BUFFALO, NY, *April 8–April 9*

JACKSONVILLE, FL, *April 8–April 9*

NILES, MI, *April 8–April 9*

SACRAMENTO, CA, *April 8–April 9*

ATLANTA, GA, *April 9*

BRIDGEPORT, CT, *April 9*

CHATTANOOGA, TN, *April 9*

HEMPSTEAD, NY, *April 9*

HOMESTEAD, FL, *April 9*

JACKSON, MI, *April 9*

LANSING, MI, *April 9*

NEW CASSEL, NY, *April 9*

PETERSBURG, VA, *April 9*

SACRAMENTO, CA, *April 9*

SHARON, PA, *April 9*

ST. LOUIS, MO, *April 9*

WATERLOO, IA, *April 9*

DALLAS, TX, *April 9–April 10*

KANSAS CITY, MO, *April 9–April 10*

NEWARK, NJ, *April 9–April 10*

NEWBURGH, NY, *April 9–April 10*

TRENTON, NJ, *April 9–April 11*

BRIDGETON, NJ, *April 9–April 12*

DOVER, DE, *April 10*

GREENBURGH, NY, *April 10*

MANHASSET, NY, *April 10*

STAMFORD, CT, *April 10*

BALTIMORE, MD, *April 11*

MERIDIAN, MS, *April 11*

CHATTANOOGA, TN, *April 11–April 12*

MANHASSET, NY, *April 11–April 12*

DES MOINES, IA, *April 12–April 13*

BALTIMORE, MD, *April 13*

PASSAIC, NJ, *April 13–April 14*

CEDAR RAPIDS, IA, *April 14*

MANHASSET, NY, *April 14*

NEW YORK, NY, *April 14*

CLARKSDALE, MS, *April 15*

CLEVELAND, MS, *April 15*

GREENWOOD, MS, *April 15*

HICKSVILLE, NY, *April 15*

MACON, GA, *April 15*

MOUNT VERNON, NY, *April 15*

TRENTON, NJ, *April 15*

WASHINGTON, DC, *April 17–April 22*

CARTERET, NJ, *April 18*

BOSTON, MA, *April 19*

WILMINGTON, DE, *April 20*

BALTIMORE, MD, *April 21*

SEASIDE, CA, *April 21*

SAN ANTONIO, TX, *April 22*

STOCKTON, CA, *April 22*

EAST ST. LOUIS, IL, *April 23*

OAKLAND, CA, *April 23*

NEW YORK, NY, *April 23–April 30*

BROOKVILLE, NY, *April 25*

BOSTON, MA, *April 26*

EAST ST. LOUIS, IL, *April 26*

OMAHA, NE, *April 27–April 29*

WILMINGTON, DE, *April 29*

KANSAS CITY, MO, *April 30*

WASHINGTON, DC, *April 30*

GAFFNEY, SC, *May 3*

MADISON, WI, *May 3*

WASHINGTON, DC, *May 5*

CAMDEN, NJ, *May 5–May 6*

NEW YORK, NY, *May 6*

NEWBURGH, NY, *May 6–May 9*

CARBONDALE, IL, *May 8*

CHICAGO, IL, *May 8*

PATERSON, NJ, *May 8*

JERSEY CITY, NJ, *May 8–May 9*

STAMFORD, CT, *May 8–May 9*

CHICAGO, IL, *May 9*

COLUMBIA, SC, *May 9*

PATERSON, NJ, *May 10*

JERSEY CITY, NJ, *May 11*

DETROIT, MI, *May 13*

LANSING, MI, *May 14*

MIAMI, FL, *May 14*

NEW HAVEN, CT, *May 14*

NEW BEDFORD, MA, *May 15*

DOVER, DE, *May 16*

NEW BEDFORD, MA, *May 16*

MEMPHIS, TN, *May 17*

WASHINGTON, DC, *May 17*

DOVER, DE, *May 17–May 20*

SALISBURY, MD, *May 18–May 20*

NEW BEDFORD, MA, *May 19–May 20*

PATERSON, NJ, *May 20*

TAMPA, FL, *May 20*

NEW YORK, NY, *May 21–May 24*

ST. PETERSBURG, FL, *May 22*

WILKINSBURG, PA, *May 23–May 24*

BATTLE CREEK, MI, *May 25*

WASHINGTON, DC, *May 25*

WILKINSBURG, PA, *May 27*

LOUISVILLE, KY, *May 27–May 31*

ANN ARBOR, MI, *May 29*

WASHINGTON, DC, *May 29*

JEFFERSON CITY, MO, *May 30–May 31*

ANN ARBOR, MI, *May 31*

NATCHEZ, MS, *June 1–June 2*

MILWAUKEE, WI, *June 3–June 4*

NEW YORK, NY, *June 4–June 5*

FLINT, MI, *June 5*

MOBILE, AL, *June 6*

PITTSBURGH, PA, *June 6*

FRANKLIN, TN, *June 8*

CAMDEN, NJ, *June 13*

PITTSBURGH, PA, *June 16*

WASHINGTON, DC, *June 16*

WASHINGTON, DC, *June 18–June 21*

*LYNDON JOHNSON SIGNS OMNIBUS
    CRIME CONTROL AND SAFE STREETS
    ACT OF 1968, June 19*

BALTIMORE, MD, *June 19*

SOUTH BEND, IN, *June 19*

DENVER, CO, *June 22*

ZONETON, KY, *June 23*

RICHMOND, CA, *June 25–June 26*

SEATTLE, WA, *July 1*

PATERSON, NJ, *July 1–July 5*

MINNEAPOLIS, MN, *July 3–July 5*

WASHINGTON, DC, *July 4*

ALEXANDRIA, VA, *July 4–July 5*

MEMPHIS, TN, *July 5*

OMAHA, NE, *July 5–July 8*

WILMINGTON, DE, *July 6*

NEWBURG, KY, *July 7*

KANSAS CITY, MO, *July 10*

NEW YORK, NY, *July 10*

TOPEKA, KS, *July 10–July 11*

YORK, PA, *July 11–July 16*

JEFFERSONVILLE, IN, *July 12*

NEW BEDFORD, MA, *July 13*

BOWLING GREEN, KY, *July 14*

JACKSON, MI, *July 14–July 17*

STOCKTON, CA, *July 17*

PASCO, WA, *July 20*

NEW YORK, NY, *July 20–July 21*

BENTON HARBOR, MI, *July 20–July 23*

NEWARK, NJ, *July 23*

CLEVELAND, OH, *July 23–July 26*

ST. LOUIS, MO, *July 24*

CHICAGO, IL, *July 25–July 26*

WHITEWATER, WI, *July 25–July 26*

MAYWOOD, IL, *July 25–July 27*

SEATTLE, WA, *July 26*

GRAND RAPIDS, MI, *July 26–July 29*

ERIE, PA, *July 27*

MIDLAND, TX, *July 27*

SOMERVILLE, NJ, *July 27*

CLEVELAND, OH, *July 28*

CROWN POINT, IN, *July 28*

GARY, IN, *July 28–July 29*

MOBILE, AL, *July 29*

MUNCIE, IN, *July 29*

KALAMAZOO, MI, *July 29–July 30*

SEATTLE, WA, *July 29–July 31*

DADE CITY, FL, *July 30*

JACKSON, MI, *July 30*

PEORIA, IL, *July 30*

GAINESVILLE, FL, *July 31–August 1*

WEIRTON, WV, *July 31–August 1*

DETROIT, MI, *August 1*

SEASIDE, CA, *August 1*

NEW YORK, NY, *August 1–August 2*

MADISON, WI, *August 3*

YORK, PA, *August 3*

GRAND RAPIDS, MI, *August 4*

TAMPA, FL, *August 4*

MOBILE, AL, *August 4–August 5*

RACINE, WI, *August 4–August 5*

INKSTER, MI, *August 4–August 8*

JACKSON, MI, *August 5*

YORK, PA, *August 5*

LOS ANGELES, CA, *August 5–August 6*

HARVEY-DIXMOOR, IL, *August 5–August 7*

RAHWAY, NJ, *August 6*

CHARLESTON, WV, *August 6–August 7*

RIVERSIDE, CA, *August 6–August 8*

YORK, PA, *August 7*

FORT WAYNE, IN, *August 7–August 9*

MIAMI, FL, *August 7–August 11*

LITTLE ROCK, AR, *August 7–August 12*

SAGINAW, MI, *August 8*

LOS ANGELES, CA, *August 9*

PITTSBURGH, PA, *August 9*

HARTFORD, CT, *August 9–August 10*

NORTH LITTLE ROCK, AR, *August 9–August 11*

HANFORD, CA, *August 11*

PRICHARD, AL, *August 11*

CHICAGO HEIGHTS, IL, *August 11–August 12*

LOS ANGELES, CA, *August 11–August 12*

KANSAS CITY, MO, *August 13–August 14*

LOUISVILLE, KY, *August 14*

ST. PETERSBURG, FL, *August 14*

CENTER MORICHES, NY, *August 15*

KANSAS CITY, MO, *August 15*

PITTSBURGH, PA, *August 15*

WATERLOO, IA, *August 15*

NEWBURG, KY, *August 16*

CINCINNATI, OH, *August 16–August 17*

NEWARK, DE, *August 16–August 17*

OWENSBORO, KY, *August 16–August 21*

PROVIDENCE, RI, *August 17–August 18*

ST. PETERSBURG, FL, *August 17–August 20*

WALTHAM, MA, *August 18*

NEW YORK, NY, *August 19*

PITTSBURGH, PA, *August 20*

PROVIDENCE, RI, *August 20*

SALISBURY, MD, *August 20*

GAINESVILLE, FL, *August 21*

NEW YORK, NY, *August 21*

WICHITA, KS, *August 21–August 23*

BLUE ISLAND, IL, *August 22*

EDGEWATER, NJ, *August 22*

PITTSBURGH, PA, *August 22–August 23*

EVANSVILLE, IN, *August 22–August 24*

BLUE ISLAND, IL, *August 23*

MUSKEGON, MI, *August 24*

YPSILANTI, MI, *August 24*

CHARLESTON, WV, *August 24–August 25*

MEMPHIS, TN, *August 24–August 25*

NEWARK, NJ, *August 25*

NEWARK, NJ, *August 26*

CHICAGO, IL, *August 26–August 29*

NEW YORK, NY, *August 27*

SAINT PAUL, MN, *August 30–September 1*

WILMINGTON, DE, *August 31*

BOSTON, MA, *August 31–September 7*

BEREA, KY, *September 1*

NEWPORT NEWS, VA, *September 1–September 2*

CHARLOTTESVILLE, VA, *September 2–
September 8*

LEXINGTON, KY, *September 4*

ST. LOUIS, MO, *September 4–September 5*

MOBILE, AL, *September 6*

NEW YORK, NY, *September 6*

ZION, IL, *September 6*

BALTIMORE, MD, *September 8*

PADUCAH, KY, *September 8*

ROANOKE, VA, *September 8–September 9*

URBANA, IL, *September 9–September 10*

SUMMIT, IL, *September 10*

WASHINGTON, DC, *September 11*

DENVER, CO, *September 11–September 13*

NEW YORK, NY, *September 11–September 13*

MIAMI, FL, *September 12*

PROVIDENCE, RI, *September 12*

SUMMIT, IL, *September 12*

HOMESTEAD, FL, *September 12–September 13*

CHICAGO, IL, *September 13*

GRAND RAPIDS, MI, *September 13*

OAKLAND, CA, *September 13*

ST. LOUIS, MO, *September 13*

WATERLOO, IA, *September 13*

DECATUR, IL, *September 14*

TOLEDO, OH, *September 14–September 15*

WEIRTON, WV, *September 14–September 15*

TEANECK, NJ, *September 14–September 16*

OAKLAND, CA, *September 15*

RAYNE, LA, *September 15*

ST. LOUIS, MO, *September 15*

WILMINGTON, DE, *September 15*

SAGINAW, MI, *September 15–September 16*

VALLEJO, CA, *September 17*

MAYWOOD, IL, *September 18*

SPRINGFIELD, MA, *September 18*

ST. JOSEPH, MI, *September 18*

ELMIRA, NY, *September 19*

MINNEAPOLIS, MN, *September 19*

ST. LOUIS, MO, *September 19*

WHEELING, WV, *September 19*

BLADENSBURG, MD, *September 20*

ORLANDO, FL, *September 20*

TITUSVILLE, FL, *September 20*

YORK, PA, *September 20–September 24*

PRICHARD, AL, *September 21*

BLADENSBURG, MD, *September 23–*
    September 24

LOUISVILLE, KY, *September 23–September 24*

BOSTON, MA, *September 23–September 27*

MONTCLAIR, NJ, *September 23–October 7*

JERSEY CITY, NJ, *September 24*

WEST PALM BEACH, FL, *September 24*

KALAMAZOO, MI, *September 25–September 26*

TRENTON, NJ, *September 26*

CHICAGO, IL, *September 27*

FLINT, MI, *September 27*

ESSEX, MD, *September 28*

NEW YORK, NY, *September 28*

KANKAKEE, IL, *September 29–September 30*

SARASOTA, FL, *September 29–October 2*

CHICAGO, IL, *September 30*

NEW YORK, NY, *October 1*

ZION, IL, *October 2*

SACRAMENTO, CA, *October 2–October 3*

NEW YORK, NY, *October 4*

HAYWARD, CA, *October 7*

SUMMIT, IL, *October 8*

PITTSBURGH, PA, *October 8–October 9*

WASHINGTON, DC, *October 8–October 9*

ATHERTON, CA, *October 9*

NEW YORK, NY, *October 9*

SAN FRANCISCO, CA, *October 11*

ST. LOUIS, MO, *October 11*

ANNAPOLIS, MD, *October 12*

CHICAGO, IL, *October 12–October 13*

NEW YORK, NY, *October 13*

WASHINGTON, DC, *October 13–October 16*

BOSTON, MA, *October 16*

MOUNT VERNON, IA, *October 17*

JACKSON, TN, *October 18*

NEW YORK, NY, *October 18*

SAN FRANCISCO, CA, *October 18*

TRENTON, NJ, *October 18*

LOUISVILLE, KY, *October 21*

HAZARD, KY, *October 22*

NEWARK, NJ, *October 22*

BLUE ISLAND, IL, *October 23*

BOSTON, MA, *October 23*

SAN FRANCISCO, CA, *October 25*

MIAMI, FL, *October 27*

WILMINGTON, DE, *October 29*

HOPKINSVILLE, KY, *October 30*

WASHINGTON, DC, *October 30*

DETROIT, MI, *November 2*

WASHINGTON, DC, *November 2*

CHICAGO, IL, *November 4*

NORTHRIDGE, CA, *November 4*

SAN FERNANDO, CA, *November 4*

WASHINGTON, DC, *November 4*

NEW YORK, NY, *November 6*

SAN FRANCISCO, CA, *November 6–November 8*

BLUEFIELD, WV, *November 7–November 9*

ROXBURY, MA, *November 12*

BLUEFIELD, WV, *November 15*

MARION, IN, *November 15*

OAKLAND, CA, *November 15*

ST. LOUIS, MO, *November 16*

MEMPHIS, TN, *November 18*

SAN FRANCISCO, CA, *November 19*

MERIDEN, CT, *November 20*

MADISON, WI, *November 21*

OSHKOSH, WI, *November 21*

BLUEFIELD, WV, *November 21–November 22*

SAN FRANCISCO, CA, *November 21–*
    November 22

CHICAGO, IL, *November 22*

SAN JOSÉ, CA, *November 26*

JERSEY CITY, NJ, *November 29*

NEW YORK, NY, *November 29*

NEWARK, NJ, *December 1*

NEW YORK, NY, *December 2–December 4*

SAN FRANCISCO, CA, *December 2–December 5*

BOSTON, MA, *December 3*

NORTHRIDGE, CA, *December 4*

ROXBURY, MA, *December 5*

MADISON, WI, *December 6*

NEW YORK, NY, *December 6*

MORGANTOWN, WV, *December 7*

NORTHRIDGE, CA, *December 8*

SAN FRANCISCO, CA, *December 9*

CHICAGO, IL, *December 10*

LOS ANGELES, CA, *December 10*

WILLIAMSBURG, VA, *December 10–December 12*

SAN FRANCISCO, CA, *December 11–December 13*

ST. LOUIS, MO, *December 12*

DEARBORN HEIGHTS, MI, *December 12–December 13*

LOS ANGELES, CA, *December 12–December 13*

MIAMI, FL, *December 12–December 13*

SAN MATEO, CA, *December 12–December 13*

CHICAGO, IL, *December 13*

NEW HAVEN, CT, *December 13*

CHICAGO, IL, *December 16*

DEARBORN HEIGHTS, MI, *December 16*

GRAND RAPIDS, MI, *December 16–December 17*

SUMTER, SC, *December 16–December 17*

ATHERTON, CA, *December 18*

SYLVESTER, GA, *December 19*

LOS ANGELES, CA, *December 20*

1969: 613 REBELLIONS

ST. LOUIS, MO, *January 4*

NEW YORK, NY, *January 6*

SAN FRANCISCO, CA, *January 6–January 9*

SYLVESTER, GA, *January 7*

LOS ANGELES, CA, *January 8–January 9*

DENVER, CO, *January 9*

SWARTHMORE, PA, *January 9–January 10*

GREENVILLE, NC, *January 13*

NEW YORK, NY, *January 13*

MINNEAPOLIS, MN, *January 14–January 15*

CHICAGO, IL, *January 15*

NEW YORK, NY, *January 15*

SAN FRANCISCO, CA, *January 15*

SYLVESTER, GA, *January 15*

DENVER, CO, *January 16*

WILBERFORCE, OH, *January 16*

LOS ANGELES, CA, *January 17*

NEW YORK, NY, *January 17*

NEW ORLEANS, LA, *January 20*

SAN FRANCISCO, CA, *January 22–January 24*

HAMDEN, CT, *January 27*

SAN FRANCISCO, CA, *January 27*

MIAMI, FL, *January 30*

DAYTON, OH, *January 31*

BERKELEY, CA, *February 3–February 5*

PROVIDENCE, RI, *February 4*

MIAMI, FL, *February 5*

NEW YORK, NY, *February 5*

GREENSBORO, NC, *February 6–February 7*

COLUMBUS, GA, *February 8*

SYLVESTER, GA, *February 8*

EDWARDSVILLE, IL, *February 10*

BERKELEY, CA, *February 13*

COLUMBIA, SC, *February 13*

DURHAM, NC, *February 13*

NEW YORK, NY, *February 13*

PITTSBURGH, PA, *February 13*

SAN FRANCISCO, CA, *February 13*

SPRINGFIELD, IL, *February 14*

MERIDIAN, MS, *February 15*

NEW YORK, NY, *February 17*

SPRINGFIELD, IL, *February 17*

NEW YORK, NY, *February 18*

CHICAGO, IL, *February 20*

NEW HAVEN, CT, *February 20*

PALO ALTO, CA, *February 20*

SAN FRANCISCO, CA, *February 20*

WORCESTER, MA, *February 20*

FAYETTEVILLE, NC, *February 21*

MIDDLETOWN, CT, *February 21*

ST. LOUIS, MO, *February 21*

ATLANTA, GA, *February 25*

LITTLE ROCK, AR, *February 25*

POMONA, CA, *February 25*

SAN FRANCISCO, CA, *February 25–February 26*

LOS ANGELES, CA, *February 26*

INDIANAPOLIS, IN, *February 27*

NEW YORK, NY, *February 27*

WILMINGTON, NC, *February 27*

SAN FRANCISCO, CA, *March 3*

BOULDER, CO, *March 3*

CHICAGO, IL, *March 3*

CHAPEL HILL, NC, *March 4*

EVANSTON, IL, *March 4*

LOS ANGELES, CA, *March 7*

NEW ORLEANS, LA, *March 7*

LOS ANGELES, CA, *March 10–March 13*

DURHAM, NC, *March 11–March 12*

ATLANTA, GA, *March 12*

HAGERSTOWN, MD, *March 14*

LAWRENCE, KS, *March 14*

PEORIA, IL, *March 15*

CHICAGO HEIGHTS, IL, *March 17*

ROCKFORD, IL, *March 17*

LOS ANGELES, CA, *March 19*

CHICAGO, IL, *March 19–March 21*

DENVER, CO, *March 20*

FORREST CITY, AR, *March 20*

READING, PA, *March 20*

ROCKFORD, IL, *March 20*

DENVER, CO, *March 21*

DeKALB, IL, *March 23*

SUMMIT, IL, *March 25*

ZION, IL, *March 26*

SAN GABRIEL VALLEY, CA, *March 26–March 28*

CHICAGO, IL, *March 27–March 28*

MONTGOMERY, AL, *March 29–March 30*

CAIRO, IL, *March 31*

NEWBURGH, NY, *March 31*

GREENVILLE, NC, *April 1*

CHICAGO, IL, *April 3*

COLUMBUS, PA, *April 3*

MEMPHIS, TN, *April 4*

ANNISTON, AL, *April 5*

WAYCROSS, GA, *April 7*

VIDALIA, GA, *April 8*

NEW ORLEANS, LA, *April 9*

PROVIDENCE, RI, *April 9*

WAYCROSS, GA, *April 9–April 11*

GAINESVILLE, FL, *April 11*

NEW YORK, NY, *April 11*

SAN DIEGO, CA, *April 11*

DES MOINES, IA, *April 14*

RALEIGH, NC, *April 14*

SAN DIEGO, CA, *April 14*

BOSTON, MA, *April 15–April 16*

NEW YORK, NY, *April 16*

MIAMI, FL, *April 16–April 17*

SAN MATEO, CA, *April 16–April 17*

HOMESTEAD, FL, *April 17*

ITHACA, NY, *April 18*

PROVIDENCE, RI, *April 18*

ATLANTA, GA, *April 18–April 19*

SYRACUSE, NY, *April 19*

BALTIMORE, MD, *April 20*

MENLO PARK, CA, *April 20*

OCALA, FL, *April 21*

ST. PETERSBURG, FL, *April 21–April 24*

NEW YORK, NY, *April 22*

YONKERS, NY, *April 22*

CHICAGO, IL, *April 23*

NEWBURGH, NY, *April 23*

NEW YORK, NY, *April 24*

CHICAGO, IL, *April 25*

ROOSEVELT, NY, *April 25*

CHARLESTON, SC, *April 25–April 27*

NORTH LITTLE ROCK, AR, *April 27*

CAIRO, IL, *April 27–April 28*

WINSTON-SALEM, NC, *April 27–April 28*

DENMARK, SC, *April 28*

MEMPHIS, TN, *April 28*

SAN FRANCISCO, CA, *April 28*

BELMONT, NC, *April 29*

PASADENA, CA, *April 30*

FORREST CITY, AR, *May 1*

LOUISVILLE, KY, *May 1*

SAN FRANCISCO, CA, *May 1*

NEW YORK, NY, *May 1–May 2*

NORTH LITTLE ROCK, AR, *May 2*

ZEBULON, GA, *May 2*

CLEVELAND, OH, *May 3*

CHICAGO, IL, *May 5*

ENGLEWOOD, IL, *May 5*

RALEIGH, NC, *May 5–May 7*

LORAIN, OH, *May 6*

NEW BRITAIN, CT, *May 6*

WEST HAVEN, CT, *May 6*

NEW YORK, NY, *May 6–May 8*

BLOOMINGTON, IN, *May 8–May 9*

BATON ROUGE, LA, *May 12–May 13*

CHICAGO, IL, *May 12–May 16*

PROVIDENCE, RI, *May 13*

SPRINGFIELD, MA, *May 13–May 14*

ATLANTA, GA, *May 14*

BURLINGTON, NC, *May 14*

CHATTANOOGA, TN, *May 14*
NEW YORK, NY, *May 14*
CHICAGO, IL, *May 14–May 15*
CLEVELAND, OH, *May 15–May 17*
STEUBENVILLE, OH, *May 16*
BURLINGTON, NC, *May 16–May 18*
WAYCROSS, GA, *May 17–May 18*
GREENSBORO, NC, *May 19*
NEWARK, NJ, *May 19*
CHICAGO, IL, *May 19–May 20*
EUGENE, OR, *May 19–May 20*
LOUISVILLE, KY, *May 20*
PORTLAND, OR, *May 20*
CINCINNATI, OH, *May 20–May 21*
CHICAGO, IL, *May 21*
NEW YORK, NY, *May 21*
PROVIDENCE, RI, *May 21*
NASHVILLE, TN, *May 21–May 22*
GREENSBORO, NC, *May 21–May 23*
NEWBURG, KY, *May 22–May 23*
PITTSBURGH, PA, *May 22–May 23*
NEW ORLEANS, LA, *May 23*
PORTLAND, OR, *May 23*
CHATTANOOGA, TN, *May 24–May 25*
REDDING, CA, *May 26*
WILKINSBURG, PA, *May 26*
CHAMPAIGN, IL, *May 26–May 28*
SAN FERNANDO, CA, *May 28–May 29*
AKRON, OH, *May 29*
BOSTON, MA, *May 29*
LONG BEACH, CA, *May 29*
PALOS HILLS, IL, *May 30*
BLACKSBURG, SC, *May 31*
KANKAKEE, IL, *June 2*
HARTFORD, CT, *June 4*
KANKAKEE, IL, *June 4*
PITTSBURGH, PA, *June 5*
CLEVELAND, OH, *June 5–June 6*
HARTFORD, CT, *June 5–June 6*
INDIANAPOLIS, IN, *June 5–June 6*
ALLIANCE, OH, *June 6–June 7*
BALTIMORE, MD, *June 7*
LOUISVILLE, KY, *June 8*
CLEVELAND, OH, *June 9*
AKRON, OH, *June 12*
CAIRO, IL, *June 12–June 13*

ROXBORO, NC, *June 13*
UTICA, NY, *June 13–June 16*
CHICAGO, IL, *June 15*
SACRAMENTO, CA, *June 15*
CAIRO, IL, *June 15–June 17*
FORREST CITY, AR, *June 17*
MANAYUNK, PA, *June 17*
MADISON, IL, *June 18*
McKEESPORT, PA, *June 19*
PARKESBURG, PA, *June 20*
CHARLESTON, SC, *June 21*
PARKESBURG, PA, *June 22*
VENICE, IL, *June 24*
OMAHA, NE, *June 24–June 26*
CHICAGO, IL, *June 25*
CAIRO, IL, *June 26*
LANCASTER, PA, *June 26*
KOKOMO, IN, *June 26–June 27*
MIDDLETOWN, CT, *June 26–June 30*
BALTIMORE, MD, *June 27*
DORCHESTER, MA, *June 27*
MARION, IN, *June 27*
WATERBURY, CT, *June 28–July 1*
SANTA ANA, CA, *June 29*
FORT WAYNE, IN, *June 30–July 1*
MIDDLETOWN, CT, *June 30–July 1*
MIDDLETOWN, OH, *June 30–July 1*
WICHITA, KS, *June 30–July 1*
MEMPHIS, TN, *July 1*
MIDDLETOWN, NC, *July 4*
MIDDLETOWN, OH, *July 4–July 5*
PHILADELPHIA, PA, *July 5*
TAMPA, FL, *July 5–July 6*
SAN MATEO, CA, *July 6–July 7*
ANDERSON, IN, *July 8*
EVANSVILLE, IN, *July 10–July 12*
TOPEKA, KS, *July 11–July 12*
SAN DIEGO, CA, *July 13–July 15*
MEMPHIS, TN, *July 14*
SACRAMENTO, CA, *July 14*
FORREST CITY, AR, *July 15*
YOUNGSTOWN, OH, *July 15–July 17*
FAYETTEVILLE, NC, *July 16–July 17*
YORK, PA, *July 17–July 22*
JACKSONVILLE, NC, *July 20*
STUART, FL, *July 20–July 23*

FAYETTEVILLE, NC, *July 21*

COLUMBUS, OH, *July 21–July 22*

CHICAGO, IL, *July 22–July 23*

BAKERSFIELD, CA, *July 23*

HARTFORD, CT, *July 23*

LOS ANGELES, CA, *July 24*

BATON ROUGE, LA, *July 26*

PRICHARD, AL, *July 26*

FRESNO, CA, *July 27*

SANFORD, NC, *July 27*

COLORADO SPRINGS, CO, *July 28*

CHICAGO, IL, *July 28–July 29*

MILLINGTON, TN, *July 30*

CHICAGO, IL, *July 31*

BATON ROUGE, LA, *July 31–August 1*

CARVER RANCHES, FL, *August 1*

LANCASTER, PA, *August 2*

CHARLOTTE, NC, *August 3*

JACKSON, KY, *August 3–August 6*

LOUISVILLE, KY, *August 5*

DECATUR, IL, *August 7–August 8*

NEW ORLEANS, LA, *August 8*

KANEOHE, HI, *August 9–August 10*

GASTONIA, NC, *August 10*

BATON ROUGE, LA, *August 11*

FORREST CITY, AR, *August 11*

OXFORD, PA, *August 11*

LITTLE ROCK, AR, *August 11–August 12*

CHICAGO, IL, *August 12*

FREEHOLD TOWNSHIP, NJ, *August 13*

SACRAMENTO, CA, *August 13*

FORREST CITY, AR, *August 14*

ANNAPOLIS, MD, *August 15*

CHARLESTON, SC, *August 15*

COLUMBIA, PA, *August 15*

LINDEN, NJ, *August 15*

CHARLOTTE, NC, *August 16*

DAYTON, OH, *August 16*

BENTON, AR, *August 17*

NIAGARA FALLS, NY, *August 17–August 20*

FLORENCE, SC, *August 18–August 20*

OKLAHOMA CITY, OK, *August 20–August 21*

PLAQUEMINE, LA, *August 25*

PITTSBURGH, PA, *August 25–August 27*

FORREST CITY, AR, *August 26*

SANFORD, NC, *August 26*

HOT SPRINGS, AR, *August 26–August 30*

CAIRO, IL, *August 27*

CHICAGO, IL, *August 27*

NEW IBERIA, LA, *August 27*

LEXINGTON, KY, *August 30*

NEW YORK, NY, *August 30*

FORT LAUDERDALE, FL, *August 31–September 2*

PARKESBURG, PA, *September 1*

HARTFORD, CT, *September 1–September 5*

COATESVILLE, PA, *September 1–September 7*

CHARLOTTE, NC, *September 2*

DAYTON, OH, *September 2*

LA GRANGE, KY, *September 2*

MIAMI, FL, *September 2*

POMPANO BEACH, FL, *September 2–September 3*

BOSTON, MA, *September 3*

PARKESBURG, PA, *September 3*

DANIA, FL, *September 3–September 4*

DENHAM SPRINGS, LA, *September 4*

NEWTOWN, FL, *September 4*

CARBONDALE, IL, *September 6*

SPRINGFIELD, OH, *September 6–September 7*

DENHAM SPRINGS, LA, *September 7*

FORT LAUDERDALE, FL, *September 7*

CHICAGO, IL, *September 8*

SHREVEPORT, LA, *September 8–September 9*

PORTLAND, OR, *September 8–September 11*

NEW YORK, NY, *September 8–September 12*

CAIRO, IL, *September 9*

COLLEGE PARK, GA, *September 9*

GAINESVILLE, FL, *September 9–September 11*

LIDO BEACH, NY, *September 10*

CAIRO, IL, *September 11*

PORTLAND, OR, *September 11*

VERO BEACH, FL, *September 11*

BATON ROUGE, LA, *September 12*

OAKLAND, PA, *September 12*

KANKAKEE, IL, *September 12–September 14*

KOKOMO, IN, *September 12–September 14*

CAIRO, IL, *September 13*

VICTORVILLE, CA, *September 13*

UTICA, NY, *September 14*

ABERDEEN, MD, *September 15*

DAYTON, OH, *September 15*

HAYWARD, CA, *September 15*

KANSAS CITY, MO, *September 15*
WINSTON-SALEM, NC, *September 15*
BOSTON, MA, *September 15–September 18*
HOLLYWOOD, FL, *September 15–September 18*
CAIRO, IL, *September 16*
JACKSONVILLE, FL, *September 16*
PITTSBURGH, PA, *September 16*
KANKAKEE, IL, *September 16–September 17*
UNION, SC, *September 16–September 17*
BOSTON, MA, *September 17*
CHATTANOOGA, TN, *September 17*
HARRISBURG, PA, *September 17*
PEORIA, IL, *September 17*
WILMINGTON, DE, *September 17*
URBANA, IL, *September 17–September 18*
ALLEGHENY, PA, *September 18*
BLADENSBURG, MD, *September 18*
CHICAGO, IL, *September 18*
FORREST CITY, AR, *September 18*
NEPTUNE BEACH, FL, *September 18*
PITTSBURGH, PA, *September 18*
BOWIE, MD, *September 18*
SAN FRANCISCO, CA, *September 18–September 19*
WILMINGTON, DE, *September 19*
HOMESTEAD, FL, *September 20*
MULLINS, SC, *September 20–September 21*
RIVERSIDE, CA, *September 20–September 21*
EVANSVILLE, IN, *September 21*
DETROIT, MI, *September 21–September 23*
EUNICE, LA, *September 22*
CHAPEL HILL, NC, *September 22–September 23*
WILMINGTON, DE, *September 22–September 23*
CHICAGO, IL, *September 22–September 26*
RIVERSIDE, CA, *September 23*
SEATTLE, WA, *September 23*
PITTSBURGH, PA, *September 23–September 24*
NEW CASTLE, DE, *September 23–September 25*
SALISBURY, NC, *September 24*
WILMINGTON, DE, *September 24*
CARVER RANCHES, FL, *September 25*
CEDAR RAPIDS, IA, *September 25*
GREENVILLE, SC, *September 25*
ELKHART, IN, *September 25–September 26*
HOLLYWOOD, FL, *September 25–September 26*

PEMBROKE PARK, FL, *September 25–September 26*
GARY, IN, *September 26*
INDIANAPOLIS, IN, *September 26*
LITTLE ROCK, AR, *September 26*
NEW CASTLE, PA, *September 26*
TOPEKA, KS, *September 26–September 27*
CAROL CITY, FL, *September 27*
LAWRENCE, NY, *September 27*
PROVIDENCE, RI, *September 27*
HAMMOND, IN, *September 29*
MIAMI, FL, *September 29*
ASHEVILLE, NC, *September 29–September 30*
ZEBULON, GA, *September 29–September 30*
NEW YORK, NY, *September 30*
RIVERSIDE, CA, *September 30*
SAN DIEGO, CA, *September 30*
DAYTON, OH, *September 30–October 1*
PEORIA, IL, *September 30–October 2*
DENVER, CO, *October 1*
NEWBERRY, SC, *October 1*
BOSTON, MA, *October 1–October 2*
FREEPORT, NY, *October 2*
SAN BERNARDINO, CA, *October 2*
SAN BERNARDINO COUNTY, CA, *October 2*
SANFORD, NC, *October 2*
TEXARKANA, AR, *October 2*
WICHITA, KS, *October 2*
CHICAGO, IL, *October 2–October 3*
SAN FERNANDO, CA, *October 2–October 3*
CAMBRIDGE, MA, *October 3*
COATESVILLE, PA, *October 3*
GOSHEN, IN, *October 3*
SAN DIEGO, CA, *October 3*
SOUTH BEND, IN, *October 3*
CHICAGO HEIGHTS, IL, *October 3–October 4*
LOS ANGELES, CA, *October 3–October 4*
TREASURE ISLAND, CA, *October 3–October 5*
ALEXANDRIA, VA, *October 4*
CHICAGO, IL, *October 4–October 5*
EDWARDSVILLE, IL, *October 5*
LAS VEGAS, NV, *October 5–October 8*
PEORIA, IL, *October 6*
PHILADELPHIA, PA, *October 6*
PITTSBURG, KS, *October 6*
CHICAGO, IL, *October 6–October 7*

SANFORD, NC, *October 6–October 7*

ROCKY MOUNT, NC, *October 6–October 8*

LAS VEGAS, NV, *October 6–October 9*

ALTON, IL, *October 7*

CHICAGO, IL, *October 7*

LAS VEGAS, NV, *October 7*

ST. LOUIS, MO, *October 7*

GALESBURG, IL, *October 7–October 8*

ECORSE, MI, *October 8*

SPRINGFIELD, MA, *October 8*

ERIE, PA, *October 9*

FORT PIERCE, FL, *October 9*

LYMAN, MS, *October 9*

MEMPHIS, TN, *October 9*

SAN FRANCISCO, CA, *October 9*

SANFORD, NC, *October 9*

STORRS, CT, *October 9*

SOUTH BEND, IN, *October 9–October 10*

CHATTANOOGA, TN, *October 10*

CHICAGO, IL, *October 10*

FORT LAUDERDALE, FL, *October 10*

FORT PIERCE, FL, *October 10*

LAS VEGAS, NV, *October 10*

LOS ANGELES, CA, *October 10*

NORTH MANCHESTER, IN, *October 10*

MUNCIE, IN, *October 10*

PROVIDENCE, RI, *October 10*

SAN BERNARDINO, CA, *October 10*

BOSTON, MA, *October 10–October 11*

PORTLAND, OR, *October 11*

ROCHESTER, PA, *October 11*

SANTA ROSA, CA, *October 11–October 12*

FORT DIX, NJ, *October 12*

FORT KNOX, KY, *October 12*

PACOIMA, CA, *October 12*

SANFORD, NC, *October 12–October 13*

HOLLYWOOD, FL, *October 13*

NEW HAVEN, CT, *October 13*

ROCHESTER, PA, *October 13*

ST. LOUIS, MO, *October 13*

PITTSBURGH, PA, *October 13–October 14*

CHICAGO, IL, *October 13–October 15*

ALEXANDRIA, VA, *October 14*

MEMPHIS, TN, *October 14*

CHICAGO, IL, *October 14–October 15*

FORT PIERCE, FL, *October 14–October 15*

SAN BERNARDINO, CA, *October 14–October 15*

LAWRENCE, NY, *October 15*

NEWBERRY, SC, *October 15*

SAN FRANCISCO, CA, *October 15*

WASHINGTON, DC, *October 15*

WILMINGTON, DE, *October 15*

PITTSBURGH, PA, *October 15–October 16*

SPRINGFIELD, MA, *October 15–October 16*

COATESVILLE, PA, *October 16*

MUNCIE, IN, *October 16*

ARLINGTON, TX, *October 17*

GOLDSBORO, NC, *October 17*

ST. LOUIS, MO, *October 17*

ALEXANDRIA, VA, *October 17–October 20*

DALLAS, TX, *October 18*

TEXARKANA, AR, *October 18*

NEW BRITAIN, CT, *October 20*

OZONE PARK, NY, *October 20*

WASHINGTON, DC, *October 20*

WINSTON-SALEM, NC, *October 20*

CLEVELAND, OH, *October 21*

WINSTON-SALEM, NC, *October 21*

OZONE PARK, NY, *October 22*

PROVIDENCE, RI, *October 22*

SUFFOLK, VA, *October 22*

SUFFOLK, NY, *October 23*

BLUE ISLAND, IL, *October 23–October 24*

NEW YORK, NY, *October 23–October 24*

GREENVILLE, NC, *October 24*

OZONE PARK, NY, *October 24*

CAROL CITY, FL, *October 26*

BELLPORT, NY, *October 27*

GREENVILLE, NC, *October 27*

CLEVELAND, OH, *October 28*

HAMMOND, IN, *October 28*

NEW YORK, NY, *October 29*

CHICAGO, IL, *October 29–October 31*

ABINGTON, PA, *October 30*

CHICAGO, IL, *October 30*

MARKHAM, IL, *October 30*

MIDLOTHIAN, IL, *October 30*

PHILADELPHIA, PA, *October 30*

ANNISTON, AL, *October 30–October 31*

PEORIA, IL, *October 30–October 31*

MARKHAM, IL, *October 31*

NEW YORK, NY, *October 31*

JACKSONVILLE, FL, *October 31–November 1*

CHARLESTON, WV, *November 3*

CHICAGO, IL, *November 3*

DUBUQUE, IA, *November 3*

TALLADEGA, AL, *November 3–November 6*

SPRINGFIELD, MA, *November 4–November 5*

CHICAGO, IL, *November 5*

LARGO, MD, *November 5*

MEDFORD, MA, *November 5*

NEW YORK, NY, *November 5*

PENDLETON, IN, *November 5*

TULSA, OK, *November 5*

NEW IBERIA, LA, *November 5–November 7*

MEMPHIS, TN, *November 6*

NEW YORK, NY, *November 6*

ST. LOUIS, MO, *November 6*

TULSA, OK, *November 6–November 7*

NEW IBERIA, LA, *November 7*

SPRINGFIELD, MA, *November 7*

GREENVILLE, NC, *November 8*

SAN BERNARDINO, CA, *November 9– November 15*

ERIE, PA, *November 10*

MEMPHIS, TN, *November 10–November 11*

CHAPEL HILL, NC, *November 11*

ALBANY, NY, *November 12*

CAMBRIDGE, MA, *November 12*

NEW YORK, NY, *November 12*

CHICAGO, IL, *November 13*

MEMPHIS, TN, *November 13*

MIAMI, FL, *November 13*

ST. LOUIS, MO, *November 13–November 14*

FREEPORT, IL, *November 14*

HYATTSVILLE, MD, *November 15*

SOMERVILLE, TN, *November 15*

CHICAGO, IL, *November 17*

SAN BERNARDINO, CA, *November 18*

SPRINGFIELD, MA, *November 18–November 19*

MILWAUKEE, WI, *November 18–November 21*

CAMBRIDGE, MA, *November 19*

LOS ANGELES, CA, *November 19*

DETROIT, MI, *November 20*

MEMPHIS, TN, *November 20*

STILLWATER, OK, *November 20*

CHATTANOOGA, TN, *November 21*

HARVEY, IL, *November 21*

LAS VEGAS, NV, *November 24*

MILWAUKEE, WI, *November 25*

NEW YORK, NY, *November 25*

SANDERSVILLE, GA, *November 26*

SEATTLE, WA, *November 26*

PHILADELPHIA, PA, *November 27*

JACKSON, MI, *November 28–December 1*

WILDWOOD, FL, *November 30*

CHAPEL HILL, NC, *December 1*

PHILADELPHIA, PA, *December 1–December 2*

GOLDSBORO, NC, *December 2–December 3*

MOBILE, AL, *December 3*

SANDERSVILLE, GA, *December 3*

CHICAGO, IL, *December 4*

JACKSON, MI, *December 4*

SPRINGFIELD, MA, *December 4–December 5*

CAMBRIDGE, MA, *December 5*

CHICAGO, IL, *December 5*

CAIRO, IL, *December 6*

SOUTH BEND, IN, *December 6*

DOUGLAS, GA, *December 7*

NEW YORK, NY, *December 7*

FORT VALLEY, GA, *December 8–December 9*

NEW YORK, NY, *December 9*

AKRON, OH, *December 10*

FORT VALLEY, GA, *December 10*

CAMBRIDGE, MA, *December 11*

LOS ANGELES, CA, *December 11*

BLUE ISLAND, IL, *December 12*

CHICAGO, IL, *December 12*

CLEVELAND, OH, *December 12*

JACKSONVILLE, AR, *December 12*

SHREVEPORT, LA, *December 12*

SPRINGFIELD, MA, *December 12*

CHAMPAIGN, IL, *December 13*

WAKE FOREST, NC, *December 13*

SHREVEPORT, LA, *December 14*

MAYWOOD, IL, *December 15*

PLATTSBURGH, NY, *December 15*

CHICAGO, IL, *December 15–December 16*

WHITEWATER, WI, *December 15–December 16*

McKEESPORT, PA, *December 16*

MADISON, MO, *December 17*

MARQUETTE, MI, *December 18*

PHILADELPHIA, PA, *December 18*

ROXBOROUGH, PA, *December 18*

SHELBY, NC, *December 23*

SANDERSVILLE, GA, *December 27*

NEW YORK, NY, *December 28*

1970: 632 REBELLIONS

SELMA, AL, *January 3–January 5*

MONTGOMERY, AL, *January 4–January 5*

NEWARK, NJ, *January 8*

TUCSON, AZ, *January 8*

EWING TOWNSHIP, NJ, *January 9*

RICHTON, MS, *January 10*

ALBANY, NY, *January 12*

GLENN DALE, MD, *January 12*

NEW HAVEN, CT, *January 12*

SUITLAND, MD, *January 12*

PITTSBURGH, PA, *January 15*

SAN DIEGO, CA, *January 15*

PINE BLUFF, AR, *January 15–January 16*

BELLPORT, NY, *January 16*

CHICAGO, IL, *January 16*

ROSELLE, NJ, *January 16*

THIBODAUX, LA, *January 16*

PITTSBURGH, PA, *January 17*

GREENWICH, CT, *January 19*

THIBODAUX, LA, *January 19*

BOSTON, MA, *January 19–January 20*

GAINESVILLE, FL, *January 20*

PHOENIX, AZ, *January 20*

SPRINGFIELD, MA, *January 22*

LOUISVILLE, KY, *January 26*

NEW YORK, NY, *January 26*

WEST POINT, MS, *January 26*

SANTA ANA, CA, *January 27–January 29*

TULSA, OK, *January 27–January 29*

GAINESVILLE, FL, *January 29*

ROYAL OAK, MI, *January 30*

LACKAWANNA, NY, *January 31*

SEATTLE, WA, *January 31*

YORK, PA, *January 31*

CAIRO, IL, *January 31–February 1*

LEWISBURG, PA, *February 1*

LACKAWANNA, NY, *February 2*

PLAINFIELD, NJ, *February 2–February 3*

BRADENTON, FL, *February 3–February 5*

GREENWOOD, MS, *February 4*

FORT COLLINS, CO, *February 5*

CHICAGO, IL, *February 6*

NORFOLK, VA, *February 6*

WASHINGTON, DC, *February 6*

CLEVELAND, OH, *February 6–February 7*

COLUMBUS, OH, *February 7*

JACKSONVILLE, MS, *February 7*

WHITEWATER, WI, *February 7*

NEW ORLEANS, LA, *February 7–February 13*

NEW BRITAIN, CT, *February 9*

PANAMA CITY, FL, *February 9*

BERKELEY, MO, *February 9–February 10*

ALGIERS, LA, *February 9–February 13*

MABEN, MS, *February 10*

WASHINGTON, DC, *February 10*

CAMP PENDLETON, CA, *February 11*

LIMA, OH, *February 11*

ORLANDO, FL, *February 11*

PANAMA CITY, FL, *February 11*

ANNAPOLIS, MD, *February 12*

BALTIMORE, MD, *February 12*

ST. LOUIS, MO, *February 12*

BERKELEY, MO, *February 12*

WASHINGTON, DC, *February 12*

ST. LOUIS, MO, *February 12–February 14*

CLEVELAND, OH, *February 13*

JACKSONVILLE, FL, *February 13*

LAS VEGAS, NV, *February 13*

LEONARDTOWN, MD, *February 13*

MIDDLETOWN, OH, *February 13*

ALLENTOWN, NJ, *February 15*

DES MOINES, IA, *February 16*

LAS VEGAS, NV, *February 16*

RAHWAY, NJ, *February 16*

BALTIMORE, MD, *February 16–February 17*

ANNAPOLIS, MD, *February 17*

WASHINGTON, DC, *February 17–February 18*

AMHERST, MA, *February 18*

BRISTOL, PA, *February 18*

LINDEN, NJ, *February 18*

MEMPHIS, TN, *February 18*

COVINGTON, KY, *February 19*

PITTSBURGH, PA, *February 19*

CAMP PENDLETON, CA, *February 20*

LINDEN, NJ, *February 20*

UNIVERSITY CITY, MO, *February 20*

CARTERET, NJ, *February 21*

DETROIT, MI, *February 21*

NEW YORK, NY, *February 21*

ST. LOUIS, MO, *February 21*

HIGH SPRINGS, FL, *February 22*

ITHACA, NY, *February 22*

ALACHUA, FL, *February 23*

CHATTANOOGA, TN, *February 23*

GRAND RAPIDS, MI, *February 24*

INGLEWOOD, CA, *February 24*

ST. LOUIS, MO, *February 24*

CARTERET, NJ, *February 24–February 25*

NORTH COLLEGE HILL, OH, *February 25*

OXFORD, MS, *February 25*

DETROIT, MI, *February 26*

HYATTSVILLE, MD, *February 26*

NORTH COLLEGE HILL, OH, *February 26*

RIVER ROUGE, MI, *February 26*

ST. LOUIS, MO, *February 26*

ALBUQUERQUE, NM, *February 27*

ALLENTOWN, NJ, *February 27*

AMHERST, MA, *February 27*

HARLEYVILLE, SC, *February 27*

SOUTH HADLEY, MA, *February 27*

AKRON, OH, *February 28*

ALLENTOWN, NJ, *March 2*

CLEVELAND, OH, *March 2*

EWING, NJ, *March 2*

LAMAR, SC, *March 2*

NEW YORK, NY, *March 2–March 3*

ST. LOUIS, MO, *March 4*

COLUMBUS, OH, *March 4–March 5*

BUFFALO, NY, *March 5*

GAINESVILLE, FL, *March 5*

HEMPSTEAD, NY, *March 5*

LAS VEGAS, NV, *March 5*

SEATTLE, WA, *March 5*

CHARLESTON, WV, *March 6*

NEW YORK, NY, *March 6*

PITTSBURGH, PA, *March 6*

CINCINNATI, OH, *March 7*

DETROIT, MI, *March 8–March 9*

BEL AIR, MD, *March 9*

CAMBRIDGE, MD, *March 9*

PLAQUEMINE, LA, *March 9*

CHICAGO, IL, *March 9–March 10*

KANSAS CITY, MO, *March 9–March 11*

ATLANTA, GA, *March 10*

CHICAGO, IL, *March 10*

PERTH AMBOY, NJ, *March 10*

ROCHESTER, NY, *March 10–March 11*

SPRINGFIELD, MA, *March 10–March 12*

CAMBRIDGE, MD, *March 11*

DETROIT, MI, *March 11*

EL DORADO, AR, *March 11*

GAINESVILLE, FL, *March 11*

PITTSBURGH, PA, *March 11*

SEATTLE, WA, *March 11*

BUFFALO, NY, *March 12*

NEW YORK, NY, *March 12–March 13*

CAMDEN, NJ, *March 13*

COLUMBUS, OH, *March 13*

JACKSONVILLE, FL, *March 13*

SAN FRANCISCO, CA, *March 13*

STAMFORD, CT, *March 13*

CARTHAGE, MS, *March 14*

HARTFORD, CT, *March 14*

INDIANAPOLIS, IN, *March 14*

CINCINNATI, OH, *March 16*

ST. LOUIS, MO, *March 16*

CLEVELAND, OH, *March 17*

PITTSBURGH, PA, *March 17*

VENICE, CA, *March 18*

BOSTON, MA, *March 18–March 21*

AUSTIN, TX, *March 19*

HARTFORD, CT, *March 19*

INDIANAPOLIS, IN, *March 19–March 20*

KANSAS CITY, MO, *March 19–March 20*

OKLAHOMA CITY, OK, *March 20*

OMAHA, NE, *March 20*

PHOENIX, AZ, *March 20*

HYATTSVILLE, MD, *March 21*

NEW YORK, NY, *March 22*

ANN ARBOR, MI, *March 23*

MIAMI, FL, *March 23*

ST. LOUIS, MO, *March 23*

CAMDEN, NJ, *March 24*

KANSAS CITY, MO, *March 24*

PITTSBURGH, PA, *March 24*

MIDDLETOWN, CT, *March 24–March 25*

MARLBORO, NJ, *March 25*

ANN ARBOR, MI, *March 25–March 26*

BEAVER, PA, *March 26*

GAINESVILLE, FL, *March 26*

CLEVELAND, OH, *March 26–March 27*

NEW YORK, NY, *March 28*

WEST HAVEN, CT, *March 29*

BEAVER, PA, *March 31*

SAN FRANCISCO, CA, *March 31*

ITHACA, NY, *April 1*

GAINESVILLE, FL, *April 2*

ATLANTA, GA, *April 3*

CLEARWATER, FL, *April 3*

YORK, PA, *April 3*

GAINESVILLE, FL, *April 3–April 4*

HAMILTON, OH, *April 3–April 4*

NEWTON, GA, *April 3–April 6*

NEW YORK, NY, *April 4*

SAN PEDRO, CA, *April 5*

CAMBRIDGE, MA, *April 6*

CLEVELAND, OH, *April 6*

OCALA, FL, *April 6*

SPRINGFIELD, MA, *April 6*

ELIZABETH, NJ, *April 6–April 7*

PHOENIX, AZ, *April 6–April 9*

ATLANTA, GA, *April 7*

HAMMOND, IN, *April 7*

ITHACA, NY, *April 7*

OCALA, FL, *April 7*

ABINGTON, PA, *April 8*

AMES, IA, *April 8*

DETROIT, MI, *April 8*

KANSAS CITY, MO, *April 8*

NEW YORK, NY, *April 8*

PHILADELPHIA, PA, *April 8*

PITTSBURGH, PA, *April 8*

SPRINGFIELD, MA, *April 8*

FRANKLIN, NJ, *April 9*

MIAMI, FL, *April 9*

WASHINGTON, DC, *April 9*

CAMBRIDGE, MA, *April 9–April 10*

KANSAS CITY, MO, *April 10*

LINDEN, NJ, *April 10*

WHITE PLAINS, NY, *April 10*

BEACON, NY, *April 10–April 13*

DES MOINES, IA, *April 10–April 16*

LAWRENCE, KS, *April 11*

NEW ORLEANS, LA, *April 11*

OMAHA, NE, *April 11*

ATHENS, GA, *April 13*

CORAL GABLES, FL, *April 13*

DETROIT, MI, *April 13*

LAWRENCE, KS, *April 13*

LOS ANGELES, CA, *April 13*

NEW YORK, NY, *April 13*

CHATTANOOGA, TN, *April 13–April 15*

SUFFOLK, VA, *April 13–April 16*

ATLANTIC CITY, NJ, *April 14*

BOSTON, MA, *April 14*

HOUSTON, TX, *April 14*

KANSAS CITY, MO, *April 14*

ST. LOUIS, MO, *April 14*

ATLANTA, GA, *April 14–April 15*

CULPEPER, VA, *April 15*

FRANKLIN, NJ, *April 15*

JACKSONVILLE, FL, *April 15*

LAWRENCE, KS, *April 15*

MIAMI, FL, *April 15*

NEW YORK, NY, *April 15*

DETROIT, MI, *April 15–April 16*

PROVIDENCE, RI, *April 15–April 16*

SANDUSKY, OH, *April 15–April 16*

HARRISBURG, PA, *April 16*

HARTFORD, CT, *April 16*

KANSAS CITY, MO, *April 16*

SANTA BARBARA, CA, *April 16*

BEDFORD, VA, *April 17*

HARRISBURG, PA, *April 17*

ATLANTIC CITY, NJ, *April 17–April 18*

EVANSTON, IL, *April 17–April 19*

ST. LOUIS, MO, *April 18*

SEATTLE, WA, *April 19*

STORRS, CT, *April 19*

BIRMINGHAM, AL, *April 20*

COVINGTON, LA, *April 20*

EVANSTON, IL, *April 20*

KANSAS CITY ,MO, *April 20*

LAKELAND, FL, *April 20*

ATLANTIC CITY, NJ, *April 20–April 21*

LAWRENCE, KS, *April 20*

LITTLE ROCK, AR, *April 21*

NEW YORK, NY, *April 21*

RICHMOND, VA, *April 21*

STATE COLLEGE, PA, *April 21*

CHATTANOOGA, TN, *April 22*

NEW YORK, NY, *April 22*

LAWRENCE, KS, *April 22–April 23*

CHICAGO, IL, *April 23*

EUGENE, OR, *April 23*

TERRE HAUTE, IN, *April 23*

HARVEY, IL, *April 24*

NEW YORK, NY, *April 24*

PALO ALTO, CA, *April 24*

PENNS GROVE, NJ, *April 24*

PEORIA, IL, *April 24*

PHILADELPHIA ,PA, *April 24*

UNION CITY, NJ, *April 24*

BATON ROUGE, LA, *April 26*

HARVEY, IL, *April 27*

NEW YORK, NY, *April 27*

DETROIT, MI, *April 27–April 29*

BERKELEY, CA, *April 28*

CHATTANOOGA, TN, *April 28*

PHILADELPHIA, PA, *April 28*

CHAMPAIGN, IL, *April 29*

HARVEY, IL, *April 29*

COLUMBUS, OH, *April 29–April 30*

BOGALUSA, LA, *April 30*

FERNDALE, MI, *April 30*

MARKHAM, IL, *April 30*

URBANA, IL, *April 30*

CHAMPAIGN, IL, *April 30–May 1*

ROYAL OAK, MI, *May 1*

GREAT LAKES, IL, *May 2*

CHICAGO, IL, *May 4*

KALAMAZOO, MI, *May 4*

NEW YORK, NY, *May 4*

ST. LOUIS, MO, *May 4*

COLUMBUS, OH, *May 4–May 6*

BEAVER FALLS, PA, *May 5*

BROCKPORT, NY, *May 5*

MIAMI, FL, *May 5*

SACRAMENTO, CA, *May 5*

CHAMPAIGN, IL, *May 6*

ITHACA, NY, *May 6*

FORT DODGE, IA, *May 6–May 7*

CLEVELAND, OH, *May 7*

VIVIAN, LA, *May 7*

MIAMI, FL, *May 7–May 8*

HOMESTEAD, FL, *May 7–May 11*

DETROIT, MI, *May 8*

ST. LOUIS, MO, *May 9*

GRAND RAPIDS, MI, *May 9–May 11*

DAYTONA BEACH, FL, *May 11*

ST. LOUIS, MO, *May 11*

TALLAHASSEE, FL, *May 11*

AUGUSTA, GA, *May 11–May 12*

PITTSBURGH, PA, *May 11–May 16*

ONEONTA, NY, *May 12*

EL PASO, TX, *May 12–May 13*

ATHENS, GA, *May 12–May 14*

BALTIMORE, MD, *May 13*

CHICAGO, IL, *May 13*

ONEONTA, NY, *May 13*

SYRACUSE, NY, *May 13*

BLOOMINGTON, IL, *May 13–May 14*

LONG BEACH, CA, *May 13–May 14*

NEW YORK, NY, *May 13–May 14*

ST. LOUIS, MO, *May 14*

JACKSON, MS, *May 14–May 15*

MIDDLETOWN, CT, *May 14–May 15*

BALTIMORE, MD, *May 15*

CARBONDALE, IL, *May 15*

NEW YORK, NY, *May 15*

LAKE PROVIDENCE, LA, *May 16–May 17*

MOBILE, AL, *May 17*

MIAMI, FL, *May 18*

NASHVILLE, TN, *May 18*

NEW YORK, NY, *May 18*

LAS VEGAS, NV, *May 19–May 20*

LINCOLN, NE, *May 19–May 20*

JACKSON, MS, *May 20*

OKLAHOMA CITY, OK, *May 20*

MIAMI, FL, *May 20–May 21*

ROCHESTER, NY, *May 20–May 21*

NORFOLK, VA, *May 20–May 22*

BATTLE CREEK, MI, *May 21*

COLUMBUS, OH, *May 21*

LAS VEGAS, NV, *May 21*

NEW HAVEN, CT, *May 21*

NEW ORLEANS, LA, *May 21*

ROCHESTER, NY, *May 21*

SEATTLE, WA, *May 21*

KALAMAZOO, MI, *May 21–May 22*

ALIQUIPPA, PA, *May 21–May 23*

DETROIT, MI, *May 22*

MONROE, MI, *May 22*

MIAMI, FL, *May 23*

JACKSON, GA, *May 24–May 25*

LANCASTER, PA, *May 24–May 27*

PITTSBURGH, PA, *May 25–May 27*

TEMPE, AZ, *May 25*

VISITACION VALLEY, CA, *May 25–May 28*

COCOA, FL, *May 26–May 27*

TEMPE, AZ, *May 26–May 27*

PHOENIX, AZ, *May 27–May 28*

SPRINGFIELD, MA, *May 28–May 29*

WILKINSBURG, PA, *May 29*

ALEXANDRIA, VA, *May 29–May 30*

CHESTERTON, IN, *May 30*

KANSAS CITY, MO, *May 31*

ALEXANDRIA, VA, *May 31–June 2*

SMITHFIELD, NC, *June 1*

COLUMBUS, OH, *June 4–June 5*

ENGLEWOOD, NJ, *June 5*

BALTIMORE, MD, *June 6*

STARKVILLE, MS, *June 6*

ST. LOUIS, MO, *June 7*

VISALIA, CA, *June 7*

CHICAGO, IL, *June 8*

SEATTLE, WA, *June 9*

FORREST CITY, AR, *June 10*

LANCASTER, PA, *June 10*

ROXBURY, MA, *June 10*

ALIQUIPPA, PA, *June 11*

SAN DIEGO, CA, *June 12–June 14*

WILMINGTON, NC, *June 15*

MIAMI, FL, *June 15–June 18*

CHICAGO, IL, *June 16*

EMERYVILLE, CA, *June 17*

DES MOINES, IA, *June 18*

PITTSBURGH, PA, *June 21*

CHICAGO, IL, *June 22*

CAIRO, IL, *June 24*

BALTIMORE, MD, *June 27*

OMAHA, NE, *July 2*

AKRON, OH, *July 4*

PHILADELPHIA, PA, *July 4*

PALO ALTO, CA, *July 4–July 5*

CHAMPAIGN, IL, *July 5*

PONTIAC, IL, *July 5*

ASBURY PARK, NJ, *July 5–July 9*

SOMERVILLE, NJ, *July 6*

BOSTON, MA, *July 6–July 7*

CHARLESTON, WV, *July 8*

NEW BEDFORD, MA, *July 8–July 13*

MICHIGAN CITY, IN, *July 11–July 12*

HIGHLAND PARK, MI, *July 11–July 13*

MALVERN, AR, *July 12*

ROSTRAVER, PA, *July 13*

PROVIDENCE, RI, *July 15–July 16*

CHATTANOOGA, TN, *July 16*

LAWRENCE, KS, *July 16–July 17*

CHICAGO, IL, *July 17*

KALAMAZOO, MI, *July 17*

AUGUSTA, GA, *July 18*

DETROIT, MI, *July 19*

HAGERSTOWN, MD, *July 19–July 20*

LAWRENCE, KS, *July 20*

NEW YORK, NY, *July 20*

CLEVELAND, OH, *July 21*

FORT WAYNE, IN, *July 22*

LAWRENCE, KS, *July 22*

NEW BRUNSWICK, NJ, *July 22–July 24*

PITTSBURGH, PA, *July 23*

PEORIA, IL, *July 23–July 26*

WEST CHESTER, PA, *July 24–July 28*

NEW YORK, NY, *July 25–July 26*

PITTSBURGH, PA, *July 26*

HOUSTON, TX, *July 26–July 27*

NEW BEDFORD, MA, *July 26–July 30*

JERSEY CITY, NJ, *July 28*

WACO, TX, *July 28*

CROWLEY, LA, *July 29*

OMAHA, NE, *July 29*

WORCESTER, MA, *July 29–July 31*

NEW YORK, NY, *July 30*

OAKLAND, CA, *July 30*

PHOENIX, AZ, *July 30*

STATESVILLE, NC, *July 30*

CHICAGO, IL, *August 1*

ATLANTA, GA, *August 2*

PENSACOLA, FL, *August 2*

LIMA, OH, *August 5–August 6*

PHILADELPHIA, PA, *August 7–August 9*

JERSEY CITY, NJ, *August 8–August 11*

NEW YORK, NY, *August 10–August 12*

AKRON, OH, *August 10–August 14*

CAIRO, IL, *August 12–August 13*

HAGERSTOWN, MD, *August 13*

CHICAGO, IL, *August 13–August 14*

POMPANO BEACH, FL, *August 14–August 16*

FORT LAUDERDALE, FL, *August 15–August 19*

CENTRAL ISLIP, NY, *August 18*

CAMP PENDLETON, CA, *August 25*

CHICAGO, IL, *August 25*

SAN QUENTIN, CA, *August 25–August 26*

NEW HAVEN, CT, *August 27*

ROCKY MOUNT, NC, *August 27*

SAN DIEGO, CA, *August 27*

DOWAGIAC, MI, *August 29*

WASHINGTON, FL, *August 29*

PLYMOUTH TOWNSHIP, PA, *August 30*

TUCSON, AZ, *August 30*

NEW YORK, NY, *August 31*

NORRISTOWN, PA, *September 1–September 2*

SAN FRANCISCO, CA, *September 2*

CHARLOTTE, NC, *September 3*

CHERRY HILL, NJ, *September 3*

DETROIT, MI, *September 7*

EARLE, AR, *September 10*

MOBILE, AL, *September 10–September 11*

BOWLING GREEN, KY, *September 11*

NASHVILLE, TN, *September 11*

PITTSBURGH, PA, *September 11*

BOGALUSA, LA, *September 14*

BOWLING GREEN, KY, *September 14*

MEMPHIS, TN, *September 14*

NEW ORLEANS, LA, *September 14–September 15*

PITTSBURGH, PA, *September 14–September 15*

NEW YORK, NY, *September 14–September 18*

JAMAICA PLAIN, MA, *September 15*

DANVILLE, VA, *September 16*

CHICAGO, IL, *September 16–September 17*

RICHMOND, VA, *September 17*

CAMDEN, AR, *September 18*

GRIFFIN, GA, *September 18*

MARION, IN, *September 18*

TOLEDO, OH, *September 18–September 19*

YANCEYVILLE, NC, *September 18–September 19*

PORTSMOUTH, VA, *September 19*

EAST ST. LOUIS, MO, *September 21*

LAS VEGAS, NV, *September 21*

NEW YORK, NY, *September 21*

PARKIN, AR, *September 21*

PEORIA, IL, *September 21*

WASHINGTON, DC, *September 21–September 22*

RALEIGH, NC, *September 22*

EVANSVILLE, IN, *September 22–September 25*

BOGALUSA, LA, *September 23*

BOURG, LA, *September 23*

LAFOURCHE, LA, *September 23*

ST. LOUIS, MO, *September 23–September 24*

DORCHESTER, MA, *September 24*

HOUSTON, TX, *September 24*

MEMPHIS, TN, *September 24*

PORTSMOUTH, VA, *September 24*

WICHITA, KS, *September 24*

DENVER, CO, *September 24–September 25*

HOUSTON, TX, *September 25*

MATAWAN, NJ, *September 25–September 28*

NEW YORK, NY, *September 27–September 27*

ASBURY PARK, NJ, *September 29*

FLINT, MI, *September 29*

ANN ARBOR, MI, *September 30*

ERIE, PA, *October 1*

PITTSBURGH, PA, *October 1*

TROUTMAN, NC, *October 1–October 2*

NEW YORK, NY, *October 1–October 4*

ANNAPOLIS, MD, *October 2*

BALTIMORE, MD, *October 2*

KALAMAZOO, MI, *October 2*

NEW YORK, NY, *October 2–October 4*

UNION, NJ, *October 3*

NEWARK, NJ, *October 5*

UNION, NJ, *October 5*

PONTIAC, MI, *October 5–October 7*

SOUTH BEND, IN, *October 6–October 7*

ALBION, MI, *October 7*

SAN RAFAEL, CA, *October 8*

SAVANNAH, GA, *October 8*

UNION, NJ, *October 8*

HUNTSVILLE, AL, *October 9–October 12*

MORRISTOWN, TN, *October 10*

PORTSMOUTH, VA, *October 10*

CAIRO, IL, *October 10–October 16*

ST. LOUIS, MO, *October 11*

MALVERNE, NY, *October 12*

ROCHESTER, NY, *October 12*

BATTLE CREEK, MI, *October 12–December 13*

BALTIMORE, MD, *October 13*

HAZARD, KY, *October 14*

COLUMBIA, SC, *October 15*

HUNTSVILLE, AL, *October 15*

ROCKLEDGE, FL, *October 15*

WELLSTON, MO, *October 15*

NEW YORK, NY, *October 15–October 16*

CHICAGO, IL, *October 17*

DENVER, CO, *October 19*

CHICAGO, IL, *October 19–October 23*

TALLADEGA, AL, *October 20*

CAIRO, IL, *October 21*

DALLAS, TX, *October 21*

SOUTHERN PINES, NC, *October 21–October 24*

BIRMINGHAM, AL, *October 22*

SAN FRANCISCO, CA, *October 22*

NORFOLK, VA, *October 22–October 23*

MONROVIA, CA, *October 23*

CAIRO, IL, *October 23–October 24*

KENT, OH, *October 24*

CAIRO, IL, *October 24–October 25*

DETROIT, MI, *October 24–October 25*

PROVIDENCE, RI, *October 25*

BATTLE CREEK, MI, *October 26*

CHICAGO, IL, *October 26*

MONROVIA, CA, *October 26*

MOBILE, AL, *October 27*

DENVER, CO, *October 28*

NEW YORK, NY, *October 28*

CHATTANOOGA, TN, *October 29*

PROVIDENCE, RI, *October 29*

TRENTON, NJ, *October 29*

MONTGOMERY, AL, *October 29–October 30*

FORT WAYNE, IN, *November 2*

ROBBINS, IL, *November 4*

BRIDGEPORT, CT, *November 5*

GREENVILLE, SC, *November 6*

LANSING, MI, *November 6*

ROBBINS, IL, *November 6*

HENDERSON, NC, *November 6–November 8*

DAYTONA BEACH, FL, *November 7–November 8*

KALAMAZOO, MI, *November 9*

MADISON, IL, *November 9*

PITTSBURGH, PA, *November 9*

PARIS, TX, *November 10*

ST. PAUL, MN, *November 10*

LAS VEGAS, NV, *November 11*

SALINAS, CA, *November 11*

BIRMINGHAM, AL, *November 12*

CARBONDALE, IL, *November 12*

CHESTER, SC, *November 12*

EAST ST. LOUIS, IL, *November 12*

BATON ROUGE, LA, *November 13*

WASHINGTON, DC, *November 13*

MEMPHIS, TN, *November 14*

CHICAGO, IL, *November 15*

GREENVILLE, SC, *November 16*

WARRENTON, NC, *November 16*

GREENVILLE, SC, *November 18–November 19*

NEW ORLEANS, LA, *November 19*

CHICAGO, IL, *November 20*

PARIS, TX, *November 20*

GRADY, AR, *November 20–November 22*

CHAPEL HILL, NC, *November 21*

CHICAGO, IL, *November 23*

FLINT, MI, *November 24*

SILER CITY, NC, *November 24*

WINSTON-SALEM, NC, *November 24*

ST. LOUIS, MO, *November 24–November 25*

NEW ORLEANS, LA, *November 26*

ROANOKE, VA, *November 26*

PROVIDENCE, RI, *November 27*

WINSTON-SALEM, NC, *November 27*

SAGINAW, MI, *November 30*

CHICAGO, IL, *November 30–December 4*

UNION, NC, *December 2*

ELDORADO, AR, *December 3*

AIKEN, SC, *December 4*

MOUNT OLIVE, NC, *December 4*

CAIRO, IL, *December 5*

LINDEN, NJ, *December 6*

CHESTER, WV, *December 9*

CHAMBERSBURG, NJ, *December 12*

TEXARKANA, AR, *December 15–December 16*

DENTON, TX, *December 18*

SILVER SPRING, MD, *December 21–December 23*

1971: 319 REBELLIONS

VICKSBURG, MS, *January 2–January 3*

SUMTER, SC, *January 5*

MOUNT CLEMENS, MI, *January 5–January 6*

SUMTER, SC, *January 7*

MIAMI, FL, *January 8*

MIAMI, FL, *January 11*

NEW ORLEANS, LA, *January 11*

CHICAGO, IL, *January 14*

BENTON HARBOR, MI, *January 15*

CHARLESTON, SC, *January 15*

MIAMI, FL, *January 15*

WILMINGTON, NC, *January 15*

CLARKSVILLE, TN, *January 15–January 18*

MEMPHIS, TN, *January 18*

NEW BERN, NC, *January 18*

BRINKLEY, AR, *January 19*

PITTSBURGH, PA, *January 20–January 22*

MURRYSVILLE, PA, *January 22*

NEW ORLEANS, LA, *January 22*

CARSON CITY, NV, *January 23*

ANCHORAGE, AK, *January 23–January 24*

COLUMBIA, SC, *January 25*

HUNTSVILLE, AL, *January 26*

OKLAHOMA CITY, OK, *January 27*

BALTIMORE, MD, *January 31*

PRICHARD, AL, *February 2*

HOUSTON, TX, *February 4–February 5*

OKLAHOMA CITY, OK, *February 4–February 5*

WILMINGTON, NC, *February 4–February 8*

LYNCHBURG, VA, *February 8*

BOSTON, MA, *February 9*

JACKSON, MI, *February 9*

CHESTER, SC, *February 10*

CHICAGO, IL, *February 10*

GREENVILLE, NC, *February 10*

HOUSTON, TX, *February 10*

BALTIMORE, MD, *February 11*

BERKELEY, MO, *February 11*

FORT PIERCE, FL, *February 11*

MOBILE, AL, *February 11*

NEW ORLEANS, LA, *February 11*

PINE BLUFF, AR, *February 11*

ANN ARBOR, MI, *February 11–February 12*

CAMBRIDGE, MA, *February 12*

HOUSTON, TX, *February 12*

PRICHARD, AL, *February 12*

RIDGELAND, SC, *February 13*

SPRINGFIELD, MA, *February 14*

ANN ARBOR, MI, *February 15*

CAIRO, IL, *February 15*

CAMBRIDGE, MA, *February 15*

CAMILLA, GA, *February 15*

CHARLESTON, SC, *February 15*

COCONUT GROVE, FL, *February 15*

NEW ORLEANS, LA, *February 15*

ATLANTA, GA, *February 15*

WILMINGTON, NC, *February 15–February 18*

HOUSTON, TX, *February 16–February 17*

MILWAUKEE, WI, *February 16–February 17*

BALTIMORE, MD, *February 17*

JACKSON, MS, *February 17*

MANATEE, FL, *February 17*

TEXARKANA, TX, *February 17*

CHARLESTON, SC, *February 18*

CHARLOTTE, NC, *February 19*

FERNDALE, MI, *February 19*

FORT PIERCE, FL, *February 19*

NEW YORK, NY, *February 19*

BALTIMORE, MD, *February 20*

COCONUT GROVE, FL, *February 20–February 21*

FORT PIERCE, FL, *February 21*

CHARLOTTE, NC, *February 22*

NEW YORK, NY, *February 22*

NORTH VERSAILLES, PA, *February 22*

ROANOKE, VA, *February 22*

STATEN ISLAND, NY, *February 22*

CAMILLA, GA, *February 23*

CHICAGO, IL, *February 23*

LENOIR, NC, *February 23–February 24*

CHARLOTTE, NC, *February 24*

NEW YORK, NY, *February 24–February 25*

GURDON, AR, *February 25*

RIVIERA BEACH, FL, *February 25*

SELMER, TN, *February 26*

ALIQUIPPA, PA, *February 27*

BALTIMORE, MD, *February 28*

MIAMI, FL, *March 1*

PITTSBURGH, PA, *March 1*

TUSCALOOSA, AL, *March 1*

PRINCESS ANNE, MD, *March 2*

KNOXVILLE, TN, *March 3*

MIAMI, FL, *March 3*

NEW ORLEANS, LA, *March 3*

PITTSBURGH, PA, *March 3*

WHITE PLAINS, NY, *March 3*

FREEPORT, NY, *March 4*

MIAMI, FL, *March 4–March 5*

ARKADELPHIA, AR, *March 8*

COLUMBUS, OH, *March 8*

FREEPORT, NY, *March 8*

ST. LOUIS, MO, *March 8*

FREEPORT, NY, *March 9–March 10*

GREENVILLE, SC, *March 10*

RICHMOND, IN, *March 10*

BOSTON, MA, *March 11*

CHICAGO, IL, *March 11*

BROCKTON, MA, *March 12*

HUMBOLDT, TN, *March 13–March 14*

COLUMBUS, OH, *March 15*

HUMBOLDT, TN, *March 15*

TARRYTOWN, NY, *March 16*

WILMINGTON, NC, *March 16–March 17*

EAST ST. LOUIS, IL, *March 17*

DETROIT, MI, *March 18*

BOSTON, MA, *March 18–March 19*

WEST POINT, GA, *March 19–March 21*

OPA-LOCKA, FL, *March 22–March 24*

HOUSTON, TX, *March 24*

JESSUP, MD, *March 29*

BELZONI, MS, *March 30–April 1*

BALTIMORE, MD, *March 31–April 1*

CHARLOTTE, NC, *March 31–April 1*

COLUMBUS, OH, *April 2*

BROCKTON, MA, *April 2–April 3*

BEDFORD, VA, *April 5*

BROCKTON, MA, *April 5*

SAN FRANCISCO, CA, *April 6*

JACKSONVILLE, FL, *April 9*

JACKSON, MS, *April 13*

MILLEDGEVILLE, GA, *April 13–April 14*

DUQUESNE, PA, *April 15*

GAINESVILLE, FL, *April 15*

NEW ORLEANS, LA, *April 15*

MOSS POINT, MS, *April 15–April 16*

ST. PETERSBURG, FL, *April 16*

MONTICELLO, AR, *April 19*

ROCHESTER, NY, *April 19*

ST. PETERSBURG, FL, *April 19*

DONORA, PA, *April 20–April 21*

MELBOURNE, FL, *April 20–April 22*

SAN FERNANDO, CA, *April 22*

HUNTSVILLE, AL, *April 22–May 1*

NEW ORLEANS, LA, *April 23*

CHICAGO, IL, *April 24*

DUQUESNE, PA, *April 24*

NEW ORLEANS, LA, *April 26–April 27*

DUQUESNE, PA, *April 27*

NEWARK, NJ, *April 27*

NEW YORK, NY, *April 27–April 28*

EL DORADO, AR, *April 28–April 29*

EASTON, PA, *April 30*

NEW YORK, NY, *April 30*

SAPULPA, OK, *April 30*

WASHINGTON, DC, *May 3*

NEW YORK, NY, *May 4*

HAMPTON, VA, *May 4–May 5*

PITTSBURGH, PA, *May 4–May 7*

NEW YORK, NY, *May 5–May 7*

JACKSON, MS, *May 7*

MERIDIAN, MS, *May 7*

OPA-LOCKA, FL, *May 7*

SEATTLE, WA, *May 9*

BALTIMORE, MD, *May 12*

DORCHESTER, SC, *May 12*

CHARLOTTE, NC, *May 14*

NEW YORK, NY, *May 17*

MOSS POINT, MS, *May 18*

BEAVER FALLS, PA, *May 21*

TULLYTOWN, PA, *May 21–May 22*

CHATTANOOGA, TN, *May 21–May 25*

CHICAGO, IL, *May 24–May 26*

COLUMBUS, OH, *May 25*

FAIRFIELD, CA, *May 25*

CHARLOTTE, NC, *May 27*

DREW, MS, *May 27*

PRICHARD, AL, *May 28*

BUFFALO, NY, *May 29*

CAIRO, IL, *May 29*

MOSS POINT, MS, *May 31*

CHARLOTTE, NC, *June 2*

ST. JOSEPH, MO, *June 4*

BALTIMORE, MD, *June 5*

PITTSBURGH, PA, *June 7*

ROCHESTER, NY, *June 7*

BUFFALO, NY, *June 8*

BALTIMORE, MD, *June 9*

EAST PALO ALTO, CA, *June 9*

NEW YORK, NY, *June 9*

BUFFALO, NY, *June 10*

JACKSONVILLE, FL, *June 10–June 19*

NEW YORK, NY, *June 11*

NEWBURGH, NY, *June 11*

NEW YORK, NY, *June 13*

WICHITA FALLS, TX, *June 13*

ALBUQUERQUE, NM, *June 13–June 14*

NEWBURGH, NY, *June 14*

COLUMBUS, GA, *June 16–June 19*

ROCHESTER, NY, *June 17*

COLUMBUS, GA, *June 21*

BUFFALO, NY, *June 22*

MACON, GA, *June 24*

ONLY, TN, *June 24*

MACON, GA, *June 29–July 1*

ROCKVILLE, MD, *July 1*

LOUISVILLE, GA, *July 2*

TARPON SPRINGS, FL, *July 2*

MACON, GA, *July 2–July 3*

TITUSVILLE, FL, *July 4–July 5*

CHATTANOOGA,TN, *July 15*

COLLINSVILLE, IL, *July 16*

ROCHESTER, NY, *July 21–July 22*

AKRON, OH, *July 22–July 23*

MIAMI, FL, *July 25*

NEW ORLEANS, LA, *July 26*

SYRACUSE, NY, *July 30–August 4*

AYDEN, NC, *August 6*

CAMDEN, AL, *August 6*

RIVERSIDE, CA, *August 8*

CHICAGO, IL, *August 9*

SOUTH MIAMI, FL, *August 13*

CHICAGO, IL, *August 14–August 15*

CHICAGO, IL, *August 17–August 18*

JACKSON, MS, *August 18*

ATLANTA, GA, *August 24*

SAN FRANCISCO, CA, *August 26*

PEORIA, IL, *August 28*

ROME, GA, *August 29*

SEATTLE, WA, *September 3*

CHICAGO, IL, *September 4–September 5*

JACKSONVILLE, FL, *September 5–September 7*

NEW YORK, NY, *September 6–September 7*

BALTIMORE, MD, *September 7–September 9*

ALEXANDRIA, VA, *September 8*

PONTIAC, MI, *September 8*

FORT LAUDERDALE, FL, *September 9*

JONESBORO, GA, *September 9*

ATTICA, NY, *September 9–September 13*

NEW ORLEANS, LA, *September 10*

LUBBOCK, TX, *September 10–September 11*

BUTLER, AL, *September 11*

JACKSONVILLE, FL, *September 11*

PASCO, WA, *September 13*

FORT WAYNE, IN, *September 13–September 14*

ROME, GA, *September 14–September 15*

AIKEN, SC, *September 15*

NEWPORT, VA, *September 15*

SEATTLE, WA, *September 15*

ROME, GA, *September 16*

MADISON, AR, *September 17*

OXFORD, PA, *September 18*

NEW YORK, NY, *September 18–September 19*

DALLAS, TX, *September 21*

HAMDEN, CT, *September 22*

PITTSBURGH, PA, *September 23*

ST. PETERSBURG, FL, *September 23*

INGLEWOOD, CA, *September 24*

SPRINGFIELD, MA, *September 24*

PHILADELPHIA, PA, *September 26*

BUFFALO, NY, *September 27*

IRVINGTON, NJ, *September 27*

PISCATAWAY, NJ, *September 27*

TAMPA, FL, *September 27*

INGLEWOOD, CA, *September 28*

GLASSBORO, NJ, *September 28–September 29*

SPRINGFIELD, MA, *September 28–September 29*

MIDDLETOWN, OH, *September 29*

NEW YORK, NY, *September 29*

JACKSONVILLE, FL, *September 29–October 2*

FLORISSANT VALLEY, MO, *September 30*

ROCHESTER, NY, *September 30*

SEATTLE, WA, *September 30*

CAHOKIA, IL, *October 1*

PROVIDENCE, RI, *October 1*

WILMINGTON, NC, *October 1–October 5*

PONTIAC, IL, *October 2*

PROVIDENCE, RI, *October 4*

NORFOLK, VA, *October 5*

NEWARK, NJ, *October 6*

PROVIDENCE, RI, *October 6*

STOCKTON, CA, *October 6*

GENEVA, NY, *October 7*

PERTH AMBOY, NJ, *October 9*

DAYTON, OH, *October 11*

ST. PETERSBURG, FL, *October 12–October 13*

FORT WAYNE, IN, *October 13*

PERTH AMBOY, NJ, *October 13*

NEW BRUNSWICK, NJ, *October 13–October 15*

ABBEVILLE, LA, *October 15*

CHELSEA, MI, *October 17*

FORT WORTH, TX, *October 18*

NEWARK, NJ, *October 18*

SEATTLE, WA, *October 18–October 19*

MEMPHIS, TN, *October 19–October 24*

HILTON, NY, *October 22*

HYDE PARK, NY, *October 22*

ROCHESTER, NY, *October 22*

JOLIET, IL, *October 22–October 23*

ANNISTON, AL, *October 26*

OKLAHOMA CITY, OK, *October 26*

CHARLOTTE, NC, *October 27*

LITTLE ROCK, AR, *October 28*

CHARLOTTE, NC, *October 29*

NEW YORK, NY, *October 29*

UTICA, NY, *November 1*

CHARLOTTE, NC, *November 2*

BALTIMORE, MD, *November 6*

NORFOLK, VA, *November 8–November 9*

PITTSBURGH, PA, *November 11*

WAUKEGAN, IL, *November 12*

FORT McCLELLAN, AL, *November 15*

PITTSBURGH, PA, *November 15*

MILWAUKEE, WI, *November 16*

MONROVIA, CA, *November 18*

RAHWAY, NJ, *November 24–November 25*

ST. LOUIS, MO, *December 2–December 3*

WESTBURY, NY, *December 6*

NEW ORLEANS, LA, *December 8*

PRICHARD, AL, *December 10*

ABBEVILLE, LA, *December 16*

1972: 71 REBELLIONS

BATON ROUGE, LA, *January 10*

NEW YORK, NY, *January 12*

MARIANNA, AR, *January 13*

STOCKTON, CA, *January 18–January 19*

DALLAS, TX, *January 20–January 21*

MARIANNA, AR, *January 23*

GALESVILLE, MD, *January 24*

AUSTIN, TX, *January 27*

HILLSBOROUGH, NC, *February 1*

MARIANNA, AR, *February 7*

KINGS PARK, NY, *February 9*

DONELSON, TN, *February 10*

FARMINGDALE, NY, *February 10*

TRENTON, NJ, *February 12*

LOS ANGELES, CA, *February 13*

CHARLESTON, NC, *February 15*

PINE BLUFF, AR, *February 15*

PORTSMOUTH, VA, *February 16*

STATESVILLE, NC, *February 17*

TRENTON, NC, *February 17*

PORTSMOUTH, VA, *February 19*

LOMPOC, CA, *February 20*

BOSTON, MA, *February 23*

WILMINGTON, NC, *February 25*

EAST ELMHURST, NY, *February 27*

WICHITA, KS, *March 6–March 8*

KEY WEST, FL, *March 7*

BATON ROUGE, LA, *March 10*

HARVEY, IL, *March 10*

HARVEY, IL, *March 15*

GARY, IN, *March 22*

DAYTON, OH, *March 22–March 23*

NEW YORK, NY, *April 1*

STARKE, FL, *April 4*

BALTIMORE, MD, *April 5*

DALLAS, PA, *April 6*

HYATTSVILLE, MD, *April 11*

COBLESKILL, NY, *April 12*

OKLAHOMA CITY, OK, *April 13*

AUSTIN, TX, *April 19*

CHICAGO, IL, *April 19*

NEW BRUNSWICK, NJ, *April 19*

MAXTON, NC, *April 20*

LONG BEACH, CA, *April 23*

NEW BRUNSWICK, NJ, *April 25*

KINGSTREE, SC, *May 4*

NEWARK, NJ, *May 8*

BORDENTOWN, NJ, *May 14*

PORT ST. JOE, FL, *May 16*

ALEXANDRIA, VA, *May 19*

NEW YORK, NY, *May 23*

COLUMBIA, SC, *May 29*

TEHACHAPI, CA, *July 14*

BALTIMORE, MD, *July 17*

HYATTSVILLE, MD, *July 18*

LA GRANGE, KY, *August 6*

DALLAS, TX, *August 23*

OKLAHOMA CITY, OK, *August 30–*
August 31

CHELSEA, MA, *September 6*

FALLS CHURCH, VA, *September 8*

FALLS CHURCH, VA, *September 10*

DEL RIO, TX, *September 15*

NEW ORLEANS, LA, *September 18*

OKLAHOMA CITY, OK, *September 21*

HARVEY, IL, *September 22*

ATLANTA, GA, *September 23*

PEORIA, IL, *October 5*

OKLAHOMA CITY, OK, *October 11*

CHICAGO, IL, *October 16–October 17*

NEW YORK, NY, *October 31*

OKLAHOMA CITY, OK, *November 30*

1980: 1 REBELLION

MIAMI, FL, *May 17–May 20*

1982: 1 REBELLION

MIAMI, FL, *December 28–December 31*

1989: 1 REBELLION

MIAMI, FL, *January 16–January 21*

1992: 1 REBELLION

LOS ANGELES, CA, *April 29–May 4*

2001: 1 REBELLION

CINCINNATI, OH, *April 9–April 13*

NOTES

INTRODUCTION

1. On the sit-in movement in Greensboro and elsewhere, see Clayborne Carson, *In Struggle: SNCC and the Black Awakening of the 1960s* (Cambridge, MA: Harvard University Press, 1981); William Henry Chafe, *Civilities and Civil Rights: Greensboro, North Carolina, and the Black Struggle for Freedom* (New York: Oxford University Press, 1981); Manning Marable, *Race, Reform, and Rebellion: The Second Reconstruction in Black America, 1945–1982* (Jackson: University Press of Mississippi, 1984); Christopher W. Schmidt, *The Sit-Ins: Protest and Legal Changes in the Civil Rights Era* (Chicago: University of Chicago Press, 2018).

2. "Statement by the President Upon Making Public an FBI Report on Recent Urban Riots, September 26, 1964," Lyndon Baines Johnson Presidential Library (hereafter LBJPL) Folder "Statements of LBJ September 26, 1964–September 28, 1964," Box 122; Lyndon B. Johnson, "July 27, 1967 Speech to the Nation on Civil Disorders." Available at: https://millercenter.org/the-presidency/presidential-speeches/july-27-1967-speech-nation-civil-disorders; Bill Simmons, "Detroit Holds Only 150 of 7200 Taken in Riot," *Washington Post*, August 29, 1967, pg. A4; "Buildings Damaged by Detroit Riot Put at 450," *Wall Street Journal*, August 3, 1967, pg. 9; Bill McGraw, "A Quick Guide to the 1967 Detroit Riot," *The Center for Michigan Bridge Magazine*, March 11, 2016. Available at: https://www.mlive.com/news/detroit/2016/03/a_quick_guide_to_the_1967_detr.html.

3. On the East St. Louis riot of 1917, see Harper Barnes, *Never Been a Time: The 1917 Race Riot That Sparked the Civil Rights Movement* (New York: Walker & Company, 2008); Charles Lumpkins, *American Pogrom: The East St. Louis Race Riot and Black Politics* (Athens: Ohio University Press, 2008); Elliott M. Rudwick, *Race Riot at East St. Louis* (Carbon: Southern Illinois University Press, 1964); Ida B. Wells, *The East St. Louis Massacre: The Greatest Outrage of the Century* (independently published 2020; originally published 1917). For accounts of riots predating East St. Louis, see Brian Butler, *An Undergrowth of Folly: Public Order, Race Anxiety, and the 1903 Evansville, Indiana Riot* (New York: Garland, 2000); David Fort Godshalk, *A Night of Violence: The Houston Riot of 1917* (Baton Rouge: Louisiana State University Press, 1976); Robert V. Haynes, *A Night of Violence: The Houston Riot of 1917* (Baton Rouge: Louisiana State University Press, 1976).

4. On the Red Summer of 1919 see Barbara Foley, *Spectres of 1919: Class and Nation in the Making of the New Negro* (Urbana: University of Illinois Press, 2003); Cameron McWhirter, *Red Summer: The Summer of 1919 and the Awakening of Black America* (New York: Henry Holt & Co., 2011); William Tuttle, *Race Riot: Chicago in the Red Summer of*

1919 (New York: Atheneum, 1970); Jan Voogd, *Race Riots and Resistance: The Red Summer of 1919* (New York: Peter Lang, 2008); Robert Whitaker, *On the Laps of Gods: The Red Summer of 1919 and the Struggle for Justice That Remade a Nation* (New York: Crown Publishers, 2008). On Tulsa see Alfred L. Brophy, *Reconstructing the Dreamland: The Tulsa Riot of 1921: Race, Reparations, and Reconciliation* (New York: Oxford University Press, 2003); James S. Hirsch, *Riot and Remembrance: The Tulsa Race Riot and Its Legacy* (New York: Houghton Mifflin, 2008); Scott Ellsworth, *Death in a Promised Land: The Tulsa Race Riot of 1921* (Baton Rouge: Louisiana State University Press, 1992); Randy Krehbiel, *Tulsa 1921: Reporting a Massacre* (Norman: University of Oklahoma Press, 2019); Tim Madigan, *The Burning: The Tulsa Race Massacre of 1921* (New York: St. Martin's Griffin, 2003). On World War II era riots, see Dominic J. Capeci and Martha Wilkerson, *Layered Violence: The Detroit Rioters of 1943* (Oxford: University of Mississippi Press, 1991); Robin D. G. Kelley, *Race Rebels: Culture, Politics, and the Black Working Class* (New York: The Free Press, 1994); Charles River Editors, *Zoot Suit Riots: The History of the Racial Attacks in Los Angeles During World War II* (CreateSpace Independent Publishing Platform, 2016); Gerald Van Dusen, *Detroit's Sojourner Truth Housing Riot of 1942: Prelude to the Race Riot of 1943* (Charleston, SC: The History Press, 2020). See also Ann Collins, *All Hell Broke Loose: American Race Riots from the Progressive Era through World War II* (Santa Barbara, CA: Praeger, 2012); Victoria Wolcott, *Race, Riots, and Roller Coasters: The Struggle Over Segregated Recreation in America* (Philadelphia: University of Pennsylvania Press, 2012).

5. James Upton, "The Politics of Urban Violence: Critiques and Proposals," *Journal of Black Studies* 15, no. 3, (1985): 243–258, pg. 245; Robert M. Fogelson, *Violence as Protest: A Study of Riots and Ghettos* (New York: Anchor Press, 1971), 28; California Governor's Commission on the Los Angeles Riots, *Violence in the City—An End or a Beginning?: A Report by the Governor's Commission on the Los Angeles Riots* (Sacramento: State of California, 1965), 6, 3. For further discussion of rioting as a pathological, opportunistic act, see Edward Banfield, *The Unheavenly City: The Nature and Future of Our Urban Crisis* (Boston: Little, Brown & Co., 1970); Banfield, "Rioting Mainly for Fun and Profit," in *Metropolitan Enigma*, ed. James Q. Wilson (Cambridge, MA: Harvard University Press, 1968); Eugene Methvin, *The Riot Makers: The Technology of Social Demolition* (New York: Arlington House, 1970).

6. In *Black Silent Majority* (Cambridge, MA: Harvard University Press, 2015), political scientist Michael Javen Fortner argues that Harlem residents' demands for a harsh "War on Crime" and draconian sentencing measures led to the enactment of the Rockefeller Drug Laws in New York City in 1973, and should be seen as a central force in ushering mass incarceration. Fortner argues that in Harlem and other Black urban areas during this period, residents mobilized to condemn the "junkies" in their midst by demanding their severe punishment and removal. He suggests that this "black silent majority" (which, given the scope of the evidence he presents, draws mainly voices from the Black clergy and middle class) privileged dealing harshly and retributively with crime above all else, including civil rights, discrimination, and police brutality. See also Fortner, "The Carceral State and the Crucible of Black Politics: An Urban History of the Rockefeller Drug Laws," *Studies in American Political Development* 27, no. 1 (2013). James Forman Jr. offers a powerful account of the Black activists and organizations that mobilized in support of punitive programs in *Locking Up Our Own: Crime and Punishment in Black America* (New York:

Farrar, Straus and Giroux, 2017). See also Forman, "Racial Critiques of Mass Incarceration: Beyond the New Jim Crow," *NYU Law Review* 87, no. 1 (2012).

7. Lyndon B. Johnson, "July 27, 1967 Speech to the Nation on Civil Disorders." Available at: https://millercenter.org/the-presidency/presidential-speeches/july-27-1967-speech-nation-civil-disorders.

8. Shriver quoted in Gareth Davies, *From Opportunity to Entitlement: The Transformation and Decline of Great Society Liberalism* (Lawrence: University Press of Kansas, 1999), 191; Otto Kerner et al., *Report of the National Advisory Commission on Civil Disorders* (Washington, DC: US Government Printing Office, 1968), 160, 162, 159, 319.

9. For a detailed consideration of the Martin Luther King Jr. rebellions and their aftermath, particularly in Washington, DC, see Clay Risen, *A Nation on Fire: America in the Wake of the King Assassination* (Hoboken, NJ: Wiley & Sons, 2009). The statistics used have been compiled by Professor Christian Davenport and his research team at the Radical Information Project (https://radicalinformationproject.weebly.com/uprisingsdisturbancesriots .html) at the University of Michigan's Center for Political Studies, based on the records of the Lemberg Center for the Study of Violence. In the summer of 2016, approximately thirty boxes of the Lemberg archives were located at the Radical Information Project in the Center for Political Studies, where Davenport and his team have used these sources for quantitative studies of the thousands of incidents documented by the Lemberg researchers. (The archives have been recently opened to the public and are now housed at Brandeis University's Robert D. Farber University Archives & Special Collections Department, although at press time a number of boxes are still at the Radical Information Project.) See "Civil Disturbances," with Adrian Arellano, Kiela Crabtree and Christian Davenport, December 28, 2020 (draft manuscript in Davenport's possession); "Riot Codebook" (in author's possession). On prison rebellions and activism during this period, see Dan Berger, *Captive Nation: Black Prison Organizing in the Civil Rights Era* (Chapel Hill: University of North Carolina Press, 2014); Berger and Toussaint Losier, *Rethinking the American Prison Movement* (New York: Routledge, 2018); Losier, "Against 'Law and Order' Lockup: The 1970 NYC Jail Rebellions," *Race & Class* 59, no.1 (2017): 3–35; Heather Ann Thompson, *Blood in the Water: The Attica Prison Uprising of 1971 and Its Legacy* (New York: Pantheon Books, 2016).

10. Countless state and local officials joined national policymakers and federal officials in targeting young Black men with new punitive programs, but low-income communities of color suffered from increasing police brutality and shared the conditions of mass unemployment, degraded housing, and unequal access to educational resources as a whole. White and Latinx Americans alike have neglected or downplayed this history—the idea that "Mexicans don't riot because we're too busy working"—advancing the view of violent protest as an irrational and pathological behavior associated with Black Americans alone. But rebellions in Puerto Rican, Mexican American and other Brown communities should be recognized as part of a much larger political dynamic, arising from shared grievances among people of color, and draw our attention to the inherent discrimination within American law enforcement and the criminal legal system. Even if the contours of inequality unfolded under distinct historical conditions in each locale, the fact of American racism leaves open the possibility that marginalized groups will revolt to dismantle the structures of inequality. "Riot Codebook"; Natalie Delgadillo, "The Forgotten History

of Latino Riots," *Bloomberg CityLab*, April 11, 2017. Available at: https://www.bloomberg
.com/news/articles/2017-04-11/mapping-the-history-of-latino-urban-riots; Aaron Fountain, "Riot Shaming by Latinos Needs to Stop," *Latino Rebels*, September 26, 2016. Available at: https://www.latinorebels.com/2016/09/26/riot-shaming-by-latinos-needs-to-stop/.

11. Stuart Schrader, *Badges without Borders: How Global Counterinsurgency Transformed
American Policing* (Berkeley: University of California Press, 2019), 137; "Project Sky
Knight: A Demonstration in Aerial Surveillance and Crime Control," Box 26, Egil Krogh
Collection, Richard Nixon Presidential Library (hereafter RNPL); "Administrative History
of the DOJ," LBJPL Folder "Administrative History of the DOJ," Box 3, Lyndon Baines
Johnson Administrative History of the Department of Justice, vol. 4, pt. 5 and Va.

12. Schrader, 197; Lyndon B. Johnson, "Statement by the President Upon Signing the Omnibus
Crime Control and Safe Streets Act of 1968." Available at: https://www.presidency.ucsb
.edu/documents/statement-the-president-upon-signing-the-omnibus-crime-control-and
-safe-streets-act-1968; Omnibus Crime Control and Safe Streets Act of 1968, Pub. L. No.
90–351, 82 Stat. 197 (1968).

13. Ashley Howard, "Prairie Fires: Urban Rebellions as Black Working Class Politics in Three
Midwestern Cities" (unpublished dissertation, University of Illinois 2012); Peter B. Levy,
The Great Uprising: Race Riots in Urban American during the 1960s (New York: Cambridge
University Press, 2018), and Thomas J. Sugrue and Andrew P. Goodman, "Plainfield Burning: Black Rebellion in the Suburban North," *Journal of Urban History* 33, no. 4 (2007):
568–601 are a few notable exceptions to the big-city focus of much of the historical litera-
ture on Black uprisings during this period.

14. Charles Koen, *My Story of the Cairo Struggle* (master's thesis, Union for Experimenting
Colleges and Universities, Cincinnati, OH, 1980), slide presentation 6 (165).

15. Here I draw from Kwame Anthony Appiah's discussion of how identities are in part constituted by scripts, or stories and models of conduct that people use to shape self-conception,
plans of action, norms of conduct, evaluative judgments, and senses of belonging. See *The
Ethics of Identity* (Princeton, NJ: Princeton University Press, 2005).

16. My definition of politics comes from Robin D. G. Kelley's discussion of James C. Scott's
notion of "infrapolitics." See Kelley, "'We Are Not What We Seem': Rethinking Black
Working-Class Opposition in the Jim Crow South," *Journal of American History* 80, no. 1
(1993): 75–112. See also Michael George Hanchard, *Party/Politics Horizons in Black Political Thought* (New York: Oxford University Press, 2006) and Charles Tilly and Sidney Tar-
row, *Contentious Politics*, 2nd ed. (New York: Oxford University Press, 2015).

17. On slave patrols and law enforcement in Early America and in the antebellum period,
see Sally E. Hadden, *Slave Patrols: Law and Violence in Virginia and the Carolinas* (Cam-
bridge, MA: Harvard University Press, 2003); Dennis C. Rousey, *Policing the Southern
City: New Orleans, 1805–1889* (Baton Rouge: Louisiana State University Press, 1996);
Philip J. Schwarz, *Twice Condemned: Slaves and Criminal Laws of Virginia, 1705–1865*
(Baton Rouge: Louisiana State University Press, 1988); Samuel Walker, *Popular Justice: A
History of American Criminal Justice* (New York: Oxford University Press, 1998).

18. Thomas Jefferson, *Notes on the State of Virginia* (1781), Query XVIII: Manners. Available
at: https://teachingamericanhistory.org/library/document/notes-on-the-state-of-virginia
-query-xviii-manners/.

19. Johnson quoted in Kyle Longley, "Our Leaders Can Look to Lyndon Johnson to See How
to Minimize Damage Today," *Washington Post*, May 31, 2020. Available at: https://www

.washingtonpost.com/outlook/2020/05/31/our-leaders-can-look-lyndon-johnson-see-how -minimize-damage-today/ and Josh Israel, "How Lyndon Johnson Responded to Baltimore's Last Riots," *Think Progress*, April 28, 2015. Available at: https://archive.thinkprogress .org/how-lyndon-johnson-responded-to-baltimores-last-riots-f3c0378909c/.

CHAPTER 1: THE CYCLE

1. Robert Nolan, "Carver Ranches Is an Early Black Enclave," *South Florida Sun Sentinel*, 1 Apr 2015. Available at: https://www.sun-sentinel.com/local/broward/fl-carver-brow100 -20150430-story.html; "Shots Fired at Police Cars," *Fort Lauderdale News*, August 1, 1969, no page given, Lemberg Folder "Carver Ranches August 1-1969."

2. Minutes of August 2, 1967 Cabinet Meeting, LBJPL Folder "Cabinet Meeting 8/2/67 [4 of 4]," Box 9, Cabinet Papers; on the rebellions before June 1968, see Janet L. Abu-Lughod, *Race, Space, and Riots in Chicago, New York, and Los Angeles* (New York: Oxford University Press, 2007); Jordan T. Camp, *Incarcerating the Crisis: Freedom Struggles and the Rise of the Neoliberal State* (Oakland: University of California Press, 2016); Max Felker-Kantor, *Policing Los Angeles: Race, Resistance, and the Rise of the LAPD* (Chapel Hill: University of North Carolina Press, 2018); Max Herman, *Fighting in the Streets: Ethnic Succession and Urban Unrest in Twentieth-Century America* (New York: Peter Lang, 2005); Elizabeth Hinton, *From the War on Poverty to the War on Crime: The Making of Mass Incarceration in America* (Cambridge, MA: Harvard University Press, 2016); Sidney Fine, *Violence in the Model City: The Cavanagh Administration, Race Relations, and the Detroit Riot of 1967* (East Lansing: Michigan State University Press, 2007); Dan Georgakas and Mavin Surkin, *Detroit: I Do Mind Dying* (1975; repr., Cambridge, MA: South End Press, 1998); Gerald Horne, *Fire This Time: The Watts Uprising and the 1960s* (Charlottesville: University Press of Virginia, 1995); Otto Kerner et al., *Report of the National Advisory Commission on Civil Disorders*, (Washington, DC: US Government Printing Office, 1968); Peter B. Levy, *The Great Uprising: Race Riots in Urban America During the 1960s* (Cambridge: Cambridge University Press, 2018); Manning Marable, *Race Reform and Rebellion: The Second Reconstruction in Black America, 1945–1982* (Jackson: University Press of Mississippi, 1984), H. Masotti and Don R. Bowen, *Riots and Rebellion: Civil Violence in the Urban Community* (Beverly Hills: Sage Publications, 1968); Malcolm McLaughlin, *The Long, Hot Summer of 1967: Urban Rebellion in America* (New York: Palgrave Macmillan, 2014); Kevin Mumford, *Newark: A History of Race, Rights and Riots in America* (New York: NYU Press, 2007); Alyssa Ribeiro, "'A Period of Turmoil': Pittsburgh's April 1968 Riots and Their Aftermath," *Journal of Urban History* 39 (April 2012): 147–171; Thomas Sugrue, *The Origins of Urban Crisis: Race and Inequality in Postwar Detroit* (Princeton, NJ: Princeton University Press, 1996) and Sugrue, *Sweet Land of Liberty: The Forgotten Struggles for Civil Rights in the North* (New York: Random House, 2008); Heather Ann Thompson, "Understanding Rioting in Postwar America," *Journal of Urban History* 3 (March 2000): 391–402 and *Whose Detroit? Politics, Labor, and Race in a Modern American City* (Ithaca, NY: Cornell University Press, 2004); Eldridge Cleaver, "Requiem for Nonviolence," *Ramparts Magazine* (May 1968): 48–49.

3. Mark Jacob, "Recordings show Daley, LBJ worked to stem 1968 riots," *Chicago Tribune*, March 30, 2010. Available at: https://www.chicagotribune.com/news/ct-xpm-2010-03-30 -ct-met-daley-lbj-0331-20100330-story.html.

4. "Granting Activity 1965–1966," pg. 42, LBJPL Folder "Volume IV, Law Enforcement

Assistance Part V, Law Enforcement Assistance—Narrative History [1 of 2], Box 3, LBJ Administrative History, Department of Justice; Congress of the United States, Congressional Budget Office, "Federal Law Enforcement Assistance: Alternative Approaches" (Washington, DC: US Government Printing Office, 1978), 9; US Department of Justice, Office of Justice Programs, "50 Years of Building Solutions, Supporting Communities and Advancing Justice," February 14, 2020. Available at: https://www.ojp .gov/ojp50/1968-beginning#:~:text=President%20Lyndon%20Johnson%20signs%20 into,grant%2Dmaking%20and%20research%20budget.

5. US Department of Justice, National Institute of Justice, "LEAA 1970: LEAA Activities July 1, 1969 to June 30, 1970," US Department of Justice, 2.

6. Mary Ann O'Connell, "Blacks See Double Standard in Justice," *Decatur Review*, August 12, 1969, no page given, Lemberg Folder, "IL—Decatur, August 7–8, 1969," Box 12.

7. Hap Veerkamp and Vickie Varnum, "Police Shot First, Blacks Say," *Hollywood Sun-Tattler*, September 30, 1969, pg. 1; Brian Patterson, "Stores Looted: Rock-Throwing Spree Disrupts East Side," *Columbus Dispatch*, June 5, 1970, pg. 1; "300 Policemen Maintain Peace in JC," *Bayonne Times*, August 11, 1970, no page given, Lemberg Folder, "NJ—Jersey City"; "Negro Youths Harass Area: York Declares Emergency," *Philadelphia Inquirer*, July 16, 1968, pg. 10.

8. Jon Gosser, "Disturbance Erupts, 2 Policemen Injured," Fort Wayne *News-Sentinel*, August 8, 1968, page number illegible, Lemberg Folder, "IN—Fort Wayne, August 7–9, 1968," Box 9; "Looting, Store Burning Follow Melee in Ghetto," *Ann Arbor News*, June 6 1969, no page given, Lemberg; "West Side Violence Subsides," *Akron Beacon Journal*, September 14, 1970, A1; William Kezziah and Donn Gaynor, "Gas Breaks Up 3rd Night of Violence," *Akron Beacon Journal*, August 13, 1970.

9. "Police Harassment Is Blamed for Violence by Black Youth," *York Gazette and York Daily*, July 17, 1968, pg. 1. Lemberg Folder "PA—York," Box 9.

10. Levy 256; "South End Cools Off as Police Get Tough," *York Dispatch*, July 17, 1968, pg. 44, Lemberg Folder "York—Pennsylvania," Box 9; "Police Harassment Is Blamed for Violence by Black Youth."

11. O'Connell, "Blacks See Double Standard in Justice"; "Arrest Three in Decatur Race Disorder," *San Francisco Examiner*, August 10, 1969, no page given, Lemberg Folder "IL—Decatur, August 7-8, 1969," Box 12; Ron Frazier, "Police End 2nd City Disorder," *Decatur Herald & Review*, August 9, 1969, no page given, Lemberg Folder "IL—Decatur, August 7–8, 1969," Box 12; Larry N. Payne, "Police Fire Shots to Disperse Crowd," *Decatur Review*, August 9, 1969, pg. 14.

12. Mark Sanchez, "Park Arrests Touch Off Violence" *New Mexico Daily Lobo*, June 17, 1971, pg. 1.

13. "Police Use Chemical Mace to Rout Crowd, Nab 2," *Baltimore Sun*, June 19, 1968, pg. C2.

14. "Mob Releases Policemen's 3 Suspects," *Baltimore Sun*, June 26, 1968, pg. C32.

15. "300 Policemen Maintain Peace in JC," *Bayonne Times*, August 11, 1970, no page given, Lemberg Folder "NJ—Jersey City"; "300 Protest Arrest of Activist Leader," *Washington Post* 29 Aug 1970, pg. A3; "Riots Flare in Hoboken; Aftermath of Drug Raid," *Hudson Dispatch*, no citation, Lemberg.

16. Peter La Villa and Peter Weiss, "Riots Hit Hoboken," *Hudson Dispatch*, September 6, 1971, Lemberg Folder "NJ—Hoboken."

17. Gosser, "Disturbance Erupts, 2 Policemen Injured"; "Chief Says Hoodlums Began Street Fight," Fort Wayne *Journal-Gazette*, August 8, 1968, pg. A3.

18. Brian Patterson, "Stores Looted: Rock-Throwing Spree Disrupts East Side," *Columbus Dispatch*, June 5, 1970, pg. 1.

19. Brian Patterson, "350 Disrupt Troubled East Side Community," *Columbus Dispatch*, June 6, 1970, pg. 1.

20. "Riots Flare in Hoboken; Aftermath of Drug Raid"; "300 Protest Arrest of Activist Leader."

21. La Villa and Weiss, "Riots Hit Hoboken."

22. "West Side Violence Subsides," *Akron Beacon-Journal*, pg. A1; William Kezziah and Donn Gaynor, "Gas Breaks Up 3rd Night of Violence," *Akron Beacon Journal*, August 13, 1970, no page given, Lemberg Folder "OH—Akron."

23. No date, no paper name given, "More Violence—Police Arrest 13," Lemberg Folder "OH—Akron."

24. Seymour M. Hersh, "Poison Gas in Vietnam," *New York Review of Books*, May 9, 1968; Schrader, 197.

25. Kerner et al., 9, see also Chapter XII "Control of Disorder"; Schrader, 197.

26. Seymour M. Hersh, "Poison Gas in Vietnam," *New York Review of Books*, May 9, 1968. Maryland State Police with assistance of a Law Enforcement Administration Association (LEAA) grant, funded by the Governor's Commission on Law Enforcement and the Administration of Justice of the State of Maryland, *Manual Civil Disturbances*, no date given (after 1971); Howard Hu, "Tear Gas—Harassing Agent or Toxic Chemical Weapon?" *Journal of the American Medical Association* 262, no. 5 (August 4, 1989): 660–663.

27. Larry N. Payne, "Police Fire Shots to Disperse Crowd," *Decatur Review*, August 9, 1969, pg. 14.

28. Mark Sanchez, "Park Arrests Touch Off Violence" *New Mexico Daily Lobo*, June 17, 1971, pg. 1.

29. "UNM Reporter Recounts Rioting in Roosevelt Park," *New Mexico Daily Lobo*, June 17, 1971, pg. 2.

30. "Indiana Avenue Sealed Off as Crowds Gather," *Indianapolis Star*, June 7, 1969, pg. 7; "82 Arrested in 2nd Night of Clashes," *Indianapolis News*, June 7, 1969, pg. 3; "Indiana Avenue Sealed Off as Crowds Gather"; La Villa and Weiss, "Riots Hit Hoboken."

31. Veerkamp and Varnum, "Police Shot First, Blacks Say."

32. Ott Cefkin, "Snipers Fire on Pembroke Police," *Pompano Sun-Sentinel*, September 16, 1969, no page given, Lemberg Folder "FL—Pembroke Park September 1969," Box 12.

33. Hap Veerkamp, "Snipers Fire on Police Station, Cars," *Hollywood Sun-Tattler*, September 26, 1969, pg. 1; Cefkin, "Snipers Fire on Pembroke Police."

34. Gosser, "Disturbance Erupts, 2 Policemen Injured"; Jon Gosser, "Vandalism, Looting Cause Arrest of 23," Fort Wayne *News-Sentinel*, August 9, 1968, pg. 1; Brian Patterson, "350 Disrupt Troubled East Side Community," *Columbus Dispatch*, June 6, 1970, pg. 1.

35. "West Side Violence Subsides"; "Ballard Lauds Parents, Youngsters for Peace," *Akron Beacon Journal*, no date, pg. A-1, Lemberg Folder "OH—Akron."

36. "Looting, Store Burning Follow Melee in Ghetto," *Ann Arbor News*, June 6, 1969, no page given, Lemberg Folder, "IN—Indianapolis June 5–6,1969," Box 12; "Indiana Avenue Sealed Off as Crowds Gather," *Indianapolis Star*, June 7, 1969, pg. 7.

37. Mary Ann O'Connell, "Blacks See Double Standard in Justice."

38. O'Connell, "Blacks See Double Standard in Justice."

39. Lawrence Reh, "Blacks Charge Ogilvie Ordered Police Acts Here," *Decatur Review*, August 12, 1969, no page number. Lemberg Folder "IL—Decatur, August 7–8, 1969," Box 12; "Police Praised for Handling of Disturbances," *Decatur Review*, August 19, 1969, no page given. Lemberg Folder "IL—Decatur, August 7-8, 1969," Box 12; Reh, "Blacks Charge."

40. "Lindsten Sees Complaint Answering as Unneeded," *Decatur Herald*, August 19, 1969, pg. 3.

41. "Officials to Prove 2 Days of Riots in New Mexico," *Washington Post*, June 16, 1971, no page given; "Officials, Puerto Ricans Confer on Ending Hoboken Disturbances," *Washington Post*, September 7, 1971, no page given, Lemberg.

42. "West Side Violence Subsides."

43. "West Side Violence Subsides."

44. "West Side Violence Subsides."

45. Veerkamp and Varnum, "Police Shot First, Blacks Say."

46. James Baldwin, "Fifth Avenue, Uptown," *Esquire*, July 1960. Available at: https://www.esquire.com/news-politics/a3638/fifth-avenue-uptown/.

CHAPTER 2: THE PROJECTS

1. Paul Good, *Cairo, Illinois: Racism at Floodtide*, US Commission on Civil Rights, Clearinghouse Publication no. 44 (October 1973): 58; G. Louis Heath, "Ghost Town Vigilantes: The Racial Pallor of Cairo," *Nation*, December 22, 1959.

2. "Soldier Shot, Fires Set in Cairo," *St. Louis Post-Dispatch*, November 9, 1970, pg. 3; David Maraniss and Neil Henry, "Race 'War' in Cairo: Reconciliation Grows as Memories Recede," *Washington Post*, March 22, 1987, pg. A1.

3. Good, *Cairo, Illinois*, 59; Molly Parker, "Senators Raise Concern About Lead Exposure in Cairo," *Southern Illinoisan*, May 15, 2017. Available at: https://thesouthern.com/news/local/acha/senators-raise-concerns-about-lead-exposure-in-cairo-hud-says-water-filters-are-precautionary-and/article_0cc5701a-7791-5ac9-b7c0-ea6364e1b740.html; G. Louis Heath, "Ghost Town Vigilantes: The Racial Pallor of Cairo," *Nation*, December 22, 1959; George Lardner Jr., "Cairo, Ill., at War with Itself," *Washington Post*, September 21, 1969, pg. 3.

4. Donald Janson, "Negroes Demand Action by Cairo, Ill.," *New York Times*, July 21, 1967, pg. 28; Jerome P. Curry, "Negro Youth Leaders Give Cairo 72 Hours to Meet Terms," *St. Louis Post-Dispatch*, July 20, 1967, pg. 3.

5. Curry, "Negro Youth Leaders," pg. 3.

6. Heath, "Ghost Town Vigilantes"; Curry, "Negro Youth Leaders," pg. 3; Janson, "Negroes Demand Action."

7. Lee Winfrey, "The Gun Is King in City of Hate," *Detroit Free Press*, September 21, 1969, pg. 1; Good, *Cairo, Illinois*; Janson, "Negroes Demand Action."

8. Kerry Pimblott, *Faith in Black Power: Religion, Race, and Resistance in Cairo, Illinois* (Lexington: University of Kentucky Press, 2017), 81–94. See also Pimblott, "Soul Power: The Black Church and the Black Power Movement in Cairo, Illinois, 1969–1974" (PhD diss., University of Illinois at Urbana–Champaign, 2012), 108.

9.   Heath, "Ghost Town Vigilantes."

10. Curry, "Negro Youth Leaders."

11. Janson, "Negroes Demand Action."

12. Janson, "Negroes Demand Action"; Jerome P. Curry, "Cairo Leaders Meet, Believe Race Crisis Has Been Averted," *St. Louis Post-Dispatch*, July 23, 1967, pg. 3.

13. "FBI Probing Black-White Clash in Cairo," *Chicago Daily Defender*, April 2, 1969, pg. 3; "Shots Fired Near Scene of Racial Tension in Cairo," *St. Louis Post-Dispatch*, April 1, 1969, pg. 4C.

14. "Races: War in Little Egypt," *Time*, September 26, 1969, pg. 29; Good, *Cairo, Illinois*, 31.

15. Maraniss and Henry, "Race 'War' in Cairo," A1; Winfrey, "The Gun Is King in City of Hate"; "Cairo, Ill. Beset by Violence," New York *Amsterdam News*, November 28, 1970, pg. 47.

16. "People's Black History, as Seen Through Retired Fire Chief G. John Parker's Eyes." Available at: https://www.peoriastory.com/peoriastory/memories-reminiscing/.

17. "Peoria Riot Offers Clues," *Edwardsville Intelligencer*, August 8, 1968, pg. 4; on the rise and deterioration of public housing, see N.D.B. Connolly, *A World More Concrete: Real Estate and the Remaking of Jim Crow South Florida* (Chicago: University of Chicago Press, 2014); David M. P. Freund, *Colored Property: State Policy and White Racial Politics in Suburban America* (Chicago: University of Chicago Press, 2007); Arnold Hirsch, *Making the Second Ghetto: Race and Housing in Chicago, 1940–1960* (Chicago: University of Chicago Press, 1998); D. Bradford Hunt, *Blueprint for Disaster: The Unraveling of Chicago Public Housing* (Chicago: University of Chicago Press, 2009); Kenneth T. Jackson, *Crabgrass Frontier: The Suburbanization of America* (New York: Oxford University Press, 1985); Douglas S. Massey and Nancy Denton, *American Apartheid: Segregation and the Making of the Underclass* (Cambridge, MA: Harvard University Press, 1993); Richard Rothstein, *The Color of Law: A Forgotten History of How Our Government Segregated America* (New York: Liveright, 2017); Beryl Satter, *Family Properties: Race, Real Estate, and the Exploitation of Black Urban America* (New York: St. Martin's Press, 2009); Thomas Sugrue, *Sweet Land of Liberty: The Forgotten Struggle for Civil Rights in the North* (New York: Random House, 2008); Keeanga-Yamahtta Taylor, *Race For Profit: How Banks and the Real Estate Industry Undermined Black Homeownership* (Chapel Hill: University of North Carolina Press, 2019); Lawrence J. Vale, *Purging the Poorest: Public Housing and the Design Politics of Twice-Cleared Communities* (Chicago: University of Chicago Press, 2013).

18. See Heather Ann Thompson, "Why Mass Incarceration Matters: Rethinking Crisis, Decline, and Transformation in Postwar American History," *Journal of American History* 97, no. 3 (December 2010): 703–758; Elizabeth Hinton, *From the War on Poverty to the War on Crime: The Making of Mass Incarceration in America*, chap. 3 (Cambridge, MA: Harvard University Press, 2016).

19. Timothy Williams, "Poverty, Pride—and Power: In Line for Federal Help, Pacoima Hides Problems Below Neat Surface," *Los Angeles Times*, April 10, 1994, pg. 5; "Melee in Pacoima Ends in Arrests," *Los Angeles Sentinel*, May 29, 1969, pg. A3.

20. "6 Officers Hurt, 11 Persons Seized in S. Stockton Battle," Stockton *Record*, July 17, 1968, pg. 1.

21. Marnoch quoted in "6 Officers Hurt, 11 Persons Seized in S. Stockton Battle."

22. "Mob Holds 2 Cops, 4 Others in S. Stockton Gym," Stockton *Record*, July 18, 1968, pg.

1; White quoted in "Police Resume Sierra Vista Rounds; Citizen Patrols Hit," Stockton *Record*, July 23, 1968, pg. 1.

23. "Mob Holds 2 Cops."

24. Doug Wilholt (former Stockton police officer) in discussion with author, April 2017; Jefferson Strickland (former Sierra Vista resident) in discussion with author, March 2017; Alice van Ommeren, *Stockton's Golden Era: An Illustrated History* (San Antonio: HPNBooks, 2015) Chapters 4 & 5; "Mob Holds 2 Cops."

25. "Mob Holds 2 Cops"; "South Stockton Quiets as Citizens Patrol Streets," Stockton *Record*, July 19, 1968, pg. 1.

26. "Black Unity Group Denies Riot Blame," Stockton *Record*, July 19, 1968, pg. 1.

27. "Black Unity Group Denies Riot Blame."

28. Minutes of the Stockton City Council, Vol. 94, June 3, 1968–December 30, 1968, City of Stockton Clerks Office; "South Stockton Quiets as Citizens Patrol Streets," Stockton *Record*, July 19, 1968, pg. 1. Representing the Black Students Association at the local Delta Community college, Vice President Gloria Smith demanded an end to the "harassment" of the Negro community by police. She said that harassment includes such things as police stopping and checking every car containing four or more Negroes.

29. "Police Resume Sierra Vista Rounds; Citizen Patrols Hit," Stockton *Record*, July 23, 1968, pg. 1.

30. "Police Resume Sierra Vista Rounds."

31. "Peoria Riot Offers Clues," *Edwardsville Intelligencer*, August 8, 1968, pg. 4.

32. Senate Committee on the Judiciary, *Assaults on Law Enforcement Officers: Hearings before the Subcommittee to Investigate the Administration of the Internal Security Act and Other Internal Security Laws*, 91st Cong., 2nd sess. (October 6–9, 1970), 109.

33. "Curfew Imposed in Peoria Melee," *New York Times*, July 31, 1968, pg. 28; "Peoria Riot Offers Clues."

34. "Curfew Imposed in Peoria Melee"; Matt Budel, "Former Peoria Police Officer Reflects on 1968 Riots at the Taft Homes," Peoria *Journal Star*, May 11, 2015. Available at: https://www.pjstar.com/article/20150511/NEWS/150519876; "Curfews Cool Off Peoria and Gary," *Newsday*, July 31, 1968, pg. 27; "Peoria Mayor Urges All to Observe Curfew," *Philadelphia Inquirer*, July 31, 1968, pg. 4.

35. "Peoria Riot Offers Clues"; "Ten Peoria Policemen Fired on by Snipers," *Newsday*, July 30, 1968, pg. 7.

36. "Peoria Mayor Urges All"; "Peoria Riot Offers Clues."

37. "Peoria Riot Offers Clues."

38. "2 Wounded, 27 Arrested in Violence," Peoria *Journal Star*, July 24, 1970, no page given, Lemberg Folder, "IL—Peoria," Box 9.

39. "2 Wounded, 27 Arrested in Violence"; "Guard Is Alerted in Peoria Clashes," *New York Times*, July 25, 1970, pg. 11.

40. "Rioting Grips Peoria After Two Evictions," *Chicago Tribune*, July 24, 1970, pg. 5.

41. "2 Wounded, 27 Arrested in Violence."

42. "Guard Is Alerted in Peoria Clashes"; "2 Wounded, 27 Arrested in Violence"; "Two Shot in Peoria Disorders; Firebombs Thrown in New Brunswick," *Washington Post*, July 24, 1970, pg. A4.

43. "Two Shot in Peoria Disorders"; "27 Arrested During Incidents," Peoria *Evening Journal Star*, July 24, 1970, no page given, Lemberg Folder, "IL—Peoria," Box 9; John Barrette and

Norm Bain, "Mayor Uses Curfew; 3 Men Shot," Peoria *Morning Journal Star*, July 24, 1970, no page given, Lemberg Folder, "IL—Peoria," Box 9. "Fire, Shooting Hit Peoria Areas After Evictions," Peoria *Evening Journal Star*, July 24, 1970, no page given, Lemberg Folder, "IL—Peoria," Box 9.

44. "Rioting Grips Peoria After Two Evictions," *Chicago Tribune*, July 24, 1970, pg. 5; "Mayor Keeps Lid on Peoria; Six Wounded," *Chicago Tribune*, July 26, 1970, pg. 2; William F. Johnson, "Curfew 3rd Night for City," Peoria *Evening Journal Star*, July 26, 1970 no page given, Lemberg Folder, "IL—Peoria," Box 9.

45. Johnson, "Curfew 3rd Night for City."

46. "Firebomb Incidents Continue on South Side; 6 Men Nabbed," Peoria *Evening Journal Star*, July 27, 1970, no page given, Lemberg Folder, "IL—Peoria," Box 9.

47. "The Black Saboteurs," Peoria *Journal Star*, July 28, 1970 pg. A-6.

48. "The Black Saboteurs."

49. Lynne Tuohy, "Father Panik Village, Where Dreams Turn to Dust," *Hartford Courant*, August 7, 1994. Available at: https://www.courant.com/news/connecticut/hc-xpm-1994-08-07 -9408070086-story.html; Teenagers Stone Cops, Firemen at FPV," *Connecticut Post*, September 24, 1968; "Bridgeport Police Seize 15 in Rioting," *New York Times*, August 8, 1970, pg. 13.

50. "On the Battlefield: Cairo, Illinois," pamphlet prepared as a public service (Concerned Community Coalition of Bloomington-Normal and Community for Social Action):13, 5, Chicago Urban League Records, Box 96, Folder 1057, University of Illinois at Chicago Library, Special Collections; "On the Battlefield," 5; See Pimblott, *Faith in Black Power*, for an excellent, comprehensive account of the development, and Black protest in Cairo during this period.

CHAPTER 3: THE VIGILANTES

1. Kerry Pimblott, *Faith in Black Power: Religion, Race, and Resistance in Cairo, Illinois* (Lexington: University of Kentucky Press, 2017), 100.

2. Paul Good, *Cairo, Illinois: Racism at Floodtide*, US Commission on Civil Rights, Clearinghouse Publication no. 44 (October 1973): 16; "Minneapolis Calls Guard to End Riots: Troops Patrol Area of Racial Violence Dozens of Fires Mark Minneapolis Rioting," *Chicago Tribune*, July 22, 1967, pg. B6.

3. Good, 15; "Minneapolis Calls Guard."

4. Lee Winfrey, "The Gun Is King in City of Hate," *Detroit Free Press*, September 21, 1969, pg. 1.

5. Dwight D. Eisenhower, "We Should Be Ashamed!" *Readers Digest* August 1967, 67–71. Eisenhower used what the philosopher Jason Stanley calls "code words" (i.e., "savage riots," "proper principles") to conceal the connections he was making to Black Americans. See Jason Stanley, *How Propaganda Works* (Princeton, NJ: Princeton University Press, 2016).

6. Good, 17.

7. "Race Hatreds Rend Dying City," Louisville *Courier Journal*, June 26, 1969, pg. A7; Pimblott, "Soul Power: The Black Church and the Black Power Movement in Cairo, Illinois, 1969–1974" (PhD diss., University of Illinois at Urbana–Champaign, 2012), 132; Good, 16.

8. Good, 29, 17; "On the Battlefield: Cairo, Illinois," pamphlet prepared as a public service (Concerned Community Coalition of Bloomington-Normal and Community for Social Action): 13, 5.

9. George Lardner Jr., "Cairo, Ill., at War with Itself," *Washington Post*, September 21, 1969, pg. 3; Good, 17; "Priest Makes Charge: Vigilante Corps in Cairo, Ill.," *St. Louis Post-Dispatch*, March 23, 1969, pg. 1.

10. Good, 17; "Shots Fired Near Scene of Racial Tension in Cairo," *St. Louis Post-Dispatch*, April 1, 1969, pg. 4C; Stephen Darst, "Cairo, Illinois," *Atlantic* 225, no. 3, (1970): 16–25; Robert H. Collins, "Bishop Backs Fr. Montroy's Goals, but Not All of His Methods," *St. Louis Post-Dispatch*, March 25, 1969, pg. 3B; "Priest Makes Charge: Vigilante Corps in Cairo, Ill.," *St. Louis Post-Dispatch*, March 23, 1969, pg. 1

11. Collins, "Bishop Backs Fr. Montroy's Goals."

12. "Blacks, Whites Trade Shots in Cairo, Ill.," *Los Angeles Times*, April 1, 1969, pg. 19.

13. Peter B. Levy, *The Great Uprising: Race Riots in Urban America During the 1960s* (New York: Cambridge University Press, 2018), 228; "Crispus Attucks Anniversary Special Section," *York Daily Record*, April 2016. Available at: https://www.ydr.com/story/news/history/2016/04/01/crispus-attucks-anniversary-special-section/82475478/; "Police Harassment Is Blamed for Violence by Black Youth," *York Gazette and York Daily*, July 17, 1968, pg. 1; Levy, 235.

14. Levy, 274, 239.

15. "Disorderly Youths Plague York, Pa.," *Washington Post*, June, 17, 1968, no page given, Lemberg Folder "York, Pennsylvania," Box 9; Levy, 235; "Witnesses Say Two White Men Fired Shots at Blacks After Disturbance," *York Gazette and York Daily*, July 16, 1968, pg. 3; "3 Held in York, Pa. as Violence Flares for Second Night," *New York Times* 5 Aug 1968, pg. 31; Levy 257.

16. Levy, 257; "3 Held in York, Pa. as Violence Flares for Second Night," *New York Times*, August 5, 1968, pg. 31.

17. Levy, 238; Stephanie L. Morrow, "Twelve Days of Hell: A Study of Violence, Historical Memory, and Media Coverage of the York, Pennsylvania Race Riots, 1968–2003" (PhD diss., Temple University, 2016), 91; Levy, 258; see also Jim Kalish, *The Story of Civil Rights in York, Pennsylvania* (York, PA: York County Audit of Human Rights, 2000).

18. Levy, 262–263, 277.

19. Levy, 266.

20. Levy, 266.

21. Morrow, 10–11; Levy, 266; "Boy's Fabricated Story of Being Set Afire Touched Off Clashes of Gangs," *York Gazette and York Daily*, July 19, 1969, pg. 1; Lauri Lebo, "York City's Summer of Rage," *York Dispatch*, July 15, 2019. Available at: https://www.yorkdispatch.com/story/news/local/2019/07/16/1969-riots-reckoning-decades-after-yorks-summer-rage/1638562001/; Levy, 267; Morrow, 11–12.

22. Jennifer McManamin, "2 Men Charged in 1969 Killing of York Policeman During Riot," *Baltimore Sun*, October 31, 2001. Available at: https://www.baltimoresun.com/news/bs-xpm-2001-10-31-0110310291-story.html; Morrow, 12; Levy, 269.

23. Levy 270, 284, 259; "Mike Hoover, the York Riots of 1969," *York Dispatch*, December 4, 2001.

24. Levy, 270–271.

25. Levy, 272.

26. "Murder on Newberry Street," *People Magazine Investigates*, Television Series, Season 3, Episode 9 (January 2019).

27. "Murder on Newberry Street"; Levy, 262; Morrow, 13.

28. Levy, 273; Morrow, 198.

29. Morrow, 186–187; Levy, 274.

30. Rick Lee, Jim Lynch, and Teresa Ann Boeckel, "York Riot Trials: In Henry Schaad Murder, Two Sentenced to State Prison Terms," *York Daily Record*, December 20, 2017.

31. Good, 19.

32. Winfrey, "The Gun Is King in City of Hate"; "Basic Problems Cited in Cairo Unrest," *Southern Illinoisan*, April 20, 1969, pg. 1.

33. Thomas Powers, "Guard, Cops Enforce Tight Cairo Curfew," April 30, 1969 pg. A4; John C. Taylor, "Firebombings, Gunfire Mark Weekend in Cairo," *Southern Illinoisan*, April 28, 1969, pg. 1.

34. Good, 18; "Another Large Fire Hits Cairo," *The Austin American-Statesman*, June 17, 1969, pg. 4; "Cairo A Feudal City: Jackson," *Chicago Daily Defender*, June 19, 1969, pg. 2.

35. Good, 19; "Race Hatreds Rend Dying City."

36. Winfrey, "The Gun Is King in City of Hate"; Good, 33.

37. George Lardner Jr., "Cairo, Ill., at War with Itself," *Washington Post*, September 21, 1969, pg. 3; Good, 18.

38. Darst, "Cairo"; Winfrey, "The Gun Is King in City of Hate"; Lardner Jr., "Cairo."

39. Pimblott, "Soul Power," 199–200.

40. Pimblott, *Faith in Black Power*, 140.

41. Pimblott, *Faith in Black Power*, 139–140, 137; Memorandum to Connie Seals from Dwight Casimere Re: United Front of Cairo, Illinois, no date given (likely December 1969), Chicago Urban League Records, Box 96, Folder 1057, University of Illinois at Chicago Library, Special Collections; "On the Battlefield," 7.

42. "On the Battlefield," 33, 14; Brian Kelly, "Lost in the Past: At the Confluence of Two Rivers," *Chicago Tribune*, July 21, 1985, pg. I10; Heath, "Ghost Town Vigilantes."

43. Quoted in Kathy McKinney, "There Ain't No Love Downtown," in "On the Battlefield."

44. "On the Battlefield," 8–9, 18; Lardner Jr., "Cairo."

45. Lardner Jr., "Cairo"; "On the Battlefield," 12.

46. Duane Lindstrom, "A Decade of Waiting in Cairo: A Report of the Illinois Advisory Committee to the United States Commission on Civil Rights" (June 1975): 12.

47. "216 Enrolled as Deputies in Salisbury," *Washington Post*, August 24, 1968, pg. D1; "Demonstrate in Salisbury," *Washington Star*, August 24, 1968, pg. B3, Lemberg Folder, "MD–Salisbury, August 20, 1968," Box 9; "Aliquippa Riot Ebbs, Parleys on Race Start," *Pittsburgh Courier*, May 30, 1970, pg. 1; "8 Arrested in Rock-Throwing," *Ann Arbor News*, July 17, 1970, no page given, Lemberg Folder "MI—Kalamazoo 7/16/70"; "Blacks Damage Yanceyville Stores," *Charlotte Observer*, September 21, 1970, pg. 1C.

48. Darst, "Cairo."

CHAPTER 4: THE SNIPERS

1. Robin D. G. Kelley, *Hammer and Hoe: Alabama Communists During the Great Depression*, 25th Anniv. ed. (Chapel Hill: University of North Carolina Press, 2015); Timothy B. Tyson, *Radio Free Dixie: Robert F. Williams and the Roots of Black Power* (Chapel Hill: University of North Carolina Press, 2000); "Negroes with Guns: Rob Williams and Black Power,"

Independent Lens. Available at: https://www.pbs.org/independentlens/negroeswithguns/rob.html.

2. Robert F. Williams, *Negroes with Guns* (New York: Marzani and Munsell, 1962), 110.

3. Williams, *Negroes with Guns*.

4. See Brandon M. Terry, "Requiem for a Dream: The Problem-Space of Black Power," in Tommie Shelby and Terry, eds. *To Shape a New World: Essays on the Political Philosophy of Martin Luther King Jr.* (Cambridge, MA: Belknap Press, 2018).

5. See Equal Justice Initiative, *Lynching in America: Targeting Black Veterans* (Montgomery: Equal Justice Initiative, 2017). Available at: https://eji.org/wp-content/uploads/2019/10/lynching-in-america-targeting-black-veterans-web.pdf.

6. United States Federal Bureau of Investigation, Uniform Crime Report 1967, available at: https://archive.org/stream/uniformcrimerepo1967unit/uniformcrimerepo1967unit_djvu.txt; 1969, available at: https://archive.org/stream/uniformcrimerepo1969unit/uniformcrimerepo1969unit_djvu.txt; 1974, available at: https://archive.org/stream/uniformcrimerepo1974unit/uniformcrimerepo1974unit_djvu.txt; Joseph Strickland, "Detroit Negro Says He Lied on NBC Show About Killing Plot," *Washington Post*, September 29, 1967, pg. A3.

7. Guardsmen quoted in Gene Roberts, "Troops Battle Detroit Snipers, Firing Machine Guns from Tanks," *New York Times*, July 26, 1967, pg. 1; Homer Bigart, "Newark Riot Deaths at Twenty-One as Negro Sniping Widens," *New York Times*, July 16, 1967, 1.

8. Michigan State Police opened fire on an apartment after a resident lit a cigarette in the dark, killing four-year-old Tonia Blanding. National Guardsmen in Newark shot and killed twelve-year-old Michael Pugh as he took out the trash in front of his house after curfew. When police received a report of a break-in at Sharp's Drug Store on Frelinghuysen Avenue during the uprising in Newark, five police cars promptly arrived on the scene. Twenty-four-year-old Raymond Hawk happened to be standing at the intersection in front of the store, and—in the style of a drive-by shooting—police fired at him from their cruisers. Gene Roberts, "Troops Battle Detroit Snipers, Firing Machine Guns from Tanks," *New York Times*, July 26, 1967, pg. 1; "The Newark Tragedy: A Week-Long Inquiry," *Washington Post*, July 24, 1967, pg. A1.

9. On the "fog of war," see Carl von Clausewitz, *On War* (New York: Random House, 1943, originally published 1831); Jonathan L. Jackson, *Racial Paranoia: The Unintended Consequences of Political Correctness* (New York: Basic Civitas Books, 2008).

10. Quoted in Russell Sackett, "In a Grim City, a Secret Meeting with the Snipers," *Life Magazine*, July 28, 1967, 28.

11. Ron Porambo, *No Cause for Indictment: An Autopsy of Newark* (New York: Holt, Rinehart and Winston, 1971), 131. See also Tom Hayden, *Rebellion in Newark: Official Violence and Ghetto Response* (New York: Vintage Books, 1967); Kevin Mumford, *Newark: A History of Race, Rights, and Riots* (New York: New York University Press, 2007); William F. Buckley, "Riots, Snipers—And Civil Rights," *The Boston Globe*, July 29, 1967, pg. 7.

12. Quoted in John Cunningham, *Newark* (New York: New Jersey Historical Society, 2002), 320.

13. Kimberly Siegal, "Silent No Longer: Voices of the 1967 Newark Race Riots," *College Undergraduate Research Electronic Journal* (July 2006). Available at: http://repository.upenn.edu/curej/31; Joseph Sweat, "Black Patrol Looks for Police Abuse," *Austin American-Statesman*, August 1, 1967, pg. 22.

14. J. Anthony Lukas, "Bad Day at Cairo, Ill.," *New York Times*, February 21, 1971, pg. 22; Kerry Pimblott, *Faith in Black Power: Religion, Race, and Resistance in Cairo, Illinois* (Lexington: University of Kentucky Press, 2017), 142–143.

15. "Kankakee Cop Answers Call and Is Shot," *Chicago Tribune*, September 30, 1968, no page given, Lemberg Folder "IL—Kankakee September 28, 1968"; "Kankakee cop hurt by sniper," *Chicago Daily News*, September 30, 1968, pg. 30; "17 Youths Are Jailed in Roanoke," *Richmond Times-Dispatch*, November 28, 1970, 1B; "Armed Negroes Attack Police Station in Cairo, Ill," *New York Times*, October 25,1970, pg. 30.

16. FBI Uniform Crime Report, 1968; "Detective, Negro Youth Slain in Detroit Suburb," *Washington Post*, August 9, 1968, no page given, Lemberg Folder, "MI—Inkster August 4–8, 1968"; Senate Committee on the Judiciary, *Assaults on Law Enforcement Officers: Hearings before the Subcommittee to Investigate the Administration of the Internal Security Act and Other Internal Security Laws*, 91st Cong., 2nd sess. (October 6–9, 1970), 136; FBI Uniform Crime Reports analyzed by Dan Wang. Available at: https://danwang.co/statistics-on-police-fatalities/; spreadsheet available at: https://docs.google.com/spreadsheets/d/10r8L CmZjxxKDpMv2SV4B9SWCJxOa0LivJkxT2PvQLJ0/edit#gid=936511667; Congressional Record—Senate August 1, 1968, 24703.

17. Paul Takagi, "A Garrison State in a 'Democratic' Society," in *Readings on Police Use of Deadly Force*, James J. Frye, ed. (New York: The Police Foundation, 1970), 195–212; Ronald H. Beattie, "Police Officer Shootings: A Tactical Evaluation," *The Journal of Criminal Law, Criminology and Police Science* 54 (1963); Joseph Goulden, "The Cops Hit the Jackpot," *Nation*, (November 1970); Ralph Knoohuizen, Richard P. Fahey, and Deborah J. Palmer, "The Police and Their Use of Fatal Force in Chicago," Chicago Law Enforcement Study Group (1972); Centers for Disease Control and Prevention, National Center for Health Statistics, "Compressed Mortality File 1968–2011." http://www.cjcj.org/news/8113; Elle Lett et al., "Racial Inequity in Fatal US Police Shootings, 2015–2020," *Journal of Epidemiology and Community Health* Epub ahead of print (November 23, 2020). http://dx.doi.org/10.1136/jech-2020-215097; for coverage of federal reporting errors see Carl Bialik, "The Government Finally Has A Realistic Estimate of Killings by Police," *FiveThirtyEight*, December 15, 2016. Available at: https://fivethirtyeight.com/features/the-government-finally-has-a-realistic-estimate-of-killings-by-police/. "Mapping Police Violence" dataset available at: https://mappingpoliceviolence.org/; "Fatal Force" dataset available at: https://www.washingtonpost.com/graphics/investigations/police-shootings-database/.

18. "Black Liberation Front Takes Credit for Harlem Ambush of Cops," *Black Liberation News* 2, no. 2 (February 1970), pg. 1.

19. *Assaults on Law Enforcement: Hearings*, 69.

20. "Riot Codebook"; Arnold Kotz et al., *Firearms, Violence, and Civil Disorders: A Research in Social Problems Study—Prepared for: the National Advisory Commission on Civil Disorders* (Menlo Park: Stanford Research Institute, July 1968), 26. Available at: https://www.ncjrs.gov/pdffiles1/Photocopy/11802NCJRS.pdf; Bill Schmidt, "Inquiry Team Named in Inkster Shootings," *Detroit Free Press*, August 11, 1968, pg. 3.

21. "News from Around the Suburbs: Inkster," *Detroit American*, July 22, 1968, pg. 5; Author Interview with Darnell Summers July 28, 2020.

22. Ferruccio Gambino, "The Transgression of a Laborer: Malcolm X in the Wilderness of America," *Radical History Review* (Winter 1993); Malcolm X, "Speech at Ford Audito-

rium," February 14, 1965. Available at: https://www.blackpast.org/african-american -history/speeches-african-american-history/1965-malcolm-x-speech-ford-auditorium/.

23. Elizabeth Esch, *The Color Line and the Assembly Line: Managing Race in the Ford Empire* (Berkeley: University of California Press, 2018), see chap. 3; "Racism Charges Return to Dearborn," *New York Times*, January 5, 1997; Malcolm X, "Speech at Ford Auditorium."

24. "Michigan Cop Slain," *Chicago Tribune*, August 9, 1968, no page given, Lemberg Folder "MI—Inkster August 4–8, 1968"; "Inkster Police Quizzed in Death," *Ann Arbor News*, August 9, 1968, no date given, Lemberg Folder "MI—Inkster August 4–8, 1968"; "Michigan Cop Slain," *Chicago Tribune*, August 9, 1968, Lemberg Folder "MI—Inkster August 4–8, 1968."

25. Mary Ann Weston and Bill Schmidt, "Shootings Probed in Inkster," *Detroit Free Press*, no date given, Lemberg Folder "MI—Inkster August 4-8, 1968;" Mary Ann Weston, "Police Cleared in Shooting," *Detroit Free Press* August 17, 1968, pg. 3A.

26. Weston, "Police Cleared in Shooting," 3A.

27. Weston, "Police Cleared in Shooting," 3A; Weston and Schmidt, "Shootings Probed in Inkster."

28. Weston, "Police Cleared in Shooting," 3A; FBI Uniform Crime Report, 1968; "Detective, Negro Youth Slain in Detroit Suburb," *Washington Post*, August 9, 1968; Lemberg Folder "MI—Inkster August 4–8, 1968"; "Michigan Cop Slain," *Chicago Tribune*, August 9, 1968, Lemberg Folder "MI—Inkster August 4–8, 1968."

29. "Detective Slain; Policemen Wounded," *Lansing State Journal*, August 8, 1968, no date given, Lemberg Folder "MI—Inkster August 4–8, 1968"; Mary Ann Weston, "Slain Boy's Kin Accuses Westland Police of Killing," *Detroit Free Press*, no date, no page given, Lemberg Folder "MI—Inkster August 4–8, 1968."

30. Weston, "Slain Boy's Kin."

31. Weston, "Police Cleared in Shooting," 3A.

32. Weston and Schmidt, "Shootings Probed in Inkster"; Manning Marable, "The Sad Case of Darnell Summers," New York *Amsterdam News*, May 14, 1983, pg. 11.

33. Weston and Schmidt, "Shootings Probed in Inkster"; "Inkster Police Quizzed in Death," *Ann Arbor News*, August 9, 1968, no page given, Lemberg Folder "MI—Inkster August 4–8, 1968."

34. Weston, "Slain Boy's Kin."

35. Weston, "Police Cleared in Shooting," 3A.

36. John Kifner, "In the Ghettos of Chicago, Policemen Are Targets," *New York Times*, August 9, 1970, pg. 40.

37. Jeffrey Haas, *The Assassination of Fred Hampton: How the FBI and the Chicago Police Murdered a Black Panther* (Chicago: Chicago Review Press, 2011); Rod Bush, *We Are Not What We Seem: Black Nationalism and the Class Struggle in the American Century*, rev. ed. (New York: New York University Press, 2000); Ward Churchill and Jim Vander Wall, *Agents of Repression: The FBI's Secret Wars against the Black Panther Party and the American Indian Movement* (New York: South End Press, 2001). See also Roy Wilkins and Ramsey Clark, *Search and Destroy: A Report by the Commission on Inquiry into the Black Panthers and Police* (Washington, DC: Metropolitan Applied Research Center, 1973) for a detailed discussion of COINTELPRO activities leading to the murder of Hampton and Clark.

38. Flint Taylor, *Torture Machine: Racism and Police Violence in Chicago* (Chicago: Haymarket Books, 2019); "'Torture Machine' Recounts 50 Years of Fighting Police Misconduct," written by Jay Shefsky, aired April 8, 2019, on WTTW News, https://news.wttw .com/2019/04/08/torture-machine-recounts-50-years-fighting-police-misconduct.

39. May 25, 1970 Memo to John Ehrlichman from Leonard Garment, Box 80, John Dean Files, (RNPL); Nick Kotz and Bob Woodward, "US Adrift in Crime Fight"; Kifner, "In the Ghettos of Chicago," 40.

40. *Assaults on Law Enforcement: Hearings 2*, 160; *Hearings 2*, 160 (statement of Edward Gurney, Senator from FL).

41. *Hearings 2*, 139.

42. *Hearings 2*, 156, (statement of Richard Schweiker, US Senator from PA), 335, 331; Bruce M. Tyler, "The Rise and Decline of the Watts Summer Festival, 1966 to 1986," *American Studies* 31, no. 2 (Fall 1990): 61–81; *Hearings 2*, 156.

43. "Ten Point Program of the Black Panther Party for Self-Defense (October 1966)," in Huey P. Newton, "War Against the Panthers: A Study of Repression in America" (PhD diss., University of California, Santa Cruz, 1980), 141–146.

44. US National Archives, Records of the FBI ca. 1966–1969, "Black Panther," Record identifier 12101. Available at: https://www.youtube.com/watch?v=IrZIEMrmVrw&feature=you tu.be. On Panther organizing in Oakland, see Donna Murch, *Living for the City: Migration, Education, and the Rise of the Black Panther Party in Oakland, California* (Chapel Hill: University of North Carolina Press, 2010).

45. *Assaults on Law Enforcement: Hearings 2*, 78.

46. Robin C. Spencer, *The Revolution Has Come: Black Power, Gender, and the Black Panther Party in Oakland* (Berkeley: University of California Press, 2016), 89.

47. *Assaults on Law Enforcement: Hearings 2*, 78; Spencer, *The Revolution Has Come*, 89; Balko, *The Rise of the Warrior Cop: The Militarization of America's Police Forces* (New York: Public Affairs, 2013), 76.

48. *Assaults on Law Enforcement: Hearings 2*, 379–380; *Hearings 2*, 135.

49. *Hearings 2*, 445; *Hearings 2*, 109.

50. *Hearings 2*, 258, 371; Takagi, "A Garrison State."

51. *Assaults on Law Enforcement: Hearings 2*, 73; *Hearings 2*, 69–70.

CHAPTER 5: THE POISONED TREE

1. Michael Bernstein and Erik Girard, "Black Whisper Turns to Shout," *Washington DC News*, October 28, 1969, pg. 7, Lemberg Folder "VA—Alexandria 10/9 Police vs. Youths," Box 13.

2. Maurine McLaughlin, "Controversial Policeman: 'I'm Paid to Defend Citizens,'" *Washington Post*, October 10, 1969, pg. C1, Lemberg Folder "VA—Alexandria 10/9 Police vs. Youths," Box 13.

3. McLaughlin, "Controversial Policeman," C1.

4. McLaughlin, "Controversial Policeman," C1; Joseph D. Whitaker, "Black Youth Tells of Chase: 'Then He Took Out His Gun,'" *Washington Post*, October 10, 1969, pg. C1, Lemberg Folder "VA—Alexandria 10/9 Police vs. Youths," Box 13.

5. Whitaker, "Death Unites Blacks," *Washington Post*, June 7, 1970, pg. D1; At $8,000, the median white family income was double that of their Black counterparts. McLaughlin, "The City Still Faces South a Century after Civil War," *Washington Post*, June 26, 1969, pg. G1.

6. "Alexandria Melee Quelled," *Washington Post*, July 6, 1968, pg. B2.

7. McLaughlin, "Controversial Policeman," C1; "Melee Shakes Alexandria," *Washington Post*, October 10, 1969, pg. C1, Lemberg Folder "VA—Alexandria 10/9 Police vs. Youths," Box 13.

8. "'A Few Bad Apples': Phrase Describing Rotten Police Officers Used to Have Different

Meaning," written by Malorie Cunningham, aired 14 June, 2020, on *ABC News*, https://abcnews.go.com/US/bad-apples-phrase-describing-rotten-police-officers-meaning/story?id=71201096; "Bad Apple Proverbs: There's One in Every Bunch," written by Geoff Nunberg, aired May 5, 2011, on NPR *Fresh Air*, https://www.npr.org/2011/05/09/136017612/bad-apple-proverbs-theres-one-in-every-bunch; Helen Rosner, "How Apples Go Bad," *New Yorker*, June 8, 2020. Available at: https://www.newyorker.com/culture/annals-of-gastronomy/how-apples-go-bad.

9. Whitaker, "Black Youth Tells of Chase," C1.

10. Whitaker, "Black Youth Tells of Chase," C1; "Melee Shakes Alexandria," C1; McLaughlin, "Controversial Policeman," C1.

11. Whitaker, "Black Youth Tells of Chase," C1; McLaughlin, "Controversial Policeman," C1.

12. Whitaker, "Black Youth Tells of Chase," C1.

13. McLaughlin, "Controversial Policeman," C1; Whitaker, "Black Youth Tells of Chase," C1.

14. Whitaker, "Black Youth Tells of Chase," C1; McLaughlin, "Controversial Policeman," C1.

15. McLaughlin, "Controversial Policeman," C1.

16. McLaughlin, "Controversial Policeman" C1; Juvenile complaints are issued by officers themselves, rather than justices of the peace; Whitaker, "Black Youth Tells of Chase," C1; "Melee Shakes Alexandria," C1.

17. McLaughlin, "Controversial Policeman," C1; Hank Burchard and Carl W. Sims, "2 Police Firings Demanded," *Washington Post*, October 12, 1969, pg. A31, Lemberg Folder "VA—Alexandria 10/9 Police vs. Youths," Box 13; Bernstein and Girard, "Black Whisper Turns to Shout," 7, Lemberg Folder "VA—Alexandria 10/9 Police vs. Youths," Box 13; Betty Jones, "Alexandria: Some Views in a Race Crisis," *Washington DC News*, October 28, 1969, pg. 7.

18. "Melee Shakes Alexandria," C1; Bernstein and Girard, "Black Whisper Turns to Shout," 7; Jones, "Alexandria: Some Views in a Race Crisis."

19. Whitaker, "The 16th Census Tract: Alexandria's Other Side," *Washington Post*, June 26, 1969, pg. G1.

20. Burchard and Sims, "2 Police Firings Demanded," A31.

21. Burchard and Sims, "2 Police Firings Demanded," A31.

22. Burchard and Sims, "2 Police Firings Demanded," A31; Bernstein and Girard, "Black Whisper Turns to Shout," 7.

23. McLaughlin, "Alexandria May Cancel Night Football," *Washington Post*, September 10, 1968, pg. A3; McLaughlin, "Negro Students Volunteer to Bar Violence at Football Games," *Washington Post*, September 12, 1968, pg. C16.

24. "Police Arrest Three Youths After Alexandria Store Fight," *Washington Post*, September 23, 1969, C7; Paul Hodge, "Fire Bombs Hurled," B1, Lemberg Folder "VA—Alexandria 10/9 Police vs. Youths," Box 13.

25. Sandee Toothman, "2 Nights of Fire Bombs Rock Area," *Alexandria Gazette*, October 20, 1969, pg. 1, Lemberg Folder "VA—Alexandria 10/9 Police vs. Youths," Box 13; Hodge, "Fire Bombs Hurled, " B1; Kevin Klose, "Alexandria Secretly Drafts Plan to Meet Most of Negro Demands," *Washington Post*, October 19, 1969, pg. 1.

26. Toothman, "2 Nights of Fire Bombs Rock Area," 1; "Fire Bombs Hit Official's Firm in Alexandria," *Washington DC Star*, October 19, 1969, pg. 3A, Lemberg Folder "VA—Alexandria 10/9 Police vs. Youths," Box 13.

27. Jones, "Alexandria: Some Views in a Race Crisis," 7; Toothman, "Columbus St. Market

Hit by Fire Bomb," *Alexandria Gazette*, October 21, 1969 pg. 1, Lemberg Folder "VA—Alexandria 10/9 Police vs. Youths," Box 13.

28. "DC Black Revolutionaries Enter Local Protests," *Alexandria Globe*, October 23, 1969, pg. 1, Lemberg Folder "VA—Alexandria 10/9 Police vs. Youths," Box 13; Toothman, "Columbus St. Market Hit by Fire Bomb," 1; John Reichman, "Council Adopts 4-Point Program to Curb Unrest," *Alexandria Gazette*, October 23, 1969, pg. 1, Lemberg Folder "VA—Alexandria 10/9 Police vs. Youths," Box 13.

29. Reichman, "Council Adopts 4-Point Program," 1; "Two Youths Are Found Guilty in Callahan-Strickland Case," *Alexandria Globe*, December 4, 1969, pg. 8, Lemberg Folder "VA—Alexandria 10/9 Police vs. Youths," Box 13; McLaughlin, "Alexandria Acts on Race Tension," *Washington Post*, October 21, 1969, pg. C1.

30. "DC Black Revolutionaries Enter Local Protests"; Joy Aschenbach, "Firing of Alexandria Policeman Asked," *Washington Star*, October 15, 1969, pg. B1; Toothman, "Columbus St. Market Hit By Fire Bomb," 1; "Firebombing Hits Store in Alexandria," *Washington Post*, October 21, 1969, pg. C1.

31. "Melee Shakes Alexandria," C1; McLaughlin, "Alexandria Lifts 'Emergency' Bans," *Washington Post*, June 7, 1970, pg. 1.

32. "Policeman, Alexandria, Being Sued," *Richmond Times-Dispatch*, November 14, 1969, pg. 13D, Lemberg Folder "VA—Alexandria 10/9 Police vs. Youths," Box 13; "Callahan, Alexandria Face Suit," *Washington Post*, November 14, 1969, pg. C9; "Alexandria Policeman in '69 Race Case Quits," *Washington Post*, June 3, 1970, pg. A4.

33. McLaughlin, "Pvt. Callahan Is Honored in Alexandria," *Washington Post*, October 30, 1969, pg. B1.

34. McLaughlin, "Pvt. Callahan Is Honored in Alexandria," B1.

35. McLaughlin, "Pvt. Callahan Is Honored in Alexandria," B1.

36. J. Y. Smith, "2 Alexandria Negroes Get Probation in Arrest Fracas," *Washington Post*, December 10, 1969, pg. 33.

37. Maurine McLaughlin and Alex Ward, "Hawes Retiring as Police Chief in Alexandria," *Washington Post*, December 17, 1968, pg. B1.

38. Bernstein and Girard, "Black Whisper Turns to Shout," 7.

39. "Week's Disorders End in Alexandria," *New York Times*, June 7, 1970, pg. 39; Vernon Miles, "Flashes of Violence in City's History," *Alexandria Gazette Packet*, June 28, 2017, pg. 1.

40. McLaughlin, "Alexandria Lifts 'Emergency' Bans," 1.

41. McLaughlin, "Alexandria Lifts 'Emergency' Bans," 1.

42. "Week's Disorders End in Alexandria," 39.

43. "Week's Disorders End in Alexandria," 39; McLaughlin, "Alexandria Lifts 'Emergency' Bans," 1; "Alexandria Slayer Out on Parole," *Washington Post*, October 16, 1971, pg. D16.

CHAPTER 6: THE SCHOOLS

1. On the history of segregation in the northern states, particularly in school systems, see Matthew F. Delmont, *Why Busing Failed: Race, Media and National Resistance to School Desegregation* (Berkeley: University of California Press, 2016); Davison M. Douglas, *Jim Crow Moves North: The Battle over Northern School Segregation, 1865-1954* (Cambridge: Cam-

bridge University Press, 2005); Ansley T. Erickson, *Making the Unequal Metropolis: School Desegregation and Its Limits* (Chicago: University of Chicago Press, 2017); David G. Garcia, *Strategies of Segregation: Race, Resident, and the Struggle for Educational Equality* (Berkeley: University of California Press, 2018); James K. Nelsen, *Educating Milwaukee: How One City's History of Segregation and Struggle Shaped Its Schools* (Madison: Wisconsin Historical Society Press, 2015); Brian Purnell et al., eds., *The Strange Careers of Jim Crow North: Segregation and Struggle Outside the South* (New York: New York University Press, 2019).

2. Robert A. Dentler, "Barriers to Northern School Desegregation," *Daedalus* 95, no. 1 (1966): 45–63; Sean F. Reardon and Ann Owens, "60 Years After *Brown*: Trends and Consequences of School Segregation," *Annual Review of Sociology* 40, no.1 (2014): 199–218; Joint Economic Committee, the United States Congress, "The Economic State of Black America in 2020." Available at: https://www.jec.senate.gov/public/_cache/files/ccf4dbe2 -810a-44f8-b3e7-14f7e5143ba6/economic-state-of-black-america-2020.pdf; Emily Richmond, "Schools Are More Segregated Today than During the Late 1960s," *Atlantic*, June 11, 2012. Available at: https://www.theatlantic.com/national/archive/2012/06/schools-are -more-segregated-today-than-during-the-late-1960s/258348/.

3. Kathryn Anne Schumaker, "Investing in Segregation: The Long Struggle for Racial Equity in Cairo, Illinois, Public Schools," *Ohio Valley History* 14, no.3 (2014): 48–67; Paul Good, *Cairo, Illinois: Racism at Floodtide*, US Commission on Civil Rights, Clearinghouse Publication no. 44 (October 1973); "200 Negroes Walk Out at Argo School," *Chicago Tribune*, September 6, 1968, pg. A2; "Negroes Protest Election: All-White Cheerleader Team Causes Walk Out," *New Journal and Guide*, May 10, 1969, pg. 16.

4. For a sustained discussion on the ties between the cheerleading issue and civil rights struggles, see Amira Rose Davis, "Black Cheerleaders and a Long History of Protest," *Black Perspectives* (n.p.: African American Intellectual History Society) January 3, 2019. Available at: https://www.aaihs.org/black-cheerleaders-and-a-long-history-of-protest/. See also Rose Davis, *"Can't Eat a Medal:" The Lives of Black Women Athletes in the Age of Jim Crow*, especially chap. 5 (Chapel Hill: University of North Carolina Press, forthcoming 2021); "Aliquippa Riot Ebbs, Parleys on Race Start," *New Pittsburgh Courier*, May 30, 1970, pg. 1.

5. "Black Students to Demand Colleagues Be Reinstated," Harrisburg *Patriot*, February 27, 1969, pg. X; "School Holiday Called," Harrisburg *Patriot*, February 18, 1969, pg. 1; on the Black student movement at colleges and universities, see Martha Biondi, *The Black Revolution on Campus* (Berkeley: University of California Press, 2014).

6. House Committee on Education and Labor, *Juvenile Delinquency Prevention and Runaway Youth Hearings before the Subcommittee on Equal Opportunities*, 93rd Cong., 2nd sess. (held in Los Angeles, March 29 and Washington, DC, April 21, May 1–2, 8, and 21, 1974); on the school-to-prison pipeline see Nancy A. Heitzeg, *The School-to-Prison Pipeline: Education, Discipline, and Racialized Double Standards* (New York: Praeger, 2016); Elizabeth Hinton, *From the War on Poverty to the War on Crime: The Making of Mass Incarceration in America*, chap. 6 (Cambridge, MA: Harvard University Press, 2016); Monique Morris, *Pushout: The Criminalization of Black Girls in Schools* (New York: The New Press, 2016); Kelly Welch and Allison Ann Payne, "Racial Threat and Punitive School Discipline," *Social Problems* 57, no.1 (2010): 25–48; Heather Ann Thompson, "Why Mass Incarceration Matters: Rethinking Crisis, Decline, and Transformation in Postwar American History," *Journal of American History* 97, no. 3 (December 2010): 703–758.

7. "Cops Arrest Eight Youths at Asbury Park High," Newark *Star-Ledger*, October 2, 1970, no page given, Lemberg Folder "NJ—Asbury Park September 20," Box 4.

8. Joseph R. McClure, "A City's Centennial: Harrisburg's 1960 Celebration as a Pivotal Event," (master's thesis, American Studies, Pennsylvania State University at Harrisburg, 2015), 66; "Crisis in Racially-Troubled Capital Schools Said Easing," Warren *Times-Mirror and Observer*, February 22, 1969, pg. 3.

9. "School Holiday Called," Harrisburg *Patriot*, February 18, 1969, pg. 1.

10. "School Holiday Called," pg. 1.

11. "Disorderly Activity Leads to School Board Action," Harrisburg *Patriot*, February 20, 1969, pg. 1.

12. "Disorderly Activity Leads to School Board Action," pg. 1.

13. "Disorderly Activity Leads to School Board Action," pg. 1; McClure, 68; "School Holiday Called," pg. 1.

14. "New Waves of Violence Shut Harrisburg Schools," *Pocono Record*, February 21, 1969, pg. 1; "City Black Coalition Terms Straub, Shafer 'Militaristic,'" Harrisburg *Patriot*, February 22, 1969, pg. 1.

15. "Harrisburg Schools Still Seething with Disorders," *Oil City Derrick*, February 21, 1969, pg. 20.

16. "Harrisburg Schools Still Seething with Disorders," pg. 20.

17. "Eleven Youths Under Arrest," Harrisburg *Patriot*, February 21, 1969, pg. 1; "White Pupils Absent at Harrisburg," *Indiana Gazette*, February 22, 1969, pg. 2.

18. "City Black Coalition Terms Straub, Shafer 'Militaristic'"; "White Pupils Absent."

19. Black Students to Demand Colleagues Be Reinstated," Harrisburg *Patriot*, February 27, 1969, pg 1; Erwin Endress, "School Board Vows to Resolve Demands of Black Students," Harrisburg *Patriot*, March 1, 1969, pg. 1.

20. "Black Student Union Charges Schools Distorted Demands," Harrisburg *Patriot*, March 19, 1959, pg. 9.

21. *Pennsylvania Human Relations Commission, Investigative Hearing Report—City of Harrisburg, Dauphin County* (1969), 44.

22. "Around the Nation: Burlington Curfew Imposed," *Washington Post*, May 18, 1969, pg. A10.

23. "Around the Nation: Burlington Curfew Imposed," pg. A10.

24. A. Howard White, "It Was a Long Tragic Night for Burlington," Burlington *Daily Times-News*, May 17, 1969, pg. 1; "High School Protestors Arrested," *Charlotte Observer*, May 17, 1969, pg. 1C.

25. "Town Quiet: Burlington Curfew Lifted, Guard Says," *Charlotte Observer*, May 20, 1969, pg. 5A; Charlie Frago, "Violence of 1969 Still Haunts Family: Thirty-Two Years after a Race Riot Tore Burlington Apart, a Family Seeks Answers and a City Ponders Race Relations Today," Greensboro *News & Record*, May 15, 2001. Available at: https://greensboro.com/violence-of-1969-still-haunts-victims-family-thirty-two-years-after-a-race-riot-tore/article_bc7e44fb-7d96-5804-921f-202668d0e21d.html.

26. Jim Lasley, "Black Youth Killed in Night of Violence," Burlington *Daily Times-News*, May 17, 1969, pg. 1; "Around the Nation: Burlington Curfew Imposed," pg. A10.

27. Frago, "Violence of 1969." Lasley, "Black Youth Killed in Night of Violence." The song "Mustang Sally" was popularized by Wilson Pickett on his 1966 album "The Wicked Pickett," although James Brown covered the song and performed it with Pickett in the late 1960s. This description is based on Zenobia Mebane's recollection—it is possible that the lyrics on Leon Mebane's coat referenced a different James Brown song, or that Wilson Pickett was in fact Leon Mebane's favorite singer.

28. Lasley, "Black Youth Killed in Night of Violence"; Frago, "Violence of 1969"; "Burlington Death Reports Differ," illegible paper name, May 18, 1969, pg. 1, Lemberg Folder, "NC—Burlington May 16–19, 1969," Box 11.

29. Timothy Minchin and John A. Salmond, *After the Dream: Black and White Southerners Since 1965* (Lexington: University Press of Kentucky), 97; "Guard Stays in Burlington," *Charlotte Observer*, May 19, 1969, pg. 1C.

30. "Court Gives Probation to Students," *Winston-Salem Journal*, June 19, 1969, pg. 28; "Town Quiet," pg. 5A.

31. Frago, "Violence of 1969."

32. "Guard Clears Snipers in Sweep of College," *National Guardsmen*, no date given, Lemberg Folder "NC—Burlington May 16–19, 1969," Box 11; Newsreel from trailer, "Walls That Bleed: The Story of the Dudley–A&T Uprising." Available at: https://vimeo.com/46754407.

33. "Trouble in Greensboro: A Report of an Open Meeting Concerning the Disturbances at Dudley High School and North Carolina A&T State University," North Carolina State Advisory Committee to the United States Commission on Civil Rights, March 1970. Available at: http://libcdm1.uncg.edu/cdm/essay1969/collection/CivilRights.

34. Senate Committee on Government Operations, *Riots, Civil and Criminal Disorders: Hearings before the Permanent Subcommittee on Investigations Part 22*, 4875, 91st Cong., 1st sess. (July 10, 1969); "Dr. Claude Barnes," Southern Oral History Program, UNC Center for the Study of the American South. Available at: https://sohp.org/2018/03/27/staff-pick-dr-claude-barnes/.

35. "From Black Power to Multicultural Organizing in Greensboro" see chap. 1 (Greensboro Truth and Reconciliation Project Final Report, 2006). Available at: https://greensborotrc.org/pre1979_blackpower.pdf.

36. See Claude W. Barnes, "Bullet Holes in Wall: Reflections on the Dudley/A&T Student Revolt of May 1969," in Barnes, Moseley and Steele, eds. *American National and State Government* (Dubuque, IA: Kendall Hunt, 1997). Available at: https://www.scribd.com/document/265782394/Bullet-Holes-in-the-Wall-The-Dudley-A-T-Student-Revolt-of-May-1969-8-21-14; Barnes, "A Consideration of the Relationship Between Ideology and Activism in the Black Nationalist Movement: A Case Study of the Greensboro Association of Poor People" (master's thesis, Atlanta University, Atlanta, GA, 1981); Steven E. B. Lechner, "Gate City Rising: Continuity and Change within Greensboro's Black Liberation Movement of the 1960s" (master's thesis, University of North Carolina at Greensboro, 2015); Eric Ginsburg, "The Forgotten History of Greensboro's A&T/Dudley Revolt," *Teen Vogue*, May 22, 2020. Available at: https://www.teenvogue.com/story/the-history-of-greensboros-aandtdudley-revolt; "Dr. Claude Barnes."

37. "Trouble in Greensboro."

38. In 1967, Black students at Texas Tech University formed a Student Organization for Black Unity, but it appears to have little or no relation to the Greensboro group, Greensboro Truth and Reconciliation Project Final Report; "Trouble in Greensboro."

39. "Trouble in Greensboro"; *Riots, Civil and Criminal Disorders: Hearings*, 4873.

40. *Riots, Civil and Criminal Disorders: Hearings*, 4874.

41. Greensboro Truth and Reconciliation Project Final Report; "Trouble in Greensboro."

42. Greensboro Truth and Reconciliation Project Final Report; Barnes, "Bullet Holes in Wall."

43. Exhibit No. 734 from *Riots, Civil and Criminal Disorders: Hearings*, Vincent S.

McCullough, "You May Be Next!," North Carolina A&T State University, Greensboro, Student Information Service, Tuesday, May 20, 1969.

44. Greensboro Truth and Reconciliation Project Final Report; *Riots, Civil and Criminal Disorders: Hearings*, 120.

45. "Willie Grimes," Bluford Library at North Carolina A&T State University. Available at: http://www.library.ncat.edu/resources/archives/grimes.html; Amy Dominello, "Who Killed Willie Grimes?" Greensboro *News & Record*, October 26, 2006. Available at: https://greensboro.com/life/community_news/who-killed-willie-grimes/article_f3a2d30f-e060-5743-bc42-b2ded1d125dd.html.

46. Exhibit No. 736 from *Riots, Civil and Criminal Disorders: Hearings*, Barnabus (Willie Drake), "Dear Brothers and Sisters," May 22, 1969; "Guard Clears Snipers in Sweep of College," *National Guardsmen*, no date given, Lemberg Folder "NC—Burlington May 16–19, 1969," Box 11; "Trouble in Greensboro."

47. "Trouble in Greensboro"; "Guard Clears Snipers in Sweep."

48. President's Commission on Campus Unrest, *Report of the President's Commission on Campus Unrest* (Washington, DC: US Department of Health, Education, and Welfare, National Institute of Education, 1970).

49. "Trouble in Greensboro."

50. "Trouble in Greensboro."

51. "Black Students to Demand Colleagues Be Reinstated."

52. "Trouble in Greensboro."

53. Barnes "Bullet Holes in the Wall"; Ginsburg, "The Forgotten History of Greensboro's A&T/Dudley Revolt."

CHAPTER 7: THE COMMISSIONS

1. Anthonly M. Platt provides the best discussions of various riot commissions and task forces in the twentieth century. See *The Politics of Riot Commissions, 1917–1970: A Collection of Official Reports and Critical Essays* (New York: Macmillan, 1971); Lyndon Johnson, "July 27, 1967: Speech to the Nation on Civil Disorders." Available at: https://millercenter.org/the-presidency/presidential-speeches/july-27-1967-speech-nation-civil-disorders; Alice George, "The 1968 Kerner Commission Got It Right, But Nobody Listened," *Smithsonian Magazine* 1 (March 2018). Available at: https://www.smithsonianmag.com/smithsonian-institution/1968-kerner-commission-got-it-right-nobody-listened-180968318/; Susan T. Gooden and Samuel L. Myers Jr., "The Kerner Commission Report Fifty Years Later: Revisiting the American Dream," *The Russell Sage Foundation Journal of the Social Sciences* 4, no. 6 (September 2018): 1–17.

2. For excellent analysis of the shortcomings of the Kerner Commission's analysis, see Keisha L. Bentley-Edwards et al., "How Does It Feel to Be a Problem? The Missing Kerner Commission Report," *The Russell Sage Foundation Journal of the Social Sciences* 4, no. 6 (September 2018): 20–40; Justin Driver, "The Report on Race That Shook America," *Atlantic*, May 2018. Available at: https://www.theatlantic.com/magazine/archive/2018/05/the-report-on-race-that-shook-america/556850/.

3. "Unrest Hits St. Paul; Several Hurt," *Ann Arbor News* August 31, 1968, no page given, Lemberg Folder "MN—St. Paul August 30–31, 1968," Box 9; "12 Officers Hurt in St. Paul Riot,"

Baltimore Sun, September 1, 1968, pg. 4; "St. Paul Quiet After Violence," *Norfolk Virginian* September 2, 1968, pg. 4; "St. Paul Quiet Again," *Ann Arbor News*, September 2, 1968, pg. 8; "St. Paul Quiet," *New York Times*, September 2, 1968, no page given, included in Lemberg Folder "MN—St. Paul August 30–31, 1968," Box 9; Nick Woltman, "50 Years Ago, St. Paul Police Tear Gassed a Barricaded Dance Hall," *Twin Cities Pioneer Press*, August 31, 2018. Available at: https://www.twincities.com/2018/08/31/stem-hall-race-riots-st-paul-labor-day-weekend-1968-50-years-ago-police-civil-rights-investigation/.

4. "Two Major Fires Hit Harrisburg," Harrisburg *Patriot*, April 9, 1968, pg. 1; Pennsylvania Human Relations Commission, "Investigatory Hearing Report—Harrisburg, Dauphin County" (1968), 6.

5. "Investigatory Hearing Report," 30.

6. Paul Good, *Cairo, Illinois: Racism at Floodtide*, US Commission on Civil Rights, Clearinghouse Publication no. 44 (October 1973): 18, 24.

7. Paul G. Edwards, "Study Blames 'Negligent White Society': Blacks Said to Cause Most Alexandria School Problems," *Washington Post*, December 12, 1970, pg. B1.

8. Plessy v. Ferguson, 162 U.S. 537, 551 (1896); Charles M. Payne, "'The Whole United States Is Southern!': *Brown v. Board* and the Mystification of Race," *Journal of American History*, 91 no. 1 (June 1, 2004): 83–91.

9. Daniel Patrick Moynihan, *The Negro Family: A Case for National Action*, chap. iv (Washington, DC: Office of Policy Planning and Research, US Department of Labor, March 1965).

10. "Investigatory Hearing Report," 15.

11. "Investigatory Hearing Report," 15.

12. "Investigatory Hearing Report," 17; Joe McClure, "Harrisburg's Race Problems to the Surface," Harrisburg *Patriot-News*, April 25, 2017. Available at: https://www.pennlive.com/opinion/2017/04/mlks_assassination_helped_brin.html.

13. "Investigatory Hearing Report," 21; "Police Board Called Good Idea Gone Bad," *Simpson's Leader-Times*, July 17, 1969, pg. 2.

14. "Sensitivity Training Ordered for Police," Harrisburg *Patriot*, July 10, 1969, pg. 1; National Education Program, "Revolution Underway." Available at: https://www.youtube.com/watch?v=4Kq-lyySptk.

15. "City Police Are Criticized—By 2 City Policemen" Harrisburg *Patriot*, July 17, 1969, pg. 1.

16. Pennsylvania Human Relations Commission, "Investigatory Hearing Report—Harrisburg, Dauphin County" (1969); "Investigatory Hearing Report" (1968), 7; "Housing in Harrisburg Blamed for Disorders," *Simpson's Leader-Times*, July 3, 1969, pg. 15.

17. "City Officials Check on Cause of 'Trouble,'" Harrisburg *Evening News*, June 24, 1969 pg. 1; "Investigatory Hearing Report" (1969), 8; "Disorder Wave Flares Through Hill, Uptown," Harrisburg *Patriot*, June 27, 1969, pg. 1; "Harrisburg Muscles Against Race Clash," *Simpson's Leader-Times*, June 24, 1969 pg. 1; "Order Restored After Harrisburg Race Riot," Sayre & Athens *Evening Times*, June 25, 1969, pg. 1.

18. On July 31, 1969, a coroner's jury absolved Kertulis of any criminal negligence in the killing of Scott. Kertulis testified that he fired a warning shot, and doctors testified that they discovered "an odor of petroleum products" on Scott's body. "Harrisburg Policeman Not Guilty," *Indiana Gazette*, August 1, 1969, pg. 45.

19. "Straub Joins Coalition in Request," Harrisburg *Evening News*, June 27, 1969, pg. 1.

20. "Straub Joins Coalition in Request," pg. 1.

21. "Straub Joins Coalition in Request," pg. 1; "ACLU Director Says."

22. Brian Kelly, "Lost in the Past: At the Confluence of Two Rivers," *Chicago Tribune*, July 21, 1985, pg. I10; "City Human Relations Panel Pressed as Start on Easing Racial Tensions," Harrisburg *Patriot*, July 3, 1969, pg. 1.

23. "Black Coalition Conducts Own Probe in Boy's Death," Harrisburg *Patriot-News* July 9, 1969, pg. 1.

24. Good, 28.

25. "City Human Relations Panel Pressed"; United Front of Cairo, Illinois, "To: All Media" press release, December 11, 1969, Folder 1057, Box 96, Chicago Urban League Records, University of Illinois at Chicago Library, Special Collections.

26. "ACLU Director Says"; "Black Coalition Conducts Own Probe in Boy's Death"; "Sensitivity Training Ordered for Police"; "Investigatory Hearing Report" (1969), 19.

27. Good, 26, 31–32.

28. Good, 26, 31–32.

29. "Sensitivity Training Ordered for Police."

30. Good, 32.

31. Joseph R. McClure, "A City's Centennial: Harrisburg's 1960 Celebration as a Pivotal Event," (master's thesis, American Studies, Pennsylvania State University at Harrisburg, 2015), 84; "Police Board Called Good Idea Gone Bad"; "City Police Are Criticized."

32. "City Police Are Criticized"; "Police Board Called Good Idea Gone Bad."

33. Good, 29, 33–34.

34. "Investigatory Hearing Report" (1969), 15, 18, 17.

35. "Investigatory Hearing Report" (1969), 4, 23.

36. "Investigatory Hearing Report" (1969), 4.

37. "Investigatory Hearing Report" (1969), 21.

38. "Investigatory Hearing Report" (1969), 53.

39. "Investigatory Hearing Report" (1969), 36–37.

40. Joseph R. McClure, 90; *Census of Population and Housing*, United States Bureau of the Census (Washington, DC, July 2, 2008). Available at: https://www.census.gov/programs -surveys/decennial-census.html; Edith Honan and Kristina Cook, "Special Report: Harrisburg: a City at War with Itself," Reuters, October 27, 2011. Available at: https://www .reuters.com/article/us-usa-harrisburg-politics/special-report-harrisburg-a-city-at-war -with-itself-idUSTRE79Q2RN20111027; "Investigatory Hearing Report" (1969), 36; Frank Pizzoli, "Analysis: Harrisburg City Reforms Human Relations Commission," *Central Voice.com* March 28, 2018. Available at: http://thecentralvoice.com/stories/analysis -harrisburg-city-reconstitutes-human-relations-commission,1434.

41. "Investigatory Hearing Report" (1969), 14, 91.

42. Duane Lindstrom, "A Decade of Waiting in Cairo: A Report of the Illinois Advisory Committee to the United States Commission on Civil Rights" (June 1975): 40, 11.

43. Lindstrom, 11.

44. United States Commission on Civil Rights, "Cairo, Illinois: A Symbol of Racial Polarization (Recommendations Based on The Cairo Hearing, March 23–25, 1972)," 10.

45. Lindstrom, 20.

46. Lindstrom, 19; Koen, *My Story of the Cairo Struggle*, 11–12, 21.

47. Lindstrom, 24.

48. Kelly, "Lost in the Past: At the Confluence of Two Rivers," pg. I10.

49. Kelly, "Lost in the Past: At the Confluence of Two Rivers," pg. I10.

50. David Maraniss and Neil Henry, "Race 'War' in Cairo: Reconciliation Grows as Memories Recede," *Washington Post*, March 22, 1987, pg. A1; Stephen Ford, "Black, Whites Live in Uneasy Peace in Cairo, Ill.," Louisville *Courier Journal*, November 6, 1977, pg. 1; "Reconciliation Grows as Memories Recede," *Washington Post*, March 22, 1987, pg. A1.

51. Otto Kerner et al., *Report of the National Advisory Commission on Civil Disorders*. (Washington, DC: US Government Printing Office, 1968), 219.

52. Maraniss and Henry, "Race 'War' in Cairo"; "Cairo, Illinois, Population 2020," *World Population Review*. Available at: https://worldpopulationreview.com/us-cities/cairo-il-population.

CHAPTER 8: THE SYSTEM

1. Bruce Porter and Marvin Dunn, *The Miami Riot of 1980: Crossing the Bounds* (Lexington, MA: Lexington Books, 1984), 53; "Riot Victim, 12, Spirited Despite Leg Amputation," *New York Times*, January 7, 1981, pg. A14.

2. George Lardner Jr. and Margot Hornblower, "Miami: Brutality Was Not Expected," *Washington Post*, May 25, 1980, pg. A1; "Riot Victim, 12"; Porter and Dunn, 52; Nicholas Griffin, *The Year of Dangerous Days: Riots, Refugees, and Cocaine in Miami 1980* (New York: 37 Ink, 2020).

3. Porter and Dunn, 53.

4. Jo Thomas, "Study Finds Miami Riot Was Unlike Those of the 60's," *New York Times*, May 17, 1981, pg. 28; Manning Marable, "The Fire This Time: The Miami Rebellion, May 1980," *Black Scholar* 11, no. 6 (1980): 2–18.

5. Porter and Dunn, 58.

6. William G. Nagel, "An American Archipelago: The United States Bureau of Prisons" (presented at the luncheon general session, National Institute for Crime and Delinquency; Statler-Hilton Hotel, Boston, MA, June 25, 1974), Folder 14, Box 78, Noel Sterrett—Issues Office Files, Jimmy Carter Presidential Library (hereafter JCPL). See also Hinton, *From the War on Poverty to the War on Crime: The Making of Mass Incarceration in America*, chap. 4 (Cambridge, MA: Harvard University Press, 2016).

7. Between 1970 and 1977, the percentage of Black and Latinx prisoners in the federal system grew from 27.4 percent to more than 38 percent, while by 1973, 48 percent of all people in state prisons were Black. In urban centers such as Philadelphia, the residents confined in the county jail went from 50 percent Black in 1970 to 95 percent four years later. In Pennsylvania as a whole—a state known for exceptionally violent and frequent rebellions during the late 1960s and early 1970s, in Harrisburg and elsewhere—Black citizens accounted for more than 62 percent of those incarcerated in state prisons in the 1970s, even though they constituted less than 10 percent of the state's population. In Florida during that period, Black residents represented 15 percent of the state's population but 55 percent of its prisoners. William G. Nagel, "On Behalf of a Moratorium on Prison Construction," *Crime and Delinquency* 23, no. 154 (1977): 154–171, 159; Bureau of Justice Statistics, "State and Federal Prisoners, 1925–1985," (Washington, DC: Bureau of Justice Statics, 1985). Available at: https://perma.cc/6F2E-U9WL.

8. Nagel, "An American Archipelago"; "Magnitude of the Wave of Jail and Prison Construc-

tion in the United States during the 1970s," *National Moratorium on Prison Construction*, (January 1977), Folder 1, Box 11, Gutierrez Files, JCPL.

9. In March 1969, a total of 994 Black men and 131 Black women held elected office across the United States. By May 1975, these numbers had increased nearly twofold for Black men (to 2,969 elected officials), and threefold for Black women (to a total of 530). By the mid-1970s, 1,438 Black Americans had been elected to municipal government positions, with an additional 939 sitting on city or county boards of education; 387 served as judges and in other elected law enforcement roles; 281 had won seats in state legislatures and state-level executive positions; and there were 18 Black politicians in the House of Representatives. Manning Marable, *Race, Reform, and Rebellion: The Second Reconstruction in Black America, 1945–1982* (Jackson, University Press of Mississippi, 1984), 117. See also J. Phillip Thompson III, *Double Trouble: Black Mayors, Black Communities, and the Call for a Deep Democracy* (New York: Oxford University Press, 2005).

10. Manning Marable, *Race, Reform, and Rebellion*, 145.

11. Shockley changed his story about the circumstances of Heath's killing: he originally told police he shot the young Black man during a struggle; he later testified that he killed Heath as he stood with his hands against the warehouse. Shockley and Hialeah police maintained that Heath was attempting to burglarize the warehouse at the time of his death. Donald P. Baker et al., "Racism Charge Stings Pioneering Prosecutor," *Washington Post*, May 23, 1980. Available at: https://www.washingtonpost.com/archive/politics/1980/05/23/racism -charge-stings-pioneering-prosecutor/c7656309-42ea-4969-a801-acb4123c754d/; "Jury Didn't Get State Request for Charges Against Policeman," *Lakeland Ledger*, April 10, 1980, pg. 24; Bill Gjebre, "Heath's Sister to Talk to Rights Jury," *Miami News*, June 11, 1980, pg. 14; Porter and Dunn, 28, 19.

12. Johnny L. Jones v. Florida, 466 So. 2d 301 (1985) No. 81–2176, (Fla. 3d DCA); Porter and Dunn, 32. After Jones appealed the 1980 decision, and on February 26, 1985, his conviction was reversed and he was granted a new trial by the 3rd District Court of Appeal. In July 1986, the Florida state attorney's office declined to prosecute Jones a second time. "Jones Won't Be Retried in 'Gold Plumbing' Case," *Orlando Sentinel*, July 5, 1986. Available at: https://www.orlandosentinel.com/news/os-xpm-1986-07-04-0230340238-story.html.

13. Porter and Dunn, 39.

14. Porter and Dunn, 36.

15. Larry Holmes, "Eyewitness Account," in *Miami: A Rebellion Against Poverty & Injustice: Selected Articles from the Pages of Workers World*, pamphlet (Workers World Party, 1980).

16. Lardner Jr. and Hornblower, "Miami: Brutality Was Not Expected," *Washington Post*, May 25, 1980, pg. A1.

17. Porter and Dunn, 49; Daryl Harris, *The Logic of Black Rebellion: Challenging the Dynamics of White Domination in Miami* (Westport, CT: Praeger, 1999), 3.

18. Daniel Patrick Moynihan, *Family and Nation* (New York: Harcourt Brace Jovanovich, 1986); Reynolds Farley, "The Quality of Life for Black Americans Twenty Years after the Civil Rights Revolution," *Milbank Quarterly* 65, supplement 1, pt. 1 (1987): 9–34; Herbert Denton, "Riot Without Rhetoric: Small Boys in Black Miami Vent Despair," *Washington Post*, July 30, 1980, pg. A1.

19. Marable, "The Fire This Time"; Denton, "Riot Without Rhetoric"; Porter and Dunn, 190, 196.

20. Porter and Dunn, 196.

21. Marable, "The Fire This Time"; Marvin Dunn, "Miami's Explosion Isn't Miami's Alone," *New York Times*, May 20, 1980, pg. A19.

22. National Commission on the Causes and Prevention of Violence Miami Study Team, *Miami Report: The Report of the Miami Study Team on Civil Disturbances in Miami, Florida During the Week of August 5, 1968* (Washington, DC: US Government Printing Office, 1969); Porter and Dunn, 15, 17.

23. Porter and Dunn, 76.

24. Porter and Dunn, 77.

25. Porter and Dunn, 80–81, 91.

26. Porter and Dunn, 79, 77, 82.

27. Denton, "Riot Without Rhetoric."

28. Marable, "The Fire This Time"; Jo Thomas, "Study Finds Miami Riot Was Unlike Those of the 60's," *New York Times*, May 17, 1981, pg. 28; Porter and Dunn, 50.

29. Harris 2; Porter and Dunn, 62–63.

30. Porter and Dunn, 64.

31. Porter and Dunn, 124.

32. Porter and Dunn, 124.

33. Porter and Dunn, 125. On the "right" of Black Americans to loot, see Eldridge Cleaver, "Credo for Rioters and Looters."

34. Porter and Dunn, 67, 145; Harris, 87; Marable, "The Fire This Time."

35. Anthony Chase, "In the Jungle of Cities," *Michigan Law Review* 84, no.4 (1986): 737–759; Porter and Dunn, 65, 97.

36. Holmes, "Eyewitness Account"; Marable, "The Fire This Time."

37. Porter and Dunn, 102.

38. Porter and Dunn, 71–72.

39. Marable, "The Fire This Time"; Porter and Dunn, 71–72.

40. Porter and Dunn, 68, 73, 167; John Crewdson, "Guard Reinforced to Curb Miami Rioting," *New York Times*, May 20, 1980, pg. A1.

41. Earl Ofari Hutchinson, *Betrayed: A History of Presidential Failure to Protect Black Lives* (Boulder, CO: Westview Press, 1996), 174.

42. Hutchinson, 171–172; Porter and Dunn, 168.

43. Porter and Dunn, 169.

44. "Rioting in a Black Area of Miami Follows a Shooting by the Police," *New York Times*, December 29, 1982, pg. A8; Sonia L. Nazario, "Ghetto Realities," *Wall Street Journal*, December 30, 1982, pg. 1.

45. Robert M. Press, "Miami Rioting Again Raises Issues of Police Misconduct," *Christian Science Monitor*, December 30, 1982, pg. 4; Robert McClure, "Miami Police Indicted in Riot Slaying," *Philadelphia Tribune*, March 4, 1983, pg. 9.

46. Lee May, "'Fear in Ghetto': Miami Riot Area Jittery as Police Trials Approach," *Los Angeles Times*, June 19, 1983, pg. 1; "Miami Officer Convicted in Slaying of Black Man," *New York Times*, September 17, 1983, pg. 7; Rick Atkinson, "Miami Jury Acquits Policeman in Fatal Shooting of Black," *Washington Post*, March 16, 1984. Available at: https://www.washingtonpost.com/archive/politics/1984/03/16/miami-jury-acquits-policeman-in-fatal-shooting-of-black/4f3b1682-1397-4fa0-b4bb-ca05dfd16414/.

47. May, "'Fear in Ghetto.'"

48. Jeffrey Schmalz, "Trial Forces Miami to Confront Its Legacy of Racial Tensions," *New York Times*, November 13, 1989, pg. A1.

49. Schmalz, "Trial Forces Miami to Confront Its Legacy," A1.

CHAPTER 9: THE PROPOSAL

1. Los Angeles Police Commission and William H. Webster, *The City in Crisis: A Report* (Los Angeles, CA, Washington, DC: Special Advisor Study, Inc., Police Foundation, 1992); Seth Mydans, "'Trial and Error' in Los Angeles as Gangs Maintain Truce," *New York Times*, May 18, 1992, pg. B8.

2. Tom Hayden, *Street Wars: Gangs and the Future of Violence* (New York: New Press, 2004), 187; João Helion Costa Vargas, *Catching Hell in the City of Angels: Life and Meanings of Blackness in South Central Los Angeles*, chap. 4 (Minneapolis: University of Minnesota Press, 2006); "Forget the LA Riots—Historic 1992 Watts Gang Truce Was the Big News," written by Frank Stoltze, aired April 28, 2012, on *89.3 KPCC*. Available at: https://www.scpr.org/news/2012/04/28/32221/forget-la-riots-1992-gang-truce-was-big-news/.

3. Author interview with Colton Simpson by telephone, October 22, 2005, and November 27, 2005; Personal correspondence with "Tim K," October 10, 2005. On rise of gangs and gang activity in Los Angeles, see Alejandro A. Alonso, "Territoriality Among African-American Street Gangs" (master's thesis, University of Southern California, Department of Geography, Los Angeles, 1999); Donald Bakeer, *Crips: The Story of the LA Street Gang from 1971–1985* (Los Angeles: Precocious Publishing Company, 1992); Yusuf Jah and Sister Shah'Keyah, *Uprising: Crips and Bloods Tell the Story of America's Crossfire* (New York: Scribner, 1995); Josh Sides, *LA City Limits: African American Los Angeles from the Great Depression to the Present* (Berkeley: University of California Press, 2003); Colton Simpson with Ann Pearlman, *Inside the Crips: Life Inside LA's Most Notorious Gang* (New York: St. Martin's Press, 2005); Stanley "Tookie" Williams, *Blue Rage, Black Redemption: A Memoir* (Los Angeles: Damamli Publishing Company, 2004).

4. On the LAPD's CRASH force, see Mike Davis *City of Quartz: Excavating the Future of Los Angeles*, new ed., (New York: Verso, 2006); Elizabeth Hinton, *From the War on Poverty to the War on Crime: The Making of Mass Incarceration in America*, chap. 6 (Cambridge, MA: Harvard University Press, 2016); Max Felker-Kantor, *Policing Los Angeles: Race, Resistance, and the Rise of the LAPD* (Chapel Hill: The University of North Carolina Press, 2018); Donna Murch, "Crack in Los Angeles: Crisis, Militarization, and Black Response to the Late Twentieth-Century War on Drugs," *Journal of America History* 102, no.1 (2015): 162–173.

5. House Committee of the Judiciary, *Organized Criminal Activity by Youth Gangs: Hearings before the Subcommittee on Criminal Justice*, 100th Cong., 2nd sess. (June 6, 1988); Wesley D. McBride, "Police Departments and Gang Intervention: The Operation Safe Streets Concept," in Arnold P. Goldstein and C. Ronald Huff, eds., *The Gang Intervention Handbook* (Champaign, IL: Research Press, 1993): 411–415, 413; National Criminal Justice Reference Service, "Homicide: 2017 National Crime Victims' Rights Resource Guide: Crime and Victimization Fact Sheets." Available at: https://www.ncjrs.gov/ovc_archives/ncvrw/2017/images/en_artwork/Fact_Sheets/2017NCVRW_Homicide_508.pdf; Alexia D. Cooper and Erica L. Smith, *Homicide Trends in the United States, 1980–2008*, Bureau

of Justice Statistics, Homicide Trends in the United States Series 2011; Manning Marable, *Race, Reform, Rebellion*, 152; Violence Prevention Coalition of Greater Los Angeles, "Fact Sheet: Gang Violence," Available at: http://publichealth.lacounty.gov/ivpp/injury_topics/GangAwarenessPrevention/Gang_Violence_VPC2009.pdf; Felker-Kantor, 230.

6. Social science research has consistently demonstrated that Black Americans, especially those who live in segregated neighborhoods with high levels of poverty, tend to be less trusting of not only law enforcement officials, but also their neighbors and romantic partners. See Monica C. Bell, "Safety, Friendship, and Dreams," *Harvard Civil Rights-Civil Liberties Law Review* 54 (2019): 703–739; Richard R. W. Brooks, "Fear and Fairness in the City: Criminal Enforcement and Perceptions of Fairness in Minority Communities," *Southern California Law Review* 73 (2000): 1219–1273; Tracey L. Meares, "Charting Race and Class Differences in Attitudes Toward Drug Legalization and Law Enforcement: Lessons for Federal Criminal Law," *Buffalo Criminal Law Review* 1, no.1 (1997): 137–174; Sandra Susan Smith, "Race and Trust," *Annual Review of Sociology* 36 (2010): 453–75. See also Robert J. Sampson, *Great American City: Chicago and the Enduring Neighborhood Effect* (Chicago: University of Chicago Press, 2012) and Sampson, "Neighbourhood Effects and Beyond: Explaining the Paradoxes of Inequality in the Changing American Metropolis," *Urban Studies* 56, no.1 (2019): 3–32; on the massive cuts from annual federal spending on social programs during the Reagan years, see Margy Waller's report, "Block Grants: Flexibility vs. Stability in Social Services" *Brookings Institute Policy Brief, Center on Children and Families*, no. 34, (December 2005): 1–8; Andrew E. Busch, *Ronald Reagan and the Politics of Freedom* (New York: Rowman and Littlefield, 2001); Richard S. Williamson, "A New Federalism: Proposals and Achievements of President Reagan's First Three Years," *Publius* 16 (Winter 1986): 11–28; Leith Mullings, "Losing Ground: Harlem, the War on Drugs, and the Prison Industrial Complex," *Souls* 5, no. 2 (2003): 1–21.

7. Vargas 199–200; Michael Krikorian and Greg Krikorian, "Watts Truce Holds Even as Hopes Fade," *Los Angeles Times*, May 18, 1997, pg. B1.

8. David Whitman, "The Untold Story of the LA Riot," *US News and World Report*, May 23, 1993. Available at: https://www.usnews.com/news/articles/1993/05/23/the-untold-story-of-the-la-riot; "The LA Riots: 25 Years Later," *Los Angeles Times*, April 26, 2017. Available at: https://timelines.latimes.com/los-angeles-riots/.

9. Mike Davis "In LA, Burning All Illusions" *Nation* 254, no. 21 (June 1992).

10. Quoted in Rubén Martínez, "Riot Scenes," in *Inside the L.A. Riots: What Really Happened, and Why It Will Happen Again: Essays and Articles*, ed. Don Hazen, (New York: Institute for Alternative Journalism, 1992), 32.

11. "Bush: He and Rights Leaders 'Were Stunned' by the King Verdict," *Washington Post*, May 2, 1992, a transcript from President Bush's nationally televised address. Available at: https://www.washingtonpost.com/archive/politics/1992/05/02/bush-he-and-rights-leaders-were-stunned-by-king-verdict/b24eb88d-e5e3-47a1-954e-e043c20161fd/.

12. "Bush: He and Rights Leaders 'Were Stunned' by the King Verdict"; Natalie Ermann Russell, "Riots in the City of Angels," *Miller Center of Public Affairs*, April 24, 2017. Available at: https://millercenter.org/riots-city-angels. Felker-Kantor, 229.

13. "Bush: He and Rights Leaders 'Were Stunned' by the King Verdict"; Russell, "Riots in the City of Angels."

14. "A City in Crisis: Voices," *Los Angeles Times*, May 3, 1992. Available at: https://www.latimes.com/archives/la-xpm-1992-05-03-mn-1958-story.html; Felker-Kantor, 231; "Los

Angeles District, United States Immigration and Naturalization Service, 1992-07-06," Folder 28, Box 9, Los Angeles Webster Commission records, 1931–1992, University of Southern California.

15. Krikorian and Krikorian, "Watts Truce Holds Even as Hopes Fade."

16. Booker Griffin, "Gangs in Seminar Announce Truce," *Los Angeles Sentinel*, December 21, 1972, pg. A1.

17. Hinton, chap. 9; Author Interview with Colton Simpson October 22, 2005.

18. "Coast Police Chief Accused of Racism," *New York Times*, May 13, 1982, pg. 24; Paul Butler, *Chokehold: Policing Black Men* (New York: New Press, 2017), 25; Jill Leovy, *Ghettoside: A True Story of Murder in America* (New York: Spiegel & Grau, 2015), 6; Alexander Cockburn and Jeffrey St. Clair, *Whiteout: The CIA, Drugs, and the Press* (New York: Verso, 1998); Rodolfo Acuña, *Anything but Mexican: Chicanos in Contemporary Los Angeles* (New York: Verso, 1996), 273.

19. Hayden, 92; Cockburn and St. Clair, 77; John L. Mitchell, "The Raid That Still Haunts LA," *Los Angeles Times*, March 14, 2001.

20. "Youth Gang Programs and Strategies," *Office of Juvenile Justice and Delinquency Prevention Summary* (August 2000). Available at: https://www.ncjrs.gov/html/ojjdp/summary_2000_8/suppression.html; Ron Dungee, "Weekend Gang Sweep Results in 352 Arrests," *Los Angeles Times*, August 24, 1989, A1; Nieson Himmel, "LA Gang Killings Put at 236—Up 15% from '87," *Los Angeles Times*, December 16, 1988, C1; Robert Welkos, "700 Seized in Gang Sweep; 2 More Die in Shootings," *Los Angeles Times*, September 19, 1988, 21; Davis, 268; Joe Domanick, *Blue: The LAPD and the Battle to Redeem American Policing* (New York: Simon & Schuster, 2016), 324–325; Felker-Kantor; Sheryl Stolberg, "150,000 Are in Gangs, Report by DA Claims," *Los Angeles Times*, May 22, 1992.

21. Bob Baker and Amy Stevens, "Pastor Hailed, Assailed on Summit to Negotiate Gang Truce," *Los Angeles Times* July 27, 1988; Guy Maxton-Graham and Bob Baker, "Gang Members in Second 'Summit,'" *Los Angeles Times*, September 1, 1988.

22. Seth Mydans, "Gangs Abiding by Cease-Fire in Los Angeles," *New York Times*, June 19, 1992, pg.1; Andrea Ford and Carla Rivera, "Rival Gangs Say Truce Is For Real," *Los Angeles Times*, May 21, 1992, pg. SDA32.

23. Marsha Mitchell, "Gang Truce Holds Despite LAPD Critics," *Los Angeles Sentinel*, May 21, 1992, pg. 1.

24. Mitchell, "Gang Truce Holds"; Michael Zinzun, "The Gang Truce: A Movement for Social Justice," *Social Justice* 24, no. 4 (1997): 258–266, 259.

25. Frank Stoltze, "Forget the LA Riots."

26. Dave Zirin, "Want to Understand the 1992 LA Riots? Start with the 1984 LA Olympics," *Nation* April 30, 2012. Available at: https://www.thenation.com/article/archive/want-understand-1992-la-riots-start-1984-la-olympics/; Max Felker-Kantor, "The 1984 Olympics Fueled LA's War on Crime. Will the 2028 Games Do the Same?" *Washington Post*, August 6, 2017. Available at: https://www.washingtonpost.com/news/made-by-history/wp/2017/08/06/the-1984-olympics-fueled-l-a-s-war-on-crime-will-the-2028-games-do-the-same/.

27. "'Bloods/Crips Proposal' in Bert X. Davila Interview, 1992-07-10," Folder 53, Box 19, Los Angeles Webster Commission records, 1931–1992, University of Southern California.

28. "'Bloods/Crips Proposal' in Bert X. Davila Interview, 1992-07-10."

29. "'Bloods/Crips Proposal' in Bert X. Davila Interview, 1992-07-10."

30. "'Bloods/Crips Proposal' in Bert X. Davila Interview, 1992-07-10."

31. Hayden, 188–189; Kamran Afary, *Performance and Activism: Grassroots Discourse After the Los Angeles Rebellion in 1992* (Lanham, MD: Lexington Books, 2009), 76.

32. Afary, chap. 3.

33. Paul Cotton, "Violence Decreases with Gang Truce," *Journal of the American Medical Association* 268, no. 4 (July 22–29, 1992): 443–444.

34. Cotton, "Violence Decreases with Gang Truce"; Andrea Ford, "Freedoms Rediscovered in Gang Truce," *Los Angeles Times*, August 14, 1992, pg. WA1.

35. "Area Community Leaders Call for Lasting Gang Truce," *Los Angeles Sentinel*, May 28, 1992, pg. A23; Russell Ben-Ali, "Police Wary of LA Gangs' Truce," *Newsday*, May 11, 1992, pg. 17; "Violence Decreases with Gang Truce," *Journal of the American Medical Association* 268, no. 4 (July 22–29 1992): 443–444; Jennifer Rowland, "Crips, Bloods Pledge Truce to Rebuild LA," *United Press International*, May 15, 1992. Available at: https://www.upi.com/Archives/1992/05/15/Crips-Bloods-pledge-truce-to-rebuild-LA/7350705902400/.

36. Mitchell, "Gang Truce Brings Hope."

37. Mydans, "Gangs Abiding by Cease-Fire"; Ben-Ali, "Police Wary of LA Gangs' Truce."

38. Ben-Ali, "Police Wary of LA Gangs' Truce"; "Area Community Leaders Call for Lasting Gang Truce."

39. John L. Mitchell, "No Letup in Random Violence During Gang Truce," *Los Angeles Times*, August 23, 1992, pg. A1; Richard A. Serrano and Jesse Katz, "LAPD Task Force Quietly Deployed Despite Gang Truce," *Los Angeles Times*, June 26, 1992, pg. OCA3.

40. Serrano and Katz, "LAPD Task Force Quietly Deployed Despite Gang Truce."

41. Jesse Katz, "Giant Step: Gang Members Join Forces to Market Their Own Brand of Shoes," *Los Angeles Times*, July 24, 1992, pg. WB1.

42. Katz, "Giant Step: Gang Members Join Forces."

43. Ashley Dunn, "Gang Members Test Capitalist Waters," *Los Angeles Times*, July 4, 1992.

44. Krikorian and Krikorian, "Watts Truce Holds Even as Hopes Fade."

45. Downey, "Between Partnership and Privatism: The Case of Rebuild LA," *Research in Social Problems and Public Policy* 8 (2001): 195–220.

46. Alonso, "Territoriality among African-American Street Gangs in Los Angeles," 5.

47. Krikorian and Krikorian, "Watts Truce Holds Even as Hopes Fade."

48. Krikorian and Krikorian, "Watts Truce Holds Even as Hopes Fade."

49. Stephen Gregory, "South-Central: LAPD's 77th Division Prepares for Move," *Los Angeles Times*, January 15, 1995; Krikorian and Krikorian, "Watts Truce Holds Even as Hopes Fade"; "Bloods/Crips Proposal."

CHAPTER 10: THE REFORMS

1. Stephanie Simon, "Mourners Pray Black Kids Didn't Die in Vain," *Los Angeles Times*, April 15, 2001, pg. A1A.

2. Kevin S. Aldridge, "Cincinnati: The Flashpoint, Unrest and Aftermath," *New Crisis* 108, no. 4 (July/August 2001): 47; Karen Juanita Carrillo, "With Thomas Killing, Cincinnati Death Toll 15," New York *Amsterdam News*, April 19, 2001, pg. 1.

3. Jerry White, "The Cincinnati Riots and the Class Divide in America," pt. 1, "Gentrification and Police Repression," *World Socialist Web Site*, May 24, 2001.

4. Aldridge, "Cincinnati: The Flashpoint"; Ron Daniels, "The Riots in Cincinnati: The City's

History Reveals Some Interesting Causes," *New Journal and Guide*, (May 24, 2001): 2; Carrillo, "With Thomas Killing, Cincinnati Death Toll 15."

5. White, "The Cincinnati Riots and the Class Divide"; Carrillo, "With Thomas Killing, Cincinnati Death Toll 15"; Robert E. Pierre, "Officer Is Acquitted in Killing That Led to Riots in Cincinnati," *Washington Post*, September 27, 2001, pg. A2; Karen Juanita Carrillo, "Cincinnati Boycott Continues," New York *Amsterdam News*, August 1, 2002, pg. 4.

6. White, "The Cincinnati Riots and the Class Divide"; Daniels, "The Riots in Cincinnati."

7. Aldridge, "Cincinnati: The Flashpoint."

8. "Community Up in Arms Over Videotaped Police Beating," Associated Press, April 29, 1995. Available at: https://apnews.com/article/4a89849a74d44b8b89a083fd03848684; Aldridge, "Cincinnati: The Flashpoint."

9. Alana Semuels, "How to Fix a Broken Police Department," *Atlantic*, May 28, 2015. Available at: https://www.theatlantic.com/politics/archive/2015/05/cincinnati-police-reform/393797/#:~:text=The%20settlement%20agreement%20for%20the,crimes%20in%20the%20first%20place.

10. Otto Kerner et al., *Report of the National Advisory Commission on Civil Disorders* (Washington, DC: US Government Printing Office, 1968), 27; "61,000 Troops Guard Riot-Ravaged Cities," *Rome News-Tribune*, April 9, 1968, pg. 1; Mark Curnutte, "Avondale Riots 50 Years later: 'It's Never Been the Same,'" *Cincinnati Enquirer*, June 9, 2017. Available at: https://www.cincinnati.com/story/news/2017/06/09/avondale-riots-50-years-later-its-never-been-same/379214001/.

11. Samuel Momodu, "The Cincinnati Riot (2001)," *BlackPast*, October 21, 2017. Available at: https://www.blackpast.org/african-american-history/the-cincinnati-riot-2001/; Andrea Y. Carter, "Calm Falls Over Cincinnati; Push for Peace Begins," *Los Angeles Sentinel*, April 19, 2001, pt. A1; "Police Shooting of Black Man Spurs 2nd Protest in Cincinnati," *Los Angeles Times*, April 11, 2001, pg. A12A; Aldridge, "Cincinnati: The Flashpoint."

12. "Police Shooting of Black Man Spurs 2nd Protest in Cincinnati," *Los Angeles Times*, April 11, 2001, pg. A12A; Aldridge, "Cincinnati: The Flashpoint."

13. Aldridge, "Cincinnati: The Flashpoint."

14. "Rioting in Cincinnati after Police Shooting," *New Pittsburgh Courier*, 28 Apr 2001, pg. 1; "Cincinnati Mayor Prolongs Curfew," *Globe and Mail*, April 14, 2001, pg. A16; Jon Yates and Kareen Brandon, "Cincinnati Under Curfew after Police Shooting, Riots," *Chicago Tribune*, April 13, 2001, pg. L1.

15. Karen Juanita Carrillo, "One life, Two Misdemeanors: Cincinnati's Blacks Shocked by Grand Jury Ruling," New York *Amsterdam News*, May 10, 2001, pg. 2; "Internal Probe Faults Cincinnati Policeman in Shooting," *Los Angeles Times*, March 20, 2002, pg. VCA29; Stephanie Simon, "Mourners Pray Black Kids Didn't Die in Vain," *Los Angeles Times*, April 15, 2001, pg. A1A.

16. Unlike the Black Panther Party, the New Black Panther Party is known for its anti-semitism, racial reductionism, and anti-Marxism. On the politics of the New Black Panther Party, see Derek Musgrove, "'There Is No *New* Black Panther Party:' The Panther-Like Formations and the Black Power Resurgence of the 1990s," *Journal of African American History* 104, no. 4 (2019): 619–656; Simon, "Mourners Pray Black Kids Didn't Die in Vain," pg. A1A. Simon.

17. Simon. "Mourners Pray Black Kids Didn't Die in Vain."

18. Daniels, "The Riots in Cincinnati"; John Iceland et al., *Racial and Ethnic Residential Seg-*

regation in the United States: 1980–2000, US Bureau of the Census, (Washington, DC: US Department of Commerce, August 2002). Available at: https://www.census.gov/prod/2002pubs/censr-3.pdf; Lucy May and G. Scott Thomas, "City's Economic Segregation High," *Cincinnati Business Courier*, December 30, 2002. Available at: https://www.bizjournals.com/cincinnati/stories/2002/12/30/story2.html.

19. White, "The Cincinnati Riots and the Class Divide."

20. White, "The Cincinnati Riots and the Class Divide."

21. White, "The Cincinnati Riots and the Class Divide."

22. Aldridge, "Cincinnati: The Flashpoint"; Daniels, "The Riots in Cincinnati."

23. Stephanie Simon, "From Cincinnati's Mayhem Come Signs of a Better Day," *Los Angeles Times*, April 14, 2001, pg. A1; Karen Juanita Carrillo, "Protest Becomes a Riot in Cincinnati," New York *Amsterdam News*, April 12, 2001, pg. 1.

24. Simon, "From Cincinnati's Mayhem Come Signs of a Better Day," pg. A1

25. Simon, "Mourners Pray Black Kids Didn't Die in Vain," pg. A1A; Nicole Colson, "John Ashcroft's Racist Hysteria," *Socialistworker.org* March 14, 2003, pg. 5.

26. Memorandum to Attorney General John Ashcroft to Evaluate Request from Mayor of Cincinnati, April 12, 2001, Archives of the United States Department of Justice. Available at: https://www.justice.gov/archive/opa/pr/2001/April/172ag.htm; Carrillo, "Protest Becomes a Riot in Cincinnati."

27. Nikhil Pal Singh, *Race and America's Long War* (Berkeley: University of California Press 2017), 7.

28. House Committee of the Judiciary, Pub. L. No. 103–771 "Violent Crime Control and Law Enforcement Act of 1994," Title XXI, Subtitle D "Police Pattern or Practice," H.R. Rep. 3355, 103rd Cong. (1994); *The Civil Rights Division's Pattern and Practice Police Reform Work: 1994–Present*, (Washington, DC: Civil Rights Division, US Department of Justice, January 2017). Available at: https://www.justice.gov/crt/file/922421/download.

29. White, "The Cincinnati Riots and the Class Divide"; Joshua M. Chanin, "Negotiated Justice? The Legal, Administrative, and Policy Implications of 'Pattern or Practice' Police Misconduct Reform" (PhD diss., American University, 2011), 53; Linn Washington Jr., "Cincinnati Blacks Endure Indignities Often," *Philadelphia Tribune*, May 1, 2001, pg. 7A.

30. White, "The Cincinnati Riots and the Class Divide."

31. Jay Rothman and Randi Land, "The Cincinnati Police–Community Relations Collaborative," *Criminal Justice* 35 (2004): 35–42, 38, 35.

32. White, "The Cincinnati Riots and the Class Divide."

33. "Collaborative Agreement," United States District Court, S. D. Ohio Western Division, Case No. C-199-317 Re: Cincinnati, Judge Dlott; Rothman and Land, "The Cincinnati Police–Community Relations Collaborative," 35–42; Jay Rothman, "Identity and Conflict: Police Community Conflict in Cincinnati, Ohio," *Ohio Journal of Dispute Resolution* 22, no.1 (2006): 105–132.

34. "Collaborative Agreement"; Rothman and Land, 38.

35. "Activists Protest Treatment of Blacks," *Los Angeles Times*, June 3, 2001, pg. A8A.

36. Lisa Cornwell, "Leaders Call for Boycott of Cincinnati," *Atlanta Daily World*, July 19, 2001, pg. 3; Stephanie Simon, "Racial Wounds Don't Heal with Time in Cincinnati," *Los Angeles Times*, December 16, 2001, pg. A26; Dan La Botz, "Cincinnati: A Decade Since the Rebellion of 2001—What Have We Learned, Where Are We Now?" *Solidarity*, April 14, 2011;

"Cosby Cancels in Face of Cincinnati Boycott," *Los Angeles Times*, February 9, 2002, pg. OCF2.

37. Saul Green, *City of Cincinnati Independent Monitor Final Report* (Washington, DC: US Department of Justice, December 2008); Semuels, "How to Fix a Broken Police Department"; Stephanie Simon, "Hope, Caution in Cincinnati," *Los Angeles Times*, April 7, 2002, pg. A18; Tony Pugh, "Cincinnati Leaders Reach Agreement on Sweeping Changes One Year After Riot," *Knight Ridder Tribune Business News*, April 4, 2002, pg. 1.

38. Pugh, "Cincinnati Leaders Reach Agreement on Sweeping Changes One Year After Riot"; "Collaborative Agreement"; Green, *Final Report*; Semuels, "How to Fix a Broken Police Department."

39. Simon, "Hope, Caution in Cincinnati," pg. A18.

40. Simon, "Racial Wounds," pg. A26.

41. Green, *Final Report*, 25; Simon, "Hope, Caution in Cincinnati," pg. A18.

42. K. Jack Riley et al., *Police-Community Relations in Cincinnati* (Santa Monica, CA: RAND Corporation, 2005). Available at: https://www.rand.org/pubs/technical_reports /TR333.html; Greg Ridgeway et al., *Police-Community Relations in Cincinnati* (Santa Monica, CA: RAND Corporation, 2009). Available at: https://www.rand.org/pubs /monographs/MG853.html; Green, *Final Report*; Semuels, "How to Fix a Broken Police Department"; "Collaborative Agreement"; Simon, "Hope, Caution in Cincinnati"; Tony Pugh, "Cincinnati Leaders Reach Agreement on Sweeping Changes One Year After Riot."

43. La Botz, "Cincinnati: A Decade since the Rebellion of 2001"; Green, *Final Report*, 29; John Seabrook, "Don't Shoot: A Radical Approach to the Problem of Gang Violence," *New Yorker*, June 15, 2009.

44. Green, *Final Report*, 36; *Police–Community Relations in Cincinnati*, (2005, 2009); Semuels, "How to Fix a Broken Police Department."

45. Semuels.

46. Semuels.

47. La Botz, "Cincinnati: A Decade since the Rebellion of 2001."

48. La Botz.

49. "Blueprint for Peace: What Ferguson Can Learn from Cincinnati," aired August 30, 2014, *NBC News*. Available at: https://www.nbcnews.com/storyline/michael-brown-shooting/ blueprint-peace-what-ferguson-can-learn-cincinnati-n191911; Mark Curnette, "Post-Riot Lessons Here Shared with Ferguson," *Cincinnati Enquirer*, August 17, 2014. Available at: https://www.cincinnati.com/story/news/2014/08/17/damon-lynch-iii-takes-cincinnatis -solution-ferguson/14210949/.

50. Chris Graves and Sharon Coolidge, "Mother at Funeral: 'I Want Justice for My Son,'" *Cincinnati Enquirer*, July 28, 2015. Available at: https://www.cincinnati.com/story/ news/2015/07/28/samuel-dubose-laid--rest/30777221/.

51. Graves and Coolidge; Nick Dutro, "Tywon Thomas: A Life After Violence," *Advertiser-Tribune*, January 7, 2017. Available at: https://advertiser-tribune.com/news/221671/tywon -thomas-a-life-after-violence/.

52. Graves and Coolidge, "Mother at Funeral"; "University of Cincinnati to pay $4.8M and Tuition of Man Slain During Traffic Stop," *Jacksonville Free Press*, January 21, 2016, pg. 12. As of June 5, 2020, the US Attorney's Office for the Southern District of Ohio said that their

review into the fatal shooting of DuBose remains ongoing, although Hamilton County Prosecutor Joe Deters indicated that he would not try Tensing for a third time on charges of murder and voluntary manslaughter. Jennifer Edwards Baker, "Federal Review Ongoing in Sam DuBose Fatal Shooting," *Fox 19*, June 5, 2020. Available at: https://www.fox19 .com/2020/06/05/federal-review-ongoing-sam-dubose-fatal-shooting-nearly-years-later/.

53. Princess-India Alexander, "Former Cop Who Killed Sam DuBose Awarded $350,000 Settlement," *Huffington Post*, March 23, 2018. Available at: https://www.huffpost.com/entry/ former-university-of-cincinnati-cop-who-killed-sam-dubose-awarded-350000-settlemen t_n_5ab521bde4b054d118e26d7c.

CONCLUSION

1. Molly Parker, "March in Cairo—'Birthplace of Civil Rights in the Heartland'—Calls for an End to Racism," *Southern Illinoisan*, June 20, 2020. Available at: https://thesouthern.com/ news/local/march-in-cairo-birthplace-of-civil-rights-in-the-heartland-calls-for-end-to -racism/article_a9b178e2-f9cd-562a-958b-786dfcf757b6.html.

2. Larry Buchanan et al., "Black Lives Matter May Be the Largest Movement in US History," *New York Times*, July 3, 2020. Available at: https://www.nytimes.com/interactive/2020/07/03/us/ george-floyd-protests-crowd-size.html; "Demonstrations & Political Violence in America: New Data for Summer 2020," (Armed Conflict Location & Event Data Project (ACLED), September 2020). Available at: https://acleddata.com/2020/09/03/demonstrations-political -violence-in-america-new-data-for-summer-2020/.

3. "Downtown Protest Turns Tense, Large Police Presence," written by Karli VanCleave, aired June 14, 2020, on *WPTA21* Fort Wayne. Available at: https://wpta21.com/2020/06/14/ downtown-protest-turns-tense/; "Protesters Call to Defund the Police," written by Gabbi Guerrero, aired June 11, 2020, on NBC *25 News*. Available at: https://week.com/2020/06/11/ protesters-call-to-defund-police/.

4. The common assumption that mainstream civil rights activists did not put forth structural critiques of racism is an unfair one. Figures like Martin Luther King Jr. and Bayard Rustin offered a deeply structural political philosophy, rooted in the kind of structural critiques often associated with activists and intellectuals who championed the politics of Black Power.

5. Between the deaths of forty-three-year-old Eric Garner in New York City on July 17, 2014 and October 20, 2020, at least two hundred fifty Black and Latinx women and men have been killed by police. They include, in chronological order: Tyree Woodson, John Crawford III, Michael Brown Jr., Ezell Ford, Dante Parker, Michelle Cusseaux, Kajieme Powell, Latandra Ellington, Laquan McDonald, Aura Rosser, Tanisha N. Anderson, Akai Kareem Gurley, Tamir Rice, Rumain Brisbon, Jerame C. Reid, Artago Damon Howard, Yuvette Henderson, Jeremy Lett, Natasha McKenna, Lavall Hall, Janisha Fonville, Thomas Allen, Charley Leundeu Keunang, Tony Terrell Robinson Jr., Naeschylus Vinzant, Anthony Hill, Bobby Gross, Brandon Jones, Meagan Hockaday, Mya Shawatza Hall, Phillip Gregory White, Eric Courtney Harris, Walter Lamar Scott, Frank Shephard, Freddie Carlos Gray Jr., William L. Chapman II, David Felix, Alexia Christian, Brendon K. Glenn, Richard Davis, Kris Jackson, Spencer McCain, Victor Emanuel Larosa, Jonathan Sanders, Salvado Ellswood, Sandra Bland, Albert Joseph Davis, Darrius Stewart, Samuel Vincent DuBose, Christian Taylor, Redel Jones, Asshams Pharoah Manley, Felix Kumi, India Kager, Jeremy

McDole, Keith Harrison McLeod, Junior Prosper, Corey Lamar Jones, Marquesha McMillan, Anthony Ashford, Bennie Lee Tignor, Jamar O'Neal Clark, Nathaniel Harris Pickett, Mario Woods, Miguel Espinal, Michael Noel, Kevin Matthews, Quintonio LeGrier, Bettie Jones, Keith Childress, Antronie Scott, David Joseph, Sahlah Ridgeway, Dyzhawn L. Perkins, Calin Roquemore, Kisha Michael, Marquintan Sandlin, Christopher J. Davis, Gregory Gunn, Akiel Denkins, Peter Gaines, India M. Beaty, Kevin Hicks, Laronda Sweatt, David Felix, Deresha Armstrong, Jessica Williams, Michael Eugene Wilson Jr., Vernell Bing Jr., Antwun Shumpert, Deravis Caine Rogers, Delrawn Small, Alton Sterling, Philando Castile, Joseph Curtis Mann, Dalvin Hollins, Paul O'Neal, Donnell Thompson Jr., Korryn Gaines, Jamarion Rashad Robinson, Sylville Smith, Levonia Riggins, Terrence Sterling, Tyre King, Terence Crutcher, Keith Lamont Scott, Alfred Olango, Christopher Sowell, Deborah Danner, Andrew Depeiza, Earl Eubanks Jr., JR Williams, Darrion M. Barnhill, Nana Adomako, Chad Robertson, Jocques Scott Clemmons, Raynard Burton, Morgon London Rankins, Alteria Woods (and the child she was carrying), Jordan Edwards, Jonie Block, DeRicco Devante Holden, Marc Brandon Davis, David Thomas Jones, Charleena Chavon Lyles (and the child she was carrying), Aaron Bailey, Dejuan Guillory, Brian Easley, India N. Nelson, Isaiah Tucker, Patrick Harmon, Charles David Robinson, Anthony Antonio Ford, Sandy Guardiola, Dewboy Lister, Calvin Toney, Lawrence Hawkins, Keita O'Neil, Jean Pedro Pierre, Dennis Plowden Jr., John Bailon, Charles Smith Jr., Geraldine Townsend, Arther McAfee Jr., Corey Mobley, Crystalline Barnes, Anthony Jacob Weber, Ronell Foster, Darion Baker, Mario Dantoni Bass, Decynthia S. Clements, Shermichael Ezeff, Cameron Hall, Stephon Clark, Danny Ray Thomas, Saheed Vassell, Juan Markee Jones, James Bauduy, Shukri Ali Said, Marcus-David L. Peters, Maurice Granton Jr., Lashanda Anderson, Robert Lawrence White, Antwon Rose Jr., Anthony Marcell Green, Rashaun Washington, Cynthia Fields, James Leatherwood, Botham Shem Jean, Dereshia Blackwell, Anton Milbert LaRue Black, DeAndre Ballard, Lajuana Phillips, Chinedu Valentine Okobi, Charles D. Roundtree Jr., Jacob Servais, Jesse J. Quinton, Jemel Roberson, Emantic Fitzgerald Bradford Jr., Jonathan Hart, Tameka Lashay Simpson, April Webster, Angel Viola Decarlo, Danny Washington, D'ettrick Griffin, Jimmy Atchison, Gregory Griffin, Willie McCoy, Latasha Nicole Walton, Sterling Lapree Higgins, Kevin Bruce Mason, Javier Ambler, Marzues Scott, Marcus McVae, Isaiah Lewis, Ronald Greene, Pamela Shantay Turner, Dominique Clayton, Miles Hall, Kevin Pudlik, Ryan Twyman, JaQuavion Slaton, Brandon Webber, Eric Jack Logan, Josef Delone Richardson, De'Von Bailey, Channara Tom Pheap, Elijah McClain, Melvin Watkins, Atatiana Koquice Jefferson, Christopher Whitfield, Eric Reason, Ariane McCree, Michael Lorenzo Dean, John Elliot Neville, Jamee Christopher Deonte Johnson, Kwame Jones, William Howard Green, Jaquyn O'neill Light, Darius Tarver, Manuel Elijah Ellis, Barry Gedeus, Donnie Sanders, Breonna Taylor, Mycael Johnson, Daniel T. Prude, Steven Demarco Taylor, Michael Brent Charles Ramos, Shaun Lee Fuhr, Dreasjon Reed, Finan H. Berhe, Yassin Mohamed, Maurice S. Gordon, George Perry Floyd Jr., Tony McDade, David McAtee, Carlos Carson, Rayshard Brooks, Julian Edward Roosevelt Lewis, Trayford Pellerin, Damian Lamar Daniels, Dijon Durand Kizzee, Deon Kay, Jonathan Price, and Marcellis Stinnette. See http://mappingpoliceviolence.org.

6. Sam Blake, "Why the George Floyd Protests Feel Different—Lots and Lots of Mobile Video," *dot.LA* June 12, 2020. Available at: https://dot.la/george-floyd-video-2646171522 .html.

7. See Keeanga-Yamahtta Taylor, *From #BlackLivesMatter to Black Liberation* (Chicago: Haymarket Books, 2016) for a history of Black Lives Matter as it became a national movement and rallying cry in the mid-2010s.

8. Joint Economic Committee, the United States Congress, "The Economic State of Black America in 2020." Available at: https://www.jec.senate.gov/public/_cache/files/ccf4dbe2 -810a-44f8-b3e7-14f7e5143ba6/economic-state-of-black-america-2020.pdf.

9. Francis Wilkinson, "As Monuments to Racism Fall, Trump's Culture War Falters," *Bloomberg*, June 7, 2020. Available at: https://www.bloomberg.com/opinion/articles/2020 -06-07/falling-monuments-to-racism-are-defeats-for-trump-s-culture-war; "Report: 59 Confederate Symbols Removed Since George Floyd's Death," written by Camila Domonoske, aired August 12, 2020, on *NPR*. Available at: https://www.npr.org/2020/08/12/901771780/ report-59-confederate-symbols-removed-since-george-floyds-death.

10. Buchanan et al.; Thomas Fuller, "How One of America's Whitest Cities Became the Center of B.L.M. Protests," *New York Times* July 24, 2020. Available at: https://www.nytimes .com/2020/07/24/us/portland-oregon-protests-white-race.html.

11. Joe Goldeen, "'Racism Is the Common Enemy'—Message of Stockton's Peaceful Protests," Stockton *Record*, June 2, 2020. Available at: https://www.recordnet.com/story/ news/local/2020/06/02/lsquoracism-is-common-enemyrsquo-mdash-message-of -stocktonrsquos-peaceful-protests/112822442/; "LAPD Officers Take a Knee to Show Solidarity with Protesters," written by Veronica Miracle, aired June 1, 2020, on ABC7 Los Angeles. Available at: https://abc7.com/take-a-knee-cops-lapd-officers-commander-cory -palka/6225950/; Maryclaire Dale, "Rethinking Police: How Camden, NJ, Reimagined Its Force," Associated Press, June 15, 2020. Available at: https://www.cbs8.com/article/news/ nation-world/rethinking-police-how-camden-nj-reimagined-its-force/103-6e0979c4-727f -4540-87f5-4cfaaf4d80ca.

12. "Some Protesters Take Issue with Police Kneeling, Calling It 'PR Stunt,'" written by Stacy Chen, aired June 6, 2020, on *ABC News*. Available at: https://abcnews.go.com/US/ protesters-issue-police-kneeling-calling-pr-stunt/story?id=71067237; "Protester Knocked Down by Buffalo Police Leaves the Hospital Nearly One Month Later," written by Rachel Treisman, 30 June 2020, NPR. Available at: https://www.npr.org/sections/live-updates -protests-for-racial-justice/2020/06/30/885780550/protester-knocked-down-by-buffalo -police-leaves-the-hospital-nearly-one-month-la.

13. Daniel Kreps, "Quaker Oats to End Aunt Jemima Brand to 'Make Progress Toward Racial Equality,'" *Rolling Stone*, June 17, 2020. Available at: https://www.rollingstone .com/culture/culture-news/quaker-oats-ends-aunt-jemima-brand-1016380/; Ben Kesslen, "Aunt Jemima Brand to Change Name, Remove Image That Quaker Says Is 'Based on a Racial Stereotype,'" aired June 17, 2020, on NBC *News*. Available at: https://www.nbcnews .com/news/us-news/aunt-jemima-brand-will-change-name-remove-image-quaker-says -n1231260; Richard Feloni and Yusuf George, "These Are the Corporate Responses to the George Floyd Protests That Stand Out," *Just Capital*, June 30, 2020. Available at: https://justcapital.com/news/notable-corporate-responses-to-the-george-floyd-protests/; "Statement by President George W. Bush," June 2, 2020, George W. Bush Presidential Center. Available at: https://www.bushcenter.org/about-the-center/newsroom/press -releases/2020/06/statement-by-president-george-w-bush.html.

14. Chris Mautner, "Harrisburg Protest over George Floyd's Death Leads to Violent Clash with Police: Recap," *Penn Live Patriot-News*, May 30, 2020. Available at: https://www.pennlive

.com/news/2020/05/harrisburg-protest-over-george-floyds-death-leads-to-violent-clash-with-police-video.html.

15. Ed Kilgore, "Trump Mulls Declaring an Insurrection and Sending Military into Cities," *New York Magazine*, June 1, 2020. Available at: https://nymag.com/intelligencer/2020/06/trump-mulls-sending-military-into-u-s-cities.html; Katelyn Burns, "Trump Called Governors 'Weak' and Said They Need to 'Dominate' George Floyd Protesters," *Vox*, June 1, 2020. Available at: https://www.vox.com/policy-and-politics/2020/6/1/21277062/trump-governors-dominate-george-floyd-protesters.

16. Tom Cotton, "Send in the Troops," *New York Times*, June 3, 2020. Available at: https://www.nytimes.com/2020/06/03/opinion/tom-cotton-protests-military.html.

17. Cotton; "ADL Debunk: Disinformation and the BLM Protests," Anti-Defamation League, 2020. Available at: https://www.adl.org/resources/reports/adl-debunk-disinformation-and-the-blm-protests; James S. Robbins, "Rioting Is Beginning to Turn People Off to BLM and Protests While Biden Has No Solution," *USA Today*, August 31, 2020. Available at: https://www.usatoday.com/story/opinion/2020/08/31/riots-violence-erupting-turning-many-away-blm-and-protests-column/5675343002/; "Do You Support Or Oppose the Black Lives Matter Movement?" *Civiqs Survey*, August 30, 2020, August 30, 2020. Available at: https://civiqs.com/results/black_lives_matter?uncertainty=true&annotations=true&zoomIn=true&net=true&race=White; Alex Ward, "US Park Police Denies Using Tear Gas on Protesters. Evidence Suggests Otherwise," *Vox*, June 2, 2020. Available at: https://www.vox.com/2020/6/2/21278559/tear-gas-white-house-protest-park-police; Thomas Gibbons-Neff et al., "Aggressive Tactics by National Guard, Ordered to Appease Trump, Wounded the Military, Too," *New York Times*, June 10, 2020. Available at: https://www.nytimes.com/2020/06/10/us/politics/national-guard-protests.html.

18. The US Park Police and other law enforcement agencies claimed that tear gas was not used against protesters in Lafayette Square on June 1, but the video evidence and the tear gas cannisters left on the scene prove otherwise. Nathan Baca, "New Video Shows Federal Police Holding Tear Gas Launchers, Rolling Stinger Grenades at Protesters," WUSA9, June 9, 2020. Available at: https://www.wusa9.com/article/news/local/protests/tear-gas-protesters-lafayette-square-park-police-new-video-evidence/65-c39fb767-b114-41d6-bcbb-530b3823d8e7; Alex Ward, "US Park Police Said Using 'Tear Gas' in a Statement Was a 'Mistake.' It Just Used the Term Again," *Vox*, June 5, 2020. Available at: https://www.vox.com/2020/6/5/21281604/lafayette-square-white-house-tear-gas-protest; Tom Jackman and Carol D. Leonnig, "National Guard Officer Says Police Suddenly Moved on Lafayette Square Protesters, Used 'Excessive Force' Before Trump Visit," *Washington Post*, July 27, 2020. Available at: https://www.washingtonpost.com/nation/2020/07/27/national-guard-commander-says-police-suddenly-moved-lafayette-square-protesters-used-excessive-force-clear-path-trump/; Marissa J. Lang et al., "Operation Diligent Valor: Trump Showcased Federal Power in Portland, Making a Culture War Campaign Pitch," *Washington Post*, July 24, 2020. Available at: https://www.washingtonpost.com/national/portland-protests-operation-diligent-valor/2020/07/24/95f21ede-cce9-11ea-89ce-ac7d5e4a5a38_story.html.

19. Jim Ryan, "Tear Gas Deployed as Federal Officers Disperse Protesters Overnight in Downtown Portland," *Oregon Live/Oregonian*, July 16, 2020. Available at: https://www.oregonlive.com/portland/2020/07/tear-gas-deployed-as-federal-officers-disperse-protesters-overnight-in-downtown-portland.html?utm_medium=social&utm_source=twitter&utm_

campaign=oregonian_sf; N'dea Yancey-Bragg et al., "'Secret Police Force:' Feds Reportedly Pull Portland Protesters into Unmarked Vehicles, Stirring Outrage," *USA Today*, August 4, 2020. Available at: https://www.usatoday.com/story/news/nation/2020/07/17/reports-federal -officers-detain-portland-protesters-unmarked-vans/5457471002/; "Demonstrations & Political Violence in America: New Data for Summer 2020"; Lindsay Nadrich, "Deputized Troopers May Snarl MultCo's Protest Prosecution Plans," KOIN 6 Portland, September 1, 2020. Available at: https://www.koin.com/news/protests/oregon-state-police-troopers-federally -deputized-amid-renewed-portland-protest-response/.

20. Matt Zapotosky et al., "Suspects Arrested after Man Shot at Albuquerque Protest," *Washington Post*, June 16, 2020. Available at: https://www.washingtonpost.com/national -security/suspect-arrested-after-man-shot-at-albuquerque-protest/2020/06/16/4ca3c8ec -afeb-11ea-8758-bfd1d045525a_story.html; Jens Gould, "Trump Announces Deployment of Federal Agents to Albuquerque," *Santa Fe New Mexican*, July 22, 2020. Available at: https://www.santafenewmexican.com/news/local_news/trump-announces-deployment -of-federal-agents-to-albuquerque/article_e80a12d6-cc34-11ea-9ab0-5b1cd8827f75.html.

21. Joe Heim, "Recounting a Day of Rage, Hate, Violence and Death," *Washington Post*, August 14, 2017. Available at: https://www.washingtonpost.com/graphics/2017/local/ charlottesville-timeline/. "Six More Defendants Settle Lawsuits After 'Unite the Right' Rally," *Georgetown Law News*, May 16, 2018. Available at: https://www.law.georgetown .edu/news/six-more-defendants-settle-lawsuit-brought-after-unite-the-right-rally/.

22. "Remarks by President Trump on Infrastructure," Office of the White House Press Secretary, August 15, 2017. Available at: https://www.whitehouse.gov/briefings-statements/ remarks-president-trump-infrastructure/.

23. Carlie Porterfield, "Who is 'Umbrella Man'? Mystery Vandal at Minneapolis Riot Spurs Conspiracy Theories," *Forbes*, May 30, 2020. Available at: https://www.forbes.com/sites/ carlieporterfield/2020/05/30/who-is-umbrella-man-mystery-vandal-at-minneapolis -riot-spurs-conspiracies/?sh=2f22502c236e; "Affidavit: Hell's Angels Member Believed to Be 'Umbrella Man' Spotted Inciting Violence During George Floyd Protests," written by Josh Skluzacek, KSTP *5 ABC News*. Available at: https://kstp.com/news/affidavit -hells-angels-member-believed-to-be-umbrella-man-spotted-inciting-violence-during -floyd-protests-/5809447/; Neil MacFarquhar, "Minneapolis Police Link 'Umbrella Man' to White Supremacy Group," *New York Times*, July 28, 2020. Available at: https:// www.nytimes.com/2020/07/28/us/umbrella-man-identified-minneapolis.html;   Haven Orecchio-Egresitz, "The Right-Wing Group Patriot Prayer, Associated with a Man Killed in the Portland Protests, Has a History of Provoking Left-Wing Groups," *Insider*, August 31, 2020. Available at: https://www.insider.com/what-is-patriot-prayer-joey-gibson-right -wing-group-2020-8; Evan Hill et al., "'Straight to Gunshots:' How a US Task Force Killed an Antifa Activist," *New York Times*, October 15, 2020. Available at: https://www .nytimes.com/2020/10/13/us/michael-reinoehl-antifa-portland-shooting.html; "Statement by Attorney General William P. Barr on the Tracking Down of Fugitive Michael Forest Reinoehl" (Washington, DC: US Department of Justice, Office of Public Affairs), Friday, September 4, 2020. Available at: https://www.justice.gov/opa/pr/statement-attorney -general-william-p-barr-tracking-down-fugitive-michael-forest-reinoehl; "Boogaloo Suspect Steven Carrillo Pleads Not Guilty to Fatal Ambush of Sheriff Sergeant in Santa Cruz Mountains" aired, October 3, 2020, on KPIX 5 *CBS News*. Available at: https://sanfrancisco .cbslocal.com/2020/08/28/alleged-boogaloo-suspect-steven-carrillo-pleads-not-guilty-to

-fatal-santa-cruz-mt-ambush/; Nate Gartrell, "'I Don't Like This, I Am Not Cool with This': Defense Releases New Details in Boogaloo-Linked Killing of Federal Officer in Oakland," *Mercury News*, October 2, 2020. Available at: https://www.mercurynews.com/2020/10/03/i -dont-like-this-i-am-not-cool-with-this-defense-releases-new-details-in-boogaloo-linked -killing-of-federal-officer-in-oakland/; Lois Beckett, "White Supremacists or Anti-Police Libertarians? What We Know about the 'Boogaloo,'" July 8, 2020. Available at: https:// www.theguardian.com/world/2020/jul/08/boogaloo-boys-movement-who-are-they-what -do-they-believe. Beyond disrupting demonstrations and inciting violence, white suprem- acists have attempted to intimidate protesters with nooses and racist messages. In Saginaw, Michigan, a Black couple discovered a noose that had been dropped through their car window with a note reading: "Accessory to be worn with your BLM T-shirt! Happy Pro- testing!" Kaytie Boomer, "Saginaw Police Investigate Possible Racially Motivated Crime after Noose Found inside Vehicle," *Michigan Live*, July 13, 2020. Available at: https://www .mlive.com/galleries/XQBSFT37FFCWBAD6YVWIEX4OTA/.

24. "House Hearing on White Supremacy Infiltrating Police Departments," CSPAN Septem- ber 29, 2020. Available at: https://www.c-span.org/video/?476341-1/house-hearing-white -supremacy-infiltrating-police-departments; "Much of Kenosha's Deadly Protest Shoot- ing Was Captured in Social Media Videos. Here's What They Show," *Milwaukee Journal Sentinel*, August 26, 2020. Available at: https://www.jsonline.com/story/news/2020/08/26/ kenosha-shooting-details-videos-show-scenes-wisconsin-protest/3442031001/.

25. Mariame Kaba, "Yes, We Mean Literally Abolish the Police," *New York Times*, June 12, 2020. Available at: https://www.nytimes.com/2020/06/12/opinion/sunday/floyd-abolish -defund-police.html.

26. Officers who resort to excessive and deadly force are very rarely punished, cities bear the costs of lawsuits for unjustifiable police killings, and together these have amounted to hun- dreds of millions of dollars in costs over recent years. See Robin D. G. Kelley, "Insecure: Policing Under Capitalism," *Spectre* 1, no.2 (Fall 2020). Available at: https://spectrejournal .com/insecure-policing-under-racial-capitalism/.

27. This concept is at the center of Tracey Meares and Tom Tyler's work on procedural justice. See Meares, "Norms, Legitimacy, and Law Enforcement," *Oregon Law Review* 79, (2000); Meares and Dan M. Kahan, "The Coming Criminal Procedure," *Annual Review of Crim- inal Procedure* 86, (1998): 1153–1184; Jason Sunshine and Tyler, "The Role of Procedural Justice and Legitimacy in Shaping Public Support for Policing," *Law & Society Review* 37, no. 3 (2003): 513–548; Tyler, "Psychological Perspectives on Legitimacy and Legitimation," *Annual Review of Psychology* 57, (2006): 375–400.

28. On how wealthy people dodge taxes, see Emmanuel Saez and Gabriel Zucman, *The Tri- umph of Injustice: How the Rich Dodge Taxes and How to Make Them Pay* (New York: W. W. Norton & Company, 2019); Emmanuel Saez and Gabriel Zucman, "How to Tax Our Way Back to Justice," *New York Times*, October 11, 2019. Available at: https://www.nytimes .com/2019/10/11/opinion/sunday/wealth-income-tax-rate.html.

29. See Robin D. G. Kelley, "What Abolition Looks Like, From the Panthers to the Peo- ple," *LEVEL*, October 26, 2020. Available at: https://level.medium.com/what-abolition -looks-like-from-the-panthers-to-the-people-6c2e537eac71; Arthur J. Reynolds et al., "Long-Term Effects of an Early Childhood Intervention on Educational Achievement and Juvenile Arrest," *Journal of the American Medical Association* 285, no.18, (2001): 2339–2346; Sara B. Heller et al., "Summer Jobs Reduce Violence Among Disadvantaged

Youth," *Science* 346, no. 6214 (December 12, 2014): 1219–1223; Congressional Research Service, "Federal Youth Employment and Job Training Programs," *In Focus*, August 31, 2020. Available at: https://crsreports.congress.gov/product/pdf/IF/IF11640; US Department of Justice, "FY 2020 Budget Request." Available at: https://www.justice.gov/jmd/page/file/1142621/download#:~:text=FY%202020%20Overview,-The%20Justice%20Department&text=The%20FY%202020%20Budget%20continues,in%20programs%20to%20assist%20them; Department of Homeland Security, "DHS Announces Grant Allocations for Fiscal Year 2020 Preparedness Grants," Official Website of the Department of Homeland Security June 30, 2020. Available at: https://www.dhs.gov/news/2020/06/30/dhs-announces-grant-allocations-fiscal-year-2020-preparedness-grants; Urban Institute, "Criminal Justice Expenditures: Police, Corrections, and Courts." Available at: https://www.urban.org/policy-centers/cross-center-initiatives/state-and-local-finance-initiative/state-and-local-backgrounders/criminal-justice-police-corrections-courts-expenditures.

30. For instance, residents can be taught to conduct CPR and heal gun shot and stabbing wounds, and they can be trained to provide care for victims of sexual assault as well as substance abuse counseling for drug addicts. Such efforts are already underway in Oakland, where the Oakland Power Projects seek to "make the police obsolete by building tools and resources to meet people's needs in other ways." See Critical Resistance, "The Oakland Power Projects." Available at: https://static1.squarespace.com/static/59ead8f9692ebee25b72f17f/t/5b6ab32e70a6ad2f21cf765c/1533719344188/TheOakPowerProj_rept_target1_v3WEB.pdf. See also alternatives to policing solutions in Kaba, "Yes, We Mean Literally Abolish the Police;" Kelley, "What Abolition Looks Like;" Derecka Purnell, "How I Became a Police Abolitionist," *Atlantic*, July 6, 2020. Available at: https://www.theatlantic.com/ideas/archive/2020/07/how-i-became-police-abolitionist/613540/; Keeanga-Yamahtta Taylor, "We Should Still Defund the Police," *New Yorker*, August 14, 2020. Available at: https://www.newyorker.com/news/our-columnists/defund-the-police?irclickid=SCsWobyysxyOWxYwUx0Mo38SUkE3yiyxyXvEVw0&irgwc=1&source=affiliate_impactpmx_12f6tote_desktop_adgoal%20GmbH&utm_source=impact-affiliate&utm_medium=123201&utm_campaign=impact&utm_content=Online%20Tracking%20Link&utm_brand=tny; "Ruth Wilson Gilmore Makes the Case for Abolition," *Intercept*, June 10, 2020. Available at: https://theintercept.com/2020/06/10/ruth-wilson-gilmore-makes-the-case-for-abolition/. All of these efforts were produced during the summer and fall of 2020.

31. "Here's What Protestors Have Been Saying for the Past Two Weeks," *DCist*, June 12, 2020. Available at: https://dcist.com/story/20/06/12/heres-what-protesters-have-been-saying-for-the-past-two-weeks/.

INDEX

Page numbers in *italics* refer to illustrations.